Sacred Sites of Sri Lanka

BAY OF BENGAL
Jaffna
Nagadipa
Trincomalee
Anuradhapura
Seruvila
Somavathiya
Sigiriya
Polonnuruva
Dambulla
Kandy
Attanagalla
Kelaniya
Colombo
Sri Pada/ Adam's Peak
SRI LANKA
Ratnapura
Kataragama
Galle
Devinuvara
N

SACRED SITES OF SRI LANKA

Donald M. Stadtner

RIVER BOOKS
SAILFISH

First published and distributed in 2025 by
River Books Press Co., Ltd
396/1 Maharaj Road, Phraborommaharajawang,
Bangkok 10200, Thailand
Tel: (66) 2 225-0139, (66) 2 225-9574
Email: order@riverbooksbk.com
www.riverbooksbk.com

Riverbooksbk riverbooksbk @riverbooks

Publisher: River Books Press Ltd., Bangkok, Thailand
EU Authorised Representative: Easy Access System Europe Oü,
16879218 - Mustamäe tee 50, 10621 Tallinn, Estonia,
gpsr.requests@easproject.com

Editor: Narisa Chakrabongse
Production supervision: Ruetairat Nanta
Design: Suparat Sudcharoen

ISBN 978 616 451 022 7

Printed and bound in Thailand by Parbpim Co., Ltd

Contents

Acknowledgements

The idea for this book began at dinner with the late Senake Bandaranayake who grumbled that too many books on Sri Lanka gave too little attention to the myths underpinning sacred sites. Without legends, he argued, sacred sites are but 'old stones'. He then jested that the Bodhi Tree at Anuradhapura would be simply another tree were it not for its ties to the Buddha, Asoka and the missionizing of Sri Lanka. He also pressed strongly that Hindu, Muslim and Christian sites should be included in order to convey the island's diversity and how Sri Lankans of all faiths, despite striking differences, largely agreed about religion's place in life. Senake's challenge shadowed me for over a decade before I mustered the courage to begin. In the end, as learned readers will recognize, this work is a scant scratch on the surface of an inexhaustible topic. These pages are then but a single brick in a stupa of millions.

Bits and pieces of the text were reviewed by Crispin Branfoot, Nandana Chutiwongs, Phyllis Granoff, Paul Halliday, Justin Henry, Vijitha Kumara, Janice Leoshko, Tamara Loos, Michel Lorrillard, Uditha Devapriya, Nicolas Revire, Davesh Soneji, Marco Ramerini, Jeffery Sundberg and Monika Zin. Stephen Berkwitz kindly reviewed my section on the Ruvanvali Stupa and Alexander McKinley shared drafts from his book on Adam's Peak. Without Kevin Trainor's unpublished translations of the *Dhatu-vamsa*, the Seruvila and Somavathiya stupas would never have made sense. John Strong reviewed several sections and sent me portions of his book on the tooth-relic. John Holt reviewed one or two chapters and guided me through the labryinthine mutations of the deity Upulvan. Others who took up red pencils were Robert Brown and Anne Blackburn. And many thanks go to Lakshika Senarath Gamage at the Norton Simon Museum of Art, Pasadena, who patiently kept answering the phone when I enquired about this or that on more occasions that I choose to remember. Above all, I want to acknowledge the support of Osmund Bopearachchi who was ever-ready to provide translations from Sinhalese sources, many photographs and invaluable guidance at every stage.

For connections between Sri Lanka and Burma, I turned to U Tun Aung Chain, Patrick Pranke and Jason Carbine who shared translated passages from the Kalyani inscription. Others were Lilian Handlin, Jacques Leider and François Tainturier. For ties with Thailand, Chris Baker, Sunait Chuttintaranond, B. J. Terwiel, and Chedha Tingsanchali were always there to help. Samerchai Poolsuwan and I traveled in Sri Lanka with Mangalika Jayatunga who guided us to remote mural sites. Also thanks go to a graduate school friend, now a retired botany professor in Chennai, Paulraj Dayanandan, who told me more than I needed to know about Bodhi trees.

After many exchanges about the Portuguese era, Chandra Richard de Silva and I became friends. Others with whom I communicated include Hugo Miguel Crespo, Jorge Flores, Zoltán Biedermann and Sagara Jayasinghe. Joaquim Santos helped with translations from a

1638-codex in Zaragosa and a former colleague from Austin, Texas, K. David Jackson, supplied a translation of the Portuguese caption on a sketch of a Buddha's footprint.

Martin Krieger shared photographs of Dutch tombstones from Tamil Nadu for comparisons in Sri Lanka. For the Dutch painter Jan Brandes, Remco Raben answered several questions. Saskia van Veen helped with the Wolvendaal gravestones and the Dutch captions on antique maps. For a photograph of Heydt's engraving of the Kelaniya Viharaya, now in the Amsterdam Museum, I am grateful to Lodewijk Wagenaar. A rare photograph of the Vishnu image at Dambulla was supplied by Ulrich von Schroeder and Darryl Lim provided images from an album on King Sanghabodhi in the Asian Civilizations Museum, Singapore. For the aerial photographs, I thank my friend Dominic Sansoni.

In Sri Lanka, many were there to help, notably my old friend Jagath Weerasinghe whose insights on a range of topics pepper these pages. Asoka de Zoysa lent a hand with mural painting and Vajira Jayathilaka furnished plans of the Kelaniya Viharaya. Others were Chryshane Mendis who shared his research on colonial forts in Sri Lanka. I am also grateful to Tharaka Ananda for a photo from Ratnapura's annual festival. For the Parsis, I corresponded with Jamsheed Choksy, and for Colombo's urban history, I turned to Locana Gunaratna. G.P.V. Somaratna and Prabo Mihindukulasuriya opened the Colombo Theological Seminary's research library. For Islam, the Chairman of the Dewatagah Mosque in Colombo, Mr Reyyaz Salley, spoke to me about the tensions between Wahhabis and the majority of Muslims. Dennis McGilvray clarified many points about Sri Lankan Islam and K. T. Silva provided information on Karunegala's syncretic shrine. And Craig Reynolds explained to me how images of the Hindu gods Kataragama and Rama at Nakhon Si Thammarat evolved into the popular deity in Thailand, Jatukham Rammathep, featured on countless amulets.

At the Temple of the Tooth, Lionel Wijesundara gave permission to River Books to photograph in the museum. Also in Kandy was Ven. Velivita Saranakara Thera who gave us complete access to the Malwatta Maha Viharaya's museum. In Colombo, I will always value meeting K.D. Paranavitana in the colonial-era J. R. Jayewardene Centre and paging through the first English edition of Baldaeus' classic Dutch work. The office visit was a wistful throwback to an era of collegiality that is fast disappearing. An important source of inspiration midway was a visit to Ranjini and Gananath Obeyesekere at their home in Kandy. Their prodigious accomplishments left me humbled, but their enthusiasm for my project lifted my spirits.

Many in Sri Lanka provided insights that my scholarly friends were unable to do. Not least was the Ven. K. Mahinda Sangharakkhita Thera at the Kelaniya Viharaya who recounted miracles performed by the relics at his famous monastery. Others were Mrs Padmini Nanayakkara and her son Amal. At her Colombo guest house, Padmini regaled me with tales from the *Mahavamsa* learned in her childhood. Also in Colombo was my neighbourhood Christian tuk-tuk driver who told me that in times of need, from anywhere, he was able to speak to the Hindu god Kataragama. Such encounters and countless others made me understand how the present is tethered to the past.

Note on Usage

Spellings of most Pali words are taken from G.P. Malalasekera's *Dictionary of Pali Proper Names* and the names of kings and locations from C. Richard de Silva's *Sri Lanka: A History*. Pali, Sanskrit and Tamil words appear as (P: *arahants*), (S: *pradakshina*) and (T: *kovil*). Sinhalese words are unidentified since they are so numerous. Diacritics are not included, since this book is intended for a general audience.

Traditional Pali sources are identified with standard initials taken from Oskar von Hinuber's *A Handbook of Pali Literature* and are not listed in the endnotes. Jatakas are numbered as they appear in the well-known *The Jatakas or Stories of the Buddha's Former Births*. For some words, the reader is referred to Malalasekera's *Dictionary of Pali Proper Names*, i.e. (Dppn: *Savatthi*). More commonly used foreign words have been preferred, such as the better-known Sanskrit *apsara* rather than the Pali *acchara* or the Sinhalese *asara*.

Spellings of certain words are sometimes split into more digestible parts based on linguistic divisions. Thus, Vimaladharmasuriya is broken down into Vimala Dharma Suriya and *Dathavamsa* becomes *Datha-vamsa*. This is not consistent, such as for *Mahavamsa, Culavamsa* and *Rajasimha*. Three sources are cited with initials: *Dipavamsa* (Dpv.), *Mahavamsa* (Mhv.)*, and Culavamsa* (Cv.).

Since regnal years are often subject to debate, I have arbitrarily used K.M. de Silva's *A History of Sri Lanka*. Dates are presented as follows: Parakramabahu I (1153-1186) and not Parakramabahu I (c. 1153 – c. 1186). The Pali or Sanskrit names for kings are generally used, such as Dutthagamani, but in some cases the more familiar Sinhalese names are adopted, such as Valagamba. In many cases, I have opted for Ceylon rather than Sri Lanka to better evoke the pre-modern era. Also, in some instances, Lanka and not Sri Lanka is used. Dates in the Buddhist Era are computed to the Western calender using the year 544/543 BCE or 483 BCE. The dates for mural painting are generally drawn from Senake Bandaranayake's *The Rock and Wall Paintings of Sri Lanka*. In the interest of brevity, the captions to J.K.L. van Dort's watercolours are cited as KITLV (Koninklijk Instituut voor Taal-,Land-,en Volkenkunde).

Tamil and Grantha characters from a stone inscription at the Temple of the Tooth (Atagade) at Polonnuruva, c. 1137-1153. *Epigraphia Zeylanica*, v. 2.

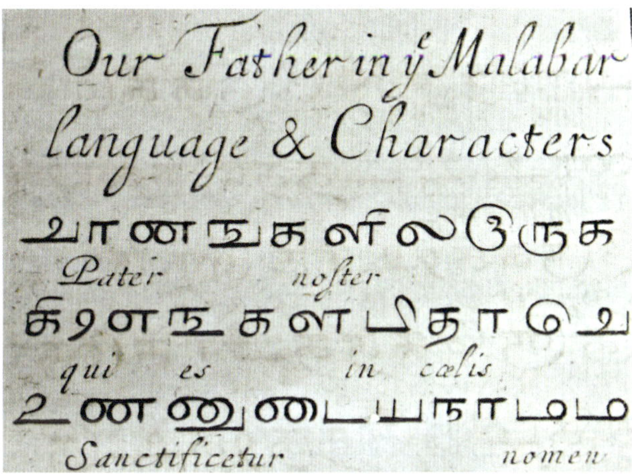

Our Father in ye Malabar language & Characters

Pater noster

qui es in cælis

Sanctificetur nomen

The Lord's Prayer *(Paternoster)* in Tamil and Roman characters. Phillipus Baldaeus, *Beschrijving der Oost Indische* (1671). After the first English edition, 1703.

The concluding page of a royal codex, 1811, the *Visuddhimagga* by Buddhaghosa. Malwatta Viharaya, Kandy. Three-line Sinhalese caption refers to the seated Buddha, Kassapa, and the kneeling figure whose future rebirth will be Gotama.

Preface

Cracking open coconuts is an Indian religious tradition found at Buddhist and Hindu shrines throughout Sri Lanka. River Books.

Friends warned me that it was madness to attend a friend's wedding in Sri Lanka. The civil war between Sinhalas and Tamils was in its thirteenth year and showed no signs of cooling. The groom, a Sinhala Buddhist named Jehan, was a university friend from California who came to the airport with another classmate, a Tamil Hindu named Ajai. Both had carved out professional niches in Colombo where the conflict had not yet touched them directly.

Leaving the airport for my hotel, Jehan said that we needed to make a detour to a temple dedicated to a goddess named Pattini. Her origins were in ancient Tamil Nadu where her husband was unjustly executed by Madurai's king. Pattini, in an avenging rage, flew over the city and burned it to the ground. This Tamil goddess was domesticated into Ceylon's Buddhist culture centuries ago, together with many other imported Hindu deities. Vendors outside the shrine hawked coconuts for cracking open on a stone slab set into the ground facing the temple. While holding a coconut, worshippers made wishes as a small piece of camphor burned on top of the hard shell. When the flame sputtered out, the coconuts were hurled against the stone slab, producing a cacophony of staccato bursts that rippled throughout the temple compound. As our coconuts cleaved open at our feet, I marveled at how a Hindu goddess was so entwined in Sinhala Buddhism when the two communities were locked in a cycle of violence. This detour to my hotel, I realized, was scarcely a coincidence, with Jehan's marriage days away. What wishes, I wondered, did my two friends put before the goddess.

The marriage party was at the colonial-era Galle Face Hotel facing the Indian Ocean. Guests once included Winston Churchill and Louis Armstrong but today's visitors were mostly Europeans

The bygone Kandyan-era is evoked by hired attire at Sinhala weddings. River Books.

A family participating in a newborn's 'blessing' at the Kelaniya monastery, a site marking the Buddha's final appearance in Sri Lanka. The child rests on a concave copper tray placed over the stone carving pictured on the right.

Beneath a copper cover is a modern stone carving with five auspicious symbols, an ancient Indian concept also mentioned in the *Mahavamsa* (Mhv: 7.16). River Books.

escaping freezing climes and tanning themselves by the pool. My friend and his bride milled about the lobby in hired faux nineteenth-century court dress, posing for photos. Then the blast struck. The epicenter was the Central Bank no more than a mile north. The reverberations drew everyone outside where a cloud of smoke rose above the business district. Within minutes, the hotel's foreign guests streamed out from the lobby for the airport. But for my friends, there was no such escape. Jehan felt terrible for inviting me to Colombo, but I reminded him that Sri Lanka's carnage was trifling compared to America's Civil War. And I reminded myself of the pernicious religious conflicts that racked Europe during the Counter-Reformation.

Returning to Colombo three years later, Jehan and his wife met me with their newborn daughter and Ajai and his wife who recently completed a degree at the London School of Economics. This time from the airport, we drove straight to the nearby Kelaniya monastery, a spot sanctified by the Buddha's visit. Parents come to the monastery with newborns who are placed on a concave copper cover set over a flat stone in the floor that is carved with auspicious ancient Indian symbols. Our turn came and a monk, standing over the infant, recited a 'blessing' in Pali and Sinhalese. The ceremony was brief and informal but an unmistakable gravitas enveloped the moment. The protective verses imparted a blanket of well-being for the child's long life ahead, like a ship's christening or a medical inoculation. As the monk's verses trailed off and the child was back in his mother's arms, I was beginning to understand how the sacred infuses so seamlessly into the lives of everyday Sri Lankans.

Pattini, from South India, was welcomed into the Sri Lankan Buddhist pantheon centuries ago. Her main shrine is outside of Colombo at Nawagamuwa. Munneshvaram Temple.

Introduction

An act of merit, providing scented water to nourish a Bodhi tree at Colombo's Gangaramaya monastary.

The Life of Sacred Sites

What makes for a sacred site? How do sacred sites come into existence and why do some flourish and others founder? And how is it that some are more sacred than others? There are no ready answers, partly because no two hallowed sites are alike. Indeed, a staggering diversity unfolds, with sacred spots sprinkled up and down the island, like raindrops. However, the birth of a sacred site is never random and each springs from diverse quarters. Some are born overnight, usually occasioned by a spectacular miracle, while others are dormant before blossoming centuries later. Sacred sites also never stand still since they are forever being re-shaped by new myths and fresh brick and mortar. The sacred landscape is then much like an open book, each generation contributing a chapter or two. But even whole chapters can go missing, since many legends have faded entirely or were transformed beyond recognition. For these reasons, each site's history offers up a jigsaw puzzle with an unknown number of missing pieces or a labyrinth with a shifting exit.

Sacred sites are difficult for us in the West to grasp because the conviction that religious rites can bend the world to our will is a thing of the past. This is why the raw emotions witnessed sometimes at sacred sites in Sri Lanka (and the world over) appear puzzling until we recognize that worshippers bring with them their most cherished aspirations and profoundest anxieties. The comforting notion that prayers, rituals and donations to churches can cure incurable diseases or win a spot in heaven or at a coveted university is no longer part of mainstream Western civilization. In Europe, doubts about divine intercession crystallized when Martin Luther tacked his manifesto on Wittenberg's church door in 1517. And later, when John Calvin famously scoffed in his *Treatise on Relics* (1543) that fragments from the True Cross of Jesus were so commonplace that they could fill an entire ship. Relic-worship, so pivotal to Medieval society, was now ridiculed. Coupled with unstoppable advances in science, older orthodox religious beliefs began a retreat still in progress. No longer were Adam and Eve thought to be real people and nor was the world created in seven days. But beneath the veneer of secular humanism was a bedrock of irrationality, illustrated by Martin Luther himself who forever fought off demons and Satan. Similar forces played out in Sri Lanka, beginning in the nineteenth century, but the notion that religion stands ready to advance our spiritual and material wellbeing is taken for granted among the majority of Sri Lankans of all faiths. It is only when we understand this that sacred sites make sense.

The Buddha's right collarbone-relic, conveyed to Anuradhapura by Asoka's grandson, was enshrined in the Thuparama Stupa.

Sacred sites are limitless in nature and in number but a common glue holding many together are miracles. For example, the Buddha's right collarbone-relic (P: *dakkhina-akkhaka*) not only replicated itself but levitated before its enshrinement, causing 'the hair of the beholders to stand on end'. (Mhv: 17. 44) This is taken from the famous fifth-century *Mahavamsa,* or *Great Chronicle*, that recorded hundreds of miracles spanning over centuries. Hindu sites were no less enveloped in the miraculous, such as a water tank near Jaffna where a princess bathed and so rid herself of her horse-face.[1] Catholic records revel in miracles, like the congregants who buried themselves up to their necks in a consecrated churchyard in 1867, awaiting the Lord to drive off Satan.[2]

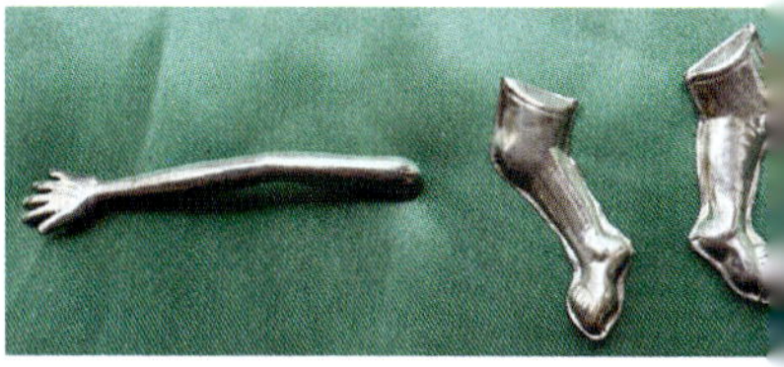

A Sinhala Buddhist soldier vowed to donate a golden arm to Colombo's Dewatagah Mosque in 2017 if he could escape the amputation of his arm. Other supplicants promised solid gold legs. Courtesy Reyyaz Salley.

Sacred sites also operate in a world with porous boundaries. This explains how both Hindus and Buddhists at St Anthony's church in Colombo pledge to make donations if their appeals are answered. Or, how a Sinhala Buddhist soldier vowed at Colombo's Dewatagah Mosque that if surgeons were able to spare his arm from amputation then he would donate an arm made of gold. He declared his oath at the mosque, kneeling in prayer before the tomb of a saint deputed to Ceylon by Islam's first caliph in the seventh century. He escaped surgery and the soldier's gift of a solid gold arm now sits in the mosque's bank vault.[3] That the lives of Islam's first caliph and a Buddhist soldier intersected in 2017 highlights the seamless intermingling of religious traditions and also how sacred sites are often so consequential in the course of a lifetime. This wondrous episode has now been added to the mosque's history. The miraculous then stands ready to be tapped by those of all faiths.

Worshippers at sacred sites must believe that their prayers and precious material offerings will advance their welfare (P: *anisamsa*), not only in this lifetime but into the next. A site's inherent power is usually set in motion by rituals and prayers that are often leavened with donations. A successful site must also be validated by the community, since its power is based partially on the perceptions of others. Few Sri Lankans for instance are unfamiliar with spectacular success stories surrounding the pilgrimage site of Kataragama. Without such features, a site is not likely to attract large numbers, in both East and West. Major national pilgrimage destinations are the most efficacious locations, but the divine is never far off, accessible each day of the year at modest neighbourhood temples, churches, mosques and domestic altars. A flickering votive candle at home or the murmur of water poured at the base of a neighbourhood Bodhi tree are among the strong sights and sounds that connect worshippers to an omnipresent sacred nexus.

Also, the sacred is never static. For example, the Buddha's tooth-relic was for centuries paired together with the Buddha's alms-bowl relic, worshipped in tandem as the pair shifted from one capital to an other. Yet the bowl-relic today is all but forgotten, for unexplained reasons. Monuments tell the same story, with some retaining their sanctity for nearly two thousand years while scores of others are now ruins on the World Heritage list. The trajectory of each sacred site is therefore unique but each speaks to how the 'past is constantly remade to suit the present'.[4]

How our lives intersect with the divine was captured by two contrasting responses to a tsunami that struck northern Ceylon on 17 December 1747. For Jaffna's Dutch governor, the deadly wave signalled 'a punishment from heaven to confuse the Heretics [Catholics] and the Pagans [Buddhists & Hindus]'. Yet, a Catholic official was only able to conclude that the 'whole of Jaffna would have been destroyed … [if] ... the Catholic father at Jaffna … had not blessed the sea'. Moreover, when God heard the priest's blessing, then 'the waters … rolled back as they had come in'.[5] Although the Portuguese and Dutch were mortal foes, these interpretations of the same event differed completely but both were in agreement that a superior will was there for all to see on the beach during that day in 1747.

The tsunami in Jaffna was also proof that bad actions always end in grief. This concept, known commonly today as *karma*, was never restricted to Buddhism and Hinduism. A Catholic chronicler in Goa for example even took the Dutch takeover of much of Portuguese Asia, or the *Estado da Índia,* as god's just chastisement for chasing profits at the expense of good governance.[6] Even the Buddha could not escape the results of bad karma, recorded in a Pali text describing twelve misdeeds in previous births that accounted for the misfortunes in his lifetime as Gotama.[7] In one case, the Buddha as a child experienced pleasurable thoughts while watching fishermen club their catch, a mean-spirited sentiment that induced pounding headaches in the Buddha's future.

'Monks should show their mirth with mouths closed'

The principal driving force behind sacred sites is the accrual of merit, based on the concept of karma that resulted in well-being and rewards in this lifetime and the next. In exchange for sustaining the Buddhist community of monks (P: *sangha*), worshippers obtained merit (P: *punna*; S: *punya*). Such support was expressed in an infinite number of ways, with donations of stupas, temples, images and monasteries heading the list. This support, however, from kings and the lay communities was predicated on the moral character of monks. If discipline among monks was lax or if schisms arose, then the balance was threatened. This explains why Buddhist history is marked by numerous reforms, or 'purification' drives. The archetype reformer was Asoka who famously expelled sixty-thousand feckless monks. Such renewal movements, for many of the same reasons, were no less transformative for Christianity, Hinduism and Islam.

A handful of reforms in Sri Lanka produced special compendiums (P: *katikavats*) spelling out directives that supplemented existing rules. The most far reaching was sponsored by King Parakramabahu I (1153-86) whose programme for renewal, noted first in a stone inscription at Polonnuruva, was circulated in the Theravada world for centuries. Monks, for example, 'should not dwell upon worldly talk or sinful thoughts, sensual and the like' nor

For her miserliness to the *sangha*, Revati was taken to the Gutha Hell by demons, a cautionary tale in the Pali canon and Commentaries. Purvarama monastery, Kataluva. Circa 1880s.

talk when worshipping stupas or the Bodhi Tree. The inscription adds that 'even if there be a just cause for laughter, the monks should only show their mirth with mouths closed and with no sound allowed to escape', borrowing one of seventy-five rules from a sub-section of an ancient Pali text, the *Patimokkha*.[8]

Fostering good behaviour among the laity were popular didactic texts that appeared as early as the thirteenth-century, such as the *Saddhamopayana* and *Pancagatidipana*. Another from the same age was the *The Stream of Delight* (P: *Rasavahini*), comprised of 103 stories, forty of which were set in India and the remainder in Lanka. An even more influential text from about the same time was *The Jewel Garland of the True Doctrine* (*Saddharma-ratnavaliya*). Stories from this collection were told and retold to children, bringing to life 'the abstract ethics and the abstruse concepts of the doctrinal tradition'.[9] Other texts describing life's do's and don'ts were the eighteenth-century *Compendium of Instruction in the Good Law* (*Saddharmovada-samgrahaya*) and a Sinhalese version of the canonical *Vimana-vatthu*. And of course the famous Buddhist birth-stories (P: *jatakas*) fostered such virtues as self-sacrifice, giving, respect for parents and so on. Even kings stood to learn from these stories. (Cv: 73. 72) Also, misbehaviour never goes unanswered, with murals in all Theravada countries depicting Buddhist hells in gruesome detail.

Expiation for misdeeds took many forms, the most popular being donations to the *sangha*. This was the backdrop for a number of Lanka's most celebrated sites today, such as the Sigiriya gardens where King Kassapa (473-495), after slaying his father, queried 'How can I be saved?'. (Mhv: 39.8) One king removed relics from a stupa at Anuradhapura and atoned by creating gardens and founding stupas while a second erected a stupa to repent for causing his rival's suicide.[10] (Cv: 44. 147) That the sole beneficiary of a long list of contrite royal supplicants was the *sangha* explains why tales of atonement amounted to a recurring theme in Buddhist chronicles.

Vows, or *bharaya* (S: *vrata*), were another driving force behind key sacred sites. For example, the massive Abhayagiri stupa at Anuradhapura was constructed to honour a pledge made by Dutthagamani if he triumphed over the Tamils. (Mhv: 33. 44) Another vow resulted in the renovation of the Dambulla caves, sworn by a king should he recover his kingdom from invaders. A description of everyday vow-making in the seventeenth century is as fresh today as it was then. In the 'House of the their Gods' oaths are sworn to donate to the temple 'Land, a Slave, Cattle, Money, Cloth, etc.' should one's wishes be granted. Supplicants 'will discourse, argue and expostulate with him [a god], as if he were there present in Person before them'. Should the entreaty fail, then the chagrined petitioner utters a 'Curse, saying He [the god] doth but cheat and deceive them'.[11] Buddhist monks even complained about Christian converts in Kandy who no longer swore vows at temples but only in churches, leaving the monasteries short of donations.[12] Certain shrines are thought to be more efficacious for declaring vows, with Kataragama leading the list.

King Kulakkottan at Trincomalee's Koneshvaram Temple. This fabled Tamil king is tied to the temple's construction.

Royal participation was also an essential ingredient in the success of sacred sites, often centred on relics that were 'latent or potential' until activated by real or imaginary monarchs imbued with 'sufficient power to actualize it'.[13] This explains the countless instances in Theravada chronicles extolling kings for founding stupas and temples, whether in the legendary past or in historical times. The founders' names then became wedded to their monuments in perpetuity, always invoked by subsequent kings in their restorations. The same held true for major Hindu sites, such as King Dappula (661-664 CE) who founded the Vishnu temple at Devinuvara, his legendary patronage even persisting into the nineteenth century.[14] Another case was King Kulakkottan and his fabled rebuilding of Trincomalee's Koneshvaram Temple.

From Outside

None of the country's major faiths were born in Sri Lanka. All came from outside but a special bond with their spiritual homelands was never broken. Buddhism's roots were in India while Tamils looked to Tamil Nadu and to myths whose backdrop was often North India. For Muslims, it was the Middle East and India from where saints made legendary visits to Ceylon. Christians looked to the Holy Land, whence St Thomas came to Ceylon, and to Europe.

The leading influence was from India, right from the beginning. Buddhism arose in India, and all of Sri Lanka's most venerated relics are thought to be from there. Even royal families generally traced their roots back to India.[15] At the same time, Hindu beliefs and customs permeated certain aspects of life, at least among the elite. One tenth-century stone inscription perfectly encapsulates this juxtaposition of Buddhist and Hindu notions, its author marveling that the incomparable Abhayagiri Stupa was graced by none other than Vishnu and the goddess Lakshmi. Or consider how a king known today for his Buddhist piety attended a ceremony lustrating the Hindu Nine Planetary Gods inside a Shiva temple at Polonnuruva in the twelfth century.[16] Was the king a Hindu during the ritual but reverted to being a Buddhist as he supervised the building of stupa? These are but two examples of how Buddhist and Hindu cultures comfortably coexisted in innumerable contexts. Such a mingling of different currents was no less true in other Theravada societies but was probably especially strong in Sri Lanka. And much like other island societies, such as Japan and the British Isles, Sri Lanka forged a unique civilization.

The Hindu god Murugan is a major deity, usually known as Kataragama in Sri Lanka. The six syllables spell out Saravanabhavan, the lake in which the deity was born.

Ceylon was known to the classical Mediterranean world as Taprobane, or Taprobana (S: Tamraparni; P: Tambapanni). The term itself probably derived from the Pali word for copper, *tamba* (S: *tamra*), taken from the copper tone of laterite clay found in Ceylon and elsewhere. (Dpv: 9. 30; Mhv: 7.41) Ptolemy used the term Taprobane in his second-century *Geographia* and an earlier Greek geographer, Strabo, noted that Taprobane exported ivory to Indian markets. The word also appeared in an even earlier work, by Megathanese, and was included in one of Asoka's famous third-century Rock Edicts. This Taprobana of classical times became forever embedded in European lore. Colombus for example thought he discovered Taprobana when he spotted Hispaniola and Cervantes' Don Quixote sought the emperor of Taprobana. Even 'a stick of cinnamon' from Taprobana was purportedly found in an ancient Roman tomb, according to a chronicler in Goa.[17] In his *Lusiads*, Camoes used Taprobane alongside Ceylon. Taprobana was also found in a treaty with England in 1815 and on an incised silver communion set given to Colombo's St Peter's Church in 1838 by George III. In some instances, the term was applied to a region or a city, located on the 'Island of Lanka' (P: 'Lankadipa'). (Dpv: 9. 30; Mhv: 6: 47)

Arumukha Navalar (1822-1879), a Hindu reformer based in Jaffna. All of Sri Lanka's religions experienced repeated reforms over the centuries.

A common name in Arab sources for Ceylon was Serendib, or literally the Island of Seren, Seren being a modification of Ceylon that in turn derived from the Pali and Sanskrit *sinha*, or lion. The word Serendib evolved in a round about fashion into 'serendipity' by the eighteenth century, based on a title of a Persian tale, *The Three Princes of Serendip*, in which Serendip was the Persian for the Arabic Serendib. Ceylon is often written in Portuguese as Ceilao or in

Buddhist lore was traditionally passed on by elders but today is transmitted in formal Sunday schools. Kelaniya Temple.

Dutch as Zeylan, both with innumerable variants. Ceylon is known to Tamils as Eelam, the word in the English name for the Tamil Tigers (Liberation Tigers of Tamil Eelam). The same word also appeared in Chola dynasty inscriptions, together with another, Illankai, deriving from Lanka. The present name, Sri Lanka, was changed from Ceylon in 1972.

Buddhists make up nearly 75 percent of the population, with Sinhalese speakers comprising the vast majority. An estimated 6,000 monasteries dot the landscape, sheltering some 15,000 monks. The religious conflicts that dogged Sri Lanka recently were present long before, witnessed in the Buddhist-Catholic Kotahena Riot of 1883 and the Buddhist-Muslim Riot of 1915. The nearly 30-year civil war between Sinhala Buddhists and Tamil Hindus ended in 2009, but tensions among all groups still simmer beneath the surface.

Islam is the third most popular faith, after Buddhism and Hinduism, adding up to nearly ten percent of the citizenry, or 2.2 million. The majority are Sunni and identify with the Shaf'i school of law. It is also the only group in Sri Lanka to define itself solely by religion.[18] There are nearly 900 mosques in Sri Lanka, with about 200 educational centres, or *madrasas*. The most sacred Islamic sites honour tombs, or *dargahs*, and legendary hermitages of saints or clerics believed to have journeyed to the island, much like the Buddha's visits. Tamil-speaking Muslims are the largest group, with smaller Islamic divisions numbering less than one percent of the total population.

Since the 1970s a rift has emerged in the Muslim community between the Sunni majority and followers of the strict Saudi Arabian Wahhabi division. The Sunni favour worship at the tombs of saints, a type of devotion that Wahhabis consider blasphemous. Another growing problem are Buddhist nationalists who too often turn their intolerance on Muslims. A fiery monk in Anuradhapura for example directed a mob to demolish a local Muslim shrine in 2011. Also, Buddhists have claimed Islamic sites, often based on skimpy archaeological evidence bolstered by the Department of Archaeology.

Most Muslim traders were based in India but others came from the Middle East. Marble tombstones found in Ceylon were commissioned and carved in distant Cambay, modern Khambaht in Gujarat and shipped to Ceylon and even as far as Java. The text of one in Trincomalee recorded the death of a Syrian noble's daughter in 1329. Another from Trincomalee is dated to 1409 and inscribed with Quranic verses.[19] Jewish merchants also participated in this long-distance commerce, forming partnerships with Muslims in Aden to construct a ship for the Ceylon trade in the early 12th century. Three Jewish goldsmiths and a cantor's son sailed aboard. The same Arab and Jewish merchants shipped 6,000 pounds of cinnamon from

This tombstone, dated to 1409, was commissioned in Gujarat and shipped over 3,000 kilometres to Trincomalee, recording the death of a jurist of the Ba 'Alavi Sufi order begun in Yemen. National Museum, Colombo.

Ceylon ('Seli') to Egypt centuries before the Portuguese dominated the shipping lanes.[20] Persian was at one time a lingua franca among certain communities, enabling the famous 14th-century Tangier traveller, Ibn Battuta, to converse with the Hindu king in the Jaffna area. Persian was also one of three languages, with Chinese and Tamil, found in the trilingual inscription of 1409 now in the Colombo Museum.

Portugal's advances in the 16th century signalled a steady erosion of Islamic mercantile dominance in Ceylon. The Portuguese objected to the 'shameful Religion' [Islam] that was spreading with 'diabolical zeal'. [21] Dutch colonialists were no less hostile when a governor decreed 'that the Moor and Muhammadan subjects of the Company receive less favour than the Christian [Calvinist] and heathen [Hindus, Buddhists and Catholics], and that they are never allowed to occupy positions of authority over Christians'. The governor continued, 'all heathen and Muhammadan superstitions must be rooted out'. The goal was to 'gradually exterminate this impudent class of people ...[and] ... those who arrive from elsewhere' should be made to return by the same vessel.[22] Such harsh dictates however were never well enforced and a sizeable Muslim population was always a part of the island's pluralistic mix.

Hindus number nearly 13 percent of the population, or close to three million and are mostly Tamils. Temples are in all the big cities, with dozens in Colombo alone. Hindu myths from India were mostly unchanged but some were transformed. For example, the myth describing the descent of the Ganges to earth was adapted to Adam's Peak and the Mahaveli Ganga River. Another case was the god Kataragama's second wife whose original birthplace in Tamil Nadu was transposed to Sri Lanka.

The demon Ravana's brother Vibhishana became King of Lanka, shown with his queen on the exterior wall of the Buddhist temple at Kelaniya. c. 1930s.

Hindu ritual practices were also borrowed from Tamil Nadu, such as the six daily ceremonies at Shaiva temples and a prescribed circumambulatory circuit within temples. Indian conventions, such as food offerings (S: *prasada*) to the deity, are the norm, together with priests or their assistants applying to the forehead a thin paste known as a *tilaka* in Pali and Sanskrit and *thilikam* in Tamil. This custom is also present among ritualists, or *kapuralas*, at Buddhist sites. The South Indian tradition of worshippers cracking open cocunuts in temple compounds is found at both Hindu and Buddhist

A brahman ritualist applying a mark, or *tilaka*, to a worshipper's forehead. Munneshvaram Temple.

sites in Sri Lanka. Even the same musical instruments for temple ceremonies in South India are used in Sri Lankan temples.

Buddhist chronicles generally characterize Hindu Tamils, or Damalas, as zealous anti-Buddhist invaders hellbent on destruction, such as sacking 'relic chambers' and carting off 'many costly images of gold' and 'violently destroying …. all the monasteries, like blood-sucking demons (*yakkhas*)'. (Cv: 55.21) These Tamil 'demons' were rhetorical foils in the chronicles that were contrasted to the virtue and piety of Buddhist kings and monks. Buddhism became a tool in what is described as a life-and-death struggle. For example, even an unspecified Buddha relic was set within a spear (P: *kunta*), used by Dutthagamani to drive the Tamils out of Anuradhapura. (Mhv: 25.1) And it was this very spear that is believed to be enshrined in one of Anuradhapura's major stupas, the Miracivatti. (Mhv.: 26: 10) Dutthagamani's mother, anticipating his birth and his war against Tamils, gruesomely relished the time when she will 'drink the water that cleansed the sword' that lobbed the head off the first Tamil soldier slain in the battle. (Mhv: 22.44)

Such anti-Tamil bias in the chronicles is irrefutable but many sources indicate that the two communities coexisted without such unceasing pernicious friction. A handful of examples suffice to suggest the degree of accord that runs counter to the narrative in the chronicles. For example, even the grandfather of the great Buddhist king Parakramabahu I (1153-86) descended from a Tamil prince from the Pandya dynasty. (Cv: 59: 41) At Polonnuruva a group of Tamil mercenaries even guarded the Temple of the Tooth and there was also a Tamil monastery, ('*demel-vehera*') at Anurdhapura. Other inscriptions speak of providing equal protection to Sinhala and Tamil coolies ('*demela-kuli*') and there were both Tamil and Sinhala workers at the Kelaniya monastery. Inscriptions now and then refer to Hindus patronizing Buddhist shrines and vice versa, notably the Buddhist king Nissankamalla constructing a Hindu temple ('*devalaya*') named after himself ('Nissankeshvara') at the Rameshvara Temple in Tamil Nadu.[23] Tamils also patronized a Buddhist site near Trincomalee where even the Chola invader, Rajendra I (1014-1044), left an inscription.[24] Researchers have neglected these signs of coexistence and many others, preferring to dwell on conventional interpretations that cast Sinhala Buddhists as the victims of unprovoked Tamil aggression.

The Buddha flanked by Vishnu, left, and Ganesha. An early 20th-century glass painting above the shrine doorway. Kotikagoda Viharaya, near Matara.

This is not to suggest that Buddhists and Hindus shared the island in ideal harmony over the ages but to propose only that the extreme animus against Tamils colouring the chronicles may not reflect actual circumstances in the premodern period. Ironically, despite the enmity between Sinhalas and Tamils that permeates the chronicles, the impact of Hindu beliefs and rituals on Sri Lankan Buddhism has been incalculable. For example, the famous annual tooth-relic procession, or *perahera*, in Kandy, is unthinkable without floats dedicated to Vishnu, Kataragama and Pattini.

Christianity left a lasting mark in Sri Lanka, beginning with Portuguese advances in the 16th century. Christians number about 7.5 percent of the total, or about 1.6 million, according to the 2012 census. Catholics are the largest group, with over six percent, with Protestant denominations making up the remainder. Christians are mostly in west coast communities where the Portuguese presence was strongest. By the time the Dutch wrested Ceylon from the Portuguese, as much as fifty percent of the population in the maritime provinces may have professed Catholicism.[25] Friars cleverly couched the gospel in dramas linked to local moral issues. One performance, for example, focussed on St John's condemnation of King Herod for taking 'his brother's wife, something which is very common among these barbarians and pagans'.[26]

A family's blessing at Colombo's St Anthony's.

Many churches have miracles explaining their foundations and there are voluminous examples of divine interventions, often foiling the Dutch. Friction among the Franciscans, Jesuits, Augustinians and Dominicans and so-called secular priests is a leitmotif in church records. There was also perennial tension between the religious orders who often promoted the welfare of the converted and corrupt Portuguese civil authority and rapacious landholders. Portuguese kings were forever called upon to settle disputes among these forces. Periodic revolts proved that converts were often quick to turn on the Portuguese and destroy churches. A Jesuit observed in 1629 that new believers 'are tender plants which shake with the wind of persecution … [and so] … might return to the worship of idols'.[27]

The hostility between Catholics and Protestants in Europe also played out throughout Asia. The Dutch feared that Catholic converts would act as the tip of a Portuguese spear in retaking the island. For example, the Dutch treaty with Kandy in 1638 enjoined that 'papists' and 'other ecclesiastics' should be 'exterminated' since they could rebel 'against their King [Rajasimha II]' with a view of aiding the Portuguese in retaking the island.[28] And the Dutch community itself was never immune from the internal squabbles that wracked Protestant Europe. One example were clandestine lay missionaries in Dutch Colombo known as Herrnutters who challenged the legitimacy of the Dutch clergy. There was even ill feeling between members of the Dutch Reformed Church and German Lutherans, many of the latter who were soldiers in Dutch employment.

Anuradhapura was a focus point in the early days of Buddhist nationalism and resistance to the British. *The Buddhist Annual of Ceylon*, 1923.

'The wish-fulfilling tree in the Island of Lanka'

Sri Lanka is the oldest continuous Buddhist nation, stretching back to the third century BCE., that is, centuries before the faith's introduction into Southeast Asia or the Far East. Thousands of short stone inscriptions in Sinhala Prakrit, a language related to Sanskrit, testify to a vibrant religious community throughout the island. However, Ceylon's history comes into sharper focus only by the 4th and 5th centuries with the rise of urban areas, such as Anuradhapura, Mantai and Tissamaharama. The country's ancient Buddhist past was never forgotten, invoked for example in a treaty with the Portuguese in 1518 that opened with references to ancient Anuradhapura ('Anu-raja-pure') and to august monarchs, such as Vijayabahu I (1055-1110).[29] And Kandy's most famous king, Kirti Sri Rajasimha (1474-1482), claimed descent from the semi-legendary king Vattagamani (89 – 77 BCE), who was himself linked to the warrior caste ('*kshatriya*'), Manu and the world's creation by Brahma. At the same time, the island's connection with the Buddha was always foremost, expressed in a sixteenth-century chronicle wherein the Buddha himself prophesied that Asoka will send the 'southern branch' of 'the wish-fulfilling tree to the Island of Lanka' where it would remain for 5,000 years.[30]

The best known is the *Mahavamsa* and its subsequent additions, named for convenience the *Lesser Chronicle* (P: *Culavamsa*), that concluded with the conquest of Kandy by the British in 1815. Another type of influential chronicle highlighted a single site, often featuring a stupa or relic. These site-histories were normally composed first in Pali and then later sometimes in Sinhalese. The best known is perhaps the 13th-century history of the Ruvanvali stupa, known as the *History of the Stupa* (P: *Thupa-vamsa*), soon followed by a Sinhalese version. Others would include the history of the Bodhi tree (P: *Mahabodhi-vamsa*) and the Buddha's footprint on Adam's Peak, *In Praise of Mount Samantakuta* (P: *Samantakuta-vannana*).[31] These chronicles were usually written by monks and often patronized by kings. Such 'histories' were also recited in probably abbreviated form in the compounds of stupas, such as one public reading at the Ruvanvali stupa sponsored by a 13th-century queen.[32] Ballads retelling the highlights of these legends were probably recited in villages, thus disseminating the legends widely over time. The large number of these chronicles surviving in monastery libraries testifies to their role in keeping alive this vast lore.

Sri Lanka's chronicles had an incalcuable influence in Southeast Asia where the *sangha* in Burma and Thailand saw themselves as part of the same missionary wave initiated at the time of Asoka. Many Pali manuscripts from Ceylon are among nearly nearly 300 listed in a 1442-inscription from Pagan, and a quick glance at Thai chronicles reveals a similar debt, such as Thailand's Emerald Buddha. Another sacred image in Thailand was was even called the 'Ceylon Buddha', or Phra Sihing. The vessel on which the image sailed was shipwrecked, but the Buddha image 'remained afloat on a single plank' until it was eventually taken to Sukhothai.[33] A Burmese tradition piggybacked on this myth wherein four Buddhas, launched from Ceylon, floated ashore in Burma where each Buddha became a regional pilgrimage spot.[34]

Four Buddhas launched from Ceylon beached in Lower Burma. This one appeared at Dawei. Shin Mokti Pagoda. Dawei. Courtesy Elizabeth Moore.

An ascetic, right, prepares protective string bracelets for Vijaya and his followers. Kelaniya Viharaya. Solias Mendis. c. 1930s.

Vijaya & His Demonic Consort

On the day of the Buddha's death in India, a prince named Vijaya landed on the shores of Lanka with seven hundred followers, thus fulfilling a prophecy uttered by the Buddha himself. This event serves as a foundation myth for Sinhala Buddhists, much like the founding of Rome by Romulus and Remus and Aeneas. The prophesy is found first in the 4th-century *Chronicle of the Island* (P: *Dipavamsa*) and then more fully in the *Mahavamsa*. (Dpv: chpt. 9; Mhv: chpts. 6-7) Vijaya's grandfather in India was a lion who mated with a human princess from Vanga, usually taken to be Bengal. Their son, Sihabahu, was born with lion paws and later slew his lion-father after he and his mother and sister escaped from a cave in which the lion-father imprisoned them. Eventually Sihabahu and his sister settled in his homeland, called Lala, thought to be Gujarat. Here, Sihabahu married his sister and produced twin sons numbering thirty-two. The eldest was Vijaya whose unspecified anti-social behaviour forced his father to banish him from Lala with his seven hundred followers. Vijaya's ships and his companions eventually made landfall in Lanka at a spot known as Tambapanni.

The Buddha instructed the chief of the gods, named Sakka, to appoint Vishnu to protect the new settlers. Vishnu's name was Uppalavanna (Pali), or Upulvan, although his early identity is debated.[35] This very myth was adapted in Burma centuries later when the Buddha also prophesied that Vishnu would appear as a sage, or rishi ('*risi*'), at the time of the Buddha's death and later establish the country's first capital at Shri Kshetra.[36]

Vijaya was greeted by Upulvan who assumed the form of an ascetic who tied magical threads, or *pirit nula*, around the wrists of the newcomers to protect them from an ogress named Kuveni (P: Kuvanna). This ogress kidnapped Vijaya's followers and later assumed 'the lovely form of a sixteen-year-old maiden'. (Mhv: 7.27) Vijaya fell for her charms and in time Kuveni gave birth to twins, a boy and girl. Her status as an ogress however disqualified Vijaya from performing a royal consecration, so he acquired a queen from Madurai in Tamil Nadu. Vijaya then banished Kuveni and the two children into the forest where Kuveni was slain by the island's demons since she had betrayed them by coupling with Vijaya. Her orphaned children escaped to Sumanakuta, that is, Adam's Peak. The brother and sister mated and their offspring became the Pulindas, an ancient Indian name given to Lanka's so-called aboriginal inhabitants, or the Vaddas. Later kings claimed descent from Vijaya.[37]

How the earlier myth of Kuveni was subject to many variations is illustrated in the 17th-century Sinhalese text named *Rajavilaya*.[38] Kuveni had three breasts but a rishi prophesied that if the middle breast vanished then she would wed Vijaya. Threatened with death by Vijaya because she kidnapped his companions, Kuveni swore an oath on her third breast that if Vijaya could spare her life then she would return his followers. The breast disappeared and Kuveni became Vijaya's queen. She then assumed the form of a horse and Vijaya, mounted, slew all of the demons who had come to a local wedding banquet. Vijaya was eventually forced to banish Kuveni since he was disqualified from assuming the throne because of her ogress status. Furious at Vijaya since he forsook her love for his own advancement, Kuveni then made for herself a diamond tongue with which she intended to cut down her consort. To protect Vijaya, the guardian gods of Lanka joined forces and severed her tongue and turned her into stone.

A male descendant of Vijaya's union with the Pandyan princess went on to wed a Sakyan princess from India, according to the *Mahavamsa*. Their son, Pandukabhaya, was therefore a full-blooded Indian and the founder of the nation's first capital, Anuradhapura. The dynastic and familial connection with India thus crystallized with the establishment of Anuradhpura. 'The Tamils are not only kinfolk [of the Sinhalas] but also co-founders of the nation' but this fundamental link between Tamils and Sinhalas has now been forgotten.[39] At least one ruler in Lanka who claimed descent from Vijaya did not identify himself with Lala but Kalinga, an example of how this flexible myth could be used to bolster political lineages.[40]

Vijaya and the demoness Kuveni on the right. Ceylon's *Mahavamsa* chronicle was well known in Thailand and Burma. Lacquer Pavilion, Suan Pakkad Palace, Bangkok. c. Late 18th century.

Vijaya's mating with Kuveni was a well-known myth outside of Sri Lanka by the middle of the first millennium. Indeed, there are so many prototypes for the legend in Indian Buddhist sources that the myth recorded in Lanka's *Mahavamsa* was a reflection of the comingled cultures of India and Sri Lanka and was certainly not completely indigenous. Even the 7th-century Chinese pilgrim Xuanzang, who never visited Lanka, recounted two legends with features nearly identical in the *Mahavamsa*. In one version, Xuanzang recorded that the son who slayed his lion-father was banished from India to the 'country of Sinhala [Lanka]' where he wed the daughter of a merchant. In the second version, Xuanzang related that 500 ogresses in Sri Lanka, disguised as lovely damsels, lured seafarers to satisfy their insatiable appetite for human flesh.[41] A merchant named Sinhala came to the island with 500 companions but a heavenly horse offered them freedom by telling them to hold tightly to his mane and to never look down at the lovely but famished maidens when they departed in the air for India. But the merchants succumbed to their charms and fell to the ground, leaving only Sinhala to escape. A similar story, in the Cloud-horse Jataka, or *Valahassa Jataka* (no. 196), claimed that half of 500 shipwrecked sailors escaped on the horse.

A Sanskrit Buddhist source mentioned the rescue of men by the horse but focussed on the chief demoness who traveled to India to woo the rich merchant Sinhala. (*Divyavadana*: 2. 252) Another version is told in the Tibetan and Chinese *Mulasarvastivadin-vinaya* in which the horse warned the sailors to never 'be bewitched at the last moment' since he would then be unable to carry them.[42] All fell victim to the damsels, except for Sinhala. The myth was brought to life with a three-dimensional stone horse at Neak Pean temple at Angkor. These examples and others, in both Pali and Sanskrit versions, indicate that Lanka was from a very early time associated with demonesses and a protagonist named Sinhala and that these tales were part of regional folklore. Indeed, it is easy to recognize Vijaya's demonic consort as part of long-standing regional traditions.

Tamils recast the Vijaya myth with a Hindu twist, recorded in a chronicle from Jaffna dated to circa 1736. Instead of Vijaya proceeding to Lanka from Lata, he traveled to Varanasi where he was instructed in a dream to settle in Lanka. Accompanied by a Varanasi brahman, Vijaya landed in Lanka and discovered only the Vadda peoples. Vijaya then called on Buddhists in Siam, who had been driven there from India, to settle in Lanka and after which they came to be called Sinhalas. Vijaya was also described as a devotee of Shiva who founded the four major Hindu temples on the island.[43] This late Tamil chronicle that incorporated many of the core elements of the Vijaya legend in Buddhist chronicles testifies to the myth's widespread currency among Tamils by the eighteenth century and a desire among Tamils to adapt the myth to their own ends.

Ceylon's Supreme Court

'The Supreme Court of Judicature in the Island of Ceylon' by James Stephanoff.
The original watercolour, c. 1818-1819, was in the Royal Asiatic Society and was reproduced in hand-coloured acquatints. Yale Center for British Art.

Sri Lanka's pluralism is captured in a watercolour titled 'The Supreme Court of Judicature in the Island of Ceylon' made for Sir Alexander Johnston who departed Ceylon in 1818 after years as Chief Justice. Sir Alexander commissioned the work in London from James Stephanoff, a well-known painter of historical scenes who never visited Ceylon but based this work on sketches from Colombo. The courthouse probably went up sometime after the British took Colombo in 1796 and was at or near the spot once occupied by the old Dutch Government House, or Landraad, in a district still known as Hulftsdorp.[44] In 1802, there were only two 'advocates and proctors', both Dutch 'gentlemen' fluent in English.[45] The classical-style building is no longer used as a courtroom and is one of a few old buildings within the modern Aluthkade Courts Complex.

A caption beneath aquatint copies recorded the presentation of the painting to Sir Alexander by your 'humble servant J Stephanoff'. Sir Alexander was praised for his 'enlightened and benevolent views' and for a 'grant made by his present Majesty while Prince Regent to the natives of Ceylon for the right of sitting upon juries … [and] … the abolition of domestic slavery'. The watercolour dates to 1818 or 1819 when King George IV was Prince Regent, but slavery was not completely abolished in Ceylon until 1844.

Two judges sit in the centre beneath a tapestry with the British royal arms. Five accused men stand in the dock, stripped to the waist, and to the left is a jury composed of 'natives' standing in two rows and clothed in velvet with metal buttons. On the far right a monk swears in a Buddhist witness, with a Hindu priest and Muslim *imam* standing by to do the same for their co-religionists. Ensuring Buddhist monks always swore to tell the truth posed a problem, since 'Budhu [*sic*] priests were always bound to speak the truth'. For guidance, the Dutch first consulted six Buddhist texts, including the *Vinaya,* but in vain. A novel proposal was to have both a Buddhist shrine and a 'Dewalle (house of gods)' [*devalaya*]' constructed near the 'court-house'. A 'capoorawla' (*kapurala*) would be in attendance within the *devalaya* and a monk stationed in the Buddhist shrine. This solution was never implemented and it was left to individual magistrates to determine by what method he 'conceives to be the most binding upon the Buddhist priests in his district'.[46]

The scores of standing figures in the foreground were never part of a real courtroom but were added to highlight the ethnic and cultural mix of Colombo at the time.

Stephanoff included diverse ethnic groups to highlight Ceylon's pluralism.

The Sixteen Sacred Sites, the two lower registers, below the Buddha's Seven Weeks at Bodh Gaya, capped by the set of Twenty-four Buddhas. Ridi Viharaya, c. 1750-1800.

The 16 Sacred Sites

All Theravada countries have an unspoken ranking of major sacred sites but only in Sri Lanka did a formal list come into existence. It is made up of 16 sites (P: *Solosmasthana*), with no prescribed sequence and no requirement to worship at any of them in one's lifetime. Indeed, few Sri Lankans have visited them all since they are dispersed throughout the island, effectively defining a national geography of consecrated ground.

Early evidence for this grouping comes from a sixteenth-century Pali chronicle from Chiang Mai that referred to 'the sixteen holy places' visited by monks from Siam and Lower Burma in about 1424. No specific sites were identified but this is strong evidence that this concept was current by that time. Augmenting this reference is a Lankan chronicle from the same century that also mentioned sixteen sacred sites; but none were specified, apart from the Bodhi Tree.[47] The set achieved a permanent place in the country's religious life by the time of Kandy's king, Kirti Sri Rajasimha, and appeared regularly in murals and on wooden manuscript covers. A clerical mission from Ayutthaya purportedly visited all the locations during this same period but the sites were not named. (Cv. 100: 128, 253) The *Culavamsa* also mentioned the 16 sites during the reign of Parakramabahu II (1236-70) but this portion of the text was probably of a later date. The sites were referred to collectively as 'relics-of-use', or *paribhogika*, meaning that the Buddha sanctified each site by virtue of his visits. (Cv: 82: 18) A group of eight sites (P: *Atamasthana*) were identified at Anuradhapura but two fourteenth-century texts, the *Pujavaliya* and the *Saddamalankaraya*, contain slightly different lists.[48]

All the sites are celebrated today in a Pali poem, or *gatha*, taught in government schools and memorised by millions, with the sites appearing in this order: Mahiyangana, Nagadipa, Kelaniya, Sri Pada, Diva-Guhava, Dighavapi, Mutiyangana, Tissamaharama, the Bodhi Tree, Maricavatti, Ruvanavali, Thuparama, Abhayagiri, Jetavana, Sila and Kataragama. This sequence was popularized by a leading monk, M. Gunananda (1823-1890), whose list appeared in his book, the *Bauddha Adahilla, or Worship of the Buddha*, issued first in 1889 and distributed in numerous editions.[49] The monk's verses were used for unique captions to murals at Colombo's Subodharama monastery.

The Jetavana Stupa at Anuradhapura, one of the sixteen sacred sites. Subodharama Viharaya, Colombo. Circa 1898.

The Checklist

This selection of sacred sites is designed to highlight a number of diverse themes. For example, the myths and histories of Anuradhapura, Adam's Peak and the Kelaniya Monastery explore the formation of Sinhala Buddhist identity in its earliest stages. The colourful meanderings of the Buddha's tooth-relic over many centuries illustrate the ways in which relics have lives of their own, subject to unexpected vicissitudes of patronage and society. Hindu sites, such as Kataragama, Devinuvara and Trincomalee, show how transplanted Indian myths were adapted to an indigenous landscape. Other destinations are windows on historical eras, such as Colombo's Dutch Wolvendaal church or a nearby monastery led by an exiled Siamese prince-turned-monk who figured in Buddhism's revival. A temple in Galle demonstrates a dispute between temple trustees and a monk that was resolved only after it went all the way up to the Surpreme Court in 1921, the judge basing his decision on a ruling found in the Pali canon's *Cullavagga*. We also visit Attanagalla where an old myth was revised centuries later and attached to the site's stupa in the thirteenth century. Another example, in the early twentieth century, centres on a charismatic monk who wedded old myths to ruinous stupas at Suruvila and Somavathiya. At Sigiriya, the legendary maidens (S: *apsaras*) are reminders of how the celestial and terrestrial realms comingled for the hundreds of ancient pilgrims who incised their poems on the famous Mirror Wall. This was a world, after all, in which a king could be seen conversing with 'Buddhist devas'. Colombo's Subodharama Monastery, though not a major site was chosen as a rare example of an urban monastery surviving intact with spectacular murals. The legendary hermitage of an Islamic saint, at Daftar Jailani near Adam's Peak, is representative of the ongoing problem of Sinhala Buddhists expropriating both Islamic and Hindu sites. Many venerated locations have been omitted but these some twenty sites, taken together, convey the rich and varied role of sacred sites in the past and their role in the formation of Sri Lankan civilization.

ANURADHAPURA

ANURADHAPURA: 'A DIVINE CITY'

Asoka's son, Mahinda, landed on this peak and began the conversion of Sri Lanka.

Anuradhapura holds a special place for Sinhala Buddhists since the state's inception and the island's Buddhist conversion began in tandem here. It was also here that the Buddha himself prophesied the future appearance of the Bodhi Tree and two of the city's major stupas. (Mhv: 1.80-83; 17.46) In addition, it is here where all the Buddha's relics (P: *sarira*) will muster at the end of the present world era. First collecting at the Ruvanvali Stupa, these relics will then proceed to Snake Island, or Nagadipa, in northern Sri Lanka, before departing for Bodh Gaya whereupon they will self-immolate. When the relics are no more, the way is paved for the Buddha of the Future, Metteyya. This narrative emerged at as early as the 5th century and was widely known, witnessed in a 14th-century inscription at Sukhothai.[1] Anuradhapura is therefore not merely another ruin-strewn World Heritage site but played an integral role in a Theravada worldview that is also central to Sinhala Buddhist identity. That a 13th-century chronicler described the ancient capital as a 'divine city resting on the terrestrial globe' is therefore scarcely surprising.[2]

Previous page:
Worshippers at the Bodhi Tree Temple.

A golden cow, with a relic inside, was enshrined within the Abhayagiri Stupa, a belief not found in the major chronicles. Mural inside worship hall beside the Abhayagiri Stupa.

The story begins when Asoka's son, Mahinda, and grandson, Sumana, flew to a mountaintop some sixteen kilometers east of Anuradhapura and converted Devanampiya Tissa (250-210 BCE). Finding the king on a hunt, a mountain-god assumed the form of a stag to lure the king to an audience with Mahinda. (Mhv: 14.4) After Mahinda's sermon, the king and his 40,000 men became Buddhists. The conversion is thought to have taken place at the peak's base, marked now by the ancient Ambasthala Stupa. Also at Mihintale are over a 100 early donative inscriptions, in caves and on rocks, one even referring to an image of Mahinda.[3]

Sumana returned to India to ask his grandfather for relics required to fulfill the nation's Buddhist destiny. He came back with the Buddha's alms-bowl filled with unspecified corporal relics that were distributed among thirty-two spots across the realm. He also visited a heaven sacred to the deity Sakka where he acquired the Buddha's right collarbone (P: *dakkhina-akkhaka*), later enshrined in the Thuparama Stupa when its brick walls were 'knee high'. (Mhv: 17. 25) The second collarbone was recovered from the Buddha's funeral pyre and enshrined at Mahiyangana. (Mhv: 1. 38).[4]

The capital's transfer to Polonnuruva at the beginning of the second millennium resulted in sharply reduced patronage. Maintenance disrupted, the stupas and monasteries inexorably fell into ruin. Much the same happened in Burma when the capital shifted from Pagan to the Ava area. However, the handful of principal monuments, both at Anuradhapura and Pagan, remained the focus of worship and restoration. For example, Nissankamalla (1187-1196) visited here from Polonnaruva where he ordered the refurbishment of 'the Miricavatti and other viharas' and also 'scattered pearls ... as if he were offering flowers on a bed of sand' in the compound of the Ruvanvali Stupa.Through such good works, kings sought 'nirvana'.[5]

The restoration of the key monuments slowed by the 14th century to the point that the large stupas at Anuradhapura were probably in no better condition than they were in the 19th century when they were 'covered with thick jungle and high trees'.[6] Though in ruins, the city was nonetheless an important religious centre, explaining why a Portuguese official was ordered to 'prevent the pilgrimages to Anu-Raja-Pure, whither Pagan [Buddhists] and Christians [converted Sinhalas] resort on the pretense of visiting those antiquities, and under such a plea a Rebellion was plotted there'.

'An Invasion of Poisonous Rats'

Rumours of ruins in fact attracted the attention of a Captain-general who deputed Father Francisco Negrão in the seventeenth-century to discover the fabled city known as Anu-Raja-Pure. The monuments were largely 'hidden in thickets' but Anuradhapura's enduring legacy assured it a place on numerous Portuguese and Dutch maps in which it usually appears as a European city in miniature with church steeples and city walls. The famous Bronze Palace (P: Lohapasada) was in ruins but the rows of surviving stone pillars were accurately tabulated by Father Negrão. The city's collapse was put down to 'an invasion of poisonous rats', a punishment for the corruption introduced by foreigners, namely, the 'Chinese, Arabs and Romans'. The populace fled into the jungle and became the 'Bedas', or Vaddas, the so-called aborigines often mistakenly identified as the first-inhabitants of Ceylon. A related but no less outlandish Portuguese report claimed that the king, after practicing cannibalism, was banished to the forest where he and his followers became the Vaddas.[8] The rise and decline of this once impressive ancient city perhaps resembled to the Portuguese the loss of Ceylon to the Dutch, a demise caused by greed and its handmaidens, corruption and mismanagement.

Anuradhapura was the longest running ancient Asian capital, extending from the third century BCE to the 11th century CE. Maps based on Ptolemy's *Cosmographia* captioned it as 'Anurogramum Regia'. Its legendary founder was the Buddha's great grand-nephew named Pandukabhaya (394-307 BCE), a scion of the Sakya clan to which the Buddha belonged. Later kings here and in Polonnoruva stressed their connection with the Sakya family that descended from the Solar Lineage (S: *Suryavamsha*). The religious environment was eclectic, flavoured with Jain ascetics, brahmans and even a benevolent horse-face demoness depicted centuries later in the Dambulla murals. There was also a 'city-god' (P: *pura-deva*). (Mhv: 10. 97; 25. 87) Strong connections with nearby South India existed throughout the centuries, in the same way as the material and spiritual culture of the British Isles was interwoven with the Continent.[9]

Our chief historical source is the 5th-century Pali *Mahavamsa*, *The Great Chronicle*, and its continuation, labelled for convenience the *Culavamsa,* or *The Lesser Chronicle*. The earliest translations of the *Mahavamsa* appeared in 1833 and 1837, and archaeologists sought to match ruins in the chronicle with monuments on the ground. The results were mixed, much like mapping out Jerusalem from Biblical passages. For example, two of the largest stupas in the chronicles, the Jetavana and Abhayagiri, were confused with one another until the discovery of a stone inscription in 1910.[10] Further, the earliest translation was quite garbled, asserting for example that the Buddha was born in Lanka and established a monastery on Adam's Peak.

The chronicles were compiled by monks belonging to the leading monastic division at Anuradhapura, known as the Mahavihara, or Great Monastery. Much of the information in the *Mahavamsa* can rarely be corroborated but scores of stone inscriptions put the city's history on firmer ground. The earliest were donations of cave-residences to monks, many from before the time of Christ. The language was Sinhala-Prakrit, akin to Indian Prakrit, written in characters adapted from India. By the third century, the preference for caves was eclipsed by brick monasteries.[11]

At the city's centre was an irregularly shaped walled enclosure whose total length stretched for nearly four kilometres. Inside were a palace and residences for the royal family and elites. Its major street was called Auspicious Great Street, or Mangul Maha-veya. The three centres of power were the king and his court, nobles and gentry, and the Buddhist community of monks (P: *sangha*). The city's large monasteries required a huge labour force to maintain the structures and to provide for thousands of monks. Land allotments were given to some workers while others were tenants, slaves or bondsmen. Craftsmen attached to individual monasteries also specialized in stone and ivory carving, roof tiles and metallurgy, with occasional references to architects and master-artisans.[12]

The two most sacred landmarks from the outset were the Ruvanvali Stupa and the Bodhi Tree, both established during the third century BCE, according to the *Mahavamsa*. Centuries later, a tooth-relic arrived from India but it merited but few verses compared to four chapters devoted to the Ruvanvali Stupa. For unknown reasons, many of the city's relics drifted out of history, such as a strand of the Buddha's hair from Bodh Gaya and the tuft-of-hair (P: *unna*) set in the Buddha's forehead.[13] (Cv: 39. 51 ; 42. 62) A monastery's prestige was probably based to some degree on the sacredness of its relics, much as relic-filled churches in Rome still are today. By the eighteenth century, a grouping of sixteen sacred sites in Sri Lanka crystalized and fully half were in Anuradhapura. These eight numbered the Bodhi Tree, the Bronze Palace and stupas (Ruvanvali, Thuparama, Miricavatti, Lankarama, Abhayagiri and Jetavana).

Three monastic divisions, (P: *nikayas*), dominated religious life. Their traditional foundation dates are known from the *Mahavamsa*, the earliest being the Mahavihara begun at the time of Asoka, followed by the Abhayagiri in 89 BCE and the Jetavana during the time of Mahasena (275-310). The Mahavihara boasted two enormous stupas, the Ruvanvali and Miricavatti, while each of the other two had a single gigantic stupa. These four stupas probably went up between the first century BCE and the third century CE and were by far the largest stupas in the ancient world, dwarfing the Sanchi Stupa and others in India.[14] The monastery grounds were extensive, with the Abhayagiri complex alone encompassing about 500 acres. Some 10,000 monks may have been in residence by the fifth century.[15] No boundaries separating these establishments are evident today but ancient residents would have been quick to recognize where one monastery left off and another began.

A figure with four arms, the Jetavana Stupa, probably from the eastern frontispiece, or *vahalkada*. Painting on stone. Possibly Kubera.

The city's earliest sculpture is found around the bases of these four ancient stupas and the smaller Kantaka stupa at Mihintale. The sculpture was set into imposing brick frontispieces abutting the stupas in the cardinal directions. These offsets were attached some time after the original stupa's construction and were the settings for offerings and rituals, as they are today. They came to be called '*ayaka*' in ancient Lanka, a term common in Andhra Pradesh where it had a different meaning; the more common Sinhalese word today for these frontispieces is *vahalkada*. Only those at the Abhayagiri can be reliably dated, by a stone inscription stating that the king established the four *ayakas* ('*catara ayika*').[16] The donor was Kanittha Tissa (167-186) and so by extension the sculpture in a similar style on the other major stupas at Anuradhapura and Mihintale can be dated to more or less the same age. All the frontispieces were in ruins and covered in jungle for centuries and were conjecturally reconstructed, starting in the late 19th century. Traces of painting once on these offsets are on view at the Jetavana Museum. These large structures were chambers for items of value, attracting ancient treasure hunters who broke into at least one. However, inside the northern and eastern projections at the Jetavana were hundreds of imported ceramics, ivory objects, and more than 300, 000 beads of various materials, together forming what is now called the Jetavana Treasure. Within one of the Abhayagiri frontispieces were two small stone stupa-like caskets donated by the wife and mother of Kanittha Tissa, now in the Colombo Museum.[17] Such offerings were made by numerous elites, probably on single occasions.

Standing Buddhas in the Ruvanvali compound, modeled on Andhra Pradesh examples. Limestone, c. Fifth or sixth century.

The early sculpture of Anuradhapura is indebted to the traditions of India's southeastern coast. The earliest Buddha images, for example, were modeled on styles from Andhra Pradesh, with larger than life-size standing Buddhas imported to Lanka. Even an inscribed coping stone for an ancient railing was made from stone imported from Andhra. Also, the famous moonstones in Anuradhapura were likely inspired by examples in Andhra. Even a handful of small marble sculptures were imported to Anuradhapura, and some stone images may have been sculpted by foreign craftsmen resident in Lanka. One figural group in marble imported from Andhra depicts Queen Maya's Dream. Another narrative sculpture at the Jetavana Stupa, showing king Sarvamdada cutting his flesh to offer a bird catcher, has direct connections with many examples in Andhra.[18] The theme of kings sacrificing their own flesh in connection with birds weaves in and of Buddhist literature and is also found in Jain traditions. There was even a 'Sinhala-vihara' at Nagarjunakonda, known from an inscription in which Ceylon is called the Island of 'Tambapamni' (Taprobana).[19]

Maya's Dream, imported from Andhra Pradesh, India, c. Third century, limestone, National Museum, Colombo.

The bulk of Anuradhapura's surviving sculpture falls largely in the city's last phase, that is, between the 8th-10th centuries. This includes scores of spectacular snake-guardian figures, moonstones and balustrades. Connections with South Indian Pallava and Chola art are evident but poorly charted. A precise chronology for the city's sculpture has yet to be worked out but the differences between the earliest and latest sculpture at Anuradhapura are readily detected.

'A Thorn in the Sangha'

The Mahavihara, Abhayagiri and Jetavana complexes represented monastic divisions that adhered to different versions or recensions of the Buddhist canon and its commentaries.[20] How these monastic lineages interacted and differed in doctrine and practice over time is however much debated. Moreover, the major surviving chronicles were compiled by the Mahavihara monks who forever disparaged other *nikayas*, thus creating a lopsided trichotomy that promoted Mahavihara virtues at the expense of the others. In fact, the pernicious conflicts among the divisions is a leitmotif in the *Mahavamsa*. The Abhayagiri monks for example were labelled 'shameless' and supported by a wicked king who destroyed the Mahavihara monasteries and carted off the materials to create the Abhayagiri complex. (Mhv: 37. 12) The Abhayagiri monastery was even described as a 'thorn' that threatened a unified *sangha*. (Cv: 36. 111) Other protagonists in the chronicles were duplicitous kings, scheming ministers, and avaricious monks who were foils to pious kings, sage ministers and self-sacrificing monks belonging to the Mahavihara. Kings who dared to act against the Mahavihara realized their error and atoned with donations to the *sangha*.

Areas of perennial contention had little to do with lofty Buddhist principles but centred on differing codes of monastic behaviour. Rules ranged widely, from how robes were to be worn to the proper method for cleaning one's teeth. Violations of rules merited punishments, with extreme infractions resulting in expulsion from the *sangha* or even exile to India 'by the king's wrath'. In fact, it was a monk's expulsion from the Mahavihara that was purportedly behind the founding of the Abhayagiri division. Not only were there

Durga, from Mihintale. c. 11th Century. National Museum, Colombo.

more than 200 rules spelled out in the *Patimokkha* section of the *Vinaya-pitaka*, but individual monasteries drew up their own norms of conduct. At least eight monasteries are known to have fashioned their own rules and recorded them in stone inscriptions during the Anuradhapura period. A good example are the Mahintale stone tablets of Mahinda IV (956-72) that instructed monks to meditate on certain 'four protective formulas' at dawn, to then clean their teeth and to dress in robes 'as prescribed in the '*Sika-karani*' (P: *Sikha-karani*), a text governing the everyday life of monasteries. In addition, certain senior monks were awarded a share, or *vasag*, of the annual 'net income' of the monastery based on their study of the of the Pali canon. For the most difficult division, the *Abhidhamma*, monks were awarded twelve portions of *vasag*, while those who mastered the *Sutta* and *Vinaya* were given only seven and five *vasags*, respectively.[21]

By the 12th century, rulers promulgated regulations (P: *katikavatas*) for the *sangha* countrywide. The first and most consequential was the Galvihara inscription at Polonuruva of Parakramabahu I that coloured the course of *sangha* history in Ceylon, Burma and Siam.

The Mahavihara division represents for many Sri Lankans today the pure Theravada orthodoxy while the dissenting Abhayagiri monastery advocated Mahayana and even Tantric doctrines. Such a contrast is oversimplified and ignores the nuanced nature of the city's centuries-long evolution and the interaction among these divisions. For example, the Abhayagiri and Mahavihara monasteries, despite their professed conflicts, shared possession of the tooth relic, if we can believe two foreign pilgrims, Faxian (337-422) and Vajrabodhi (671-741). No sacred texts attributed to the Abhayagiri monastery have survived, so its beliefs must be conjecturally reconstructed.[22]

Another monastic group was known as the Pamsukulikas that existed in both the Mahavihara and Abhayagiri divisions. By the ninth century this group formed its own school (P: *gana*). (Cv: 51. 52) Another group was the Arannikas, or 'forest-dwellers', that were connected to the Mahavihara. This group was based near Polonnaruva at Dimbulagala and came to play a major role in Thailand and in Lower Burma under the name of the Udumbaragiri. By the 12th century, the Mahavihara division was supplanted by eight groups, known as *mulas* or *ayatanas*.

The term Mahayana is nowhere found in ancient Sri Lankan sources but the Abhayagiri monks were described as followers of the *Vetulla*, a term encompassing Mahayana scriptures. (Cv: 78. 221) A 3rd-century inscription from the Jetavana extolls the views of the *Vetulla*, or 'books of the Vayatudala [Vetulla]' and alludes to conflicts with the Mahavihara. The Abhayagiri had connections with distant Buddhist communities outside of Sri Lanka, such as Java, suggesting that it was more open to new ideas than the Mahavihara *nikaya*. One Sanskrit text that may have been important was the *Sarva-tathagata-sattva-sangraha*, classified as a *yoga tantra*.[23]

Concrete evidence for Mahayana traditions are seven gold sheets

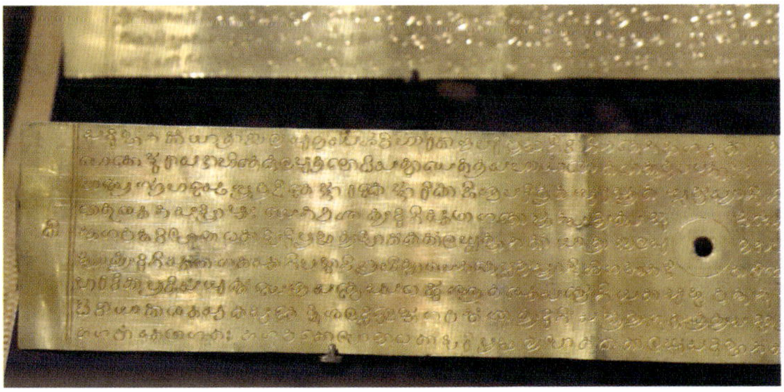

Gold plates inscribed with a portion of the *Twenty-five Thousand Verses*. c. 10th or 11th centuries, from the Jetavana Monastery, National Museum, Colombo.

inscribed in Sinhala characters with a portion of the 'Twenty-five Thousand Verses' (S: *Pancha-vimshati-sahasrika-prajna-paramita Sutra*). This text was known throughout the Mahayana world, together with the more popular 'Eight Thousand Verses'. The gold plates, datable to the 10th or 11th century, were discovered in a clay bowl within the base of the Jetavana monastery in 1982, probably interred at the time of a later refurbishment. Fragments of another Mahayana work, incised on copper sheets, have also come to light inside a brick stupa at Mihintale. This Sanskrit text is known in Central Asia and in later Chinese translations (S: *Kashyapa-parivartta*). In addition, eight small stone blocks were discovered near the Abhayagiri Stupa inscribed in North Indian *nagari* characters. Six blocks present a *dharani*, that is, a brief prayer-like summary of a longer text. The original Sanskrit Mahayana text has not survived but is known from a Tibetan translation compiled by the ninth century and is a dialogue between the Buddha and the Bodhisattva Vajrapani on the efficacy of enshrining texts within stupas. A copper plate incised with 10th-century *nagari* characters was found among the Jetavana ruins, with a two-sentence text drawn from the *Vattaka Jataka* (no. 35).[24] This is the only Pali inscription known to be in *nagari* characters. One object associated with the Mahayana is a gilded bronze thunderbolt (S: *vajra*) in the Colombo Museum, with another at the Abhayagiri Museum.

A gilded bronze *vajra* found in Anuradhapura is among tangible evidence for Mahayana ritual practices. National Museum, Colombo.

Anuradhapura participated in the wider Buddhist Mahayana world but the nature of these contacts is uncertain. Whatever the differences among the three *nikayas*, the community of monks were unified, at least in theory, under the Mahavihara mantle during the reign of Parakramabahu I (1153-1186) in Polonnuruva.

Stupas are associated with relics but certain examples were known for commemorating special occurrences or acts of atonement. Two unrelated narratives, for example, underpin the huge Miricavatti stupa. One commemorates the king's victory over the Tamils, or Damilas, using a special lance (P: *kunta*), which contained an unspecified relic (P: *'dhatu'*). Officials drove this victory-spear into the ground but no one had the strength to withdraw it, thus providing an auspicious omen for erecting a stupa to enshrine the spear. (Mhv: 26. 13) The second legend described the king enjoying a tasty pepper pod curry without a thought of sharing it with monks. (Mhv: 26. 17) For this oversight, the stupa symbolized both expiation and a reminder to never put one's own interests above the *sangha*. The stupa's Pali name, Maricavatti, was taken from the word for pepper pod (P: *marica*). These two completely disparate legends say nothing about relics in the traditional sense but the myths, which probably arose at different times, were paired together in the *Mahavamsa*.

Another example is the giant Abhayagiri stupa that owes its origin to a Jain ascetic named Giri who taunted a Buddhist king as he fled the capital in the face of a Tamil invasion. The king vowed that upon his victorious return he would construct a stupa directly over the spot of the Jain's hermitage. (Mhv: 33. 44) Relics were certainly enshrined inside the stupa but chronicles and inscriptions contain no descriptions and focus solely on the comeuppance of the Jains. Only the Chinese pilgrim Faxian remarked that the stupa was built over a footprint of the Buddha but this legend is not repeated elsewhere.[25] A much later legend about the same stupa, however, added that a gold cow, with a relic inside, was enshrined in the stupa, according to the *Saddharma-ratnavaliya*.

For the Jetavana stupa, the early chronicles also make no mention of relics but the monastery was founded as an act of atonement by Mahasena (277-304) for his destruction of the Mahavihara's Lohapasada and further pillaging of the Mahavihara. For these wicked acts, the king asked a minister to 'forgive me my fault' and restoration work was begun. (Mhv: 37. 24) In the next millennium, fresh myths were added. For example, the Buddha's cloth belt was believed to be enshrined in the Jetavana. A later myth reintroduced Mahasena whom the gods teased by keeping the precious belt-relic just out of his reach. Enraged, the king rose in the sky and cut the belt in two, one half deposited inside the Jetavana Stupa and the other remaining in heaven.[26]

Each of the three monastery complexes was comprised of numerous individual monastic units, or *pirivenas*, acting somewhat like separate colleges within a university. These *pirivenas* usually included a modest stupa, an image-hall, a chapter-house, a Bodhi tree and sometimes a relic-shrine. The residence of the *pirivena's* chief monk was in the centre of the square compound, with four smaller units arranged symmetrically for monks less senior. Nearby was a refectory and living cells for the remainder of the monks. Stone urinals have also been found amidst the monasteries. The greater part of Anuradhapura's sculpture is associated with these *pirivenas*. Land grants were generally gifted to these units that were subsumed under one of the three major monastic divisions.

Little is known about nunneries but prominent nuns are named in an early chronicle, the *Dipavamsa*. (Dpv: 18) Also, Chinese annals record that nuns from Ceylon reached Nanking in 426 CE and began China's order of nuns. Nuns enjoyed support from all three monastic divisions. One king donated a hundred 'monastery helpers' to a convent, suggesting how extensive nunneries were. However, by the end of the tenth century references to nuns peter out for unexplained reasons.[27]

Foreigners were drawn to Anuradhapura for commercial and religious reasons. The nearest port on the west coast was Mantai, near Mannar. Sassanian ware from Persia was found in excavations at the Jetavana monastery. Even a Roman visited Anuradhapura for six months at the time of Claudius (41-54 CE), and a Lankan mission was sent to Rome, according to Pliny the Elder. Also, an undated stone pillar at Anuradhapura, sculpted with a cross, is tangible evidence of a small Nestorian community who were referred to as 'Persian Christians' by the sixth-century *Cosmas Indicopleustes*. Excavations at Mantai yielded a terracotta seal, or *bulla*, impressed with a cross nearly identical in shape to the one on the pillar.[28]

Bronze seal belonging to a Hindu temple at Padaviya, north of Anuradhapura. c. 12th-13th century. Maritime Museum, Galle.

The city's most momentous event was the take over of much of northern Sri Lanka by the Chola dynasty from Tamil Nadu. Precise dates for this occupation are uncertain but it was for no more than a century, usually taken to be from circa 993 to 1070. The Cholas occupied Anuradhapura but more important centres were Polonnuruva and Trincomalee. The chronicles paint a picture of wanton destruction by Tamils, with the foreign invaders sacking 'relic chambers' and carting off 'many costly images of gold' and 'violently destroying ... all the monasteries, like blood-sucking *yakkhas* [demons]'. (Cv. 55. 21) But the archaeological evidence suggests otherwise and no signs of deliberate destruction have emerged after decades of exploration.[29]

A Nestorian cross appears on a stone pillar but the the size and nature of this community are unknown. Discovered in 1912, it is now in the Archaeological Museum, Anuradhapura.

Tamils were in Sri Lanka long before the Chola occupation and long after. In the 'southern part' of Anuradhapura the Chola king Rajendra II (1054-1064) dedicated a Vishnu temple but no remains have been found. One Tamil stone record, found at the Ruvanvali stupa, was a dedication of an image of an unknown deity by a Tamil donor described as a lay Buddhist (P: '*upasaka*'). Near Anuradhapura is an inscription referring to a Tamil Buddhist monastery as a 'demel-vehera', or Damila Vihara. This small sampling indicates a substantial Tamil presence and a degree of interaction unmarred by friction. And the Buddhist king, Nissankamalla (1187-1196), patronized the famous Hindu shrine of Rameshvaram in Tamil Nadu.[30] Had the Tamil invaders wished to raze Anuradhapura, they had ample opportunity. Hindu temples still stand in Polonnaruva but no Hindu shrines are intact at Anuradhapura. Two eight-arm Durgas now in the Colombo museum, dating from between the 8th-11th centuries, are convincing proof of a Hindu presence in the city before the Tamil invasion. Nearby to the north was the Chola centre of Padaviya, a site with Hindu temples and home to the Nanadesis, a well known mercantile guild in Tamil Nadu. Hindu temples had land holdings and used bronze seals for commercial transactions; only one has survived, from the 11th or 12th century, with a Sanskrit inscription.[31]

King Asoka severing the 'southern branch' of the Bodhi Tree at Bodh Gaya. A detail from a mural located in the southern corridor of the Mahamuni Temple, Mandalay. Circa 1892.

The Bodhi Tree: 'the southern branch'

The Bodhi tree at Anuradhapura ranks today in sanctity with the tooth-relic in Kandy and only the nearby Ruvanvali stupa equals it at Anuradhapura. The tree's planting was included in the prophesy made by the Buddha during his visit to Anuradhapura. (Mhv: 13. 163) And even Asoka himself ordered the 'southern branch' of the Bodhi Tree to be conveyed to Lanka by his daughter Sanghamitta. That she took the 'southern branch' (P: *dakkhina-sakha)* to the island is unlikely but a Bodhi Tree reaching Anuradhapura from Bodh Gaya sometime during the third or second century before Christ is feasible.

Daily rituals begin at sunrise with monks offering rice-milk on the topmost terrace and conducting a ceremony inside the shrine room on the ground level. The same rituals are repeated at midday and in the early evening, each time accompanied by drums and horns. The site is busiest on full-moon days and during the four annual festivals whose dates are fixed by the Committee of the Custodian of the Eight Great Sites. The festival in January-February is for newly harvested rice offered to the tree. The March-April festival features flowers and incense offered to the tree and eight-types of liquid allowed to monks (*gilanpasa*). The focus at this time is on a local deity named Kalu Devata Bandara, or Black God Bandara. His genesis is obscure but he was ordered by the goddess Pattini to Bodh Gaya to accompany the Bodh Tree to Lanka. The deity is thought to reside within the offering-shrine on the first terrace but no images are present. The third festival involves bathing the Buddha image in the worship hall and offering jewellery to the oldest tree on the top terrace. The last festival is Karitka Mangalaya in October-November when thousands of clay lamps are lit within the compound. One ancient festival consisted of offering cloth to the Bodhi Tree.[32]

Popular devotion takes place inside the covered shrine on the first terrace. Offerings are placed on tables beside which stand several ritualists, or *kapuralas*, who tie strings around the wrists of devotees and also apply a coloured paste to the forehead, modeled on Hindu worship. The *kapuralas* chant short prayers to the Black God Bandara and also to Kalu Kumara, a deity identified as Vishnu. When both gods became attached to the Bodhi Tree here is unknown but the two are absent in ancient sources.

How old is the tree ?

The life of a Bodhi tree (*Ficus religiosa*) can be as much as 1,500 years, making it unlikely that the sacred tree on the top terrace is the actual tree that purportedly came from India over 2,000 years ago. However, the present trees on the terraces possibly grew from generations of seeds produced from the original. A comparison between the chloroplast and nuclei of leaves from any of the trees on the terraces and even a single leaf from the live tree at Bodh Gaya could establish if the descendants in both locations were once related. Such questions are of no consequence for worshippers, since it is a matter of faith that the most sacred tree on the terrace grew from the 'southern branch' of the original.

The tree is situated in a large, walled, rectangular compound measuring 103 metres, from east to west, or just short of a football pitch. The stone boundary wall went up during the reign of Kandy's Kirti Sri Rajasimha (1747-82). In the centre of the north wall is today's principal entrance, probably datable to the eighth or ninth century judging by its sculpture. This entry is aligned with the centre of the top terrace, suggesting that the present Bodhi Tree is in one of its ancient locations. A similar gateway was noted on the south side but has left no trace. Attached to the lowest terrace on the east side is a large worship hall constructed in 1907 by a 'Buddhist gentleman of Galle'. Its stone foundation and central stone doorway are probably from the 8th or 9th century, together with four pillars supporting the temple's porch. Four shorter pillars have been built into a modern building nearby and are perhaps the same as those noted within the compound in the 1890s, as 'eight recumbent pillars of excellent workmanship'. The compound has a number of ancient stone objects but it is hard to know how they were used. A large stone Buddha, his right hand lowered to indicate the defeat of Mara, was once in the compound but is now missing.[33] There are also some modern copies. A medley of ancient stone sculptures stand outside the Mahavihara Oriental Library built in 1932 (BE 2475), located just outside the compound wall. The modern entrance gate replaced one built by the Bulankulama family that appeared in *The Buddhist Annual of Ceylon* (1923).

In the centre of the compound are superimposed terraces of diminishing size. A number of Bodhi trees are on the terraces but the one taken to be the 'original' is on the top terrace and is a single long thick branch rising low from the ground at a sharply inclined angle. This single branch meanders many metres but is hard to pick

A Bodhi leaf from St Helena, captioned '*Ficus religiosa*'. By Jan Brandes. 31 March 1787. Rijksmuseum.

The Bodhi Tree, by Solias Mendis, c. 1930s. Kelaniya Temple.

Bodhi tree worship, a detail from a parchment painting, 1734. Lund University Museum.

out from below amidst the other trees. It is a vestige of a fully grown tree that probably started life in the early 19th century. All of the trees on the terraces are venerated but only this branch is singled out for rituals. It was marked long ago for special attention by a short raised rectangular brick enclosure placed off centre on the top tier. Large healthy Bodhi trees on this terrace were captured in early photographs and in a British Museum watercolour dated from 1889. This painting, taken on the north side, shows a large Bodhi tree on the first terrace that was removed long ago. Storms in 1907 and 1911 further damaged the trees and a deranged man attempted to cut down the tree in 1929.

The trees on the top terrace showed signs of stress in the 1980s, prompting scientists to replace the soil to a depth of three metres. This re-soiling required earth infused with a special solution containing methyl bromide devised at the Perandiniya Botanical Garden lab outside Kandy. The treated soil was conveyed in forty truckloads and then placed around the roots at an auspicious time chosen by the chief monk. The lead scientist reported that 'we got lots of seeds to plant more Bo-trees', underscoring the importance of maintaining a direct lineage from the very tree sent by Asoka. Seeds collected at Bodh Gaya were styled 'the young scions of the parent tree' in the nineteenth century.[34]

The Bodhi Tree Temple. By Lt.-Col. Harry Hemersley St George. 1889, British Museum.

That the Bodhi Tree shrine assumed many forms over two millennia is certain but imagining their appearance is guesswork. The history of the modern terraces can be pieced together, however. A visitor in 1829 for example found that a single tree was enclosed in 'four receding walled terraces'. Five major branches from this tree 'grew out of the terraces at different points and seem to be held in equal reverence with the sacred tree'. The total height of the terraces in the 1820s was only 'about sixteen feet', far lower than the present terraces. The branches of the most sacred tree on the top terrace were later reduced to two and then eventually to the single branch worshipped today. By the 1890s, this branch was 'withering .... [with] scant life in its branches'. In 1908 there were ten separate Bodhi trees on the two top terraces and no less than 50 within the large compound. By the 1930s the tree looked 'weak and fragile as it stands surrounded by giant *bo*-trees three to four times as big'.[35] Access to the top terrace is restricted and so worship takes place on the terrace below and throughout the sandy compound.

Posts supporting branches from trees on the top terraces. A 5th-century Chinese pilgrim, Faxian, noted a post propping up a sagging branch on the southeast side of the Bodhi Tree.

The arrival of the Bodhi tree in Anuradhapura is told most fully in the *Mahavamsa*, though its basic outline appeared in the earlier *Dipavamsa*. It begins when a princess named Anula requested Mahinda to ordain her. He replied that the ceremony required a quorum of ten nuns, that is, performed 'at the hands of dignitaries of their own sex'.[36] Mahinda then called for his sister Sanghamitta to come to Lanka with nuns and a branch of the Bodhi Tree. Mahinda prophesied that the new tree would be planted at the same spot marking the 'enlightenment-trees' associated with the three Buddhas who visited Anuradhapura before Gotama. These three previous branches were removed from trees at Bodh Gaya by legendary nuns, but the cutting destined for Sri Lanka was special since it came from Gotama's tree and was prepared by Asoka's own hands. The trees associated with the three Buddhas preceding Gotama were of different species and did not include the Bodhi.

Since Bodhi trees were inviolate, Asoka drew a line around the 'southern branch ... with a pencil of red arsenic', after which the limb rose in the air. (Mhv: 18. 39) Roots then grew at the branch's severed end by more strokes of the pencil. The branch then sprouted a 'hundred roots' and placed itself in a golden vase in a boat that sailed down the Ganges into the Bay of Bengal. At the shore, Asoka entered the water and lifted the tree onto the outward-bound vessel.

Devanampiya Tissa welcomed the tree at Jambukola, a spot now identified with a remote beach on the north side of the Jaffna Peninsula. Emulating Asoka, he waded into the water and received the tree upon his head before placing it in a cart for its journey to Anuradhapura. Here, the tree was planted in the special Mahameghavana Park within the Mahavihara complex where the previous three enlightenment-trees had once stood. This happened in the eighteenth year of Asoka's reign, reckoned at 251 BCE. When the tree was planted in Anuradhapura there soon emerged from its 'east branch' a 'faultless fruit' from which eight saplings emerged. (Mhv: 19. 56) Four more fruits appeared and produced 32 trees. These trees, a total of 40, were distributed throughout the realm and to locations within Anuradhapura.

A legendary tree also played a major role in Western Civilization, namely, the tree that brought so much grief to Adam and Eve. Seeds from this tree were planted by their son Seth that grew into the tree that furnished the wood fashioned into the cross used for the crucifixion, thus linking the Old and New Testaments. Jewish and Islamic legends about the tree in the Garden of Eden are no less miraculous than those surrounding the Bodhi Tree.

Faxian in the 5th century claimed that a local king had sent to India long ago for the tree, with no mention of Asoka. This may indicate that the legend about Asoka's daughter had not yet gained much traction. In time, according to Faxian, the tree bent toward the southeast, requiring a post for support, resembling the supports used for the trees on the terraces today.

The earliest tree-shrines in Lanka were probably simple square stone railings with the tree in the centre. A small section of such a railing, nearly two metres in height, was discovered in 2010 beneath the worship hall.[37] Its base moldings are similar to a large railing at the Jetavana monastery, usually dated to the ninth or tenth century, but this smaller railing may be far earlier.

Anuradhapura's Bodhi Tree weaves in and out of the island's chronicles, beginning with watering festivals inaugurated by Devananampiya Tissa. (Cv: 34. 58; 38. 56) There was also a watering festival marking each king's twelfth regnal year. (Mhv: 38. 57) One king set up a stone railing (P: '*vedi*') for the tree and an arched gateway at the northern entrance. In the compound's four corners were pillars surmounted with wheels representing the Buddha's teachings (P: *dhamma*), reminiscent of the famous Asokan pillar at Sarnath. (Mhv: 38. 103) One 4th-century king constructed three gateways, or '*toranani*', that perhaps resembled the famous gateways at Sanchi. (Mhv: 36. 126) These are but some of the many references in the *Mahavamsa* but few can be confirmed since so little has survived. References to the tree in the chronicles dwindled by the 10th century, probably explained by the court shifting to Polonnaruva.

Inscriptions add to what can be gleaned from the chronicles. For example, seven nuns watered the tree daily in the 9th century. There were also expenses pertaining to a stupa (P: '*dagoba*') at the Bodhi Tree temple and there were Bodhi Tree festivals at nearby Mihintale. A 10th-century inscription records donations of gold for curd and honey to be offered daily to the Bodhi Tree. The famous Gal-vihara inscription at Polonnaruva admonishes monks to remain silent while worshipping the Bodhi Tree.[38] No references indicate that cuttings or seeds from from the Bodhi Tree in Anuradhapura were transferred to Polonnaruva.

By the 8th century elaborate Bodhi-temples (P: *bo-gehas*) arose in Sri Lanka. These could be square or circular, with the tree in the centre. The most complex were partially roofed with a large opening for the tree top. This form perhaps started in the 6th century when a king at Anuradhapura 'had a roof put over its golden house'.

Inscription on the plinth included the term *bodhi*-temple (*bodhighara*). c. ninth century. Nilakkama, close to Yapahua.

(Mhv: 41. 94) The best preserved of these early Bodhi temples is at Nilakkama, close to Yapahua, dated to the 9th century; a stone inscription on its base uses the term bodhi-temple (P:'*bodhighara*').[39]

Bodhi-shrines were often designed with four seated Buddha images placed on each side, facing outward. The capital's most famous Buddha image belonged to such a shrine, the so-called Samadhi Buddha. Bodhi-shrines continued at Polonnaruva but were mainly square in shape with only the foundations surviving.

The Devil's Tree

Among the earliest scientific notices of the Bodhi Tree is the twelve-volume *Hortus Indicus Malabaricius*, or *The Garden of Malabar*, compiled between 1678 and 1693. The tree's roots were prescribed for cholera and its leaves, 'decocted in oil' and rubbed on the skin, relieved rheumatic fever, according to the *Hortus*. The tree was associated with Vishnu in Malabar and was called the Devil's Tree by local Christians. When Dutch envoys to Kandy in 1768 saw the Bodhi Tree in front of the palace they also called it the Devil's Tree, or *Duivels Boom*. This 'Devil's Tree' was first tied to Vishnu and it was for this reason that Linnaeus likely assigned the tree its scientific name, *Ficus religiosa,* without reference to the tree's role in Buddhism.[40]

The Bodhi species is named *assattha* in Pali, or *ashvattha* in Sanskrit. Another Sanskrit name is *pippala,* also in the *Hortus,* which is found today in India as *pipal*. Each Bodhi species requires a unique type of minute wasp to pollinate its flowers that then grow into small berry-like fruits, or *syconium,* the size of a pencil eraser, each containing hundreds of seeds. The fertilized berries are consumed by birds and animals and carried far and wide.

Another Bodhi Tree legend in Sri Lanka started when a monk in India caught a seed in midair as it was falling from the tree at Bodh Gaya, according to a *jataka* (no. 479). The seed was then delivered

A monk catching a *bodhi* seed at Bodh Gaya, planted at the Jetavana Monastery (*Jataka* 479). c. Nineteenth century. Wat Kamphaeng Bang Chak. Bangkok.

to the famous disciple Ananda who placed it in an earth-filled jar at the Jetavana monastery in India where it grew to full height instantly. The tree was known as the Ananda-bodhi and certain trees in Lanka are traced to this lineage, such as at Sithulpawwa in the southeast.

The Bodhi tree was first introduced to the West by Robert Knox at a meeting of the Royal Society in 1683. He wrote in his *Historical Relation* (1681) that the 'Buddou' sat beneath the tree and that Bodhi trees were planted by older men as they approached death. A related Asian species, also important in the Buddha's life, is the banyan, or *Ficus bengelesis*, mentioned by John Milton in his *Paradise Lost* (1667). Worship of the Bodhi Tree was said to be among the reasons that native Christians 'turned aside to idolatry'.[41]

The Bodhi Tree & a Peacock's Egg

The Bodhi Tree was accompanied to Lanka by 18 men related to Asoka. (Mhv: 19.1) Some protected the tree, others oversaw rituals and others were were formed into trade guilds, such as weavers and potters. This reference to Asoka's family opened the door for subsequent Lankan elites to trace their lineages to these Asokan kinsmen. For example, a later legend arose wherein eight of these royals were identified as brothers of one of Asoka's wives. Six of these eight were then wed to daughters of Devanampiya Tissa who were 'royal virgins'.[42] The most influential brothers were the two eldest. One descended from the clan known as Moriya and the other from the Lambakanna and both clans produced many rulers between the 3rd and 11th centuries.

Another related and far-reaching myth began when a miserly brahman buried a treasure of gold. As punishment for his cupidity, his daughter was born in the womb of a peacock that abandoned her egg that was discovered by a farmer who saw within a lovely infant who 'shown like a golden image'. He presented this egg to Devanampiya Tissa and a child hatched instantly upon his lap. He called her Mayurvati, after the word for peacock (P: *mayura*). As the Peacock Queen came of age, he gave her in marriage to one of the brothers from Asoka's family. He coupled with her and from this offspring, many generations later, was born the founder of Kandy. The origin of the peacock-lineage can perhaps be traced to the 10th century when a king's epithet means 'born from a peacock'.[43]

This connection with Asoka's descendants continued even into modern times when a mother, whose son was imprisoned by the English, 'alluded to the antiquity of her ancestors who had accompanied the branch of the sacred tree from from Patlipoor', or Pataliputra, Asoka's capital. And later, James Tennent had an audience with 'a youth' whose family 'accompanied the Bo-tree to Ceylon', leading Tennent to marvel poetically that even the 'most renowned peerages of Europe ... were but creations of yesterday' compared to this ancient lineage.[44]

The Bodhi tree was also the subject of a Pali prose work of 12 chapters known as the *Mahabodhi-vamsa*, or *The Story of the Great Bodhi*, attributed to the 10th-century monk Upatissa. It drew upon the version in the *Mahavamsa* and the *Samantapasadika* by Buddhaghosa and became a 'classic' with a later commentary in the 12th century by Gurulugomi titled *Dharmapradipika*. A Sinhalese version was composed in the early 14th century by a monk named Vilgammula based at the Kelaniya monastery near Colombo. Over the centuries the tree at Anuradhapura was also the subject of no less than 50 Pali and Sinhalese works in verse and prose, together with nearly 30 ballads.[45] Other Sinhalese works treating the Bodhi Tree were made by monks during the Kandyan period.

Bodhi seeds and saplings exported from Sri Lanka were treasured in Southeast Asia and were the kernels of many legends. A Sukhothai inscription recorded that a king planted a Bodhi seed from Anuradhapura and a Chiang Mai chronicle mentions monks bringing from the 'Island of the Sinhalas' 'a seed from the southern branch'. Monks in Lower Burma returning from Lanka came with Bodhi 'branches, leaves and seeds' (P: *'sakha, patta, bijani')*. There are numerous references in Burma to Sri Lanka's 'southern branch' and a legend in which king Mindon of Mandalay himself carved Buddha images from the 'southern branch'. Also, many missions from Lanka in the nineteenth century brought Bodhi plants to Burma that were planted at major sacred sites in Upper Burma.[46]

Whether these transplants from Ceylon were branch cuttings, saplings or even fertilized berries is usually unspecified. Keeping Bodhi saplings or cuttings alive over long sea journeys must have been challenging but records prove huge numbers of plants of many species were transshipped throughout the Bay of Bengal in the colonial period. In one example, two to three thousand coconut plants were loaded on a single Dutch ship bound from India to Sri Lanka.[47]

The 'southern branch' of the Bodhi Tree carved by King Mindon of Mandalay into Buddha images. Shwe Kyi Myin Pagoda. Mandalay.

The Buddha's corporal relics were divided into eight portions. One portion is believed to be enshrined within the Ruvanvali Stupa. On the right, frontispiece, or *vahalkada.*

The Ruvanvali Stupa: Relics from the Sea

The Ruvanvali stupa is neither the oldest or even the largest at Anuradhpura but it is the most sacred. Its present height and girth conform more or less to its original size, despite extensive repairs in British times. The city's largest stupa is the Jetavana whose estimated 62 million bricks could form a wall ten feet high from London to Edinburgh, a trivia tidbit that has been repeated for over 100 years.

The stupa's founder is Dutthagamani (161-137 BCE) whose other principal monuments still survive: the Miricavatti Stupa and the Bronze Palace, or Lohapasada. The king saved the Ruvanvali Stupa for last. The construction dates for the stupas attributed to him cannot be fixed but they probably fall between the first century BCE and the fourth century CE. This conclusion is reinforced from Tl-tested brick from the the Miricavatti stupa and others.[48]

The stupa was predestined in as much as Devanampiya Tissa raised a stone pillar on the future site to signal to his grand-nephew, Dutthagamani, where to erect his stupa. (Mhv: 28.) Divine intervention guided the project from the beginning, with the celestial architect, (P: Visvakamma), preparing millions of brick at kilns in a hidden location known for its ideal clay. The bricks were revealed by a hunter who was led to the site by a deity disguised as an iguana. (Mhv: 28. 9)

To lay out the diameter of the stupa, the king ordered a circle to be drawn by a court minister walking with a taut rope tied to a post. A senior cleric suddenly appeared and counselled the king that such a huge stupa was too big to complete in one lifetime and that moreover huge stupas would bring huge headaches for future generations responsible for repairs. (Mhv: 29. 53) The king bowed to the monk's advice and reduced the dimensions. This cautionary tale hints that kings often bit off more than they could chew in a single reign. Even with its smaller size, the stupa's dimensions vastly surpassed any rival monuments in the Buddhist world at the time and for centuries to come. The king, on his deathbed, gazed at his unfinished stupa whose completion was entrusted to his brother. This theme of an unfinished stupa completed by a kinsman was adapted in Buddhist communities abroad, the two best-known examples being Yangon's Shwedagon Pagoda and Pagan's Shwezigon Pagoda. Even the trope of a pillar discovered by later generations underpinned the founding of Pegu by the Mon in Burma.

Dutthagamani enquired about the stupa's final shape from the master builder who then took water from a golden bowl and let a drop fall on the surface, producing a 'great bubble ... like unto a half-globe of crystal [a semi-hemisphere]'. (Mhv: 30. 13) The largest stupas at Anuradhapura and Polonnaruva were never exactly semi-circular in shape but stupas assumed a number of different contours that were described in later palm-leaf manuscripts.[49] The stupa's foundation was prepared by laying crushed stone pounded into place by the leather-bound feet of elephants, according to the *Mahavamsa*. Next came layers of clay, brick and iron covered by sheets of copper and silver. The relic chamber was prepared from six large stones from a mythic region in North India. Inside were placed precious objects including a Bodhi Tree made of jewels and a golden Buddha and scenes from the Buddha's life were painted on the chamber walls. Description of the Ruvanvali Stupa range over four long chapters in the *Mahavamsa*, contrasted to the *Dipavamsa* which accorded the stupa less than ten verses. (Dpv: 19. 2-10)

Once the relic chamber was completed, the king promised to supply the relics by the next day. (Mhv: 31.2) The task fell to a junior monk named Sonuttara who journeyed to an underwater kingdom of snakes that venerated the relics. These relics had been enshrined originally at one of the eight stupas in which the Buddha's corporal relics were dispersed in North India. This stupa, built on the bank of Ganges at Rajagama, was destroyed by a flood and the relics were washed down river into the ocean where they were placed within a stupa by a *naga*-king. To foil Sonuttara, the snake-chief asked his nephew to remove the relic-urn from the stupa and swallow it before

Wrapping the bands of coloured fabric around the Stupa base.

An enormous band of multi-coloured cloth is carried in procession to the stupa.

Music frequently accompanies ritual activities.

coiling himself around Mt. Meru. The crafty *naga*-king then pleaded that his subterranean kingdom had no relics. But Sonuttara was neither a dummy nor a coward and he thrust his arm into the snake's mouth to remove the urn and then presented it to the king back home. Once the urn was deposited in the relic chamber, the relics rose up and assumed the form of the Buddha. The king then placed the relics on a 'precious couch' inside the relic-chamber. (Mhv: 31.107)

By the 13th century the monument merited its own Pali chronicle, the *Thupavamsa*, followed soon by a Sinhalese version. A public reading of the Sinhalese text took place in the early 13th century sponsored by a Queen named Kalyanavati. In attendance were service-groups assigned to the temple, such as scribes, brahmans, painters, and dancers. Also, 8,808 pieces of cloth were placed around the drum of the stupa, foreshadowing the practice of wrapping the base of stupa drums in long bands of cloth seen today all over Lanka.[50]

The stupa was known by many names, such as Mahacetiya and Hemamali, but after the 12th century the most common was Ruvanvali, the Sinhalese for the Pali Ratanamali, or 'necklace of gems'.[51] Other large stupas were built in Lanka at this early age, such as at Mahiyangana and Tissamaharama, but none surpassed the four at Anuradhapura in size. Only the Rankot and Kiri stupas at Polonnaruva rival those in Anuradhapura. Other stupas of impressive dimensions were begun but never finished. The era of immense stupas came to an end after the Polonnuruva period.

Stone models symbolizing Mt. Meru have been found inside some stupas. One from Polonnuruva is divided into seven horizontal divisions representing the Seven Continents of our world known as Jambudvipa. Another feature commonly associated with relic chambers were flat stone slabs divided into small compartments containing auspicious metal objects. Such compartments usually numbered nine or twenty-five. These stones are known today in Sri Lanka as *yantra-gala*, or '*stone-yantra*', and similar examples are found widely in Asia.[52] They were usually placed below relic chambers or beneath the pedestals of Buddha images in Sri Lanka. Metal objects inside the compartments varied in Sri Lanka but some were *nagas* or sets of animals (horse, bull, elephant and lion); others were the Guardians of the Directions. Similar stones with compartments were found in Thailand but none are known in Burma.

Stone models of Mt. Meru have been found within stupas. c. Twelfth century. Topavava Stupa, Polonnuruva. National Museum, Colombo.

'There will be no Grass on our Stupa'

The simple shapes of stupas belie tremendous engineering complexity. The major Anuradhapura stupas were designed with a sloping ellipsoidal contour, unlike the semi-hemispherical shape of the Sanchi Stupa. How ancient builders produced such a graceful curve is nowhere spelled out but it was probably achieved by many evenly spaced ropes stretched from the base to the top, a technique still used for making stupas in Sri Lanka and Southeast Asia.

Stupas were subject to many types of stresses and strains and poorly designed or badly constructed stupas proved disastrous. The restoration of the Miricavatti stupa in 1987 for example resulted in the structure's near total collapse. A perennial threat was the growth of vegetation on the exterior, caused by chips and cracks in the plaster. Seeds of the *Ficus* genus were especially destructive since roots burrowed deep into the interior. Breaches in the surface then allowed rain water to penetrate the interior, producing an imbalanced internal fabric creating centrifugal forces. Such stresses caused entire sections to tumble down. Such failures are viewed as bad omens traced to bad karma so faulty stupas often carry grave political consequences.

Lanka's ancient builders ingeniously divided the stupa's interior into six vertical zones to diminish the stresses from sinkage, earthquakes, extreme weather and centrifugal forces. Each zone was comprised of materials with different structural properties. Certain zones were 'soft pockets' made up of sun dried bricks, brickbats, soil and a special pliable clay; other zones were made up of hard fired bricks of various sizes. The central zone, extending from the base to the top, consisted of brickbats set in a mixture of clay and soil.[53] The zones interacted in a way that ensured stability under adverse conditions, much as modern skyscrapers are designed today.

Sinking foundations under the tremendous weight of the dome was forever a problem, made clear in a Chiang Mai chronicle.[54] This explains why the foundations of the Jetavana Stupa were a full eight metres below ground and why layers of brick were installed so that the stupa does 'not sink down of itself'. (Mhv: 30. 54) There was also the danger of exterior plaster chipping that could lead to water filtering inside the stupa. The king raised this very problem by declaring that 'There will be no grass .... on our *ceitya* [stupa]'. (Mhv: 30. 11) A quest for the best plaster and mortar prompted a competition, described in connection with the Ruvanvali stupa. The winning proposal included sand that was first pounded and then sifted, producing a pliable mortar described as 'butter-clay' (P: *navanita mattika*). (Mhv: 29. 6) The clay was then mixed with crushed limestone and was able to withstand stresses in ways that standard plaster could not. One king ordered that the plaster at the Ruvanvali Stupa measure eight fingers in thickness. Occasional replastering was accompanied by a festival. (Mhv: 34. 43, 58) A 19th-century recipe for the plaster finish for the Anuradhapura stupas included coconut water, lime and the juice from the fruit of

The Abhayagiri Stupa's restoration required thousands of new bricks and specially designed scaffolds. Four frontispieces, or *vahalkada*, were established in the cardinal directions during the time of Kantittha Tissa (167-186), noted in an inscription ('*cater ayika*').

Sculpture attached to one of the four frontispieces at the Jetavana Stupa. Circa second century CE.

Miniature stupa showing octagonal pillar beneath the umbrella. From Dalivala, Kegalla District. c. Third-fourth CE. Gifted from the Colombo Museum to Dalivala monastery, stolen in 2022. Osmund Bopearachchi.

Ropes placed equidistantly along the circumference of the stupa base ensured the stupa's symmetrical contour. A detail from the *Mahajanaka Jataka*, Subodharama Viharaya, Colombo. Circa 1890.

the jasmine tree. South Indian architectural manuals refer to a mortar made of eight ingredients (S: *ashtabandha*).[55]

The Jetavana masons applied mortar, made of 'butter clay', to only the tops and bottoms of each brick, thus allowing bricks to move unimpeded, slightly to the right or left, in the event of any shifting, such as in an earthquake; in a standard brick course, each brick is locked in on all sides by hard mortar. This 'butter clay' mortar was also used in the Ruvanvali and Abhayagiri stupas. The bricks themselves were made mostly of fine sand and clay, having great tensile strength. Ancient building manuals from South India describe the best materials for bricks. Baked bricks were submerged in water and those that absorbed any water were considered unfit.[56] These engineering solutions evolved over many centuries of trial and error and building techniques varied over the centuries and in different regions. That the *Mahavamsa* itself speaks directly to many of these construction challenges is testimony to their importance.

No early stupas have retained their original superstructures, but their appearance can be conjectured from a handful of miniature stupa-shaped reliquaries. All were made of hammered sheets of gold, with one exception in bronze. Highly fragile, these small reliquaries were usually placed within small stone containers inside stupa basement terraces or inside the stupa frontispieces described above. Each differs slightly from the other but the summits of many are marked by an umbrella beside which is an octagonal post with a rounded top. Such posts in these miniature examples can be linked with numerous surviving stone posts at stupa sites throughout Sri Lanka. These posts are slightly rounded and fluted at the top, indicating that they were not load bearing columns. The largest was found at the top of the Abhayagiri stupa, its three broken pieces totaling over nine metres in length.[57] Outside the Ruvanvali Stupa compound is a tall octagonal pillar that may have been installed originally at the top of the stupa or in another stupa. Only a short portion of each tall post protruded above the square platform at the top, roughly matching the height of the umbrella. (Similar posts are found in Andhra Pradesh and at the stupa site of Kanaganahalli and some are shown on the stupa drums from Amaravati.) One partially restored brick stupa, at Dematamal in Uva Provence, still retains its stone post that appears to be circular in shape.

No chronicles or inscriptions refer to these posts atop stupas, stimulating speculation about their function and symbolism. Some have called the pillar a *yupa-yatthi* (P), but how they were identified in ancient times is uncertain.[58] By the beginning of the second millennium this tradition of octagonal posts protruding from the top was no longer in vogue. The stone umbrellas were however still in use and were crowned by a metal spire, or *kota*, sometimes topped with a crystal ornament. There is also reference to a metal spire at the top of a stupa that may have functioned as a lightning rod but is known only in a single reference. (Cv. 38. 74) Hoisting the spire was never as important in Sri Lanka as it was in Burma, but a 'precious

Pillar originally embeded toward the top and center of the Abhayagiri Stupa. Such pillars were common during the first millennium. Osmund Bopearachchi.

ring of crystal' was raised at the Ruvanvali Stupa during one of its ancient renovations. (Mhv: 36. 67)

The most common Sri Lankan stupa design is characterized by several features, beginning at the base with three encircling rings or terraces. These were not used for circumambulating since they are too narrow and slightly sloped. They are described as 'a place for depositing flowers' (P: *pupphadhana*) and the lowest ring is even today used for offerings. (Mhv: 30. 51; 56: 22, 333) The dome is capped by a square brick section known as the '*harmika*' in India but styled a 'four cornered-pile' in early Sri Lanka. (Mhv: 31: 124) By the beginning of the second millennium the superstructures assumed a very different shape. The octagonal posts at the top of the stupas were no longer visible but were perhaps embedded unseen within the top of the dome. The square section above the dome remained the same but a short circular member was placed above that was surmounted by multiple thin rings forming a conical shape, symbolizing umbrellas. An example is the miniature stone stupa in the courtyard of the Ruvanveli stupa and the current stupa's top. Many slight variations on this basic model are known but the three-part shape remained remarkably consistent over the ages. The major early Anuradhapura stupas were rebuilt in the second millennium and reflected this new design. These survived into the early 20th century in ruins but drawings and antique photographs reveal that they were rebuilt much earlier in what can be considered the standard style. Other examples are the Kiri and Rankot stupas at Polonnaruva.

Miniature stone stupa in the courtyard of the Ruvanveli stupa.

The Sri Lanka stupa had an incalculable influence in Burma and Thailand, beginning in the 11th century, if not much earlier, the form probably derived from the small metal

Gold reliquaries in Burma based on Sri Lankan stupa designs. Rangoon, Burma, c. 1400-1420.
After Sykes, '*Account of some Golden Relics ...*' (1860).

reliquaries imported from Sri Lanka. Such caskets containing relics were found within a brick stupa near the Shwedagon Pagoda in colonial Rangoon, dating from the early 15th century.[59] At Pagan the best example is the Sitana-gyi Stupa, though the majority of stupas at Pagan followed Pala dynasty examples from Eastern India. The Sri Lankan-style stupa was far more influential in Thailand, such as at Sukhothai and Ayutthaya. Both Burma and Thailand, however, also developed indigenous stupa designs in which Lankan influence is absent.

The fame of key Sri Lankan stupas was also kept alive in Southeast Asia through Pali texts. An inscription from Burma dated to 1650 claimed that the famous Khaung-Hmu-Daw stupa near Mandalay was modelled on the Thuparama. Another inscription, from 1431, claims that another stupa near Mandalay emulated the 'Ratanacetiya' Stupa, that is, the Ruvanvali.[60] Such comparisons were symbolic since the shapes of these two Burmese stupas bear no resemblance to any stupas in Sri Lanka.

The brick bell-shaped stupa of Wat Tra Kuan, Sukhothai, early 15th century. River Books.

The 1903-Religious Riot

Anuradhapura represented the 'golden age' for Sinhala Buddhists during the later British period. Rebuilding the ancient capital hence became a matter of national pride by the 1870s. Leading the movement was Walisinghe Harischandra (1877-1913), a lay celibate, or *brahmacari*, who set up a branch of the Maha Bodhi Society in the ancient city in 1899 and who was also President of the Ruwanweli Restoration Society started in 1902 with the great Buddhist nationalist, Anagarika Dharmapala.[61] Restoring monuments accrued merit and if the British prohibited renovations by private donors, then this was tantamount to withholding merit. Moreover, the backdrop was a relentless attack on Buddhism by Christian missionaries and Tamils outnumbered Sinhalas in Anuradhapura by 1891.

Harischandra also railed against the sacred city's saloons selling arrack, meat-stalls, churches, a mosque and a Hindu temple. Tensions ignited in 1903 when some of the thousands attending the town's annual festival charged the meat-stalls, a Catholic church and other properties. A riot ensued when a Sinhala official on horseback accidentally knocked down a Buddhist woman. Over 80 pilgrims were arrested, including Harischandra.

During the riot in 1903, Harischandra was prosecuted. After his *Pura Vidyawa* (1912).

Other threats came when increasing amounts of cash were donated to the *sangha* by pilgrims in the 1840s, resulting in 'fertile sources of intrigue'. For example, Anuradhapura's chief monk was defrocked for corruption in 1842 by his home monastery in Kandy. A perennial problem stemmed from two branches of a family that claimed descent from Asoka's ancestors who accompanied the Bodhi Tree to Lanka. Both branches litigated for decades about 'the rights ... to the Bo-tree shrine' and the leadership of the Eight Great Sites Association.[62] The case eventually came down to a dispute between a son and daughter begot by two different mothers and the head of one of these families. The final judgement in 1872 did little to dampen the friction and the government effected a compromise, ruling in 1881 that the city's chief monk should belong to the Malwatta monastery but must be approved by representatives of the families descended from service groups attached to the Bodhi Tree. One shudders to think if the pious Asoka could have witnessed his Sri Lankan kinsmen squabbling over the spoils left by pilgrims at the Bodhi Tree. It would be comforting to attribute such avarice to the evils of colonial rule but 'purse-proud' monks plagued the ancient *sangha*.[63]

The worst modern conflict erupted when Tamil Tiger commandos took possession of the Bodhi Tree and other sites for a day in 1985, resulting in over 140 fatalities. More recently, in 2011, a mob led by monks destroyed a mosque. The offensive butcher shops and arrack vendors have long since been replaced at this World Heritage site by tawdry souvenir stalls and aggressive touts hawking postcards. The Buddha easily reconciled powerful snake-kings and defeated demons but how much more daunting would his tasks be in our own age.

SIGIRIYA

Sigiriya: 'Heaven has Lost its Appeal'

The genetle slop of the gardens ensured that water from the Rock above and the adjacent reservoir flowed down into the garden.

Sigiriya's fame owes nothing to relics or to the Buddha's visits to Sri Lanka. Instead, this World Heritage destination highlights the role of atonement in the creation of sacred sites, since the backdrop is a prince who sought redemption after murdering his father. The celebrated murals feature some twenty celestial maidens whose impenetrable gazes have entranced terrestrials for centuries.

The story begins with a coup in Anuradhapura when a minor prince named Kassapa forced his father to reveal a rumoured hidden treasure. The king replied that his only wealth was a water tank excavated for his subjects. Furious, Kassapa ordered his father placed alive within a wall, resulting in his death. Meanwhile, the legitimate crown prince, Kassapa's half-brother, fled to India. Fearing his return, Kassapa 'betook himself through fear to Sigiriya which is difficult of ascent'. (Cv. 39. 2) The king spent the next eighteen years in self-exile at Sigiriya, traditionally but conjecturally reckoned between 477 and 495 CE.[1]

Dreading retribution for patricide, Kassapa asked himself from the mountain fastness 'How can I be saved?'. The immediate answer was by 'meritorious works', the first of which was listed as the 'gardens' that now unfold below the towering granite monolith, or Rock. (Cv: 39. 8-9) Meanwhile, the rightful heir to the throne returned from exile in India and confronted his half-brother on an open field at Sigiriya. The battle turning against him, Kassapa severed his own head, with his opposing kinsman departing for Anuradhapura and leaving Sigiriya abandoned. Whether the king really slayed his father will never be known but a heap of legendary material was later piled onto his biography in order to stress how sins (P: *papas*) never go unanswered. Indeed, one later text concluded that Kassapa fell into the worst of hells (P: Avici) for slaying his father, 'to suffer torment for a period of a *kalpa*'.[2]

King Kassapa's palace at Sigiriya was likened to Alaka, (P: *Alakamandan*), the celestial home of the God of Wealth. (S: Kubera; P: Kuvera) This connection is found in the *Culavamsa* and confirmed by the king's sole surviving stone inscription wherein he is styled the 'Great King Kassapa, Master of Alaka' (P: 'Kasabala-Alakapaya-maharaja'). (Cv: 39.5) Kasabala is old Sinhalese for Kassapa whose name also appears as Kasuba, such as 'Sigiri-Kasubu' or as 'Kasub-giri'.[3] Kubera was once ruler of Lanka before being deposed by his half-brother, the demon Ravana. Kubera's Alaka-city also pops up in other places in the *Culavamsa* and in the Pali canon. Scholars have made much of the site's association with Kubera, but since a number of Lanka rulers likened themselves to Kubera perhaps its significance at Sigiriya has been overstated.[4] (Cv: 37.106:74, 208: 80.5)

Previous page:
Celestial maidens and a water-garden combine in this unique World Heritage site. Courtesy Dominic Sansoni.

The site dropped out of history after Kassapa's reign for about a hundred years until a ruler was imprisoned 'in the secure and safe Sihagiri' and then executed. (Cv: 44. 32) The Rock was then a place for finishing off rivals, with symbolic ties to the celestial city of Alaka invoked when it was convenient. Interpretations today agree that Sigiriya was never a fortress nor the nation's capital but rather a pleasure retreat for Kassapa during the second half of the 5th century.[5]

Ancient Buddhist caves are situated amidst massive boulders.

One likely source of inspiration for Sigiriya was the king's legendary ancestor, Sihabahu, who was the father of Sri Lanka's founder, Vijaya, and the son of a lion (P: *siha*). Like Kassapa, Sihabau also killed his father and founded the legendary Lion City, or Sihapura, in India. (Mhv: 6.35) Kassapa's debt to Sihabahu is probably evoked by the enormous Lion Entrance to the the summit and the site's name, Lion Mountain (P: 'Sihagiri'), attested in the *Culavamsa* and inscriptions on the Mirror Wall.[6] (Cv: 39. 2) The ancient name Sihagiri is now the Sinhalese Sigiriya. Sihagiri was also the name of an unidentified stupa, probably at Anuradhapura.[7]

The Gardens

Unfolding at the base of the Rock is the only surviving Asian landscape garden of its kind from the first millennium, beginning just steps beyond the modern footbridge at the entrance. Its elaborate layout is difficult to make out at ground level but the dimensions are staggering. The outer moat alone is 24 metres wide and five metres deep while the inner moat's length is some 900 metres. How labour was organized at Sigiriya to excavate such a prodigious project is uncertain but an 11th-century inscription near Anuradhapura describes 'tank-work' that was assigned to tenants who violated agreements, in lieu of fines. Each offender was assigned sixteen cubits in circumference and one cubit in depth.[8]

Engineers worked hand in hand with garden planners to integrate water into the design, much like Versailles. A massive reservoir, named Sigiriya Wewa, bordered the moat on the south and was fed by the Sigiriya River and monsoon rains. Work on the gardens began by removing all the unchecked vegetation in order to lay the underground conduits, somewhat like installing a sprinkler system before a lawn is planted. When the trenches were finished, small rectangular-shaped stone conduits were placed below ground.

Government archaeologists began exploring Sigiriya in the late nineteenth century. The large tank at the summit.

The reservoir's water level needed to be roughly twenty metres in order for the force of gravity to discharge water into the conduits, working on the same principle underpinning the Twin Ponds at Anuradhapura and Roman aqueducts. The water level is lower today

Identified as a storage area. Viewed from the Mirror Wall.

since the huge stones forming the dam wall have shifted and so water is unable to reach the required height. Stratigraphic radiocarbon datings indicate that the retaining wall 'could very well coincide with the short period' of Kasyapa's reign.[9] On the Rock's irregular plateau were at least six tanks and a large pool that collected water and diverted it down the hill into a tank on the terrace just below the Lion Entrance. From there, it flowed down into the garden in semi-circular stone pipes held together by metal bands.

Upon entering the modern entrance a slight rise in elevation creates a gentle slope down which water still flows. How much of this incline is natural or artificial is hard to tell but calculating the slope's precise incline for water to flow required sophisticated mathematical modeling. Similar water engineering fed a long aqueduct at Anuradhapura that was designed with a sloping gradient of about ten centimetres per kilometre. Once the underground water system was in place at Sigiriya, there was little room for major changes.

The garden's symmetrical layout may have been influenced by pre-Islamic Near Eastern gardens, since the four prominent L-shaped pools are reminiscent of the Persian garden in four equal quarters, or *chahar bagh*. Departing from the symmetry are two narrow meandering 'streams' of shallow water running over quartz pebbles to an underground 'pressure chamber' from where the water emerges as four small fountains. Such hydraulic accomplishments reflected centuries of experimentation in irrigation.[10] That Colombo is the only Asian capital with a National Irrigation Museum testifies to these achievements.

The Nandana Garden

The backdrop for Sigiriya's designers were legendary gardens in India and Sri Lanka. The most famous in Theravada lore was the Nandana Garden (P: *nandana-vana*), situated in the Heaven of the Thirty-three Gods. Overseen by its chief deity, Sakka, the garden was enlivened by nymphs (S: apsaras; P: accharas) Even bliss itself was unobtainable without visiting the Nandana Garden, as a deity remarked to monks. It was from this garden that Gotama Buddha departed to begin his life on earth in the Lumbini Grove (P: 'Lumbini-vana').[11] This legendary garden was important in Sri Lanka, proved by the conversion of an Anuradhapura king at a spot named Nandana Garden. (Mhv: 15. 2) But how exactly were Lanka's gardens influenced by this famous celestial counterpart is nowhere stated. (Mhv: 15. 2)

There was also a Nandana Garden at Pollonuruva whose 'crown jewel' was a shower-bathing area fed from pipes. (Cv: 73. 104) and a garden at Anuradhapura, the Great Cloud Garden, or Mahameghavana, whose only features were 'fruit-trees and flowering-trees'. (Mhv: 11. 2) King Kassapa is said to have designed a small garden at Anuradhapura at a monastery dedicated to his two daughters, but this is known from a much later source. (Mhv: 39. 11) This garden included the Issarasamana monastery whose small tank is overlooked by rock carvings of elephants and an enigmatic seated male figure beside a horse. Nearby is a tank known now as the Ranmasu Uyana, but this small complex shares little with the garden at Sigiriya. Other gardens in antiquity would include the Kalinga-vana where Nissankamalla enjoyed dancing and singing.[12]

Hindus also knew a Nandana Garden, associated with 'twenty thousand apsaras who could madden with passion any man they took in their arms' and Kubera's Alaka was inhabited by 'hosts of apsaras'. Sri Lankan Tamils also recognized a Nandana Garden, as a place where flowers were grown to offer to temples.[13]

The Murals & the Mirror Wall

The murals are reached by two restored stairways leading to a narrow open-air corridor between the cliffside and the ancient Mirror Wall. Made of brick and coated with burnished plaster on both sides, the Mirror Wall extends nearly the entire length of the Rock's western face. Both sides 'shine as if they had been but a few years completed', an observation no less true today as it was in 1853.[14] This long corridor once led to a staircase reaching the Lion Entrance on the north side. The garden below is not visible from inside the corridor, since the wall's height is just over two metres; even from within the corridor the frescos are not visible since they are in a recessed pocket high above. The hundreds of poems on the Mirror Wall were therefore not composed as a reaction to the *apsaras* seen today in the upper pocket. However, painted *apsaras* directly opposite the Mirror Wall were likely only steps away from the pilgrims as they proceeded. When the murals began to chip off the huge wall surface of the Rock is hard to say but the fact that the poems from the eighth and ninth centuries speak of the *apsaras* suggests that the murals were intact then.

To understand ancient mural techniques, the site's first archaeologist, H.C.P. Bell, consulted painters in the village of Nilagama who were employed by the Kandyan kings at Dambulla and other sites. The rock surface was first prepared with a layer of plaster composed of clay mixed with rice husks and straw; current research has determined that this layer at Sigiriya consisted of plant-gum, clay, sand and fiber.[15] This layer was then covered by a layer of smoothed mortar made of lime, or *chunam*. Compositions were first sketched out by thin dark lines and colour lastly applied as a filler. Light washes of different tones form the background for the apsaras. Many examples of preparatory sketches are seen at Dambulla but the single noticeable underdrawing here is a raised hand visible on an *apsara* carrying a tray of flowers. Artists relied on basic colours, such as red, yellow ochre and green, with many blended

A small section of the water gardens. The Sigiriya Rock in the distance.

'a firm hold and a sure head'

The frescos were first copied by A. Murray of the Public Works Department during a single week in 1889. The pocket's floor was too sloped for normal scaffolding so 'iron stanchions were let into the floor and a strong trestle made secure to them'. This trestle supported a platform that required Murray to lie 'at full length on his back or side' to complete his copies of thirteen maidens in 'coloured chalks'.[18] None of these works have survived but five years later, the Head Draughtsman of the Archaeological Survey, D.A.L. Perera, completed copies on canvas over five months in 1896-1897. The originals are kept in the National Museum in Colombo.

Perera used a system of supports with an 'improvised chair' in which he 'swung in the air upwards of 150 ft above the ground and 50 ft clear of the cliff'. This swinging chair was connected to a rope suspended from the top of the Rock. A better system was devised for the next season during which Perera copied the murals 'in mid-air … tied to a rough cage of sticks connected to a cantilever of jungle-timber, firmly lashed to a stout iron cramp let into the rock floor'. These ingenious supports required 'a firm hold and a sure head'.[19]

The surviving *apsaras* are remnants of a single massive painted surface that once extended across the entire rock face. A protective drip-ledge high above the pocket indicates the point where the frescos terminated. The total painted surface was roughly 13,500 square metres and was the largest single continuous mural in the world. Two or three tiny pockets with traces of painting were noted on the western face but these were 'inaccessible without elaborate preparations'.[20] The surviving murals are perhaps no more than five percent of the total. The original composition would have been a profusion of apsaras numbering in the hundreds, if not thousands, set amidst painted clouds. Whether the Nandana Garden, with its celestial maidens, was meant to be evoked is possible but no traces of painted vegetation have survived.

The earliest illustrations of the *apsaras* were made by A. Murray in 1889. After Foucher (1896).

The entire rock face was once covered with hundreds, if not thousands, of such *apsaras*.

Oil paintings by D.A.L. Perera, from 1896-97, are now in the Colombo Museum. National Museum, Colombo.

Two *apsaras*, perhaps in procession with floral offerings. The lines of a raised hand above the bodice indicate that the original design was altered.

Enormous scaffolds set against the cliffside were required to support hundreds of artisans. The painting was probably accomplished in a single campaign in the 5th century since re-erecting the scaffolding would have required tremendous effort. A special challenge for those installing the scaffolding was the uneven rock surface but crews were experienced from plastering Anuradhapura's enormous contoured stupas.

shades. Blue pigment, traces of which are found only in the Cobra Hood cave at the base of the rock, was made from lapis lazuli (P: *veluriya*) imported from Afghanistan and it was also employed among the murals inside the relic chamber at Mahiyangana and at Ajanta. A lapis lazuli stone also played an important role in the famous *Vidhura Jataka* (no. 545) and the Buddha's throne at Nagadipa was made of lapis lazuli. (Dpv: 1. 38) Jewellery of lapis lazuli was known at Polonnuruva, together with diamonds and pearls.[16]

The inner face of the Mirror Wall is inscribed with over 2,000 short poems. Most are addressed to the painted *apsaras* but others speak of the palace on top of the Rock, the Lion Entrance or the site as a whole. The poems probably begin in the 6th century, that is, in the century following Kassapa's reign, but the majority belong to the 8th and 9th centuries. A small number refer to Kassapa himself.[17] About 30 or 40 date to between the 11th and 13th centuries, but how much of the mural painting was still in evidence then is hard to know.

The poems are in unrhymed Sinhalese verse but a smattering are in Sanskrit. Most are two lines but some have as many as three or four. A few are signed, but the majority are anonymous. There are also about 150 signatures unattached to poems. A small number are inexplicably cut off midcourse. Most are incised at eye-level in small characters. Those leaving poems belonged to society's literate elites and included at least one prince, a governor of an unnamed city and several Buddhist monks and nuns.

Queens, Courtesans, or Celestial nymphs ?

The mural painting is in one long pocket some forty metres above the floor of the Mirror Wall. Early visitors, such as the Pali scholar W. Rhys Davids, had no access to the pocket and he resorted to using a telescope from the garden below. Access in the early days was by 'iron ladders and steps cut in the rock' and it was only in 1938 that the present circular iron staircase went up.[21] The murals became known to the public only in the late 19th century, as visitors increased and when Murray's pastels were displayed along the double staircase of the Colombo Museum in 1893. His works triggered speculation about the damsels that has never stopped: Who are they? Are they celestial maidens or real women attached to the court or something else altogether?

The murals would not have survived the elements if they were not protected in the recessed pocket. The *apsaras* were never in view from the Mirror Wall and also poorly visible from the base of the rock because of the recessed pocket. Some figures are in fragmentary condition. One figure, for example, is indicated only by a single hand. The majority are poised as if in procession, moving to the left, in the direction of the Lion Entrance. Their lower extremities are concealed by a light coloured wash simulating wavy clouds; other clouds are dark red. Most carry flowers, perhaps capturing the act of bringing offerings. Some are paired, with one woman presenting flowers to the other from a tray. Their faces appear in one-quarter or three-quarter view, except for a few in complete profile. The garments and jewellery convey the opulent nature of contemporary court life. Other first-millennium painting sites share the same high quality, such as within the relic chambers of stupas at Mihintale and Mahiyangana and murals on rock surfaces at Hindagala, Gonagolla and Puligoda.

Bell felt that the women represented Kassapa's queens and courtesans who were depicted with 'individual likeness'. He went so far as to see 'the staid older sister, accompanied by a dusky maid of unattractive mien'. Other notables had their own interpretations, such as Alfred Foucher who studied Murray's pastels. Foucher accepted Bell's identification of Kassapa's queens ('*reines sinhalaises*') and added that the ladies of darker skin ('*coleur foncee*') were Tamils. However, the range of skin tones probably reflected the elite at the time who were 'not physically homogeneous'. Moreover, the poems on the wall also express an appreciation for both light complexion, or 'golden-hued' ('*ravan*'), and darker skin, likened to the blue lily ('*mahanel*'), or *Nymphaae stellata*'. Sources from the second millennium, such as the *Saddharamalankara*, also confirm that shades of skin colour reflected an 'heterogeneous society'. But skin tone was at least an issue in one Pali text in which brahmans boasted that 'Only brahmans are the light caste; others castes are dark'.[22]

Paranavitana suggested that the ladies could be Kubera's own daughters, since the Rock was compared to this god's city, while another scholar proposed that the ladies represented Tara, the female companion of the Mahayana bodhisattva Avalokiteshvara. An opposing analysis came from the great Sri Lankan Tamil savant, Ananda Coomaraswamy, who proposed that these were celestial nymphs. The scholarly consensus today follows Coomarswamy in taking the women to be *apsaras*, with no specific references to Kubera's heavenly city or to the king's court.[23]

There were over 1,500 inscriptions on the Mirror Wall and most were diverse reactions to the *apsaras* but all visitors were motivated by 'a romantic mind in search of love and pleasure'. They represent a one-way conversation between the maidens and the presumably predominant male audience. One poem concluded: 'Now that I have seen these resplendent ladies, heaven has lost its appeal'. The love however was always unrequited and so poems often take on a wistful longing. Emotions were also imputed to the apsaras. For example, one visitor apologized to the damsels for his uninvited intrusion as he passed before them. The wall was thus an open book to visitors over the centuries. Clever, witty and seasoned with repartee, the poems were meant to be relished by others. The Sigiriya maidens still enjoy a life of their own, since the ladies are rumoured to spring to life after midnight and jest about the amusing tourists who streamed by during the day. This could be dismissed as tittle-tattle but the night watchmen report hearing howls of laughter descending down the cliffside.

Apsaras dancing in Sakka's heavenly realm, Wat Pathum Wanaram, Bangkok. Apsaras play a role in Buddhist, Hindu and Jain literature.

The Celestial Maidens

Apsaras were among a huge number of demi-gods weaving in and out of Buddhist, Hindu and Jain texts and secular literature. They inhabit a heavenly sensual realm (P: *kamadhatu*) but can appear on earth to mix with terrestrials, for both good and bad effect. Joining *apsaras* in heaven was also a reward for performing good deeds, as the famous *Nimi Jataka* makes clear. (no. 541); but *apsaras* were able to ensnare ill-disciplined earth-bound ascetics with deadly repercussions. (no. 537) Apsaras were also residents of Sakka's heaven, such as those dancing on lotus petals at Bangkok's Wat Pathum Wanaram temple.[25] Even a servant girl could be reborn as an *apsara*. (Mhv: 27. 13) These diverse stories indicate how nymphs played roles in innumerable settings, with no division between the religious and secular worlds.

Folklore recently unearthed in villages surrounding Sigiriya paints a slightly different picture than the standard narrative in the *Culavamsa*.[26] The core story was the same but the villagers' tales included many additions that probably arose before and after the *Culavamsa*. One such episode was Kassapa's queens throwing themselves off the cliffside after hearing of the king's suicide on the battlefield. It would be natural to dismiss such lore about the leaping maidens as a recent variant myth but it is confirmed among a dozen or so of the ancient poems on the Mirror Wall:

> 'Why is this rock dear to her who, having been aggrieved
> as the kings dies ...[she] appears as if she is hurling herself
> from the summit'.[27]

In fact, this theme of royal woman throwing themselves off heights belonged to popular unwritten lore for centuries. One instance from the 17th century was a queen and her daughter in Sitavaka who 'flung themselves down head long, having received the news that 'that the king had lost the Battle'.[28]

Other modern folklore absent in the *Culavamsa* was Kassapa's rebirth in the Avici Hell, recorded also in a Sinhalese chronicle from the thirteenth century.[29] These examples and others highlight how today's standard 'history' around Sigiriya, based on the *Culvamsa*, was only one slice of a much larger picture. Other episodes, now lost, were surely jettisoned for unknown reasons. There was therefore no single historical or legendary 'truth' about Sigiriya but many coexisting 'truths'.

The Palace

Access to what is now called the Palace required passing into an enormous lion made of brick covered by stucco. Inside the lion was a steep staircase that zigzagged up the treacherous rockface to the top of the Rock. Into the surface were carved 'horizontal grooves' three to six inches in depth and set at three to five foot intervals.[30] The metal stairway visitors climb today generally follows the ancient stairway.

This enormous lion lent the site its ancient name, the Lion Mountain (P: 'Siha-giri'), attributed to Kassapa who 'built a staircase in the form of a lion'. (Cv: 39. 3) Senake Bandraranayake and others have conjectured that the two enormous feet were forepaws but forepaws have five claws while these at Sigiriya have four; the diminutive fourth claw is set well behind the other three, deliberately placed there to enhance the lions' versilimiltude. The colossal lion therefore rested on its haunches, not on its front legs as previously proposed.[31]

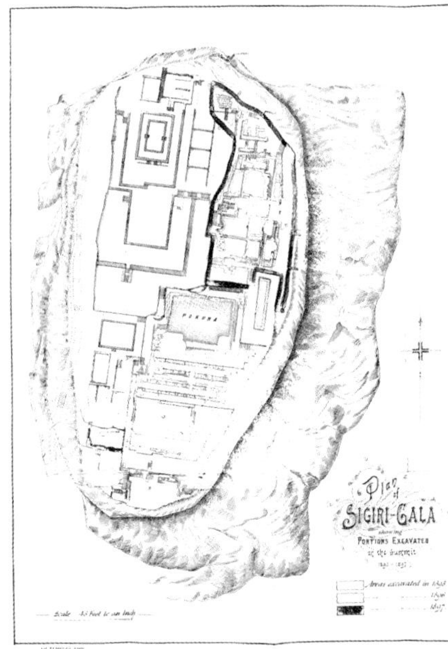

The summit's uneven contours and haphazard design suggest that there was no overarching plan. After the *Journal of the Ceylon Branch of the Royal Asiatic Society*, vol. 15, 1897–1898.

The summit's long uneven plateau slopes sharply downward from the entrance on the north and is filled with brick structures and cisterns that were 'covered with jungle' when the foundations were exposed in 1895 by H.C.P. Bell. The highest point has now the ruins of a small stupa, built in perhaps three stages, the earliest of which may date to Kassapa's reign. Few structures survive above waist level but they were once topped by tiled wooden roofs. A marble walkway cuts an uneven path from north to south. There is also a huge 'throne' cut from the living rock. Some have seen an underlying scheme based on a modular grid but the plateau's plan argues for a haphazard development. There was even an attempt to link the Rock to the solstice. But the most madcap notion was that the summit was Ravana's palace, reflecting the 'booming Ravana epidemic originating in Hindu India and diffused to ardent Ravanaists of Sri Lanka'.[32]

King Kassapa still maintains a firm grip in the nation's Buddhist imagination. For example, a feature film in 1974, *The God King*, situated Kassapa holding court on the summit. And Kassapa's conflict with his half-brother proved irresistible to the late science fiction author based in Sri Lanka, Arthur C. Clarke, who integrated both Sigiriya and Adam's Peak into his *The Fountains of Paradise*. Even hair styles modelled on those worn by the *apsaras* were adopted by women in Colombo in the 1960s.

H.C.P. Bell and his family and the painter D.A.L. Perera suspended on a swinging bamboo gondola.

Life Without a Drip-ledge At the foot of the Rock is the Boulder Garden where some 30 monastic caves are set amidst cyclopian boulders. Caves were among the five acceptable types of residences, noted in the *Vinaya-pitaka*. Short inscriptions between the third and first century BCE within the Sigiriya caves were commissioned by donors. A typical example reads 'This cave is a co-donation of the male lay-devotee Uttara and the female lay-devotee Tissa'. Most caves here were presented to the *sangha* by local chiefs, called '*paramaka*'.[33] Small communities nearby provided the monks with food and necessities. No inscriptions at Sigiriya refer to nuns. The caves were probably inhabited as late as the eighth century.

The Mirror Wall and the circular iron staircase, installed in 1938, leading to the murals.

The Lion Entrace, through which one proceeded to the palace on the summit. A fourth claw on the outer side of the paws, not visible in the photograph, indicates that the lion stood originally on its hind feet.

Conjectural drawings, such as this one, have assumed that the lion was prone on its front feet but a fresh interpretation suggests otherwise.

Also at Sigiriya, between the gardens and the Rock, are traces of at least one stupa, image-houses, Bodhi Tree shrines and an ordination-hall. Arranged in an asymmetrical layout, it seems that they were built at different times. Buddha images from Sigiriya are on view at the site museum, together with terracotta architectural ornaments. Within the buried debris of the Boulder Garden were found a number of fired clay figurines that have been identified as souvenirs to remind pilgrims of the apsaras. The site museum was designed by Chandana Ellepola, with recent didactic displays planned by Jagath Weerasinghe.

The caves at Sigiriya would likely be similar to this ancient cave at Hatthikuchchi whose outer wall was reburbished centuries later.

Naturally formed caves were partially excavated to adapt them for habitation. The open exterior was then enclosed by the addition of an outer screen wall made of fired brick or adobe blocks, combined with rubble. Walls could also be made with wooden lattices daubed with a mixture of soil and clay. Several caves at Sigiriya have retained the lower portions of their original brick walls. The cave interiors were covered with unpainted plaster during the early phase, much of which still adheres to the rock surface.

Monsoon rain was diverted from dripping down into the cave by a shallow narrow depression cut just above the top of the cave; water then ran off to the side, much like a modern gutter. This device is now called a drip-ledge (P: *mariyaya*), or *kataram* in Sinhalese, and drip-ledges are found wherever there are Buddhist caves. The donative inscriptions usually appear just below the drip-edge. The king associated with the Dambulla caves for example was praised for 'drip-ledges cut over hundreds of rock caves'.[34]

Caves with protective outer walls and drip-ledges were far more commodious than natural caves inconvenienced by the elements. A drip-ledge came to be a conventional marker, or manner of speech, for caves fitted with an exterior wall and a drip-ledge. The distinction between caves with or without a drip-ledge even entered scholastic Buddhist commentary in which monks seeking a strict ascetic life were forbidden to occupy caves with the luxury of drip-ledges. Caves fitted with drip-ledges were however considered acceptable.[35]

At least five of these early caves at Sigirya were refurbished in the fifth century and later. The insides, with fresh coats of plaster, were often enlivened with murals but only a few tantalizing fragments survive. Even a full-length female figure can be seen inside Cave 7. Painted decorative bands in Cave 9 reveal motifs originating in India but which were found widely in Southeast Asia. Such brightly painted interiors indicate that a monk's life was scarcely as severe as the present appearance of the caves suggests. By the nineteenth century, bears had replaced the monks.[36]

KELANIYA

KELANIYA: THE BUDDHA COUNSELS A SNAKE KING

The Buddha's final visit to Sri Lanka was here, on the bank of the Kelani River. A Bodhi tree and the central temple.

This monastery marks the hallowed ground where the Buddha's final visit to the island took place. Its namesake is the Kelaniya Ganga River that rises near Adam's Peak. The word *kelaniya* is Sinhalese for the Pali *kalyani*, meaning beautiful. The earliest mention of the site is the fourth-century *Dipavamsa* that situated the monastery at the 'mouth of the Kalyani', though the monastery is actually about fifteen kilometres from the coast. (Dpv: 2: 53) Nearby caves, with stone inscriptions, indicate a Buddhist presence in the region around the time of Christ, centuries before the monastery's beginnings.[1] The complex sits atop a broad mound whose high sloping sides are reinforced with roughly chiselled stones of uncertain age. The temple's formal entrance faces the Kelani river.

Our story begins when the Buddha journeyed to Ceylon to mediate a conflict between two snake-kings (P: *naga-rajas*) over possession of a jewelled throne. One was Mahodara and the other his nephew, Culodara. This throne was a dowry gift from Mahodara's father to Culodara's mother but upon her death, Mahodara demanded its return. (Mhv: 1.50) The two forces assembled on Nagadipa, or Snake-Island, but the Buddha delivered 'a doctrine that begets accord'. (1. 60) Bloodshed averted, the contested throne remained in Nagadipa. (1. 68) Three years later, Mahodhara's uncle named Maniakkhika, literally 'Gem Eyes', invited the Buddha to deliver a sermon from a 'precious throne' at Kelaniya. This throne is now thought to be enshrined in the monastery's stupa but the throne in Nagadipa was never said to be transferred to Kelaniya. (Mhv: 1. 45, 75) In fact, little is known about what was believed to be enshrined in Kelaniya's stupa in antiquity, contrasting with the many descriptions of relics in certain stupas at Anuradhapura. Although the *naga*-king Culodara played only a cameo role in Sri Lanka, his fame spread widely in the Theravada world, appearing in Burma in a Pagan inscription from 1131 and the entire legend was summarized in a 15th-century Chiang Mai chronicle.[2]

A glass encased reliquary is believed to contain Buddha relics conveyed here from Kandy during the site's reconstruction. This hall, from the 1930s, was attached to the nineteenth-century antechamber with the reclining Buddha.

The basic legend emerged first in the *Dipavamsa* and later in the 5th-century *Mahavamsa*, with some variations. (Dpv: 2.1-60; Mhv: 1. 45) For example, the contested throne in Nagadipa was made of lapis lazuli (P: '*veluriya-pallanka*'), according to the *Dipavamsa*, but was designated a 'gem-set throne' (P: '*mani-pallanka*') in the *Mahavamsa*. (Dpv: 2. 38; Mhv; 1. 45) Snakes, rivers and thrones were combined in a Sanskrit text where a '*naga* maiden' presented the Buddha a gem-studded throne on a river bank at Bodh Gaya.[3]

Previous page:
The snake-king Maniakkhika dominates the wall leading to the reclining Buddha. c. 1850.

The Kelani River empties into the Indian Ocean just above Colombo. A Dutch map, circa 1770. National Archives, the Netherlands.

The Buddha preaching from his 'gem-set throne' (Mhv. 1.45), now believed to be enshrined in the monastery's stupa.

The Buddha was accompanied to Lanka by the deity Samiddhisumana who resided within a kingstead tree (P: *rajayatana*), or *Buchanania latifolia,* at the Jetavana monastery. Uprooting the tree, the god held it above the Buddha like an umbrella in Nagadipa. Later, this same tree was planted where the Buddha preached on Nagadipa. (Mhv: 1.53, 67) The tree and the throne were said to be enshrined in a stupa named after the tree, the 'Rajayatana cetiya', according to the 13th-century Pali text, the *Rasavahini.*[4] The *Mahavamsa*, however, says nothing about enshrining the throne or the tree in Nagadipa. Nagadipa's importance was sealed however by the 5th century when Buddhaghosa wrote that at the end of our current eon all corporal relics of the Buddha will assemble at the Rajayatana shrine on Nagadipa after first collecting at Anuradhapura and then proceeding to Bodh Gaya where they will be consumed by fire and usher in the Future Buddha, or Metteyya.[5] The story of the tree and the throne on Nagadipa is largely unknown today and rarely depicted but was highlighted in three stucco panels above the temple's main entrance, thus cleverly uniting Nagadipa and the Buddha's stay at Kelaniya.

A snake-queen's death provoked a war over her dowry, a 'gem-set throne'. Nagadipa Purana Vihariya. Nainativu Island.

A legendary throne was also found in South India in the 6th-century Tamil Buddhist classic about the courtesan Manimekalai.[6] This heroine paid homage to the jewelled-throne (T: *mani-pallavam*), situated on an island identified as Sri Lanka. By circumambulating the throne, she acquired a magic bowl from the local goddess before returning to Tamil Nadu and recreating an identical throne. Another Buddhist tale from Tamil Nadu, known as the *Kundalakesi*, also referenced the throne. These two Tamil works suggest that certain themes usually thought to originate in Lanka may in reality have developed in tandem in South India. Also, the contested jewelled-throne underscores how secular themes blended into religious traditions and how craving and attachment to possessions, like the jewelled-throne, only beget strife. The site's earliest patron was the legendary Yatthala Tissa whose uncle welcomed Asoka's children to Anuradhapura. He was credited here with a five-storied temple, (P: *'panca-pasada')*.[7] (Cv. 85: 64) Although no evidence points to his rule at Kelaniya, his name was invoked over the centuries by royal patrons at Kelaniya piggybacking on his fabled fame. But the first king to call Kelaniya home was Kalyani Tissa whose daughter gave birth to Dutthagamani, the warrior-king who drove the Tamils from Anuradhapura. (Mhv: 22. 13) Kalyani Tissa is not mentioned in the *Mahavamsa* but later commentators tied him to Anuradhapura's royal family to enhance the monastery's prestige.[8]

What Kelaniya looked like in the first millennium is guesswork, since only a few tantalizing fragments survive. For example, two fragmentary Buddha images from about the 7th century have been discovered, one now in the sculpture garden beside the Bodhi tree and the second in the compound of the Kit-siri-mevan stupa across the river. Another possible early survival is a stone urinal in the sculpture garden. Two *naga*-guardian figures of inferior quality in the sculpture garden date perhaps to the 12th century. The single major surviving monument is the stupa but it has been rebuilt so often that its original shape is uncertain. The Colombo environs were within Anuradhapura's orbit, proved by the large 7th- or 8th-century stupa base nearby at Attanagalla.

Bathing in the river

Two 10th-century inscriptions refer to the Buddha bathing in the river here but this episode was never included in the early chronicles. This incident is commemorated by the small stupa complex Kit-siri-mevan named after a 4th-century king of the same name who had no connection with Kelaniya but who received the tooth-relic in Anuradhapura. The first inscription mentions a stupa containing the Buddha's bathing-robe, or '*uda-kas-da'.* The second was found at the Kelaniya itself and refers to a donation to what was called the Auspicious Stupa, (P: '*mangala-dagoba*'), at the 'Kalani–vehera'. Also, a 'lamp with a stand of precious stones' was donated from funds diverted from female dancers attached to the Ruvanvali Stupa at Anuradhapura.[9] This bathing episode is another example of how certain popular legends were never recorded in the island's chronicles.

The story of the Buddha's bathing extended well outside Lanka. A king in Pegu in Burma for example told his monks sailing to Lanka that their ordinations would be conducted on the 'Kalyani River where the Blessed One [the Buddha] enjoyed a bath'. A northern Thai chronicle also recorded that monks from Siam and Cambodia were ordained 'on a flotilla of boats tied together .... in the Kalyani river'. The Pegu mission, though never recorded in the *Culavamsa,* was well known in Ceylon in the 19th-century.[10] This bathing and the resultant 'sacred water-drops' also appeared in poems, such as the *Mayura Sandesaya.*

A Footprint in the River

The bathing episode is tied to another tradition in which the Buddha impressed his footprint in the river bed for the community of snakes, a legend appearing as early as the 13th-century *Pujavaliya.* Even a nineteenth-century English visitor at Kelaniya described a 'deep eddy in the stream' where the footprint was said to be at the bottom.[11] This legend probably stems indirectly from a well-known Pali tradition in which the Buddha bestowed one footprint to a snake-king and another to a heretic, along a river bank in Western India. The two foot impressions in India were in fact directly likened to the footprint at Kelaniya.[12]

Kelaniya also played a key role vis a-vis Adam's Peak, as it was from Kelaniya that the Buddha flew to the mountain belonging to the god Sumana. (Mhv: 1.78) In the *Mahavamsa,* the Buddha's transition from Kelaniya to Adam's Peak appears arbitrary and abrupt, almost as an afterthought, but the legend was later adjusted and the god Sumana himself was placed at the Kelaniya.[13] In this version, Sumana first reminded the Buddha that he granted two footprints in India, after which he then invited the Buddha to impress a footprint on his mountaintop. Situtating Sumana at the Kelaniya thus established a poignant link between the monastery and Adam's Peak.

Solias Mendis also designed the stucco work for the temple's exterior that enveloped the nineteenth-century temple. These impish figures were likely modeled on those at the Tivanka Temple, Pollonuruva.

Kelaniya Through the Ages

The monastery's history comes into sharper focus only in the 12th century when it was the most sacred location on the west coast. Testimony comes from a royal pilgrimage by the famous Polonnuruva ruler, Nissankamalla (1187-96), who recorded his visit here in no less than six stone inscriptions. 'Kalani' was grouped together with the island's most venerated sites, such as Anuradhapura and Dambulla.[14] The monastery received attention from many subsequent monarchs and was also included among the Sixteen Sacred Sites, a list standardized by the 18th century.

The great patrons at Kelaniya included Vijayabahu III (1232-36) who rebuilt the stupa, said to be destroyed by the Tamils, or 'Damilas'. (Cv: 81. 59-63) Tamils desecrating Buddhist sites is a cherished theme in Sinhala chronicles but no facts support a destructive Tamil role at Kelaniya. Vijayabahu III's successor, Parakramabahu II (1236-70), restored the five-storied temple attributed to Yatthala Tissa and a recumbent Buddha. He also repaired a temple containing a '*Tivanka*' image, signifying a standing Buddha with a flexed hip, creating a 'thrice-bent' curve, or *tivanka*. (Cv: 85. 64-72) This image likely represented the Buddha's descent from the Tavatimsa Heaven, reminiscent of the brick image inside Polonnuruva's Tivanka Temple. The same king restored a stupa at Attanagalla, only 30 kilometres northeast of Kelaniya. Many structures noted in the *Culavamsa* as being at Kelaniya are also described in the *Pujavilaya* but nothing of significance from this period survives.[15]

The sole inscription from this period was found at the Kit-siri-mevan stupa, from 1344. Its short text recorded repairs to the 'Kit-sir-meavan [*sic*] Kalani viharaya' and the construction of a temple for the Bodhi tree. The donations were funded by a land grant from an unnamed king and managed by a chief monk at Kelaniya named Vilgammula. This same cleric was the author of the Sinhalese *Bodhivamsa*, or *Chronicle of the Bodhi Tree*, composed on behalf of Parakramabahu IV (1302-1306). The monk Vilgammula was also based at Kelaniya for a time, according to the *Bodhivamsa*, in agreement with the inscription. He belonged to a monastic group named Vilgammula, one of the eight fraternities blended together by Parakramabahu I at the Jetavana Monastery in Polonnuruva.[16]

Calm Before The Storm

The Kelaniya complex probably reached its zenith in the 15th century under patronage from the nearby capital of Kotte. Kelaniya was by then a commercial centre and home to villas used as retreats by Kotte's elites. From Kelaniya to Kotte is no more than eight kilometres as the crow flies and both were connected by narrow waterways. Poets painted the town in vivid colours with its 'broad streets thronged with men of many climes' and its mansions rivalling those on the celestial Kailasa Mountain. It was further graced with 'virgins wondrous that tempt the gallants', one of many hyperbolae in the *Mayura Sandesaya.* In another poem, its citizens were blessed with 'amorous husbands and wives, each with no thought but for the other'.[17] No villas in the township have survived, being of perishable materials.

An inscribed slab at the Kelaniya from 1509 described the complex in detail. This inscription, nearly two metres in height, was probably the same panel noted amidst Kelaniya's ruins by a German traveller in the 1730s.[18] It was issued by Parakramabahu IX (1489-1513) who ruled in Kotte. This epigraph and others are built into an exterior wall of the chief monk's residence.

This Kotte king renewed the plaster on the stupa's exterior, built a stone wall on the north side and a flight of steps on the eastern side with a moonstone ('*sanda-kada-pahana*'). Two nearly identical moonstones are found in the temple compound and one is perhaps the very moonstone mentioned in the inscription. The king also rebuilt the image hall ('*samadhi-pilima-geya*'), a shrine commemorating where the Buddha put on his robe after bathing ('*siwaru-da-geya*') and a shrine commemorating the monk in the cauldron of oil ('*telkatara-geya*'). Repairs were also made to a small shrine named Tivanka-geya that probably contained an image depicting the descent from the Tavatimsa Heaven. There was also a shrine for the Future Buddha, or '*na-pilima-geya*', '*na*' being an abbreviation for Natha, that is, Avalokiteshvara, that was interpreted as Metteyya.[19] He also refurbished the five-storied hall, or '*pas-mahal-paya*', and installed a latrine. For upkeep, the inscription specified amounts of paddy required from those who occupied temple lands and who served in the kitchen, bath houses and elephant and horse stables. These included both Tamils and Sinhalas, implying a mixed population at the time in the Colombo area. Many shrines in the inscription also match the generalized descriptions from a 15th-century poem, *Salilhini Sandesaya.* Apart from the main stupa, nothing can be identified today but the inscription reveals a flourishing monastic community in 1509.

Detail of mural showing the Portuguese, who purportedly razed the monastery in 1575, during the war with nearby Sitavaka.

The Portuguese

The court at Kotte and the Kelaniya monks in 1509 could scarcely foresee the storm on the horizon triggered by the arrival of the Portuguese. The monastery's fortunes began to decline with the reign of a converted Kotte king named Dom João Dharmapala (1551-97) who transferred revenues from the 'lands at Calane [Kelaniya] on both sides of the river' to the Franciscans in 1557, together with revenues from Kotte's Temple of the Tooth.

This moonstone was possibly a royal donation, referred to in an inscription dated to 1509 ('*sanda-kada-pahana*'). Now placed at the entrance to the main temple.

The monastery's death knell is usually ascribed to Diogo de Melo who in 1575 pursued Sinhala troops from nearby Sitavaka who were attempting to overthrow Dharmapala. This commander destroyed 'that City [Kelaniya] and the 'Temple of great pilgrimage', according to the Portuguese chronicler Queiros. His history, however, was compiled nearly a century after the purported event and no contemporaneous evidence has corroborated this pillaging. So did such total destruction really occur at Kelaniya? Queiros himself stated that lodging for the Sitavaka troops was being prepared in the 'ruins of Calane', implying that at least part of the site was derelict before the alleged destruction. The 'ruins of Calane' were probably a result of the rupture of patronage decades before 1575 with the transfer of property to the Franciscans.

Discovering no opposing troops at Kelaniya, De Melo then went on an alleged rampage. During the pillaging, the enemy arrived and the Portuguese drove some Sinhala soldiers into the river who drowned. The destruction so briefly referred to by Queiros was taken up with relish by P.E. Pieris in his influential *Ceylon: The Portuguese Era* (1913). This nationalist historian greatly embellished the incident by claiming that 'villagers' defending the sacred shrine were 'driven into the river and drowned'.[20] The soldiers in the Portuguese chronicle were hence turned into defenceless villagers in this patriotic retelling. This dramatic version by Pieris, based solely on a few lines in Queiros, then slipped comfortably into the nation's history books. However, if the Portuguese were so bent on destroying the monastery, why did the pillage only begin as late as 1575, years after the Portuguese controlled nearby Colombo in the 1560s and long after the 1550s when the Christian king sympathetic to Portugal assumed the thrown?

That Sinhala and Portuguese documents of the 16th century are silent about the destruction of Kelaniya is another strong reason for doubting Queiros's account. Most probative is that the Sinhalese chronicle, the *Rajavilaya,* says nothing about the temple's fate, and this in a text which never missed a chance to describe destruction wrought by European invaders. The same is also true for the Sinhalese *Alakeshvara Yuddhaya* covering much the same period.[21]

The real culprit in the site's decline was likely the abrupt cessation of patronage in 1557. Without a tireless removal of vegetation, even the mightiest monuments lapse quickly into ruins, as 19th-century photographs of Anuradhapura's monuments illustrate. Trees, especially the *Ficus* genus, wreak havoc in brick or stone monuments. Anuradhapura's ruinous state was never attributed to Portuguese malice, but nationalist historians have been too quick to blame Iberian barbarians for Kelaniya's slide into ruins.

'Others say it was an accident'

An unsolved murder occurred at Kelaniya in 1551. The victim was King Bhuvanekabahu II (1521-51), the Buddhist king in Kotte and grandfather of the converted king Dharmapala. The Portuguese had been leaning hard on him to forsake Gotama for the Gospel and his staunch refusal generated much chagrin, revealed in letters to and fro between Ceylon to Goa and even to King João III in Lisbon. This Buddhist king went so far as to declare that he would rather 'become a Moor than a Christian'.[22]

Who exactly pulled the trigger on the 'firelock' and for what reasons are still debated but the incident transpired when Portuguese troops purportedly friendly to the king assembled at Kelaniya to protect his kingdom from an attack by the king's brother based at nearby Sitavaka. All accounts agree that the king was shot while either standing on an upstairs verandah or when he appeared before an open window. On which side of the river the villa was located is unclear too but the palatial retreats, or '*Bom Retiro*', were probably in the vicinity of the present temple complex.[23]

The most convincing explanation is that the assassination was ordered by a local official, Gaspar de Azevedo, who came to the king's villa in Kelaniya 'with 80 Portuguese with their muskets' and the king was shot 'when he came to the verandah to see the Portuguese have their meal'. Bad blood between De Azevedo and the king began as early as 1548. The assinassation led to an 'enquiry' by the governor of Goa who ordered the arrest of De Azevedo. Despite the arrest of the likely guilty party, gossip about the incident took on a life of its own. A later Portuguese source named the shooter as Antonio de Barcelos, a mulatto slave of the Viceroy of Goa. Barcelos, on his deathbed, took responsibility for the shot but claimed he was aiming at a pigeon! A juicier later twist claimed Barcelos was hired by the king to shoot his queen's secret lover. The paramour was expected to stand at a certain hour by a certain window but failed to appear. The king, standing by the window in error, was in the wrong place at the wrong time. The shot 'passed through his head' and he expired three hours later. The truth about his death was never settled, confirmed by a Dutch account that concluded that the king was killed 'as some say, purposely, but as other say, by mistake'. A Sinhala source stated that the king's death was payback for his bad karma for 'joining hands with the Portuguese [Pratika]' and thereby endangering Buddhism. But this same source summed up the ongoing ambiguity: 'Some say this evil deed was deliberate; others say that it was an accident'.[24]

The assassination of a Sinhalese king at Kelaniya in 1555 was recorded in Portuguese, Dutch and Sinhalese accounts. After Francois Valentijn's *Old and New East-India.*

The Renewal: fifty thousand bricks

The Kelaniya monastery passed into Dutch control after the Portuguese were forced from the Colombo fort in 1656. Although the structures were in ruins, Kelaniya itself never lost its hallowed stature, much like the most sacred ruinous stupas at Anuradhapura. The Dutch were keenly aware of Kelaniya's symbolic importance as the 'seat of Buddhism in the Company's territories', as observed in 1682; another Dutch notice, in 1692, stated that the Kelaniya is the 'most renowned and frequented *dagoba* [stupa] in the Island'. That this major sacred site was so firmly under Dutch control was a painful reminder of Kandy's impotence and vulnerability, much like the Shwedagon Pagoda in British hands in Lower Burma when the Burmese court was restricted to Upper Burma.

The Dutch trading company, the VOC, was keen not to jeopardize commercial contacts between the coast and the highland Kandyan kingdom and so monks were allowed to remain at Kelaniya. Pressure from the Dutch Reformed Church grew, however, and the government ordered the clerics to vacate Kelaniya in 1692. Tension between the church and the VOC's commercial relations with Kandy is a leitmotif in Dutch archives. This evidence proves that Buddhist activity persisted at the site, despite the withdrawal of royal support in the previous century and the derelict condition of the monuments.

Two European eye-witnesses visited Kelaniya shortly after the monks departed in 1692. The first was a Swabian named Martin Wintergerst who was there around 1700 'to collect large stones from an old ruined *pagoda* (or idol-temple)' for use in a gate in Colombo. He 'came to a hill on which such a pagoda once stood, its stones strewn about' and removed 42 stone posts, about 8, 10 and 12 feet in length and a half a foot across.[25] A few stray crude posts fitting this description still remain at Kelaniya. That Wintergerst was sent to Kelaniya for building materials suggests that the Dutch in Colombo knew that the site was in ruins.

Wintergerst found 'common folk' squatting amidst the stone ruins, burning candles and worshipping. He was also struck by a group of brahmans ('Barmanen') who were Hindu ascetics who 'behaved in all imaginable ways'. Wintergerst saw 'one who wept, another who did all sorts of acrobatic tricks, laughing and shouting; and thereto they use a certain herb, named *hatto*, which they eat or smoke like tobacco and when this takes effect it causes either violent laughter or pitiful lamenting and crying. We saw some of them even beat their heads so pitifully on these stones that one might think they would burst into 1,000 pieces, so greatly did it excite them that we took their stones away [to Colombo]'. This *hatto* was cannabis (*Cannabis indica)*, and a similar description was noted in 16th-century Goa, in Garcia da Orta's classic, *Colloquies on the Simples* [*sic*] *and Drugs of India*; the drug was called '*bangue*' in Goa, or *bhang* in Hindi. It also 'provoked lust' and made a 'man drunke or in a manner out of his wits' when mixed with the arecca nut. These brahmans may have been ascetics from South India; a Dutch priest had complained

The image hall, circa 1850, was refashioned and enveloped in the present temple, begun in 1927, preserving the murals dating to 1851.

about such holy men in 1704 and the governor Van Goens ordered that the 'heathen yogies' be forbidden to enter the country, together with Moors.[26]

Robert Knox, once a captive in the Kandyan kingdom, told the famous Robert Hooke of the Royal Society in London that he 'so often experimented with it [cannabis] himself, that there is no Cause of Fear, tho' possibly there may be Laughter'. Knox brought a sample to England and it was introduced to a Society meeting in 1689, the first learned notice of cannabis in the West.[27]

A German, Johann Wolfgang Heydt, visited Kelaniya in the 1740s, and found the mound 'called by the natives Galana or Calana … overgrown with crooked bushes, which have spread over the whole hill … [with] many stones lying upon and around it'. This mound was probably the main stupa that we see today. Heydt noted further that worshippers gathered 'in great numbers …. with the lighting of 1,000 lamps'.[28] Heydt prepared a sketch, turned into an engraving. The site's fortunes reversed within a few decades, after support flowed from Kandy.

Though the site was in ruins it remained a major focus of devotion. Johann Wolfgang Heydt. 1744. National Library of the Netherlands.

Occasional clerical missions to the Kelaniya monastery were dispatched from the court in Kandy. A monk was deputed here with palanquin bearers and four drummers, with Dutch approval, both in 1699 and 1703. The cleric also carried a reliquary, or '*dhatu karanduva*'. His presence caused an 'incredible mass of Company's subjects, nominally Christians, [who] also came flocking and made heathenish offerings'. Much later, in 1750, an embassy of 32 monks came to Colombo led by a senior monk who sought Dutch medical assistance. He requested to be lodged at the Kelaniya monastery but was refused since the Dutch 'apprehended difficulties getting him away when once settled at Calanie [Kelaniya]'. Further, the Dutch declared him 'in perfect health, and … only simulating illness'.[29] These instances suggest the enduring sacred nature of Kelaniya, both for the court in Kandy and for low-country residents, despite its ruinous state.

Colonial policy relaxed in the next decade and Kandy's Kirti Sri Rajasimha (1747-82) was authorized by the Dutch to rebuild the complex. The head of the *sangha*, Velivita Saranankara, appointed a senior monk, Dehigaspe Atthadassi and his pupil, Mapitigama Buddharakkhita, to supervise. A stone inscription, dated to 1767, noted Atthadassi's repairs to the stupa and the monastery's terraced enclosure and a ceremony for 'fitting eyes to a stone image'.[30]

Work was still in progress twelve years later, since another stone inscription, in 1779, recorded that the Kandyan king supplied 50,000 bricks and powdered lime for mortar to repair the stupa ('*caitaya*') and that he repaired the image-house, pavilions ('*mandap*a'), refectories and preaching halls. For upkeep, the proceeds of paddy land were granted. The epigraph ends by noting repairs and

The stupa's reconstruction sponsored by the court in Kandy. 1785. John Brandes. Rijksmuseum.

improvements at the Kit-siri-mevan-Kelani-Viharaya. This grant was made during the time of Buddharakkhita, the pupil of the former head.

A now lost copperplate grant issued in 1780 repeats this information and adds that the stupa was to be 40 cubits in height, that is, about 18 metres; a cubit is about 46 centimetres. 40 cubits was a conventional measurement assigned to many structures and even to the Bodhi Tree. The stupa today measures about 27 metres. A sculpture adorned with 'the ten accessory emblems' was donated, together with an image-house with 'a portico and stone steps'. The king in Kandy also ordered 'thousands of gold coins' to be used for 'the repair of dilapidated and ruined structures'.[31]

A watercolour from about five years later, in 1785, by Jan Brandes, shows how the desolate mound sketched by Heydt in the 1740s had been transformed. The painting shows a nearly completed stupa and a two-storied structure on the right with a tile roof that was later removed. The whitewashed structure on the left has been plausibly identified as the Vibhishana shrine. Destructive vegetation can be seen sprouting from the fabric of the stupa even in the course of rebuilding. The painting's caption reads, 'The highest section of the Sinhalese pagoda named Kelaniya on the island of Ceylon two hours from Colombo. No. 2. This mound is constantly enlarged by the priest by the application of layers of stone and plaster one around another, and it is thought that great treasure lies hidden within it, since it said to have made by human hands'. Brandes never visited the site but relied on sketches made by another.[32]

Pax Britannica

The Dutch capitulated to the English in Colombo in 1796 and in the next year a Scottish army officer visiting Kelaniya submitted a report to Calcutta's *Asiatick Researches* that stated that 'The stupa was finished then [in 1797] but its outer layer was "of no great thickness of bricks … [and] was damaged and partly destroyed by the rain".

The gateway facing the Kelani River, frontispiece to *Scenery and Reminisces of Ceylon*. John Deschamps. 1845. London.

To the south of the stupa were two brick temples with tile roofs. One had murals which included "Hooneman [Hanuman], Brama [Brahma], Vishnu", and "sixteen representations of Daghopes [stupas]', that is, the Sixteen Sacred Sites. A nearly life-size seated Buddha was in both temples. In one temple were three stone images protected by a glass case.[33]

These two adjacent temples described in 1797 were dismantled and replaced with a single structure by about 1850, next to the stupa. This temple, seen in old photographs, was enveloped in the 1930s by the building seen today. Antique photographs show the original, with its encircling portico covered with a sloping tile roof. This old temple was decried as 'painfully modern' in 1915. A small structure, located beside the monastery's Bodhi tree, gives an idea of the original appearance of the temple now encased by the new one.

The temple's signature gateway facing the river was built in the first quarter of the 19th century, captured in a watercolour made between 1828 and 1838 by a British officer, John Deschamps.[34] The gate is of European design but for a typical Sinhala 'face of glory' placed at the apex. A new matching gateway next to the old one went up in 1988.

Helene Dep Wijewardene (1864-1937) donated new flooring to the temple in 1888 and later sponsored the present temple.

Helene Dep Wijewardene

The prime mover behind today's temple was Helene Dep Wijewardene (1864-1937) whose husband, Don Philip, traced his family to 14th-century royalty. His lumber business on the nearby Kelani River left a fortune to Helene upon his death in 1903. The family switched faiths during the colonial era, from Catholic to Dutch Reformed and then from Anglican to Buddhist. Her descendants played leading national roles, notably her grandson, J.R. Jayewardena, Sri Lanka's President from 1978-89. Under Helene's stewardship, the small temple dating to about 1850 was completely enveloped within a new one begun in 1927. Helene's patronage, however, started decades earlier with the gift of the temple's present stone floor in 1888, commemorated by a stone block embedded in the floor just inside the main entrance, inscribed with her initials and a date: 'H.D.W. 5/25/88'.

Groundbreaking was on 1 January 1927, with the temple's completion ten years later in January 1937. Helene attended the ceremony, recorded in sketches by Mendis that were later used in his murals.[35] A Sinhalese stone inscription set into the rear exterior wall, dated 1934 (Buddhist Era 2417), records her donation. A Scottish architect in Colombo, H.H. Reid, was commissioned for the project. Helene knew Reid before the Kelaniya project when he designed her European-style residence, called Sri Ramya, now the library of the American Center on Galle Road. Here, Helene entertained Rabindranath Tagore and Nandala Bose from Calcutta.

Helene's first act of patronage was new stone flooring, commemorated by this block embedded in the floor at the main entrance, dated May 25 1888.

Reid harmonized the exterior of the Kelaniya temple with traditional Sinhala architecture. The eight-sided cupola for example is a quotation of the famous 'octagon' at Kandy's Temple of the Tooth. Reid was a member of the firm Edwards Reid and Begg that also designed the addition to Kandy's Temple of the Tooth that is now a museum. The famous Geoffrey Bawa joined this group in the 1950s but decried what he dubbed the 'Kelaniya style'. A copycat version of the Kelaniya temple is the popular Bellanwila temple in Colombo from the 1940s.

The project's muralist, Solias Mendis, also designed the stucco sculpture ornamenting the temple's exterior.[36] Nine nearly life-size images reflecting the island's eclectic traditions ring the walls. From the entrance going clockwise is Ganesha, followed by the goddess Ganga. The rear wall has Vishnu, Vibhishana's coronation and Natha, a deity in Sri Lanka once associated with Avalokiteshvara but now with the Future Buddha, or Metteyya (a seated Buddha in the headdress can signify the Buddha of the Future, or Metteyya, in Sri Lanka). On the other side, facing the stupa, is Kelaniya's snake-king Maniakkhika, the six-headed Hindu god Kataragama, the Buddha with Sumana on Adam's Peak and lastly the god Rama with his bow. The whimsical figures around the base were likely modeled on the frolicking stucco imps at Polonnuruva's Tivanka temple. The cramped narrow space between the temple and the stupa is a result of the enlargement of the temple in the 1930s.

Entrance hall, with the inner sanctum in the rear. The reclining Buddha is in the chamber on the right.

The 1851 Murals

The mid-19th-century temple consists of two parallel oblong chambers of equal size, one room serving as the entrance hall for the shrine room containing a reclining Buddha. A painted Sinhalese inscription above one of its doorways reads: 'The chief incumbent of Kelaniya, Mapitigama Sangharakkita, has completed the construction of the temple on the Full Moon Day in the year 2394 [1851] of the Buddha's Era'.[37] This chief monk was sent from Kandy to Kelinaya and belonged to a distinguished clerical lineage.

Murals feature eight *Jatakas*, each identified by a single painted caption in the middle of its register. Only two are drawn from the revered last ten, the Sama and Vessantara, 540 and 547. The narrative flows from left to right, or counter-clockwise, beginning on the front wall to the right of the central doorway leading to the inner shrine. The temple's six original doors are still intact, two on each long side, one in the front and one in the rear. One of two original windows in the adjoining chamber with the reclining Buddha was enlarged into a door in the 1930s.

The room with the reclining Buddha and its adjoining antechamber formed the temple dating to circa 1851. This modest temple was incorporated into the present temple begun in 1927. Courtesy Vajira Nalinda Jayathilaka.

One of two unidentified possible donors. Circa 1851.

Front Wall

Just beneath the ceiling is the seven-week period at Bodh Gaya during and after the Buddha's defeat of Mara and the Enlightenment. The Buddha is shown seated or standing and accompanied by different trees associated with specific weeks. The Enlightenment beneath the Bodhi Tree is first, on the right. The series is captioned, 'Sat Sathiya', or 'Seven Weeks', a grouping found as early as the fifth-century Pali *Nidanakatha* and known in Mahayana traditions, with many variations.

Two standing male figures to the right of the doorway turn towards the reclining Buddha. The pair are thought to be ancient kings but their individualized features suggest that they were real temple patrons and that the artists worked from sketches drawn from life. Whether the pair were local donors or members of the Kandyan elite is unknown. Four *Jatakas* in parallel rows take up the remaining space on the rear wall. From top to bottom are the *Culla-Dhammapala*, *Devadhamma*, and *Sama jatakas* and the *Vessantara* (nos. 443, 6, 540, 547). The *Vessantara Jataka* occupies the lowermost register and is the only one extending over all three walls. It begins to the left of the shrine doorway, with Vessantara and his family departing from the palace. Small portions of the murals surrounding the door are hidden by a raised border of ornamented stucco added sometime in the early twentieth century.[38]

Side Wall

The top register depicts the Sixteen Sacred Sites, starting on the right, each identified by a caption. The register below is devoted to the *Mahasilava Jataka* and below is the *Telapatta Jataka* (nos. 51, 96), both extending the full length of the wall.

The Telapatta tale centres on the Buddha-to-be (P: *bodhisatta*), and five of his brothers who were enrolled at university in Taxila

Tempting damsels turned into ogresses gorged themselves on Taxila's king and his court. Circa 1851. *Telapatta Jataka.*

Mara and his demons and the Earth Goddess. Circa 1851.

in distant Gandhara. Their journey proved fatal since the boys were seduced en route by ogresses disguised as enticing maidens, each lad falling victim to his own weakness, such as melodious music, haute cuisine or the pleasures of the flesh and so on. The Buddha-to-be was promised by a special Buddha (P: *pacceka*) that if he resisted these sirens, then he would become Taxila's king. The painters revelled in the demonesses consuming the poor victims. The *bodhisatta* was the lone survivor of this carnage but the most beautiful of the ogresses shadowed him all the way to Taxila. Even the king of this university town was 'snared by her loveliness' and so put her up in the lodgings of a queen-consort, despite the *bodhisatta's* dire warnings that 'she is an ogress and has eaten my five companions'. Then, with nightfall, this beguiling damsel transformed herself into a demoness who gorged herself on the king's 'skin, tendons and flesh, leaving only the bare bones'. Moments later, her goblin sisters flooded into the palace and satiated themselves on the entire royal staff while leaving 'not even a fowl or a dog alive'. (no. 96: 236) The sensible citizens of Taxila then recognized the self-control of the *bodhisatta* and anointed him king. This same *Jataka* also enjoyed popularity in Burma and was the subject of a unique cloth painting from ancient Pagan.[39]

The central bay highlights Buddha's defeat of Mara whose demons approach on the right and scamper off on the left, their faces and contorted poses showing as much bewilderment as terror. The earth goddess pops out from the ground, only too ready to deliver Mara a lesson he will never forget. The goddess announced that she witnessed the Buddha's last life as prince Vessantara, a reference reinforced by this very *jataka* appearing below on the lowermost register. Beginning to the left of the adjacent doorway in the adjoining bay, above the Vessantara story, is the *Mahakanha Jataka* (no. 469).

Rear Wall

The register beneath the ceiling shows the Buddha's visit to Kelaniya, accompanied by 15 'worthy-ones' (P: *arahants).* In the centre is a large seated Buddha, the thumb and index finger of his raised right hand touching to form a circle. A caption explains the action: 'Having been invited … [the Buddha]… arrived by air accompanied by 500 *arahants*', agreeing with the description in the *Mahavamsa.* (Mhv: 1.73) Five *arahants* sit to either side. Next to the Buddha are three snake-hooded figures, perhaps representing the three *naga* protagonists connected to the Buddha's visit here. On the left is a seated princely figure, perhaps the Buddha of the Future, matched on the other side by a dark ogre-like figure; but these two characters are not part of the Buddha's visit to Kelaniya in the *Mahavamsa.*

Jataka scenes take up the remaining registers. The topmost tells the story of Varanasi's king Dhammasonda who craved to hear the Buddha's teachings but Gotama Buddha had not yet come into the world. This tale was never part of the early Pali *jataka* series but first appeared in a 13th-century collection from Lanka known as the *Rasavahini,* or *Stream of Delights.* It remains popular in Sri Lanka and was also known in Southeast Asian non-canonical *jataka* collections; the version in Thailand largely conforms to the one in Lanka.[40] Below is the *Saccamkira Jataka*, (no. 73), on both sides of the entrance. To the right of the door is the conclusion of the *Mahakanha Jataka*. The *Vessantara* tale continues at the bottom of this wall. The last frame shows the death of the wicked Jujaka and Vessantara's daughter being weighed on a scale, counterbalanced by a food-offering that will win her release from Jujaka. Measuring her weight on a scale is nowhere mentioned in the standard Pali *Vessantara Jataka* but calculating donations on a scale equal to one's body weight reflects an ancient Indian tradition (S: *tulabharaya*), a custom found widely in texts and inscriptions and also known in Ceylon.[41] The lowermost frame shows three monks facing toward the reclining Buddha. The trio has been identified with the temple's former chief monks but this is uncertain.

Ceiling

Painted wooden panels feature the Twelve Zodiacal signs, the Guardians of the Ten Directions and *avataras* of Vishnu. These groupings derived from South India but variations in India and Sri Lanka abound.[42] Each of the eight guardians are labelled, apart from the figure in the centre, shown emerging from a coiled snake and holding a palm-leaf manuscript and a string of beads, two attributes of

Four *avataras*, from left to right (Rama, Balarama, Parashurama, Krishna). Rama holds an unusual bow and Krishna is shown with his flute. Ceiling panel detail.

The Buddha addresses snake-kings and *arahants* at Kelaniya. Circa 1851.

the deity Brahma. Brahma and Vishnu are considered the ninth and tenth guardians in some formulations, the former representing the zenith and the latter the nadir. The artists have cleverly united these two guardians in a single composition. None of the ten avataras are captioned. Vishnu is shown on a snake, holding the discus and the conch in his upraised hands. Krishna is pictured fluting while Rama, with a diminutive Hanuman at his side, holds an unusual bow with multiple holes for adjusting the bow's tautness. Absent is the avatara of the future, the horse-riding Kalki, and the Buddha, an avatara added now and then to the varied lists. The zodiacal figures appear in separate frames, all captioned. In the centre are a man holding an image of sun and a woman holding the moon. Four panels feature a tree in their centre, with animals and human figures, likely influenced by earlier imported South Indian printed cottons in Lanka. Copious references to textiles and dyes traded between India and Ceylon are found in reports by Dutch governors.[43]

A ceiling detail showing three of the Guardians of the Ten Directions. A composite of Brahma, holding a palm-leaf manuscript and beads, and Vishnu upon the snake named Anantasayana, are the last two Guardians.

The painting at Kelaniya belongs to what has been called the 'Southern style' but the convoluted strands of Sinhalese painting are a Gordian Knot that has yet to be untangled.[44] Other mural sites in the environs of Colombo are in Kotte and at the Subodharama Temple. The last sputter of this tradition are murals at Sapugaskanda, near Kelaniya, dated to 1896.

Zodiacal signs, Guardians of the Ten Directions and the *avataras* of Vishnu, painted on hundreds of narrow wooden slats comprising the ceiling. Circa 1851.

The Reclining Buddha was the major focus of devotion in the 19th century. The top row of murals show the 24 Buddhas, with below rows of *arahants*.

The Reclining Buddha Image

The wall separating the two chambers is an arresting juxtaposition of painting and sculpture. Dominating the centre is a colossal image of Kelaniya's snake-king, his tiny snake-hood peeking out above his headdress. The dedication of the temple, in 1851, is found above the doorway on the right in an oval cartouche. Above the other doorway is a seated crowned image of the Future Buddha. The deities above the arch on the right are Brahma, with his three heads and holding an umbrella, and an orange-hued four-arm Vishnu holding a conch. Two bearded ascetics occupy the centre. Above the door on the left is a dark-coloured Vishnu grasping a discus and on the right Shiva holds an axe in one of his four arms.

The reclining Buddha was part of the original temple in about 1850 but has been refurbished many times. Near the feet are three colossal standing images in high relief against the wall, each labelled by Sinhalese captions ('Natha', 'Sri Vishnu' and 'Kadasyami' [Skanda]). Just below the ceiling are murals with the group of 24 seated Buddhas, with identifying captions. Rows of *arahants* continue on the adjoining wall.

Opposite the reclining Buddha are the Four World-Guardians (P: *lokapalas*). (DN 20) From left to right is Dhataratthi, followed by Viruppakkha, Virulhaka and Kuvera, each with attendants and captions. Such an arrangment in a row is not an uncommon in temples from this period. To the left are Shiva and Ganesha. On the adjoining wall is Hanuman and at the hall's opposite end is a two-arm Saman and Vibhishana.

A small stone slab set into the floor is sculpted with five auspicious symbols (bow and arrow, trident, sword, conch and discus; see page 11). The concept of five weapons is ancient and the founder of Lanka, Vijaya, was armed with five unspecified weapons. (Mhv: 7. 16) The types of weapons varied, and here Vishnu's mace is replaced by a trident, usually associated with Shiva. The theme of 'five weapons' is usually connected to Vishnu and is the subject of a famous Sanskrit *Hymn of of the Five Weapons* (S: *Panchayudhya*

Detail of Shiva with his third eye. The mural faces the reclining Buddha.

Stotram). Some of these weapons were also featured on a banner seized during the British assault on Kandy in 1815 and now at the Royal Hospital Chelsea, London.[45] The stone is protected by a removable metal covering on which newborns are placed and 'blessed' by a monk. The stone was probably placed here sometime in the twentieth century since it went unmentioned in earlier accounts.

Solias Mendis (1897-1975) began the murals in 1930 and did not finish until 1946.

Solias Mendis

When Helene Wijewardena requested Solias Mendis (1897-1975) to decorate the walls of her new temple, she scarcely foresaw that this commission would result in the country's most remarkable artistic achievement in modern times. Mendis devoted over 15 years to the project, beginning in 1930, at the age of 33, and not stepping down from the scaffolding until 1946. Mendis apprenticed with his uncle and his early projects attracted the attention of Helene's son, Don Charles Wijewardena, who supervised much of the Kelaniya project.

Mendis likely began the murals with small sketches that were later made into full-size drawings that numbered at least forty-two, the number preserved in the National Archive. In some cases, changes were made to the initial sketches. For example, in the sketch showing a famous Kandyan king presenting a fan to a head monk, the position of the two figures are reversed in the final mural (compare to the book cover). Other changes were minor. Once Mendis finished the life-size drawings, he likely copied them free-hand onto the primed walls. In some sketches, parallel lines crisscross the compositions, suggesting that they were later to be used as modules to guide the size of the final mural. However, these lines are not present on the life-size drawings in the National Archive.

The murals are governed by twin overarching themes. The first is Kelaniya's place in the Buddha's relationship to Sri Lanka, while the second is the monastery's history from its inception to its refurbishment by Helene. What sources did Mendis turn to for his diverse subject matter? Did he himself select all or most of the subjects or did Helene or the Kelaniya monks offer suggestions? It seems that Mendis himself was responsible for most, if not all, of the imagery.

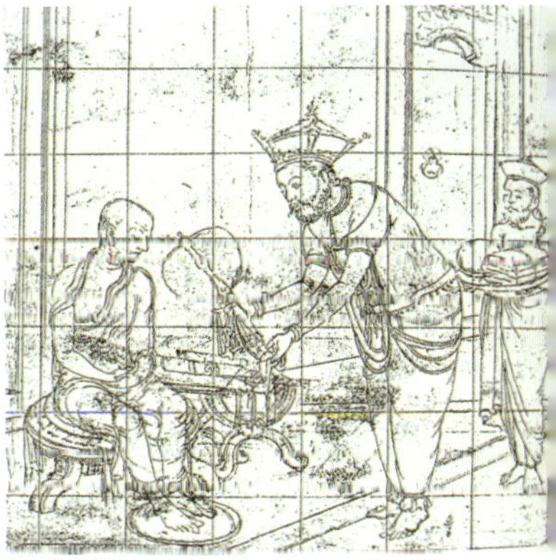

A sketch by Mendis of King Kirti Sri Rajasimha presenting a fan to the Kandyan monk, Velivita Sri Saranakara whose disciple oversaw the rebuilding of Kelaniya. The two characters are reversed in position in the finished mural.

The principle source was the *Mahavamsa*, easily available in printed Sinhalese editions, but there are also many themes from unknown sources. For example, the espisode of a monk within a cauldron is not part of the *Mahavamsa* but appeared only centuries later. Other themes were completely outside the traditional chronicles, such as certain incidents from the Portuguese and Dutch periods and the ordination of Burmese monks on the Kelaniya River. For many of these historical subjects, Mendis may have turned to a rare Sinhalese 'guide', *A History of the Kalyani Monastery* (*Kalyani Vihara Varnanava*) published in Colombo in 1890.[46] Other panels have no direct connection to the Kelaniya's history, such as a tale about Asoka and his wife in a previous existence.

Years before the Kelaniya project began, Solias Mendis developed his own special style. Meddepola Raja Maha Viharaya, Giriulla. 1923.

In 1934 Helena invited the Bengali painter, Nandalal Bose (1882–1966) to Colombo. He heartily endorsed the frescos in progress at the Kelaniya, but must have been struck by how Mendis departed completely from the contemporary styles modeled on European conventions and which clothed Buddhist subjects in pseudo-Roman or Victorian attire in compositions based on single-point perspective. (A painted work by Bose in silk is now at the Sapumal Foundation in Colombo.) Mendis drew unflattering depictions of the Portuguese and Dutch but the British are nowhere to be seen. It is as if the British had vanished, perhaps speaking to a growing nationalism that sought a clean break from Britain in the context of a Buddhist revival.[47]

Mendis was sent by Helene in 1930 to India to study painting at the famous Santiniketan art academy outside Calcutta sponsored by the Tagore family. He also toured sites in India known for ancient Buddhist frescos, such as Ajanta. It is often written that the Kelaniya murals were influenced by his Indian experience but his earlier work suggests that the roots of his Kelaniya style began before his foreign travel. This earlier work can be traced at a cave-temple complex named Meddepola Raja Mahaviharaya just outside of Giriulla, about 65 kilometres northeast of Colombo. A painted inscription there by Mendis is from 1923 (BE 2466), seven years before the Kelaniya project. Here one can detect the artist's pre-Kelaniya style. A few rarely depicted *Jatakas* also appear, such as the Matuposaka (no. 455), signaling Mendis' familiarity with a wide range of Buddhist topics. But his genius came to fruition only by the time of the Kelaniya project in the 1930s.

The Buddha's Three Visits to Lanka

Single large panels dominate the centre of each wall of chamber at Kelaniya. Each focus on the Buddha's three visits to Lanka, based closely on the opening chapter of the *Mahavamsa*. The narration unfolds in a loose chronological sequence and moves clockwise within the chamber, starting on the rear wall. Surrounding these four panels are dozens of smaller frames, some supplementing the panels focussing on the three visits and others treating unrelated topics. The ordering of episodes is not always straightforward but a unified narrative unfolds. A few subjects begin on one wall and continue on the next, while the monk-in-the-cauldron tale is the only episode extending over three walls. Short Sinhalese captions identify the scenes.

The Buddha's first visit is featured on the rear wall where the Buddha dispels the demons (P: *yakkas*), by setting ablaze his hide mat. The panel is captioned, 'Mahiyangana'. On a side wall is the second visit when the Buddha meets the snake-kings on Nagadipa to resolve the dispute over the Jewelled Throne. The scene is captioned 'Nagadipa'. The third visit, on the front wall, shows the Buddha preaching from the disputed Jewelled Throne. The large glass-encased shrine projecting into the hall was never part of the original design and now obscures a small portion of the mural. The metal reliquary inside the glass shrine contains unspecified bodily relics of the Buddha said to have been given to the temple in the time of Sri Kirti Rajasimha.[48] The central panel on the remaining side shows the Buddha's visit to Adam's Peak that followed the Buddha's departure from Kelaniya. It is labeled, 'Mark of the Foot' (P: '*pada lanchana*').

A minor prince died from a poisoned mango intended for his half-brother, the crown prince.

The Story Unfolds: Supplementary Frames

Surrounding the large panels are dozens of smaller frames augmenting the Buddha's three visits to Lanka. Beginning on the side wall at the top is a long frame showing the Buddha flying from Kelaniya to Adam's Peak. Below is the Kelaniya snake-king offering a large bowl to the Buddha, just prior to his departure for Adam's Peak. (Mhv: 1. 76) In the adjoining small panel the god Sumana invites the Buddha to visit his mountaintop. Two parallel frames on the right take up the action. Here the Buddha preaches in a 'hidden cave' captioned 'Divaguhava'. The caption on the right reads, 'The Buddha stops at several places including Dighavapi'. The last scene in this sequence on this side wall shows the Buddha returning to the Jetavana monastery. (Mhv: 1. 83) Sumana's invitation to the Buddha and the 'hidden cave' are not part of the *Mahavamsa* but appear in a 13th-century Pali chronicle devoted to Adam's Peak, the *Sumanakuta-vannan*.

Kelaniya's snake-king offers the Buddha a bowl before the Buddha departs for Adam's Peak.

The remaining panels on this wall link the Kelaniya monastery to Anuradhapura's royal family, the introduction of Buddhism and the

Kalyani Tissa and his younger brother Uttiya being taught to read and write by a monk.

birth of Dutthagamani. Between the two doors is Anuradhapura's king, Devanampiya Tissa, kneeling with his bow before the monk Mahinda, followed by Mahinda. The king makes a donation by pouring water over Mahinda's right hand. The second and last segment shows the Bodhi Tree sapling in mid-air.

The other panels begin with the failed assassination of Devanampiya Tissa's brother, Mahanaga. The king's wife attempted to kill her stepson Mahanaga with a poisoned mango so that her son could inherit the throne but her own son inadvertently ate the fruit. Next to the lifeless boy stands his father. The scene is labeled, 'Plot to kill Mahanaga'. The following scene shows Mahanaga's son, Gothabhaya, headed for the city of Mahagama in the south on an elephant. Next comes Gothabhaya's infant son, captioned 'Prince Yathala Tissa', who grew up in the south and became Dutthagamani's father. (Mhv: 15. 170) The stupa on the right is labelled, 'The Kelaniya Viharaya built by King Yathala Tissa'.

Solias Mendis prepared sketches for his large compositions. Some forty are preserved in the National Archives, Colombo.

The two lower frames to the right of the doorway set the stage for the scene of the boiling cauldron on the rear wall. The top panel is captioned, 'King Gothabhaya ruling in Kelani town'. To the right, Gothabhaya is shown sending off his brother, Prince Kalyani Tissa, on an elephant, to assume the throne in 'Magampura' (Mahagama) in the 'Ruhuna Kingdom'. The bottom panel shows prince Kalyani Tissa as a child with his younger brother, Uttiya, learning to read and write from a monk, captioned 'Learning Letters'. The same tutor-monk is shown arriving at the palace when Kelaniya Tissa has been later made king at Kelaniya. The last scene on this side wall depicts the king hearing about the loose behaviour of his brother Uttiya with the queen.

Rear Wall

The narrative then skips to the rear wall where the top register shows the king's brother Uttiya going into hiding after the king was told of his adulterous overtures. The next frame shows Uttiya's trusted courier receiving a love-letter intended for the king's wife. Next is the same courier, now dressed as a monk, sneaking into the palace at Kelaniya behind the blameless senior monk. (Mhv: 22. 15) The king then spotted the love-letter that fell to the floor. The shamed queen walks away, the king realizing that the love-letter is hard evidence of his brother's cuckoldry. The king's mind was so clouded with rage that he failed to recognize his brother's handwriting and accused the unwitting monk of the wrongdoing. On the right the guiltless monk is led off by two men, to face the cauldron shown on the rear wall. This version most closely resembles a narrative found in a thirteenth-century Sinhalese chronicle. A later version has a slightly different twist with the king's brother imitating the handwriting of the innocent monk.[49]

The king's wife fleeing from a tsunami striking Kelaniya. The king is about to fall off his elephant, a punishment for placing the monk in the cauldron.

The monk is described in the caption, 'sitting in meditation in a hot oil cauldron', the flames stoked by two men. Both the messenger-monk and the senior monk are slain and thrown into the nearby sea, according to the *Mahavamsa*, but Mendis departed from this narrative by adding the monk in the cauldron. The end of the panel follows the *Mahavamsa* by showing the countryside engulfed in rising sea water, the gods wreaking havoc for slaying a monk, confirmed by the caption. The motif of a flood avenging a wrong is also found in the Tamil classic, the *Manimekalai*.

The queen bends to pick up a love-letter from the king's brother, dropped by the monk who was a courier, centre.

Side Wall

The central panel shows the Buddha visiting Lanka to mediate the conflict between the two snake-kings. On the lower left, the king's daughter prepares to embark on a boat to escape the floodwaters. The king is seen tumbling off his elephant near the shore, payback for his treatment of the innocent monk, a detail found in at least one chronicle.[50] The last scene shows the princess arriving in southern Lanka where she is wed to Kakavanna Tissa. She will soon give birth to Dutthagamani and become the national heroine under the name of Viharamahadevi.

The scene above shows the island's demons resettled on an island called Giridipa. The Buddha then preached to the gods. To the right the seated Buddha presents hair-relics to the god Sumana. The Buddha is then shown returning to Uruvela in India where he meets the three converted Kassapa heretics. Next to the central panel, snake-kings make offerings to the Buddha, followed by the Buddha preaching. In the last segment, the Buddha returns to the Jetavana monastery. The panel below shows the Buddha in India receiving an invitation to visit Ceylon from the chief naga-king at the Kelaniya, presaging the central panel on the front wall.

Two long parallel registers below the central panel skip to events relating strictly to the Kelaniya monastery. The first on the left shows the destruction of the stupa by King Kalinga Magha, an invader from India. The next shows the rebuilding of the stupa by Vijayabahu III, purportedly destroyed by Tamils. (Cv. 81. 59) The next segment skips centuries to the mission sent from Pegu in the 1470s from Lower Burma for the re-ordination of monks on a barge tethered on the Kelani River. The caption reads, 'The king of Buruma-rattaa [Burma country] says to the monks, 'go for your ordination (P: '*upasampada*') to Lankadipa'. The last segment shows a Burmese lay official kneeling before Bhuvankabahu VI (1469-77) welcoming the Pegu mission. The caption reads, 'Ritual of Upasampada at the Kalyani river with monks from Ramanyadesa', or Ramannadesa, an old term for Lower Burma.

The panel at the end of the wall, just beyond the door, shows Dutch officials conferring with Sinhala leaders, captioned, 'Rejection of the request to renovate the temple by Holland officials'. Next

The Dutch in Colombo rejected the appeal from Kandy to restore the Kelaniya monastery.

Helene Dep Wijewardene, her family and monks at ground breaking in 1927, left, and entering the finished temple in 1937.

comes the arrival of a Kandyan monk with an entourage, the caption stating, 'Arrival of a Kandyan monk, disregarding the opposition of the Dutch'. A sole Dutchman is shown standing on a ruinous brick temple. In reality, the Dutch reception of monks from Kandy varied greatly during that period since both the Dutch and the court in Kandy had common commercial interests. A Dutch governor in 1697 for example granted a visit of five 'High Priests' [monks] and 34 'ordinary Priests' to Colombo, conceding that 'His Majesty [in Kandy] may be best won by kindness and courtesy'.[51] Many of these lesser-known temple incidents may have been known to Mendis in the aforementioned 1890 guidebook.

The panel below features Helene at a ceremony celebrating the beginning of the new temple in 1927. The caption mentions the 'image house that was covered with stone [flooring] blocks' at the request of the chief monk, Mapitigama Buddharakkhita', referring to Helene's donation of flooring in 1888. The caption continues: 'Helene Wijewardena lays the first stone to renovate the temple on request of Mapitigama Dhammarakkhita'.

Helene is next to her daughter and son-in-law and their two boys, Hector and Junius. The two children, however, appear too young to be set into this scene from 1927. Other family members stand amidst a group of monks. A brahman priest kneels, ready to blow a conch. An indistinct object in Helene's hands was intended for the open stone reliquary on the ground. This small stone box in the mural perhaps now lies beneath a large stone lotus panel embedded in the floor of the main sanctum. Later, during the dedication ceremony in January 1937, Helene poured water from a conch shell on top of this lotus, signifying the formal donation of the monastery to the sangha. A huge conch in a glass case next to the reclining Buddha may be the very one used in the ceremony. Helene attended the ceremony in a wheelchair but she is shown standing.[52]

The adjacent scene shows Helene again, entering the finished temple in 1937, holding a small gilded stupa-shaped reliquary, with the caption, 'Arrival of *dhatu karundawa* [relic casket]'. The turbaned gentleman is Don Walter, Helene's son and the founder of the temple's annual procession. The relics inside the casket are nowhere recorded. The same reliquary is shown atop an elephant in the adjacent panel depicting the temple's first *perahera*. This same small reliquary is perhaps now inside the large reliquary worshipped in the glass encased shrine set against the temple's front wall.

Front Wall

The lower panels on this wall are continuations of those on the sidewall. The topmost shows a monk sweeping a courtyard, captioned 'The start of renovation of the Kelaniya Viharaya by Monk Dehigaspe'. This is the first monk sent from Kandy. The next shows the partially reconstructed stupa, with two piles of bricks slated for the rebuilding. The caption reads, 'Mapitigama [Buddharakkhita] arrives with the support of king Sri Kirti Rajasimha of Kandy'. The last scene, concealed by the projecting shrine, shows the nineteenth-century temple and Bodhi tree, with the caption stating that this was the state of the temple in the Buddhist Era, 1469 [1926]. The panel below shows the temple's inaugural procession, with two elephants, captioned, 'The start of perahera by Don Walter Wijewardene with approval of his mother, in 1469 [1926]'. The last scene shows the procession trailing off in the distance.

The monk Dehigaspe, from Kandy, sweeps a courtyard before the restoration of the stupa, indicated by the stacks of bricks.

On the side wall are two parallel panels treating the emperor Asoka and his chief queen during their previous lives, first told in the *Mahavamsa*. (5. 48-69) In an earlier birth, Asoka was a *pacceka* Buddha, garbed as a monk, who sought honey for a sick fellow *pacceka* Buddha. Lost in the forest, a simple country lass guided the future Asoka to three brothers who were honey-merchants. One brother eagerly gave away honey to the future Asoka, but his two brothers berated him for his generosity at their expense. In a future life, the altruistic honey-merchant became Asoka and the woman who guided the future king to the merchants became one of Asoka principal wives in a future birth under the name Asandhimitta. The three scruffy chaps at the far right are the honey-merchants, with the caption, 'Examining the income and expenditure by three merchants'. The conclusion is shown on the left with the caption, 'Offering of Bee Honey', to the ill monk. The last figure in the panel is an ascetic, leading off a goat, labeled 'Story of Tebhatika', another name for the three heretical Uruvela Jatila brothers converted by the Buddha. The episode with the three honey-merchants had taken a different twist by the 13th century by claiming that one of the mean-spirited brothers was in a future birth none other than Devanampiya Tissa, the king who was converted to Buddhism by Asoka son.[53]

Before Asandhimitta married Asoka, she gave birth in a previous life to a son named Nigrodha who in a subsequent life as a novice converted Asoka. He is named after the Nigrodha tree, that is, the banyan (*Ficus benghalensis*). Amidst the branches is the tree deity who becomes the child's namesake in a future birth. The next scene shows the king Devanampiya Tissa converted by Asoka's son. The

A monk sentenced to death for facilitating a tryst between the queen and the king's brother.

presence of Nigrodha who converted Asoka echoes the conversion of Devanampiya Tissa by Asoka's son. The queen Asandhimitta makes one of her earliest appearances in the *Mahavamsa* but she weaves in and out of post-canonical Pali literature. She played an important role in the famous cosmological text attributed to King Lithai in Sukhothai where cloth is substituted for honey.[54]

'like a royal goose in an emerald vase'

Trysts and adultery in palaces rarely ripple beyond the royal boudoir but the legendary episode of this cuckolded king at Kelaniya shaped a nation's history in as much as it provided the context for the birth of Dutthagamani. This basic queen-is-caught-with-a-lover story in the *Mahavamsa* was the kernel around which far more elaborate myths grew in the second millennium. The chief addition was a cauldron of boiling oil into which the king ordered the monk. A number of slightly different versions emerged and it is hard to be sure which, if not several, Mendis drew upon. In one version the oil refused to boil due to the monk's resolve but the monk recalled from his previous life as a cowherd that he knowingly flicked a fly into a 'pot of boiling hot milk'. The monk then reasoned that the king was not to blame for his punishment but his ill-fortune was proof of his own bad karma. Coming to this realisation, the oil then boiled and the monk expired. It was then that the gods, in sympathy with the monk, flooded the king's realm. The version is recorded in the 13th-century *Sinhalese Thupavamsa* and is similar to the 14th-century Pali work, the *Rasavahini*, in which the monk remained unruffled in the boiling vat, 'like a royal goose in an emerald vase', and recited 98 verses before passing away. A 14th-century text, the *Saddharmalankaraya*, also connected the monk in the cauldron to this grouping of 98 verses that had long existed but with no link to the monk. This collection was later named the 'The Oil Cauldron Stanzas', or *Tela-kataha-gatha*. The verses themselves had wide appeal, since passages were found in a Pali and Khmer inscription from Thailand, dated to 1061, but with no mention of the monk in the cauldron nor to the *Tela-kataha-gatha* collection.[55]

A boiling cauldron is also a theme in the early Sanskrit text, the *Ashokavadana*, wherein a cleric underwent the punishment in Asoka's prison known as 'Asoka's Hell'. The monk emerged unscathed, seated upon a lotus that sprouted from the bottom of the vat. It was in fact this miracle that prompted the conversion of Asoka, retold in a number of different ways. In one of the several Chinese versions, the monk is compared to a goose hovering in the air, resembling the passage in the Pali *Rasavahini*. The Chinese pilgrims Faxian and Xuanzang also noted in India the site of this legendary prison near the king's capital and referred to the incident of the cauldron.[56]

The Kelaniya monastery had by the early 15th century memorialised this oil-cauldron episode with a separate temple. The structure marked the spot where the king 'immersed the faultless arahant in the cauldron of boiling oil'. There was also, by 1509, even a sculpture of the monk placed inside a special temple at Kelaniya known as 'Tel-katara-geya'.[75] By the late 19th century, no shrine commemorating this episode is recorded.

The tale lingered for centuries, even coming to the attention of a Portuguese chronicler in Goa who recorded that the monk remained in the cauldron unhurt for seven days until he expired. These 'seven-days' appear also in the 17th-century *Rajavilaya* where boiling oil miraculously became cold water. The story survived into the 19th century when it was repeated to an English traveler. A king's brother enamoured with his brother's wife is hardly new but in one case the secret lover triumphed, reversing the outcome of the Kelaniya story. (Mhv: 36. 42) In Thailand the theme took an unexpected twist in fourteenth-century Sukhothai when a nobleman actually encouraged a marriage between a married woman and her secret lover, a servant, in order to enable both to attend upon the servant's aged mother. Even cuckoldry, it seems, can be transformed into Buddhist merit under the right conditions. The ribald Kelaniya story even caught the attention of two British princes who visited Ceylon who cited the story to mock Edwin Arnold's 'vaunted *Light of Asia* of which Europeans of the Arnold stamp are so much enamoured'.[58]

The Sanctum

The enlargement of the temple begun in 1927 called for the addition of a sanctum at the rear showcasing the principal image, a gilded Buddha. At the entrance, just beneath the ceiling, are four large panels treating the history of Lanka beginning chronologically with the Buddha at the moment of his death. The Buddha informed the god Sakka that Vijaya has arrived on Lanka's shores and that he was to be 'handed over the guardianship of Lanka to the god who is the colour like the lotus', the deity commonly identified as Vishnu, or Upulvan.

The birth of the Buddha's horse, Kanthaka, and its groom, Channa.

(Mhv: 7. 5) Upulvan kneels on the right, cast in a pale bluish hue, evoking his namesake, the blue-lotus (P: *uppala*). On the opposite wall, Vijaya is shown reaching the shores of Lanka with his male retinue. The god Sakka, disguised as an ascetic, is preparing special protective string bracelets for the arriving men. A dog in one corner is a demoness in disguise who is an attendant of Vijaya's soon-to-be wife, Kuveni. (Mhv: 7. 6-9). The neighbouring panel shows the king laying out the boundaries of the Mahavihara at Anuradhapura with a plough. Along on the same wall are monks copying the Pali scriptures at the Aluvihara monastery north of Kandy.

Before the entrance to the main shrine is the monk Buddhaghosa presenting three palm-leaf manuscripts, his famous *Vissudhimagga*, to the chief priest of the Mahavihara. The second panel shows Kirti Sri Rajasimha from Kandy gifting a fan to the famous monk Velivita Sri Saranakara whose disciple was sent to Kelaniya to supervise its rebuilding. The original fan is said to be in the museum at the Malwatta Viharaya in Kandy.

A separate chamber on the left showcases the Bodhi Tree, starting with Asoka removing the 'southern branch'. The principal composition depicts Asoka's daughter, Sanghamitta, standing in the ship from India, the Bodhi Tree in the prow and Devanampiya Tissa wading into the sea to receive the tree. Another panel shows Sanghamitta, receiving the robes of a nun, since the origin of nunneries in Lanka is traced to her. A small panel shows the tree at Anuradhapura, as it appeared in photographs from the first half of the last century.

The second chamber highlights Kandy's tooth-relic. The principal panel shows Hemamala and her husband escaping from India with the relic hidden in her glowing headdress. A panel on one side shows a wicked Indian king directing the destruction of the tooth, his smith striking the tooth on an anvil. All these scenes are drawn not from the *Mahavamsa* but from the 13th-century *Chronicle of the Tooth Relic* (P: *Datha-vamsa*).

The adjacent corridor has episodes from the Buddha's early life, beginning with Maya's dream. Another shows the sage Kaladeva inspecting the infant for auspicious physical signs, followed by the young Buddha-to-be seated beneath the Jambu tree whose protective shadow miraculously remained stationary while his father conducted the ploughing ceremony. Later the school-age future Buddha is learning to read and write with his male classmates while a young female pupil peers from behind a tree.

The Buddha identified this barking dog as a deceased miserly brahman named Todeyya, a rebirth unbeknownst to his son standing by. In one of two small chambers normally closed to the public.

The Buddha's life history continues in the chamber on the other side. The Buddha-to-be is shown seated in the Tusita Heaven with three gods. The caption refers to the *bodhisatta* 'searching for the five considerations' that will determine when he will appear in the world.[59] Other panels show Sujata offering food to the Buddha's at Bodh Gaya and the grass-cutter whose offering was used as a cushion beneath the Bodhi Tree. Another panel shows the birth of the Buddha's horse, Kanthaka, and the Buddha's groom, Channa, both of whom shared their birthdate with the Buddha.

Two small chambers at the rear of the temple are normally closed to visitors but contain murals reflecting Mendis' familiarity with Buddhist subjects. One panel shows the Buddha standing before a dog that in a past life was a greedy merchant named Todeyya but reborn as a dog in his own home, a post-canonical Pali story but rarely depicted. A nearly identical version occurs in Sanskrit and Jain sources and was taken up by the stone carvers of ancient Gandhara. Another mural shows a young child offering a bowl of dirt to the Buddha, a spontaneous kindly act that resulted in the boy's rebirth as king Asoka. This theme is not part of the Theravada world but is found in the Sanskrit *Ashokavadana* and was a popular theme in Gandhara. Elsewhere in the two chambers we see the Buddha Dipankara and the ascetic Sumedha, the groom preparing for the flight from the palace, the taming of the elephant Nalagiri, and the god Indra playing a three-string instrument. The single *jataka* chosen by Mendis was the Chaddanta (no. 514), about feuding female elephants, for which he may have drawn upon a composition he witnessed at Ajanta.

The Estonian Communist : 'A Hammer Blow to Good Taste'

Solias Mendis' crowning achievement was planned for the sanctum's rear wall. The theme was to be Mara's defeat, a subject not treated elsewhere by him. By this time, late in 1936, his patron, Helene, had died and her descendants instructed Mendis to scrap his original concept in favour of a faux Himalayan landscape. The artist refused and withdrew from the commission. A local painter was found, Karl Kasman, an Estonian who had been part of the Colombo art scene since the late 1920s. His powder blue landscape is 'out of tune with the rest of the paintings … a hammer blow to good taste'.[60]

The sanctum's Himalayan backdrop by a left-leaning Estonian, Karl Kasman.

Kelaniya is home to the major shrine dedicated to Vibhishana. This 1851 mural of Vibhishana faces the reclining Buddha.

Little is know about Kasman but he contributed a newspaper review of an art exhibition in 1930. He was a Communist and may have been chosen by radical monks at the Kelaniya inspired by Marxism. He was first married to Doris Kalenberg, a piano instructor at the Girls' High School, Kandy. When this marriage failed, he took up with Claudine Leibowitz, a Belgian leftist heiress in Colombo. She was later deported for political activities in the early 1950s, together with an American named Rhoda Miller de Silva. Kasman's whereabouts cannot be traced in the 1950s but he was monitored by Russian intelligence and merited his own classified file now buried in Soviet archives, together with dozens of prominent Sri Lankans of all political persuasions.[61]

A Demon's Kindly Brother – Vibhishana

The country's most sacred Vibhishana shrine is also located here. Vibhishana broke ranks with his demonic siblings and joined with Rama to recover Sita and eventually became Lanka's overlord in the *Ramayana*. It is believed that Rama's brother Lakshmana crowned Vibhishana here at Kelaniya. Vibhishana was included among the major deities protecting Lanka, beginning in the 14th century and also appearing among the sculpture at the Lankatilaka temple near Kandy, dated to 1332. Perhaps the earliest recorded association between Vibhishana and Kelaniya is a poem, the *Vuttamala-sandesaya*, from the time of Parakramabahu V (1344-59) that ended with a prayer to Vibhishana at Kelaniya for the king's welfare.

Later, Vibhishana became especially popular for the kings of nearby Kotte and their royal patronage probably explains how Kelaniya became the *locus sanctus* for this deity. The greatest patron was Parakramabhu VI (1411-1466) whose very birth was due to the 'caring divine eye' cast by Vibhishana on his mother.[62] Other poems from this period referring to the shrine are the *Hamsa* and *Mayura Sandesayas*.

There were certainly several Vibhishana shrines at Kelaniya over the centuries but none left a trace. The modern shrine is a narrow room where offerings are made before a sanctum concealed by three modern cloth paintings depicting Vibhishana in the centre, with his white horse, flanked by Vishnu and Kataragama. Lay ritualists, or *kapuralas*, receive offerings and recite formulaic prayers, or *yatikas*. Some Buddhists, mostly urban educated elites, will not make offerings here, believing that Vibhishana is an interloper in a 'pure' Buddhist Sinhala environment.

Kelaniya's Declaration of Independence

The monastery saw a dispute in British times over ordinations between certain lowland monks and the established sangha in Kandy. The lowland monks formed the Kalyani Fraternity in 1855 that sought to perform higher ordinations at the Kelaniya monastery, a direct riposte to the Kandyan establishment that dictated that valid ordinations were to be conducted only in Kandy. The Kelaniya head monk sided with the Kandy faction.) The Fraternity responded by purchasing land in Kelaniya where 21 novices were initiated in defiance of Kandy.
That Kelaniya was chosen as the group's base testifies to the location's

Sri Lanka's most sacred Vibhishana shrine, opposite the Buddhist temple.

symbolic importance. The influential monk, Hikkaduwe Sumangala (1827-1911), strove to unite the low-country and Kandy fraternities.

The founder of the Buddhist Theosophical Society, H.S. Olcott, lectured at the Kelaniya and attended the ceremony marking the start of the monastery's restoration in 1888 when Helene donated the stone flooring. Also speaking at the monastery was the monk M. Gunananda, the star of the famous Panadura Debate. The new Buddhist flag, designed by Olcott and others, was hoisted at the Kelaniya and was called at the time 'the glorious standard of our Lord Buddha'.

In the struggle against British domination, a Kelaniya Declaration of Independence was read aloud here on 6 January 1947, modelled directly on the document from the United States. The same year saw a succession dispute triggered by the death of the head monk who amended his will in favour of a young monk named Buddharakkhita, bypassing a more senior cleric. The matter became so heated that it was litigated in court. The younger monk won out but soon disgraced the temple and the robe by his flamboyant lifestyle that included a liaison with a prominent married woman in Colombo. This same monk persuaded a junior monk in 1959 to turn a .45 Webley revolver on Prime Minister S.W.R.D. Bandaranaike, ostensibly for his policy of favouring Tamils but the real reason was likely a business partnership gone sour.[63] Buddharakkhita was found guilty and died in prison. A co-conspirator was the wife of Don Charles Wijewardana, Wimala, but she was released for lack of evidence.

Sri Pada: Adam's Peak

Sri pada: The Jewelled Crown of Lanka

The Buddha's footprint. Courtesy World Pilgrimage Guide.

The Buddha could scarcely have foreseen that his footprint atop a mountain peak in Sri Lanka would one day be venerated by millions of pilgrims thousands of years later. It is also fair to say that the Buddha would be astonished to learn that his footprint would later be mistaken for Adam's, our 'first ancestor' in the *Old Testament* and *Quran*. Even Hindus embraced the Buddha's footprint, taking it to be Shiva's. Hence pilgrims of all persuasions trod up the same mountain trails but were inspired by different beliefs. There are several major sacred footprints in Burma and Thailand but these stemmed from early Pali sources; the Buddha's footprint in Sri Lanka, however, was indigenous in origin. The favoured name for the site is Sri Pada, or Sacred Footprint, but outside of Sri Lanka it is commonly known as Adam's Peak. The peak's fame spread widely in the Buddhist world; in China an Indian monk called it 'Lanka-Mountain' and in Sukhothai it was lauded as 'the jewelled crown of Lanka'.[1] Guidebooks tout the site's inclusivity but pilgrims these days are overwhelmingly Sinhala Buddhists.

The stone impression itself bears little resemblance to a foot's contour. Whether it is a natural shallow cavity or partially fashioned with hammer and chisel, as skeptics argue, is impossible to say. It is roughly 170 centimetres in length, or 5 feet 6 inches, and 76 centimetres wide, or 2 feet 6 inches. Its depth is about 5 centimetres, or close to 2 inches. It caps an irregularly shaped boulder-like outcrop near the centre of the peak's flat summit whose dimensions were likened to a tennis court. The peak was often included in Portuguese and Dutch maps, with various names, such as Pico de Adam or Adam

Previous page:
The god Sumana welcoming the Buddha to his mountain in the distance. Solias Mendis.1930s. Kelaniya Monastery.

The Buddha impressing his footprint and resting 'during the heat of the day' (Mhv: 1. 78). Late 19th century. Sapugoda Mahavihara, Beruwala.

Piek. Among the earliest surviving illustrations is a drawing made in 1638 by Constantino de Sã de Miranda, preserved in a codex at Zaragoza's University Library.[2]

The story of Sri Pada unfolds in the opening chapter of the *Mahavamsa* treating the Buddha's three sojourns to the island. It was on the final visit, after preaching on the bank of the Kelani River near Colombo, that the Buddha 'rose [in the air] and left his footprint on Sumana-kuta', that is, Sumana's Mountain. (Mhv: 1. 78) These few simple words are the meagre narrative background for one of Buddhism's most venerated sites. After visiting the peak, the Buddha then proceeded to his last Sri Lankan stop, at Dighavapi in the southeast, before returning to India's Jetavana monastery. (Mhv: 1. 78)

The peak's popularity grew over the ages and by the 13th century merited its own Pali chronicle, *In Praise of Mount Samanta* (P: *Samantakuta-vannana*).[3] This poem of nearly 800 verses was an expansion far beyond the single sparse passage in the *Mahavamsa*. For example, the *Mahavamsa* made no reference to a left or right foot but this later chronicle noted that it was the left foot, indicating that some significance was attached to this but for unexplained reasons. The cold stone yielding beneath the Buddha's foot was likened to hot wax receiving a signet ring. Why Sumana came to be tied to this particular mountain is nowhere stated, but the indigenous deity was associated with this region by the mid-fifth century. (Mhv: 7. 67)

How did Sri Lankan Buddhists come by the notion of the Buddha impressing his foot into stone? It was likely inspired by a Pali Commentary, the *Punnovadasutta-atthakatha*, which described the Buddha granting a footprint to a snake-king (P: *naga-raja*) on the bank of the Narmada River in western India and another nearby to a converted heretic named Saccabandha on a hilltop. Each footprint served as a relic of the Buddha meant for worship after the Buddha's return to his homeland in India; this same motivation was no less true for ancient Ceylon. Some elements of this Pali Commentary

FORMA DO PICO D'ADAÕ

The earliest European depiction of the peak, 1638. After *Plantas das fortalezas, pagodes & ca. Da ilha de Ceilão*, Biblioteque National, Madrid. Folio 35r.

The Buddha, with the heretic Saccabandha on his mountain, left, and the snake-king by the Narmada River. c.13th century. Pagan. Burma. Temple no. 585. Courtesy Samerchai Poolsuwan.

appeared in a Sanskrit tale, the *Purna-avadana*, but no mention was made of footprints for a *naga* or a heretic. However, the Pali tradition was well known in Ceylon, attested by the fifth-century scholastic Buddhaghosa who situated the two footprints in India's Yonaka region in his *Samantapasadika* ('Jambudipe Yonakaratthe').[4]

The Buddha met the god Sumana at the Kelani River just north of Colombo where Sumana reminded him of the foot impression he presented to the converted heretic Saccabandha in India. Sumana then requested that this special 'favour of Yours be towards me also!'. Honouring the appeal from Sumana, the Buddha then set off immediately from Kelaniya 'on the road through the sky' to the peak whose summit was compared in size to a threshing floor. The two footprints in India remained known in Lanka and continue to underpin major footprint-sites in Burma and Thailand but these footprints belonged to a narrative tradition that stood apart from Sri Pada. Early Sinhalas were aware of these two footprints in India, reflected in a myth about the Buddha bestowing a footprint to a snake-king at the Kelani River. This lore of a footprint at Kelani survived into the 19th century but is no longer remembered. A similar association between the Buddha, a snake and a riverbank appeared too in a Sanskrit biography of the Buddha but with no mention of a footprint.[5]

Replicas of the Buddha's footprints, made of stone, metal or even wood were commonplace throughout the Buddhist world and are still produced today and donated to monasteries and classified as replicas (P: *uddesika*). In Sri Lanka, hundreds of such small footprint replicas in stone were placed in stupa compounds in the first millennium, usually showing both soles together, incised with a handful of auspicious marks. In later depictions, the soles are often ornamented with 108 auspicious symbols, perhaps listed first in a Sri Lankan 12th-century commentary, the *Jinalankara-tika*. One of the earliest examples with the 108 symbols is now in the Pagan Museum in Burma. A 14th-century Sukhothai inscription even listed each symbol and the symbols appear on a 15th-century example from Wat Phra Ram, Ayutthaya, now in the Bangkok Museum.[6]

The Buddha's footsteps never left a trace unless it was for a specific purpose, contrasting with the popular perception that every footstep taken by Muhammad on stone was made permanent by an impression. Examples include the brahman named Dona who followed footprints leading to the Buddha and who was then liberated from rebirths.(A.2.37; AA.2.505) A popular 13th-century Sinhalese tale was based on an ancient Pali Commentary. (DhA.1.202) It begins when a mother spotted a foot impression that she recognized as belonging to a special being free of passions. Her spouse belittled her discovery and later unwittingly offered his daughter to the Buddha in marriage, unaware that he was the very man free of passions. The Buddha then mocked his proposal and moreover remarked that his daughter looked like a corpse bristling with revolting impurities. (Sadly, the daughter never recovered from the slight and lived out a miserable life tormenting others since 'loathing came to possess her', as a Sanskrit version phrased it.) The Buddha's footprint in Lanka was in a different class altogether, since it functioned as a relic for the newly converted nation to worship upon the Buddha's return to India, serving as a permanent 'sign of remembrance'.[7] The footprint acted thus as a tangible proxy for the Buddha himself, belonging to a class of relics designated as *paribhoga-dhatu*, or 'relics of use', that encompassed objects that came into contact with the Buddha, such as an alms-bowl or water-strainer.

Adam and Eve, in Ceylon, clothed in banana leaves after the Ex[ulsion. The paired elephants and other animals re[resent the creatures that God requested Adam to name in *Genesis*. By Jan Brandes, circa 1784. Watercolur. Courtesy Arader Galleries, New York.

The Peak through the Ages

When exactly Adam's Peak attracted Buddhist worship is difficult to fix but the fourth-century chronicle, the *Dipavamsa*, omits any mention of Sri Pada, hinting that the peak's prominence arose only by the time of the *Mahavamsa*. Whatever the starting point, the footprint enjoyed a wide early regional reputation. A reference for instance appeared in the sixth-century Tamil poem from South India, the *Manimekalai,* wherein the mountain is called Samonoli, a name also used in Lanka and where a goddess venerated a pair of feet. The text also mentions supernatural beings who flew to Lanka and circumambulated the peak.[8] Its fame was thus part of regional lore shared by both Sri Lanka and South India by the middle of the first millennium.

References to Sri Pada following the *Mahavamsa* are few in Sri Lanka, probably because Adam's Peak was so isolated from major patronage centres, such as Anuradhapura. A handful of Chinese notices however attest to the peak's importance in the wider Buddhist world. The earliest is the fifth-century Chinese pilgrim in Anuradhapura, Faxian, who noted that the Buddha planted one footprint to the north of the city and a second atop an unnamed mountain fifteen *yojanas* away. The seventh-century Chinese monk Xuanzang never visited Ceylon but referred to 'Mount Lanka' where the Buddha preached the *Sutra on the Visit to Lanka* (S: *Lankavatara-sutra*). This text placed the Buddha on the 'peak of Mt. Malaya' which likely is meant to be Adam's Peak. Among those present at the sermon was Ravana, the demon chief of the Ramayana and king of Lanka. Further, a seventh-century Indian monk, Vajrabodhi, ascended Lanka Mountain (S: '*Lanka-parvata*') where he paid homage 'to the Buddha's foot'. There is also a sixth-century inscription at Bodh Gaya referring to a Sinhala monk who lived on 'the lower slopes of Lanka Mountain'.[9] These notices testify to the footprint's growing fame during the second half of the first millennium.

The historical picture comes into sharper focus only by the time of Vijayababu I (1055-1110) when a stone inscription from a village just north of the mountain recorded the king's pilgrimage from Polonnaruva. He offered 'various adornments studded with beautiful gems of seven kinds to the Sacred Footprint impressed on the summit of Samanola rock'. The footprint here is called a 'relic in the form of a footprint', or '*pas las-da*' (S: *pada-lanchana-dhatu).* Even the king placed his own 'bejewelled crown' on top of the stone cavity. The inscription described two 'terraces' on the summit. The topmost contained the footprint and the lower terrace was reserved for 'people of inferior status'. This perhaps meant that those of lesser social standing were unable to ascend the boulder on the summit or were more likely not permitted on the summit itself. The inscription also described two gateways 'fitted with locks and keys' leading to the top. A near duplicate of this inscription was found on the mountain's south side.[10] The inscription named the three Buddhas who preceded Gotama in this eon and who also left their footprints on the mountain but these earlier footprints were never thought to be visible here. Linking these three previous Buddhas to sites sacralized by Gotama Buddha was commonplace in the Theravada world, even in the first millennium. The king's gifts were also described in the *Culavamsa*. (60. 64)

The next major royal pilgrim was Nissankamalla (1187-96) who made an ambitious tour from his capital in Polonnaruva to a number of sacred sites 'that were inaccessible due to forests, water and mountains' and Sri Pada was listed as 'Samanola'. He also left an inscription in a cave about thirty metres below the summit on the north side, much as he did at Dambulla. This record confirmed a land grant by Vijayabahu. Next to the inscription is an incised outline of a standing figure who is the king himself, described in a nearby inscription reading 'this is the manner in which Nissankamalla stood worshipping the footprint'.[11]

Various Sri Lankan chronicles now and then recorded royal donations to the footprint. One gift from the 13th century refers to a canopy (P: '*mandapa*') above the footprint held down by 'strong chains [affixed] to iron pillars', foreshadowing chains used centuries later in the same way. The same king established on the summit an image of 'Sumana-deva', perhaps the first in a tradition that continues today. He also spent a night on the summit circumambulating the footprint. (Cv: 86.18-36) Another patron was a mid-16th-century king from Kandy who constructed 'bridges and roads' to facilitate travel.[12]

Sri Pada may have even attracted the Chinese emperor whose trilingual inscription from 1410 on the south coast referred to 'the shrine of the Buddhist temple on the mountain of Ceylon'. The emperor offered precious objects, such as pieces of gold and silver and 50 rolls of silk. These gifts were probably not hauled up the mountain but perhaps deposited in the small hamlet of Pelmadulla in the foothills near Adam's Peak and which had become important by the 19th century for storing metal covers for the footprint. The Tamil and Persian portions of the inscription do not mention the mountain but a Chinese Muslim in the 15th century ascended the peak and reported that the footprint belonged to a holy man known as 'A-tan [Adam]', thus reflecting Muslim and Christian views.[13]

The only purported break in patronage came when Sri Pada

came under the notorious anti-Buddhist Rajasimha I (1581-93). This 'impious fool … placed miscreant ascetics [devotees of Shiva]… on Sumanakuta to take for themselves all the profit accruing therefrom'. (Cv: 93. 9-12) This rupture in patronage is probably legendary, casting Rajasimha as a foil for a later king, Kirti Sri Rajasimha (1747-82), who took credit for liberating Sri Pada from the Hindus. Indeed, in one Sinhalese text, *The Sitavaka War* (*Sitavaka Hatana*), Rajasimha is described as a supporter of Adam's Peak. Other Kandyan rulers also patronized Sri Pada and a ruler in Kotte, Parakramabhu VI, donated iron rails for pilgrims in the 15th century.[14]

Casting the 'Shadow of the Peak'

Two major routes to the summit are used today, the more difficult from Ratnapura, on the south side, where the distance is 12 kilometres from the trailhead. From the north, the climb is only some six kilometres. The longer approach still accrues more merit, as attested already in the 14th-century by Ibn Battuta. Lesser-known paths up the peak were described in 1908. Many ascend after midnight in order to reach the summit in time to see the sun cast a triangular-shaped shadow over the countryside. This spectacular effect was even given a name, 'Shadow of the Peak', and first photographed in about 1900.[15]

This shrine shelting the footprint grew increasingly elaborate in the late nineteenth century. After *The Graphic*, 30 August 1879.

By 1815 the footprint was protected by 'a small building formed of the most durable wood' whose roof was capped with tiles. By 1819 the shrine was held fast to the rock against strong winds 'by means of heavy chains' suspended from the roof. A sketch in 1833 by the botanist, Anna Maria Walker, shows the chains holding down the shrine. Old photographs show how this 'wooden shed' grew increasingly elaborate but the roof chains remained in place into the twentieth century. Pilgrims stood outside the simple shrine and 'deposited in the sacred impression … copper-money and rice,

These two large inscriptions were thought to be on Adam and Eve's tombs. Parchment. Signed by J.S. Croppenbergh. Dated 1734. Lundt University Museum

cotton-cloth, betel-leaves and flowers'. Votaries also chanted the Five Precepts in concert with a monk and then lit strips of cloth 'dipped in oil' that were then suspended from metal stands. Less than a handful of monks resided on the summit. Pilgrims included 'the professed Christian Catholic, as well as *Christian reformados* [Protestants] and Mussulman of Hindoostan [Indian Muslims]'. A small wooden shrine just below the footprint housed an image of the god Saman. The footprint was framed in the early 19th century by a shallow border made of molded lime, or *chunam,* and is visible in the earliest photograph of the foot. Toes were added at some time by a mixture of 'lime and sand', appearing in a sketch made in about 1900, indicating a left foot.[16]

'Like Christians going to Santiago de Compostela in Galicia'

Numerous manuscripts of Marco Polo's famous *Travels* circulated in Europe for centuries but one Burgundian example, attributed to 1475-1525, included perhaps a unique depiction of the peak, accompanied by a text in Middle French. Marco Polo (1254-1325) likened the pilgrimage to Adam's Peak to Christians going to 'Santiago [de Compostela] in Galicia'.[17] Polo never once mentioned a footprint on the peak, only a Muslim belief that Adam's tomb was located on the mountain and that Adam's 'hair, teeth and bowl' that were interred inside. This very tomb is pictured in semi-profile on this illustration at the top of the mountain. (No tombs of any sort have been found on the summit.) Polo discredited this idea and claimed that the items in the tomb belonged rather to 'Sergamoni Borcan', a name for Sakyamuni Buddha he learned in Mongolia.

The Burgundian artist shows the Buddha, as prince Sakyamuni before his enlightenment, serving food to four women who were 'the most beautiful to be found', according to the accompany text. The prince's father 'commanded them [the maidens] to cavort with him all day and night ... to turn his heart to worldy things'. These modest damsels reflect the sensitivities of the French nobility and are a contrast to two local women in loincloths who the text reports 'go quite naked except that they cover the middle [with loincloths]'. Polo also probably confused Adam's Peak with the Buddhist monastic cave site of Mulgirigala that was thought to be the burial place of Adam and Eve. Mulgirigala is east of Galle and about twenty kilometres inland and was called Adam's Berg, or Adam's Peak, by the Dutch.

Pilgrims ascending Adam's Peak. A page from a Marco Polo manuscript produced in fifteenth-century Burgundy. Bibliotheque de l'Arsenal, Paris, ms-5219, Folio 133v.

A depiction of this peak on the south coast appears in a parchment painting in Lund, dated to 1734 and signed by J.S. Croppenbergh. The two outsized inscriptions are labelled, 'The Sepulchre of Adam' and 'The Sepulchre of Eve', said to be incised on their graves. The script is indecipherable but is perhaps a poor transcription of Armenian tombstones found widely in Burma, Thailand and India; none have yet to be discovered in Ceylon. The twenty steps leading to the top and the two small caves side-by-side match two written descriptions from this period.[19]

Polo also noted 'many iron chains … arranged so that men can climb' to the top. Chains were certainly in place by his time but since Polo never visited Adam's Peak he perhaps drew on regional lore that claimed that Alexander the Great visited the tomb of Adam and established the chains. Alexander's visit to Adam's tomb on the peak is found in a 13th-century Persian text. Alexander's associations with the chains was also widely known in the West and the chains were depicted in Fr Mauro's famous 15th-century map and also described in Duarte Barbosa's travelogue. Some chains were fashioned into ladders, visible in the 1638 sketch by Miranda and also in a mural depicting Adam's Peak at Wat Phuthaisawan in Ayutthaya. Ibn Battuta mentioned as many as ten chains, one named Chain of the Profession of Faith. The real donors of these chains in antiquity are unknown but one Sinhala king was said to have made a donation of chains in the 15th century.[20]

A visitor reported in 1817 that without these chains 'small indeed would be the number of those who would complete their pilgrimage'. In some cases, the rungs were 'made solid' and engraved with the names of the donors. Many devotees offered chains and so

Rusty chains of indeterminate age can still be seen on the mountain paths at Adam's Peak. Courtesy Chryshane Mendis.

Chains suspended from the mountain aided the ascent of pilgrims. Subodharama Viharaya. c. 1896. Colombo.

there were 'eight or nine sets [of chains] hung one above the other in bunches'. The chains were still in use in the 1920s and many rusty and redundant chains of indeterminate age can be spotted today en route to the top.[21]

Batatota cave

The *Mahavamsa* recorded that the Buddha came down after impressing his footprint and 'spent the day … at the foot of this mountain … for a rest during the heat of the day'. (Mhv: 1. 78) Centuries later, this resting area was identified as The Cave of the Midday Rest, or 'Divaguha'. Its exact whereabouts was unknown but it was included among the Sixteen Great Sites and was usually depicted with the Buddha inside, recumbent. A large cavern, called Batatota-lena, is now believed to be this lost cave and was 'discovered' in 1995 about 15 kilometres north of Ratnapura. Within the cave is small room containing a Vishnu image with a painted inscription above the doorway dated to 1907 (BE 2450). Another tradition was that Sumana met the Buddha in a cave at Adam's Peak where he prophesied to the deity Sumana that a righteous universal ruler named Divyasena would appear 2,500 years after the Buddha's demise. This legend is recorded in Sinhalese manuscripts known as the *Sumana-sutraya*, dating from the Dutch era.[22] Some proclaimed in the 1950s that the Prime Minister S.W.R.D. Bandaranaike was this very Divyasena.

The Buddha resting within a cave at the foot of Adam's Peak. A Pali manuscript, *The Path of Purification. (Visuddhimagga)*, a detail. Copied on Dutch paper in the Buddhist Era 2354 (1811). Donated to the nephew of Velivita Sri Saranakara. Malwatta Viharaya. Kandy.

The Batatota Cave where the Buddha rested after visiting Adam's Peak. A sculpture of the monk who 'discovered' the cave in 1995 stands on the right. Courtesy: Samerchai Poolsuwan.

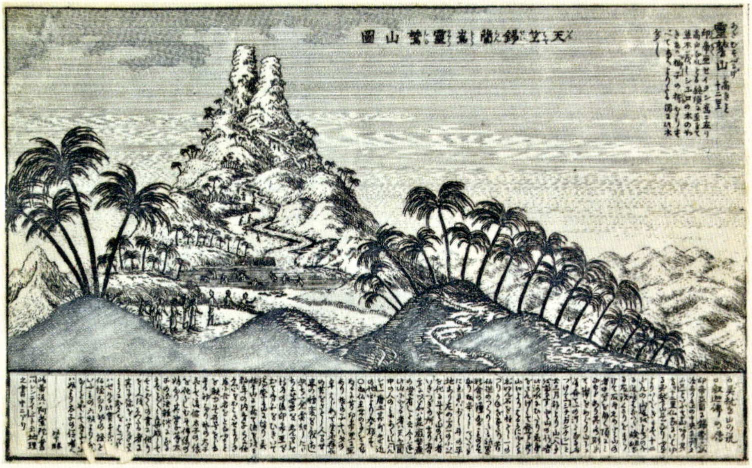

Artists in Japan came to know of the Peak by way of Francois Valentijn's illustrated account of the Dutch East Indies, *Oud en Nieuw Oost-Indien* (1726). This Dutch classic was translated into Japanese by Takano Choei in Nagasaki who worked with a German botanist and physician, Philipp von Siebold. A copperprint engraving by Matsumoto Yasuori (1786-1867) loosely followed Valentijn's plate XIII. The text of the engraving confused Adam's Peak with the familiar Vulture Peak (P: Gijjhakuta) in India where the Buddha delivered famous sermons. The title of the engraving translates: 'In India [Teniku] on the Island of Ceylon [Seiran], Vulture Peak [Ryojusen], zu [image]'. (pers. comm., Ryuiji Okudaira) Japanese intellectuals at the time located Vulture Peak and certain famous Indian Buddhist sites in Ceylon.[24]

The Descent of the Mahaweli River

Conventional wisdom today is that Hindus have worshipped at the peak from time immemorial, accepting the footprint as Lord Shiva's, but exactly when Hindus venerated the footprint is nowhere stated until the appearance of Tamil texts in the 17th or 18th century. The work with the fullest information is from Jaffna, the *Tirikonacala Puranam*. The mythology adapted the ancient Indian myth about the descent of the Ganges from heaven and its torential thrust broken on the matted locks of Shiva, thus protecting the earth from calamity. For Lanka's Tamils, Shiva's footprint on Adam's Peak marked the spot from where the mighty Mahaweli River sprung. Hindus undertook the pilgrimage over the centuries, and there was a group of '*jogis*', or yogis, and brahmans who accompanied Ibn Battutta. But by comparison to Christian and Muslim notices, far less is known about Hindu pilgrimages.

Hindu interpretations of the peak were probably never uniform. In the eighteenth century, for example, an ascetic, or 'sunyassi', from Varanasi named Purana Poori reminisced in 1792 to Jonathan Duncan about his visit to Kataragama and to Sri Pada

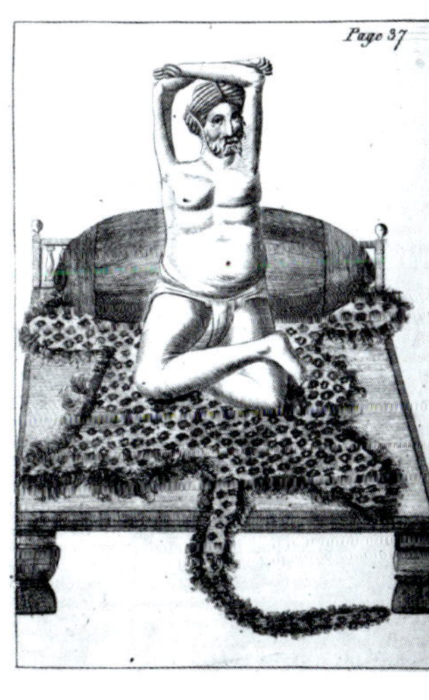

A Hindu pilgrim from Varanasi visited Adam's Peak in the late 18th century. After Jonathan Duncan, *Asiatic Researches* (1799), p. 39.

where he took the footprint to be that of Rama.[23] He also saw a cave on the mountainside where Rama hid Sita during his struggle with Ravana, perhaps one of the same caves that Ibn Battuta understood in a Quranic context. No standard *Ramayana* traditions associate Rama with a footprint in Ceylon but this Varanasi pilgrim's account illustrates how diverse religious traditions adopted the footprint as their own.

Trouble in High Places

This once remote pilgrimage spot changed dramatically in the 20th century after new roads opened and the rail line came to nearby Hatton in 1884. In the 20th century, the site became emblematic of Ceylon, together with the Tooth Relic, and the Peak appeared on a postage stamp with King George VI in 1938. The mountain's catchment area today takes in over a million residents from Colombo and Kandy alone, and local coach operators began special tours to Sri Pada long ago. In 1906 pilgrims numbered close to 8,000 and by 2001 the estimate had risen to over 2 million. This mass influx irreversibly altered the character of this once sleepy site. Indeed, the mountain top became so tightly congested that new structures are now suspended over the summit's edge. A helipad perches off the summit, for VIPs zipping in for a speedy ritual before scooting back to Colombo for a board meeting or a parliamentary debate. The footprint itself is the sole forelorn survival from yesteryear, now completely encased by a wide cement rim and painted breeze blocks (USA: cinderblocks).

The pilgrimage seasons begins from the middle to late December on a full moon day and ends in May on a full moon day before the monsoon sets in, with the summit closed to the public during the off-season. Access to the footprint itself is gained by two staircases built within a tall platform amost fully encasing the large boulder. Worshippers enter one side and step down on the other. On busy days, votaries are permitted no more than a second or two in front of the foot's impression before shuffling on. Photographs of the footprint are not allowed and it is usually covered with a cloth that is removed twice weekly for ritual washing. The footprint has been recently painted in a gold colour. Many visitors lay wishes before the impression and make vows, much like at other sacred sites, but the peak's ambiance contrasts completely from Kataragama. Pilgrims once sang ballads during the climb and Sinhalese pilgrims' poems were also published. Many legends grew up about the footprint but few have been recorded. One credits the footprint's discovery to a hermit who secretly followed celestial damsels, or *apsaras*, who flew to the site with floral offerings. Other lore located the brief presence of a Bodhi tree on Adam's Peak, or 'Samanalla-Sripada', that came from a cutting made at Bodh Gaya by a female hermit. There was also a Sinhalese poem, in 1912, that acknowledged that the footprint was the Buddha's but noted that Adam was preceded in Sri Lanka by the demon Ravana.[25]

A hermit accompanying celestials en route to Adam's Peak, once a popular folk tale. Subhodharama Viharaya, Colombo.

Control of the footprint was disputed among the various faiths in the nineteenth century but 'while their respective claims may have be equally good … the Buddhist have got possession'. Thus, the old adage, 'possession is nine-tenths of the law', transferred easily from land disputes to the ecclesiastical realm. Indeed, Buddhists had enjoyed at least nominal control of Adam's Peak since the time of Kirti Sri Rajasimha who awarded the peak to the monk Valivita Saranamkara, head of Kandy's Malwatta monastery. A Malwatta monk was appointed to be 'High Priest of the Peak' in 1826, a decision taken by George Turnour (1799-1843), the antiquarian who first translated the *Mahavamsa*.

The stakes were high since donations at Sri Pada grew to exceed those at other sites, such as the Temple of the Tooth. For example, in 1867 the number of pilgrims was estimated between ten and twelve thousand, depositing nearly two thousand pounds sterling in donations, all flowing into the Malwatta coffers in Kandy. Also, the value of the acreage in the area belonging to Sri Pada was rising. A challenge to Malwatta hegemony came from the Committee of Monks that represented low country monks in opposition to the Kandy establishment. Control of Sri Pada then passed to a low country monk by a judgement issued by the same government agent, George Turnour, but the site was later passed back to the Malwatta establishment where it remains today.[26]

By the 1860s the sacred mountain was plagued by fresh disputes, as piety and profit so often commingle in litigation. The Malwatta 'high priest' administering the Peak in the 1860s was accused of misappropriating the 'revenues of his office'. Malwatta monks launched legal action, with six members testifying against the accused. The Crown ruled against the monk and he was replaced by H. Sri Sumangala (1827-1911). This appointment was challenged by the former incumbent in court in Ratnapura in 1870 and Sumangala was prevented from assuming the post. Eventually, Colombo's Supreme Court ruled on appeal in favour of Sumangala's reinstatement. The case reveals how the *sangha* resolved problems among multiple competing interests within a backdrop of colonial authority.[27]

Ratnapura: Saman's Temple

Ratnapura: Saman's Temple

The Buddha's footprint is inextricably linked to the guardian of Adam's Peak, the god Saman, much like Moses is paired with Mount Sinai or Muhammad with Mount Arafat. The deity is unknown in the Pali canon, but his relationship to the Buddha assured him a place in the nation's religious life, beginning as early as in the fifth-century *Mahavamsa*. His most sacred temple is but a short distance outside the town of Ratnapura and some 90 kilometers inland from Colombo. From here to the mountain's base is only 20 kilometres but to the summit the rise is over 2,000 metres. Ratnapura, or 'City of Gems', refers to the area's precious stones, a hallmark of ancient Sri Lanka. The current temple, officially named Sri Saman Deva Devalaya, was largely built in the 19th century but its foundation goes back to probably the 14th. The temple is a popular stop for many pilgrims heading to Adam's Peak.

The Pali name for Saman is Sumana but the deity is addressed today as Saman Deviyo. He is a benevolent subordinate of the Buddha, unlike more ambiguous gods, such as Kataragama who can effect harm.[1] His temple outside of Ratnapura arose no earlier than the 14th century. For example, the famous kings Vijayabau I (1055-1110) and Nissankamalla (1187-1196) visited Adam's Peak but their inscriptions and the chronicles say nothing about nearby Ratnapura. Saman's status grew over the ages and by the 14th century he was counted among the protective deities of Sri Lanka. By then, Saman was matched with a consort and the duo merited a sculpture at the Lankatilaka Temple near Kandy, dated to 1344.[2] The temple's location was probably chosen because of its proximity to Sri Pada and the commercial rise of nearby Ratnapura near the bank of the Kalu Ganga waterway that empties on the west coast just below Kalatura.

The current temple was largely constructed during the reign of Kandy's last king, Sri Vikrama Rajasimha (1798-1815), in connection with his pilgrimage to Ratnapura and Kataragama in 1812. A royal order commanded the surrounding villages to repair and reconstruct 'the buildings … belonging to the Sapragomuwe Dewale [Sabaragamuwa's temple]' in preparation for the royal visit.[3] Nearly ten years before, British troops bivouacked at the 'pagoda [temple] of Saffragam' after retreating from the assault on Kandy in 1803. The temple complex at that time appeared 'even of greater extent than any other which now remains entire in Ceylon', likening it to the extensive India temple complex at 'Rammisseram' (Rameshvara). For example, the 'towers above the gateway are buildings of much solidity, labouriously ornamented'. Two covered corridors supported 'stone pillars' that intersected 'in the form of a cross' and the entire complex was protected by a 'high stone wall'.[4] This description bears no resemblance to the temple today that

Previous page:
The temple was built during the 19th century but its origins are in the 14th century. The panel with the Portuguese soldier in the outer wall is on the right.

occupies a modest raised earthen mound that was perhaps too small to accommodate such a grand complex as was described in 1803 or a Dutch fort. The temple noted in 1803 was perhaps built in the vicinity of the present one but has left no trace, apart from perhaps a handful of stone fragments in the government site museum. Other large temple complexes that have left few traces include the monuments at Trincomalee, the Vishnu shrine at Devinuvura and the tooth-relic temple at Kotte.

A steep stairway leads to the entrance whose stone lintel does not match its jambs, indicating how building material from earlier constructions were reused in the work that commenced around 1812. This door opens to a colonnade whose Doric brick pillars support a new timber roof. An entrance at the end is surrounded by figures in high relief made of brick and painted plaster, resembling countless others from this period. Behind this doorway are wooden pillars in a long hall which once kept miniature cannon known in colonial Asia as *jingals*. The sharp cracks of discharging *jingals* enhanced the festive mood of the temple's celebrations in yesteryear. A doorway at the end of the hall leads to the inner sanctum, access to which is so restricted that there are no reliable descriptions of the chief image. Old reports say that a 'golden bow and arrow' were kept inside the sanctum, together with a 'silver-stemmed umbrella'

Saman and his consort in the inner corridor of the Lankantilaka Temple, near Kandy. c. 1344 CE. Courtesy: Osmund Bopearachchi.

This doorway leads to the sanctum's antechamber. The Goddess of Fortune, Lakshmi, is in the centre.

Mahabamba Kolama, representing Rajasimha I (1581-1592). This side of his mask is benign but a demonic face is on the opposite side. Courtesy Tharaka Anand.

that once was placed above the footprint on Adam's Peak. Above this inner sanctum are two floors that may have been 'where the paraphernalia of the deity' was stored.[5]

To either side of the main shrine are two small temples. The Buddhist one contains a reliquary, with an unspecified relic, borne by an elephant in the temple's annual procession, while a pair of Pattini's fabled anklets were added to the pageant, at least by the early 19th century. However, the only firm evidence for the Pattini temple dates from 1848.[6]

The shrine's two-week annual festival culminates with a procession, or *perahera*, that includes a costumed figure on stilts known as Mahabamba Kolama, taken to be Rajasimha I (1581-92), the legendary founder of the pageant. The figure's double-sided mask shows a benevolent face on one side and a demonic face crowned by snake hoods on the other; in one hand is a sword.[7] Rajasimha ruled in Sitavaka and was cast in chronicles as a wicked foe of Buddhism and a devotee of Shiva, but he was in reality a staunch Buddhist. He not only started the festival at Ratnapura but also began a procession at the Saman temple for the tooth-relic that was kept for some time in the nearby village of Delgamuwa; this tooth is now believed to be the one in Kandy.[8]

A procession from the 1850s probably included two images of Mahabamba Kolama, with fangs and holding swords. After *Illustrated London News*, October 16 1852.

A Hymn to Samana

The temple's fortunes probably peaked during the 15th and early 16th centuries when it enjoyed the patronage of the Kotte dynasty whose capital, Jayawardenapura, was just outside Colombo. A poem extolling the temple and a manuscript recording donations fill in critical gaps. The poem of 290 verses, *A Hymn to Samana*, or *Saman Sirita*, is known from a 19th-century palm-leaf manuscript discovered in 1905. It was probably composed at the time of Kotte's ruler Bhuvanekabahu VII (1521-51) since the recorded events concluded during his reign. The poem speaks of a monk living at the time of Parakrambahu II (1234-69) who saw the god Saman in a dream on Adam's Peak and who informed him about an image of the god hidden in a cave. Discovering this sculpture, the monk then returned with the image to his own temple-monastery. Parakramabahu was also said to have built the first Saman temple, a token of thanks for a profitable expedition to find gems.[9] This king made donations at Adam's Peak, but his construction of a temple at Ratnapura is unlikely since such an important donation would probably have been included in his benefactions recorded in the *Culavamsa*. He was a devotee of Samana however since he established an image of the deity in the vicinity of the Buddha's footprint. (Cv. 86. 29)

A second source came to light in 1894 when a transcription of a palm-leaf manuscript was discovered listing donations at Ratnapura by the Kotte king Parakramabahu VI (1411-66) during his 39th regnal year, that is, 1454 CE. The text was a copy of a large stone inscription now missing, apart from three small fragments today inside the main temple. The grant was issued in the Sumangala Palace in the capital of Jayawardenapura. The donations in 'Sabaragamuwa' were to the Great Temple, or 'Maha Devale' of Saman, and a Buddhist temple called a '*vihara*'. For the temple's upkeep, a grandson of a famous brahman was awarded 26,000 coins for 'furnishing it with ramparts, gates... image-houses, *dagobas* [stupas], monasteries ... and pleasure-gardens'. The grant included a ritualist, or *kapurala*, with the title 'Kapuwa Deva', who held 'the gem-set crown and other ornaments in the presence of the image of the god [Saman]'. A monk appointed to the vihara was 'acquainted with the whole body of Buddhist doctrine' and was ordered to recite protective verses, or *pirith* (P: *paritta*) inside Saman's temple. The expenses of the two establishments were separate but were ordered to be pooled for emergencies. There was also a fund for the annual procession, or '*esala perahera*'. The grant further assigned to the temple the 'five kinds of musical instruments' and musicians to accompany dancing girls. The descendants of these very dancers were perhaps among the 50 entertainers attached to the temple in the nineteenth century who were 'remunerated from the lands belonging to the temple'. [10] The same manuscript also refers to Saman's unnamed queen and son who also appeared in a late 16th-century poem, the *Savul Sandesaya*.[11] Saman's consort and their son never attained lasting popularity and depictions of the three together have yet to be identified.

The Colonial Era

The temple's fate during the Portuguese and Dutch eras likely followed a similar tumultuous trajectory as many other temples and monasteries. The Portuguese lost Ceylon to the Dutch in the second half of the 17th-century, with the Dutch occupying Ratnapura from 1665 to about 1680. However, no traces of a Dutch or Portuguese fort in the town of Ratnapura nor at the Saman temple site have come to light. Ratnapura was twice visited by the famous Father Vas (1687-1711) who baptized 500.[12] A treaty with the Dutch in 1766 left Kandy's Buddhist rulers in control of the region but little is known about the Saman temple in these years, apart from its rebuilding in 1812.

Two very different ground plans of the fort are known from Portuguese times, one labelled Forte d'Sofragao (1624) and the other Forte d'Sofragam (1638), but whether one or both of these forts successively occupied the present raised temple mound or were established somewhere nearby is unclear.[13] A visitor to the temple in 1817 reported that 'a temple ('dewale') of some size ... [was] ... built on the ruins of an old Portuguese fort, and dedicated to Samen, who seems to be the provincial god of Saffragam'.[14] Fixing the original locations of the Dutch and Portuguese forts and the temple is further clouded since the name Saparagamawu was used interchangeably for Ratnapura and also for the entire region in colonial documents.
A stone block in the site museum bears Portugal's coat-of-arms and the armorial crest of Ceylon's two-time governor, Constantino de Sã de Noronha, 1618-22 and 1623-30. The stone probably belonged to the fort but its find-spot is unrecorded. The Portuguese permitted access to the region by Kandyan kings and a copy of the footprint on Adam's Peak was taken to Kandy during the time of Vimala Dharma Suriya I (1592-1604).[15]

Portugal's coat of arms, above, and the arms of Contantino de sã de Naronha. Its find-spot unrecorded. Site museum, Ratnapura.

The temple's location often appears in old documents as Saparagamuwa, that is, the Town of Sapara, or Sabaragamuwa in modern Sinhalese. (Cv: 94.7) The name derived from Shabara, a Sanskrit term for hunters and so-called tribals; *gamuwa* is the word for village (P: gama). The Shabaras, according to the *Mahabharata,* were born from the dung and urine of a cow belonging to the sage Vasishtha. The same word for 'backward' peoples is found in Pali and was likely attached to this region because of its 'primitive tribal' inhabitants, known as Vaddas. Other 'backward' people in this same region are thought to have descended from the demoness Kuveni and her two kids who fled after their mother was rejected by Ceylon's legendary founder, Vijaya. These became the Pulindas, another Sanskrit term for 'tribals'. (Mhv: 7.68) The Pulindas of India were even mentioned in the famous Asokan Rock Edicts. Saman is a favourite deity among the Vaddas who have long been associated with this province. Vaddas perform ritual dances in the procession at Mahiyangana's Saman temple where a tribal chief carries a bow and arrow, two attributes in the past connected to Saman. A mid-15th-century poem, the *Paravi Sandesaya*, refers to the daughters of Vaddas in the area below Adam's Peak.[16]

Saman

The god Saman seen on posters today usually stands before his white elephant, a flower in one hand and the other pointing toward Adam's Peak. This standardized rendition probably arose in the 20th century but his depictions varied widely before then. The surviving examples date mainly to the 19th century and are known mostly from murals where he is shown in narrative scenes receiving hair-relics from the Buddha intended for the stupa at Mahiyangana. Other works feature the god alone, independent of a narrative. The best-known example is a life-size image at Dambulla in Cave 2, with one hand in the teaching-gesture (S: *vitarka-mudra*) and the other signifying the removal-of-obstacles (S: *karana-mudra*). A 1726-manuscript names this deity at Dambulla as Saman. Early painted examples show a bow and arrow in the god's left hand, with the right hand lowered. The god could

Sumana is usually represented today with a white elephant against the backdrop of the god's mountain. A ritualist, or *kapurala*, stands by waiting to receive worshippers. Mahiyangana.

A 19th-century hand-coloured illustration shows Saman, his elephant and bow and arrow. After Upham (1829).

also have four arms, one with a sceptre and the other with a flower.[17] A two-armed example found among the Kelaniya murals from about 1851 shows the god with a spear or perhaps a long arrow. Enormous images of Saman, usually with two arms and made of brick and painted plaster, stand to the side of reclining Buddhas in temples from the Kandyan period and later, often paired with Vishnu.

Two Saman images are kept in a small temple on the summit of Adam's Peak today but are obscured by offerings. One is said to be silver, while the other of sandalwood. Both have two arms. The pair are removed from the summit at the end of the visiting season and taken briefly to the Pelmadulla Raja Mahavihara before being shifted during the off-season to a Saman temple at the nearby Galpottawela Raja Mahvihara.[18]

Saman was also woven into numerous myths, many of which blended indigenous, Hindu, and Buddhist themes. These narratives were current in the 19th century and earlier, but are less well known today. Many feature Saman's relations with demons. One legend has Saman ready to slay a demon named Riri Yaka and his wife but they presented him a golden bow and were spared. Another version has Riri Yaka tied to a wheel by Saman but he was offered his freedom if he forsook killing humans. In another, Saman was asked by the jealous Rama to slay his wife Sita since she had painted a flattering picture of her abductor, Ravana; Saman spared her because she was with child. Saman was also the king of a certain group of demi-gods known as 'Koombandeo' (P: *kumbhandas*), classed together with demons; but Saman 'renounced his wickedness' when he met the Buddha at Mahiyangana. Saman had other connections to demons, many with Adam's Peak as a setting.[19] The connection with the demonic is perhaps the context for the huge demons painted on the temple's whitewashed interior walls. These figures may be those noted in 1852 or more probably painted later in the century or even in the early twentieth century.

Simão Pinhão

A Portuguese soldier about to slay his Sinhala foe is the subject of a panel set into the temple's outer compound wall, with the following Portuguese inscription on its base, translated:

> 'With this [sword] I overcame this [man], it being 23 (?) years that I have been in India and 15(?) that I have served as captain; and as soon as the kings … and the king of Jafanapatao [Jaffna], I Simão Pinhão, conquered him'.[20]

A Portuguese soldier named Simão Pinhão. Original find-spot unknown. Now in the outer wall of the temple.

Simão Pinhão's colourful career started with inflicting a 'sword-cut' across the face of a fellow in a village brawl in Portugal that resulted in his banishment to Africa. His father, a nobleman, purchased his freedom but not before his son escaped from his cell. He then popped up in Goa in 1591 but landed in jail for a robbery committed near Bombay. He then served in Ceylon where he attained fame in the skirmishes between Portuguese and Kandyan forces. He was first in Ratnapura in 1599 but then assigned to various trouble spots in the ongoing guerrilla conflict, being called back to the Ratnapura area when a Sinhala revolt erupted in 1616.

The inscription stated that he triumphed over the king of Jaffna, then in the hands of a Hindu king, but this was a boast. He eventually wed a Sinhala woman whose Christian name was Dona Maria Pereira. He and his wife may have resided in or around the fort, since he was granted two villages not far from Ratnapura. The proceeds of these villages were even the subject of a petition to the Portuguese king by his niece in 1653, long after her uncle's death. He died probably around 1619 under undisclosed circumstances.

The fallen Sinhala soldier lacks any marks distinguishing him as a nobleman or a specific individual. The simple short cloth covering below his waist resembles that of a foot soldier, as does his topknot, that features in a watercolour belonging to the *Codice Casanatense* captioned 'People that are called Chingualas [Sinhalas] of the island of Ceylon, where the cinnamon comes from'. This Codice, preserved in Rome, was created around 1540.[21] How this panel, over a metre in height, was originally displayed is guesswork. And why did the Sri Lankan builders place such a deprecative depiction of Lankan soldiery into the exterior wall to lament the country's subjugation or were there other reasons?

The Buddha's footprint, metal, with 108 symbols. The wide rim was probably designed to fit over a natural or artificially created stone footprint. c. 14th or 15th century. From Kamphaeng Phet, National Museum, Bangkok.

'A much-spoken-of-representation of the sacred footprint'

A tradition arose by the 14th century, if not earlier, of honouring the footprint with a metal cover ornamented with the well-known 108 auspicious symbols. Such covers, copied in drawings, were then recreated on stone or on a metal sheet that could be placed over a natural or artifically created depression in stone. One likely example from this period is now in the National Museum, Bangkok, but no early examples have survived from Sri Lanka or Burma.[22]

These covers at Adam's Peak were removed during the pilgrimage season and kept at a temple in Pelmadulla, a village only ten kilometres from Ratnapura and an important station on the way to the peak. Another object kept here was the small wooden image of Saman that resided on the hilltop during the pilgrimage season. Other 'relics' from the peak were displayed in Pelmadulla during the pilgrim season, noted by the Prussian prince, Frederich Waldemar in the 1840s. Sometime later, nearly 60 of the most distinguished monks in Ceylon were assembled at this remote monastery to edit the various versions of the Pali canon, such as those from Burma and Siam.[23]

Evidence of a possible cover at Adam's Peak is found in a Dutch governor's report from 1707 that stated that 'the late king' (Vimala Dharma Suriya II) offered 'a massive silver *Sombreiro*' at the peak; this Portuguese word probably meant a cover, in light of the context. By the nineteenth century many references appear. Perhaps the oldest was by John D'Oyly who noted in his 1812-diary that the cover was made of gold and adorned with 'precious Stones' and kept at the temple at Pelmadulla for some time of the year. This cover was probably recent since visitors to the area before then make no reference to it nor is it mentioned in early Pali or Sinhalese sources. It also may have been a donation made by the Kandyan king whose pilgrimage to Adam's Peak and Ratnapura was made in the same year. An eyewitness in 1817 probably saw the same metal covering and described it as brass, 'studded with a few gems of little value' and without any of the 108 symbols.[24]

Another more elaborate metal cover, probably a replacement, was noted in Pelmadulla in 1848. It was divided into four separate sections that were 'laid out on the floor of the [temple] verandah for me to look at'. The rims of the four metal sheets were folded at a perpendicular angle in order to fit snugly over the raised edge that surrounded the stone footprint, the metal covering acting as a cap. It was designed in four sections to make it easier for transporting up and down the mountain. The rim was embedded with 'precious stones' of inferior quality. This cover drew much attention, described in 1848 as a 'much-spoken-of-representation of the sacred foot-print'. Later, in the 1860s, a visitor to the village remarked that a 'facsimile in copper' had replaced an earlier one that was 'lost or destroyed'.[25] These covers were without the 108 symbols, only 'lotus buds and flowers', and their whereabouts are unknown. This tradition was so well known and respected that an embossed silver cover for the footprint was presented by the English governor of Ceylon, Sir Robert Wilmot-Horton.[26]

Placing metal covers over stone footprints was a practice that can be traced to much earlier times. One example was a cover made of 'a Plate of Gold' that was examined by 'Hollanders' in 1654 at Saraburi, near Ayutthaya, the site of Thailand's most sacred footprint. It was made to the same 'length and breadth' of the stone footprint and was adorned with 68 auspicious symbols, according to the clergyman Baldaeus who received a report from his countrymen, listing each category of symbol. The symbols on the cover at Saraburi probably numbered 108, but the 'Hollanders' likely listed only one symbol rather than enumerating others in the same category.[27]

Other artistic examples representing footprints were never intended as covers. These usually contain the 108 symbols and are ubiquitous in Theravada societies where they continue to be offered to temples. A fragment of a small metal footprint was discovered at Sigiriya but is of indeterminate age.[28]

SERUVILA AND SOMAVATHIYA: THE BUDDHA'S FOREHEAD BONE AND TOOTH-RELIC

These two sites illustrate how ruinous and deserted stupas found in the 20th century became attached to old myths that were never linked to them originally. Discoveries of lost monuments and precious relics enjoy a solid place in Theravada history. The most celebrated case was the uncovering of 84,000 relics in a secret chamber by Asoka. In some instances, lost sites were found propitiously by hunters, such as the Dambulla caves and Thailand's most sacred Buddha footprint at Saraburi. Even Yangon's Shwedagon stupa was hidden and was only brought to light when two special beings (P: *arahants*) found the ruinous stupa amidst 'jungle, brambles and creepers', as the stupa's 15th-century inscription phrased it.[1] While the rise of Seruvila and Somavathiya occurred during the 20th century, linking new legends to stupas also took place in antiquity, as demonstrated in the chapter on Attanagalla. In Thailand, legends underpinning the grand first-millennium stupas at Nakhon Pathom and Nakhon Si Thammarat were supplanted centuries later by the myths known today.

The two sites are no more than 40 kilometers apart and not far inland from Trincomalee. The Seruvila stupa is known for the Buddha's forehead-bone, while the Somavathiya stupa is venerated for one of the Buddha's eye-teeth. Both monastic sites are strewn with first-millennium stone fragments dating to a time in the 13th century when a number of sites in the Trincomalee area, such as Welgama and Thiriyai, fell into ruin. Seruvila was nothing more than 'a mound of earth 25 feet high' by 1905 with a few stone steps and pillars. Little had changed by 1920 when the site 'became the abode of wild animals'. Although in ruins for centuries, Seruvila's legendary fame ensured its inclusion in an 18th-century list of sacred sites.[2] The same was true for the Kelaniya stupa near Colombo which also retained its sacredness during the Portuguese and Dutch periods, despite its ruinous state.

The key source underpinning these two stupas is the *Chronicle of the Relic* (P: *Dhatu-vamsa*), commonly assigned to the 14th century, also known as the *Chronicle of the Forehead Relic* (P: *Nalatadhatu-*

The Seruvila Stupa, containing the Buddha's forehead bone. Reconstructed in the twentieth-century, preserving its original compound wall and entrance ways.

vamsa or *Lalitadhatu-vamsa*).[3] The full text has not been published in English, but bits and pieces from it are recounted in the 15th-century inscriptions at the Shwedagon and a 16th-century Chiang Mai chronicle. The Pali text was followed somewhat later by a Sinhalese version that differed only slightly. The text was of southern origin and highlighted the role of King Kakavanna whose capital was Mahagama, or Great City, now an archaeological site famous for its Tissamaharama Stupa in southeastern Sri Lanka. Short inscriptions found in the nearby Yala National Park likely referred to Kakavanna. In northern traditions, represented by the *Mahavamsa*, Kakavanna was viewed as weak and timid, in contrast with his heroic son Dutthagamani. The southern chronicle tradition, however, paints him as a nation-builder combining courage and wisdom. He was also a great Buddhist patron in antiquity, gifting to the *sangha* silk cloth from foreign ships reaching his realm, according to an inscription.[4]

Dutthagamani's mother, forced to flee from Kelaniya to the south coast, wed King Kakavanna. The plaster images, resembling Mary cradling Jesus, suggests how patrons in both traditions employed the same artists. Kataragama.

The story unfolds in the *Dhatu-vamsa* when the Buddha foretold that both his forehead-bone and right canine tooth were destined to be entrusted to King Kakavanna. The predictions were uttered on the Buddha's third visit to the island but the *Mahavamsa* made no mention of this episode or these two relics. The Buddha declared this prophesy at Seru, an unidentified location that was probably Mahagama or its environs in southern Ceylon.[5]

The history of the forehead-bone relic (P: *Nalata-dhatu*) begins at the Buddha's cremation when the relic was presented to the Malla kingdom in northeast India. (The forehead bone is the skull's frontal section extending to the upper part of the eye sockets.) The relic was passed on from the Malla realm to locations in India where the Buddha had resided. It was eventually given, in the second century BCE, to Kakavanna in Lanka by a local king who was related to a brother of Anuradhapura's Devanampiya Tissa. Although Kakavanna was based in the south, his queen came from the Kelaniya monastery and became the mother of the warrior-king Dutthagamani. The chronicle also added that the forehead-bone-relic would set itself on the forehead of a Buddha. Additionally, there were two hair-relics of the Buddha obtained from a snake-king named Jayasena who snatched them from the brothers Tapussa and Bhallika; these hair-relics, according to the prophecy, were to be placed on the head of the same Buddha image with the forehead-bone-relic.[6] It is tantalizing to speculate that these descriptions in the *Dhatu-vamsa* recount an earlier real-life enshrinement in Sri Lanka.

Sakka, above, removing a stolen tooth-relic from Dona's turban. Only a single relic was taken in standard versions but Dona secreted away three tooth-relics in the *Dhatu-vamsa*.

The Suruvila and Somavathiya stupas were linked together in modern times since the two were connected in the *Dhatu-vamsa*. The connection was Kakavanna's sister, Somadevi, who was entrusted with enshrining the tooth-relic in the stupa that now bears her name, Somawathiya. This tooth-relic was taken from the Buddha's funeral pyre by the brahman named Dona who in standard Pali and Sinhalese sources secreted in his turban only a single tooth-relic later taken from him by the god Sakka. In the *Dhatu-vamsa*, however, Dona took three tooth-relics away from the pyre, one hidden in his turban,

The original myths attched to the two ancient stupas were lost but legends in the *Dhatu-vamsa* chronicle were questionably tied to the two stupas in the twentieth century by D. Sumedankara (1894-1984).

another inside his clothes and the third between his toes. One is now thought to be enshrined at Somavathiya. In the *Dhatu-vamsa*, the stupa was located in Soma-nagara, or Soma City.

The fortunes of these two abandoned stupa sites changed overnight when a young monk named D. Sumedankara (1894-1984) ventured from his base in the south into the jungle in search of Seru in the early 1920s. His discovery, near Trincomalee, was also prompted by a dream of a ruinous stupa at Seru. This dream is scarcely surprising since the connection between the forehead bone and Seru, told first in the *Dhatu-vamsa*, was also repeated in a Sinhalese version of the same chronicle published in 1890. It was likely this 1890-text that Sumedankara used for his journey north. Moreover, he was at that very time editing a Sinhalese version of the Pali text that was published in 1924 and the legends must have been swirling in his mind as he set forth on his mission of discovery. But the most important tip for locating the stupa was that the memory of Seruwila survived in the early 19th century. However, it is hard to explain how Seru came to be located in northeastern Sri Lanka since Seru was placed in the south, or Ruhana, in the *Dhatu-vamsa*. Also, the few inscriptions found at Somavathiya make no mention of King Kakavanna or any relics but only to a monastery founded by a prince.[7]

Like Seruvila, the Somavathiya Stupa was home to scores of first-millennium stone fragments and inscriptions stretching over acres. Cleared by the Department of Archaeology in the 1960s, the original stupa was found to be only some two metres high with bricks dated to the first century BCE.[8] The belief today is that the stupa contains one of the Buddha's canine teeth, based on the *Dhatu-vamsa* narrartive, but excavations have yielded no relics. The stupa has no surviving ancient myths and any connection with a tooth-relic is overshadowed today by mysterious lights seen shooting from the stupa's spire. Other strange lights were interpreted as flying saucers paying homage. Large posters throughout the compound depict such extraterrestial events while the site's association with the tooth-relic is now consigned to a small signboard set up by the Department of Archaeology.

Guards outside a bunker in which a relic was sent for safety by a deity. The narratives of certain sacred sites feature hidden or lost relics. Myathalun Pagoda, Magwe, Burma.

A discovery in 1960 of a stone inscription nine kilometres miles from Tissamaharama confirmed the southern origin of the *Dhatu-vamsa*. The inscription was a 10th-century land grant to the nearby Tissamaharama stupa, or 'Tisaramrad Maha-vehera', said to be built by the King Kakavanna to contain the Buddha's 'left tooth of the lower jaw [lower left canine]'. In the *Chronicle of the Tooth Relic* (P: *Datha-vamsa*), another canine tooth was also said to be from the left side but did not specify if it was an upper or lower canine; this tooth is now thought to be in Kandy. Since the relic in Kandy is believed to have arrived in Anuradhapura in the fourth century CE, this lower left canine tooth was, in legend, in southern Ceylon long before, during the reign of Kakavanna in the second century BCE. Perhaps this southern tooth-relic legend arose in the tenth century as a response to Anuradhapura's tooth-relic whose fame increased during the same period. Today, the Tissamaharama stupa is said to

The tooth-relic at the Somavathiya stupa has been recently overshadowed by mysterious lights and flying saucers hovering above the stupa.

enshrine the forehead-bone.[9] The southern origin of the *Datha-vamsa* is further evidence that the two ancient stupas in the northeast near Trincomalee were never associated with this original narrative.

Palm-leaf manuscripts of the *Dhatu-vamsa* were also transmitted to Southeast Asia where Kakavanna became widely connected with the enshrinement of the forehead-bone and the tooth- and hair-relics. The late 15th-century trilingual inscriptions at the Shwedagon Pagoda wove in select portions of the *Dhatu-vamsa*, while in Thailand, the early 16th-century Chiang Mai chronicle summarized the *Dhatu-vamsa* in a long section. The attention given to this Sri Lankan tradition in Burma and Thailand shows how the *Dhatu-vasma* had become an integral part of the *sangha's* collective history. Even in 19th-century Burma the *Nalatadhatu-vamsa* was invoked to distinguish between the forehead-bone-relic and the cranial-protuberance-relic (P: *unhisa*).[10]

Sumedankara belonged to a loose movement of 'pioneer monks' that began in the mid-19th century and continued into the 1940s, living among neglected archaeological sites such as Anuradhapura. Sumedankara formed the Seruwila Mangala Maha Chetiya Society whose mission was to rebuild the stupa. The 'mound of earth' found by the monk in 1921 was transformed ten years later into a large whitewashed stupa, with the finished project featured in *The Buddhist Annual of Ceylon* of 1932. The site's fame never stopped growing and by 1979 the government declared Seruwila a 'sacred city', a provocative decision since many Tamils and Muslims lived in the region.[11] Sumedankara was eventually appointed head of the *sangha* in the Eastern Province before his death in 1984.

The snake-king Jayasena stealing two hair-relics became part of Burma's Shwedagon Pagoda legend by the 15th century. The relics are enshrined in a stupa on Haigyi Island, south of Pathein in the Irrawaddy Delta.

The discovery and rebuilding of the stupas at Seruvila and Somawathiya demonstrate the tenacity of old legends which even in the 20th century can become attached to ruinous monuments to which they never belonged. It is also a reminder of how the miraculous uncovering of lost sites becomes part of a site's aura. These two stupas also highlight the critical role of charismatic monks who marshalled private and government investment. Abandoned stupas and temples whose legends were lost are then like books with blank pages, waiting for later generations to furnish the text. How many temples or stupas over the millennia have adopted myths that had little or nothing to do with their original foundation legends?

ATTANAGALLA

ATTANAGALLA: THE KING WITH NEITHER A HEAD NOR A KINGDOM

Sanghabodhi's cremation is marked by a stupa within this octagonal structure. The outer circular stone base dates from the seventh or eighth century.

This pilgrimage site outside of Colombo commemorates a king named Sanghabodhi (247-249) who severed his own head for the good of the realm. No archaeological finds are connected to this ruler but his biography became attached centuries later to a surviving stupa base at Attanagalla dating to the late Anuradhapura period. This site is another example of how centuries-old legends can be revived and tied to stupas to which they never belonged. Attanagalla also shows how even secular themes, such as a king's life-story, are adapted into a religious context. Few Sri Lankan Buddhists are unfamiliar with the king's tale and keeping his memory alive are paintings and sculptures of Sanghabodhi on view in countless temples up and down the country.

Sanghabodhi's life highlights the juxtaposition of good and bad actions (P: *papas*). The former is always rewarded and the latter never goes unanswered. For his compassion (P: *karuna*), Sanghabodhi was described as a 'great being' (P: *'mahasatta'*), suggeting that he could be considered 'an earthly, royal bodhisattva'. (Mhv: 36: 90) Other kings also modelled their lives on bodhisattas and others aspired to Buddhahood. (Cv: 37. 109, 180; 42.1; 50. 65) Indeed, the Buddha himself even prophesied that 'none but ... Bodhisattas would become kings of prosperous Lanka'. The king's fame was sealed since his name was prefaced to the titles of every other ruling monarch for

Previous page:
Sanghabodhi's father presenting his son to the monastery's abbot as a novice monk. Watercolour. 1890-1910. Asian Civilizations Museum, Singapore.

much of the second millennium, alternating with the title of another ruler named Silameghavanna.[1] The Sanghabodhi moniker was also adopted by Sri Lankan Tamil kings as Shri Cankapoti-varma.

His birthplace was Mahiyangana, the first spot the Buddha visited in Lanka. (Mhv. 36. 58-97) He and two friends, Sanghatissa and Gothabhaya (249-262), travelled to Anuradhapura to play out their destiny. En route, a blind man uttered a prophecy overheard by only Gothabhaya: that the three friends will become successive rulers but that his reign would be the longest. The three reached Anuradhapura where they slew the sitting monarch. Sanghatissa was then raised to the throne but soon succumbed to a poisoned *jambu* fruit. The crown then passed to Sanghabodhi, the blind man's prediction unfolding, like the fateful prophecy that shadowed Achilles.

Sanghabodhi, about to remove his head and hand it to the peasant.

Sanghabodhi, now king, was forever quick to sacrifice himself for the common good. On one occasion, when a drought afflicted his kingdom, he vowed that he would prostrate himself in the compound of the Ruvanvali Stupa until it began to rain. (Mhv: 36. 76) Despite such compassionate acts, the king's former friend, Gothabhaya, turned on him. Fearing bloodshed, Sanghabodhi fled to an unnamed location in the forest where he was offered food by a peasant. To repay this kindness, Sanghabodhi severed his own head and handed it to the poor man, realizing that the king would be only too glad to pay a handsome penny to the one bringing him proof of his rival's demise. Presenting the king's head at court, the peasant was rewarded with a sack of gold, proving how a trifling act of kindness can lead to riches. None of these episodes in the *Mahavamsa* appeared in the earlier *Dipavamsa* that accorded only two verses to Sanghabodhi which even omitted the conflict with his arch-enemy. (Dpv: 22. 53-54)

The king's sacrifice of his head belonged to a deep well of lore in the Buddhist world in the first millennium. One strong parallel is the legendary king Chandraprabha who presented his head to a villainous brahman in Gandhara. A stupa in Gandhara even commemorated where 'Chandraprabha gave his head as alms to a Brahman'. The tale also appeared in the *Sutra of the Wise and Foolish*, a Sanskrit work translated from a Central Asian language into Chinese in the fifth century and depicted among the Dunhuang murals. Another parallel was Asoka's brother, as a monk, who allowed himself to be beheaded in order for a poor cowherder and his wife to collect a reward from Asoka; a repentant Asoka, then ordered the cessation of capital punishment.[2] These examples indicate that Sanghabodhi's sacrifice of his head was part of a much larger tradition. However, why the legendary events in this king's brief two-year reign grew to be of such significance in Sri Lanka has no ready answers. In truth, Sanghabodhi may have been dethroned and killed by a rival, but, like Kassapa of Sigiriya, myths swelled around his biography later to mould the king into a model of Buddhist deportment.

A *naga*-guardian from perhaps the time when Parakramabahu II (1234-1269) restored the seventh-or eighth-century stupa.

A Stupa for a Crown

This aforementioned brief *Mahavamsa* account was centuries later vastly expanded into a Pali chronicle extolling Attanagalla. This work in mixed verse and prose is *The Chronicle of Elephant Rock Forest* (P: *Hatthavanagalla-vamsa*). The place name, Hatthavanagalla, was shortened to the Sinhalese Attanagalla, or Elephant Rock. The text was composed at the behest of Parakramabahu II (1234-1269) and can be considered a shrine-chronicle, similar to the *Thupavamsa* focussed on the Ruvanveli Stupa. Why the Sanghabodhi legend, though likely popular over the ages, blossomed at this king's court cannot be easily explained. Nevertheless, Sanghabodhi was a paragon of virtue that any ruler would wish to emulate.[3]

Parakramabahu's capital, Dambadeniya, was only 40 kilometres north of Attanagalla, and there is every reason to think that this king sponsored the restoration of an ancient stupa there. The only surviving portion of the original stupa is the circular stone foundation, over a metre high, that is probably dated to the seventh or eighth century.[4] A pair of *naga*-guardian figures may belong to the time of Parakramabahu's restoration but otherwise no sculpture from that period can be identified.

Why this specific location came to attract so much attention in the 13th century was likely its ancient but semi-abandoned ruinous monuments. In as much as the king's story was interpreted literally, there understandably arose a desire to locate the very spot in the hoary past where his death occurred. Many parallels can be cited, such as how a Roman amphitheatre in Wales was taken to be King Arthur's Round Table or how the pyramids were thought to be the granaries of Alexander the Great. Although Attanagalla was never connected to Sanghabodhi, Parakramabahu commanded his minister to perform the cremation of his father there, honoured by a stupa, and to construct a three-storied temple. (Cv: 85. 76) Over the spot where Sanghabodhi was cremated, the king erected a stupa enclosed within a circular shrine of two stories, said to serve as a 'a crown' for Sanghabodhi's head.[5] Inside the stupa were enshrined unspecified relics of the Buddha.

The brief episodes in the *Mahavamsa* were expanded into separate chapters, with some passages drawn from a Sanskrit collection of *Jatakas* known as the *Jatakamala*. Sinhalese translations from the Pali followed in the next century, the earliest being commissioned in 1392. Another was composed at Kotte in the 15th century. The numerous 19th-century Sanghabodhi palm-leaf manuscripts testify to the story's enduring popularity. Also, sharply abbreviated versions of his life now and then also appeared in various sources. The 13th-century chronicle was translated into English in 1866 by the antiquarian James d'Alwis (1823-1878) whose introduction included his first-hand observations at Attanagalla.[6]

The chief difference between the *Mahavamsa* and the later Pali chronicle is the emphasis on the redemption of Sanghbodhi's rival for driving the king into the forest and his resultant suicide.

The rival king's sin only grew since it included the death of Sanghabodhi's queen who died upon discovering her headless husband. In the *Mahavamsa*, the king's nemesis showed no remorse but his penance becomes a major theme in the later chronicle. He thus openly queried 'How shall I be released from such a sin?' He reasoned that only 'highly meritorious acts' could expiate his wrongdoing.[7]

This later chronicle also differs in small details from the *Mahavamsa*. For example, Sanghabodhi was described as a prince and given his name when his father placed him in a monastery as a child. Other differences from the Mahavamsa was the king venturing into the forest and discovering the beheaded Sanghabodhi and the deceased queen. Also, in the chronicle, the king fastened a head of gold to Sanghabodhi's body and staged a lavish cremation ritual for the former king and queen.

The cremation of Sanghabodhi and his queen. The remorseful king presides on the right. Watercolour. Circa 1890-1910. Asian Civilizations Museum, Singapore.

Sangahbodhi's queen expired when she discovered her husband. Attanagalla.

Sanghabodhi's head hovering in the air in the court of his nemesis. Mural by H. Mendis Silva. Circa 1930s. Image-house, Attanagalla.

The Stupa today

The only surviving portion of the original stupa construction is the circular stone foundation that can probably be dated in the seventh or eight century, that is, toward the close of the Anuradhapura period. Two concentric rows of stone pillars now encircle the stupa, with an inner ring of eight and an outer one of sixteen. These pillars are usually taken to be of the same age as the stupa's foundation and were identified with an ancient building type known as a stupa-temple [P: *cetiya-ghara*], or *vatadage*.[8] However, these simply designed pillars show no connection with others at Anuradhapura or at other sites. Moreover, it is unlikely that all 24 pillars would survive in such pristine condition and in their original positions. For the same reasons, it is unkikely that these pillars can be connected to Parakramabahu's restorations in the 13th century. It is true that Parakramabahu constructed at Attanagalla a covered circular stupa, known as a *vatadage*-style stupa, attested in the *Pujavaliya* and in the Pali chronicle where an equivalent term is used (S: '*vattula-vimana*').[9]

The pillars probably belong to the second half of the 18th century in the Kandyan period when the present octagonal brick wall enclosing the stupa was built. The murals on the inner face of the wall feature the Twenty-four Buddhas, each identified by captions, and two parallel rows of *arahants,* each standing beneath a semi-circular arch, a borrowing from European design. The site's patrons during this era may have been connected to Kandy since the Dutch gave permission for a Kandyan king to restore the nearby Kelaniya stupa in the mid-eighteenth century. The distance between the Kelaniya monastery and Attanagalla is only 30 kilometers so both monuments were within the same cultural orbit.

The two inner circles of stone pillars still supported a sloping tiled-roof in the 1860s. The stupa was heightened sometime after 1928 and required an extension of the wooden roof. A photo from the 1920s shows the temple from the exterior before the roof was heightened sometime in the 1930s.[10] The stone pillars were too short to support the new higher roof and therefore horizontal steel beams were installed on top of the eight inner pillars, topped by eight vertical metal posts that supported the roof. The outer row of sixteen pillars were also too short to support the new roof and today appear awkwardly supporting nothing. A third but shorter circular row of pillars supported the roof's overhang but these were replaced probably in the nineteenth century. When the stupa was heightened and the roof extended, a wooden cupola was added to enclose the stupa's spire, with painted panels. A caption on one reads in English 'Drawn by S. Peris, Alawwa'. Alawwa is a small town nearby and the artist is otherwise unknown.

Recently, some have argued that Sanghabodhi's legendary suicide did not take place at Attanagalla but at Hattikucchi, an ancient Buddhist site only 30 kilometers south of Anuradhapura. This is unlikely since the *Pujavaliya* of 1266 located the Sanghabodhi

The two rows of pillars encircling the stupa are probably from the time the octagonal wall was established. Circa 1750.

incident to 'the northeast' of the Kelaniya Vihara in 'Maya-ratta', that is, a division in western Lanka that included Attanagalla.[11] (Cv: 87. 24)This modern attempt to relocate an ancient site, with no proof, echoes how Parakramabahu identified this location with Sanghabodhi. History is then repeating itself, right before our eyes.

H. Mendis Silva and 'Offering Head for Charity'

Highlights of the later Pali chronicle are told in murals inside a small temple next to the enclosed stupa. This temple was not mentioned by d'Alwis in the 1860s so it was probably built around 1878, suggested by a fragmentary painted inscription next to the recumbent Buddha that opens with 'In the Buddhist Era 2421 [1878] the Attanagalla chief monk named Walpola'.[12] The monk's full name was Walpola Indrajoti whom d'Alwis met in the 1860s. A second but undecipherable date perhaps listed the temple's

A reclining Buddha concealed by a curtain in Attanagalla's image-hall. Murals, by H. Mendis Silva. Circa 1930s.

Sanghabodhi offers himself to a man-eating ogre. Mural by H. Mendis Silva. Circa 1930s. Image-hall. Attanagalla.

completion date. A possible portrait sculpture of this head monk projects from a wall in a specially created niche, a rare if not unique feature in temples of this period. The large recumbent Buddha set against the long rear wall is the chief focus, like numerous temples of this age. Original murals from the late nineteenth century may have been completely painted over in the 1930s by an opaque layer of red paint, seen in numerous spots where the last layer of painting has chipped off. The murals we see today are probably from the 1930s.

The chief artist was H. Mendis Silva who signed his work twice, once on each wall in minuscule English characters. He is otherwise unknown but his work is likely to come up in field surveys. The Twenty-four Buddhas begin above the reclining Buddha and run clockwise, each identified by a Sinhalese caption and an English numeral. On the rear wall are the Buddha's Seven Weeks at Bodh Gaya. In connection with the seventh week the god Sakka is shown with four arms, with two of Vishnu's attributes, the conch and the discus. A lower hand holds tooth-picks (P: *dantakattha*) made from a stiff portion of the betel-leaf vine, known as *nagalata*, presented by Sakka to the Buddha. Next, Sakka presents water to the Buddha from the celestial Anatotta Lake, shown with the usual four creatures, as it appears at Dambulla. Painters were probably guided by an unidentified Sinhalese text based ultimately on the Pali *Nidanakatha*.[13]

The Twenty-four Buddhas and *arahants* on the octagonal wall surrounding the stupa. Circa 1750.

A stylish gent of the times. Muralists blended ancient myths into modern settings. Above the central doorway.

A mural on one side wall shows the god Kataragama with his six heads and twelve arms. To the right is an unidentified figure with a snake face who holds a garland in both hands. A snake-headed figure, known as Ketu, is one of the Guardians of the Eight Directions but this deity usually holds a fish. Above the central doorway is a roundel with a dashing gent sporting a necktie and moustache.

Key episodes in Sanghabodhi's biography are described by short Sinhalese captions. The scenes may have been based in whole or in part on illustrations in pamphlets that ultimately drew upon the later Pali chronicle and its many recensions. One long panel shows the peasant going to the capital with the king's head in both hands, with an English caption 'Offering Head for Charity'. The wicked king was unwilling to recognize the head until the peasant tossed it into the air where it miraculously hovered before the king's eyes. Struck by terror as much as remorse, the king vowed to expiate his treachery and the head was placed on a throne and cremated with due ceremony. The most dramatic caper features the king facing off with a red-eyed demon (P: *yakkha*). In the *Mahavamsa* this takes up less than ten verses but it runs into an entire chapter in the later Pali and Sinhalese versions. (Mhv: 36. 73) The demon infected villagers with a fatal red-eye illness and a burning fever. After an agonizing death, the afflicted became the demon's tasty morsels. The ogre cleverly defended himself, arguing that he never ate living victims but only those who had expired. By this logic, he argued that his *modus operandi* accrued no more bad karma than a jackal surviving on carrion. Sanghabodhi offered himself up to the demon in exchange for saving the realm. The demon relented but only if the king ordered daily food offerings, or *bali*, to be placed outside village entrances. (Mhv: 36. 73)

The last three chapters of the late Pali chronicle describe various monastic structures built by the repentant king, together with a list of the monuments constructed by subsequent kings. A panel at the bottom of the wall shows four of these benefactions. One is a circular temple containing a stupa, with the caption '*vatadage*'. The freshly painted inscriptions beneath the structures are probably copied from the original captions.

Sanghabodhi's Legacy

The memory of the headless king never faded and in 1903 the story was taken up by the famous playwright John de Silva (1857-1922). And in our own time, the Cultural Affairs Ministry groundlessly claimed that the king's ashes had been discovered.[15] Even a popular hip-hop song about the pious king hit the charts in 2000.

As Sanghabodhi severed his head in the second century, a Roman governor in Paris ordered the beheading of the city's bishop who was canonized as St Denis. He later became the patron saint of France, earning a spot among the portal sculptures of Notre Dame Cathedral. The gruesome biographies of the headless Sinhala king and the French saint are reminders of the best and worst in humanity.

Moments before Sanghabodhi severed his head, he threw fingerlings into a nearby pond that immediately 'started to swim about and play'. Into the same pond, he tossed rice prepared by the wife of the peasant whom he met in the forest and the rice immediately sprouted. Seeing these miraculous omens, Sanghabodhi knew that his quest for Buddhahood would succeed and so he severed his head. This incident was not part of the *Mahavamsa* nor in the Pali chronicle but appears, *en passant*, in the seventeenth-century *Rajavilaya*.[14] A pond with fish and water vegetation is therefore often included in murals featuring the headless king. At Attanagalla these two omens are brought to life by a long low stone outcropping next to the temple with a wide artificial cavity always filled with water and flowers.

The fingerlings in the pond were part of an omen. Raja Maha Viharaya. Kotte. Circa 1880. Courtesy Samerchai Poolsuwan.

DEVINUVARA

DEVINUVARA: 'IN THE GUISE OF A WANDERING ASCETIC'

Sinhala Buddhists are now the principal worshippers.

Although now a small sleepy town at Sri Lanka's southernmost tip, Devinuvara was for centuries Sri Lanka's foremost centre of Vishnu worship. No myths explain why this location came to be associated with Vishnu, but the deity's popularity here grew in tandem with the town's rise as a coastal commercial hub. It was once the home of one of Ceylon's grandest temples but only meagre stone fragments have survived and even these cannot be safely attributed to the temple. The present temple went up in the 1950s and Sinhala Buddhists are the predominant worshippers.

The temple is dedicated to a Hindu deity but brahman priests are nowhere evident, only Sinhala ritualists, or *kapuralas,* who receive fruit, flowers or bank notes that are gifted to the deity. Above the sanctum's entrance is a painted Sinhalese inscription, 'Residence of the God Vishnu' and another, in Sanskrit, 'Homage to the God Vishnu' in North Indian characters. Access to the inner sanctum is strictly controlled and photography is forbidden.

The trajectory of Vishnu worship among Sinhala Buddhists began in the first millennium when the god was known as Upulvan. The earliest reference appears in the fourth-century *Dipavamsa* wherein the Buddha 'handed over the business of guarding the island' to Upulvan. (Dpv: 9.24) The Sinhalese Upulvan derives from the Pali Uppalavanna (S: Utpalavarna), meaning 'blue-lotus-hued', one of Vishnu's many epithets. This god Upulvan, 'in the guise of a wandering ascetic', greeted the island's first settlers and tied protective threads, or *pirit nula*, on their wrists to protect them from an ogress. (Mhv: 7.5-9) Upulvan's role as Sri Lanka's guardian was thus fixed very early and was interlaced with the island's legendary founding, thereby grafting an indigenous myth with the life of the Buddha. How Upulvan was transfigured over the centuries into Vishnu is an intellectual Gordian Knot that has been brilliantly unraveled.[1]

The earliest solid information about Devinuvara, or City of God, is a ninth-century inscription referring to villages donated to a Buddhist establishment called the 'Kihirali-*pirivana* of Giriyala'. Both Kihirali and Giriyala were used interchangeable in ancient sources for the same location, with many variations. A king named Dappula I (661-664) is credited with constructing the 'Khadirali-vihara' in the *Culavamsa* and

Previous page:
The site began in the middle of the first millennium but today's Vishnu temple was constructed in the 1950s.

for making an offering to an unnamed deity, presumed to be Upulvan. This king's connection with the temple is repeated in *Praise of the Tooth-Relic* (*Dalada-sirita*) wherein the deity is named Upulvan.[2] Dappula ruled in the south, in ancient Ruhuna, but his role in the site's formation is known only in the *Culavamsa*. (Cv: 45.48) Dappula's legendary association with Devinuvara was never forgotten and was even recounted in the 19th century.[3] Such linking of a site's foundations to semi-legendary kings was commonplace in the Theravada world.

A peacock with a palm-leaf text refers to the Sinhalese poem, the *Mayura Sandesaya*.

The rebuilt stupa, just steps away from the Vishnu temple, was probably founded in the seventh century, lending weight to Dappula's association with the site. Stone pillars in two concentric rows originally supported a sloping circular wooden roof over the stupa, conforming to an early building type known as *vatadage*. A handful of these pillars have survived, along with a standing limestone Buddha.[4]

Devinuvara joined the island's most venerated spots by the 12th century, proved by a visit by Nissankamalla (1187-96) whose pilgrimage from Polonnuruva included Anuradhapura and Kelaniya. This king left no trace here but no more than fifty years later a Sinhalese record, from the time of Parakramabahu II (1236-70), indicates the presence of a Buddhist and Hindu trading centre. It opens with homage to the Buddha and mentions 'Devinura' and a port named Tendira, or 'Tendira-tota'. Officials were commanded to enforce the levies on goods 'coming from foreign countries' and warned that no 'improprieties' should befall the town's '*viharas*, *devalas* [*devalaya*], *agraharas* and *kovils*'.[5] A *vihara* is a Buddhist establishment, while a *devalaya* is a shrine that can be associated with one of the island's guardian deities that included Upulvan. An *agrahara* is land gifted to brahmans or a brahman settlement and a *kovil* is a Tamil term for a Hindu temple. The major *devalaya* at Devinuvara was then probably dedicated to Upulvan and the *kovils* were Hindu temples patronized by Tamils. This inscription now stands near the temple's entrance, with a stupa incised on the top of one side and the sun and moon on the other. Parakramabahu is also credited with rebuilding a temple here honouring the lotus-hued god, 'Uppalavanna', also called King of the Gods, or '*devaraja*'; this king was also the first to sponsor Devinuvara's annual procession. (Cv: 85-89) No reference is made to Islamic traders whose role greatly expanded on the coastline in the following centuries.

Deities on horses above the shrine doorway, on the right. Rabbit in the moon, above.

Later, a rebuilding of the temple of the 'god-king' (Vishnu), was attributed to Parakramabahu IV (1302-26). Upulvan's popularity extended far from the south coast by then, indicated by a donated image of Upulvan east of Colombo. (Cv: 90. 101) A few decades later, a minister donated a 'three-storied image house for a standing image', probably a sculpture of Upulvan.

Upulvan and his consort. Inner corridor, Lankatilaka Temple. Dated 1344. Courtesy Osmund Bopearachchi.

The same king also made a donation of a 'stone image house' at Kanchipuram in Tamil Nadu, underscoring Sri Lanka's close ties to South India.[6]

By the 14th century, Upulvan and Vishnu were assigned to separate classes of deities within the Sinhala-Buddhist pantheon, attested by two inscriptions dated to 1344, near Kandy. One category included major pan-Hindu and Buddhist deities, such as Vishnu, Shiva and Maitreya, while the second was comprised of 'divine kings', or deities that were linked in a special way to Lanka, namely, Kihireli-Upulvan (at Devinuvara), Sumana (at Mahiyangana), Vibhishana (at Kelaniya), and Ganesha-Kanda-Kumara (at Kataragama). The second inscription, also from 1344, labels these deities Great Kings and describes them as Supreme World Protectors. (S: 'Adi Lokapala') Two later stone inscriptions from near Kandy also refer to Upulvan (S: '*Utpalavarnna*'), and 'Kihirali-Upulvan', in connection with the World Protectors.[7] The term 'Kihirali-Upulvan' is still in use among prayers that *kapuralas* recite at various sites.

These World Protectors are represented by sculptures found within the inner corridor of the Lankatilaka temple (Ganesha, Vibhishana, Upulvan, Saman, and Kataragama).[8] Upulvan is shown with four arms, one holding a discus, and standing with his consort. The temple's inscription and the context make it clear that this deity was known as Upulvan. These two figures, made of brick and painted plaster, are probably original to 1344 but with numerous refurbishments.

Upulvan was also important to the Kotte kings, ruling near Colombo, suggested by a stone inscription dated to 1429 at Devinuvara that granted a coconut grove to the '*maha-vihara*' and to an 'image-house' that was presumably for Upulvan. One donation recorded a land grant to 'Utpalavarnna' the Divine King, or '*divya raja*', during the reign of Kotte's Parakramabahu VIII (1477-89). Another record, a copper-plate land grant dated 1520, provided further support to the temple from the Kotte rulers. Vishnu and Upulvan eventually coalesced by the 16th century, with the deity playing a major role in Kandyan state rituals under the name Vishnu. Partly responsible for this was a wave of Hindu influence introduced into Sri Lanka from South India, especially from Kerala where Vishnu worship was longstanding. In Kotte itself large temples were dedicated to the four major protective deities, listed as Kihireli-Upulvan, Saman-Boksel, Vibhishana and Kanda-kumara.[9]

Shaiva worship was also present at Devinuvara, known from an inscription dated to 1510 referring to a Hindu temple, or '*kovil*', named Nagarisha. There was also a stone Ganesha and a *linga* found here. In the 20th century, Devinuvara was one of five principal Sri

Lankan Shiva temples, known as the Pancha Ishvaram, modeled on a group of five in South India. The temple was called Tondeshvaram but no evidence points to its physical existence and its inclusion within this group was probably a Tamil attempt to tap into Devinuvara's countrywide fame. It was the Vishnu temple here that always overshadowed any other temples.[10]

How artists depicted Upulvan is guesswork, since early images or brief descriptions of the god are unknown, apart from the rare example from the Lankatilaka temple. Upulvan's appearance certainly took many guises over the centuries but a rare, if not unique, example, was shown on a lost cloth painting from Devinuvara copied in about 1805. It was found in the chief temple that was then a 'humble sanctuary built of mud with a thatched roof, dedicated to Vishnu'. The deity is captioned 'Vishnu'. The two-armed god (normally shown with four arms) stands upon his vehicle, Garuda. Also, the deity holds weapons not usually associated with Vishnu, such as a bow. His left hand grasps perhaps a long arrow or spear or cane, the latter a key attribute of a related deity named Dadimunda. (see below) In later traditions, Upulvan was known as the only god strong enough to assist the Buddha in his defeat of Mara, using his bow. Images of Vishnu in Tamil temples are completely different in appearance, following standard Hindu models.[11]

Devinuvara was also a place where vows were sworn, much like oaths declared before the Vishnu sculpture in Cave 1 at Dambulla. In fact, the Dambulla standing Vishnu image was believed to be originally from Devinuvara, thereby linking the Dambulla image with the famous Vishnu site in the south. Vishnu and Upulvan also

Ancillary shrines contain a number of deities. Vishnu centre, with Pattini, left, Sarasvati, centre, and Dadimunda, right.

A now-missing cloth painting showing Vishnu on his Garuda and Kataragama astride his peacock. After Cordiner, p.116.

appear in numerous verse-incantations and ballads in connection with defeated demons. Vishnu was also even entwined in the story of Kataragama's local wife.[12] These examples indicate how major deities were absorbed into an expansive pantheon that existed alongside orthodox Hindu and Buddhist traditions.

'Five hundred women who sing and dance all night'

The fullest account of Devinuvara comes from Ibn Battuta who arrived here in 1344, the same year that the Lankatilaka Temple went up near Kandy. He observed: 'Dinawar [Devinuvara] ... is inhabited by merchants. In this town is an idol known as Dinawar, in a vast temple, in which there are about a thousand Brahman and *jugis* [yogis], placed in a large temple and about 500 women, daughters of the Hindus, who sing and dance every night in front of the idol ... The idol itself is of gold, about a man's height, and in the places of its eyes it has two great rubies'. 500 dancers may seem like hyperbole but an 11th-century South Indian inscription recorded the personal names of exactly 400 dancers assigned to a new royal temple in Tanjore. Even as late as the 17th century, Devinuruva was known for its dancing girls, recorded in Catholic documents.[13]

A 14th-century doorway. Its original location at Devinuruva is unknown.

Ibn Battuta saw no Muslim or Tamil traders, suggesting that the city's role as an international coastal emporium was yet to come. Also, he says nothing about Buddhist worship, probably indicating that it took second place. Buddhism was present at the time, however, attested by a two-storied image-house with a recumbent Buddha built by a king in the 'City of God' (P: 'Devapura'). (Cv: 90. 94) A large stone doorway may be from this time. Its original position is unknown but it was in this same location during the early British period.[14] In the lintel's centre is the seated goddess Lakshmi. Other remains, such as four matching 16th-century stone balustrades, are tangible proof of continuous building. There is however no sure way to connect any of these finds to any temples or stupas.

The Ming Connection

The temple's growing importance is highlighted by a trilingual inscription issued here by the Ming emperor, Yongle (1402-25), exactly 65 years after Ibn Battuta's visit. The inscribed tablet stands nearly two metres high and is a centrepiece in the Colombo Museum. It was removed from Devinuruva and taken to Galle where it was discovered outside the city walls in 1911. It may have been carved and incised in China and brought to Lanka, or sculpted locally; the stone has not been subject to scientific testing. A Chinese source from 1436 noted that a stone tablet was erected in Sri Lanka in the seventh year of the king's reign and so this is likely the very inscription now in the Colombo Museum. A Portuguese account from 1638 also refers to a Chinese inscription in Devinuvara. There may also have been other multilingual inscriptions since a Portuguese chronicler noted that at a temple near Matara, probably Devinuruva, were 'stone pillars which the Kings of China ordered to be set up with Letters of that Nation'.[15]

Composed in the emperor's seventh regnal year, or 1409, the text records donations in Chinese, Tamil and Persian. The absence of Sinhalese suggests that Sinhalas were on the margins of this international trade. The mission to Devinuvara was the second of seven Ming expeditions to the region between 1405 and 1433, led by the famous Muslim eunuch Zheng He whose name appears in the Tamil portion. Zheng He was also in Thailand, in 1408, and metal plaques inscribed in Chinese were found in the crypt of Wat Ratchaburana in Ayutthaya.[16]

The Chinese portion is dedicated to the Buddha, the 'Merciful and Honoured One', with 'oblations of gold and silver, gold embroidered jewelled banners of variegated silk … together with many other offerings'. The fame of Chinese silk in Lanka was even noted by the fifth-century Pali commentator Buddhaghosa. The inscription made no mention of the temple at Devinuruva but 'the Mountain of Ceylon' (Sri Pada?) is referred to in the context of the gifts. The Tamil portion details offerings made to Tenavari-nayinar, or God of Tenavarai (Devinuvara), in the kingdom of 'Ilankai', that is, Lanka. The donated gifts closely follow the list of objects contained in the Chinese portion but adds five standing lamps from Java, or *'cavan'*, together with ten pieces of sandalwood, or *'cantana'* (S: *candana*) The text's dialect is peculiar to the Tamil international trading community.[17]

The Persian section is badly weathered but followed the format of the Tamil and Chinese, with objects including embroidered articles and incense burners. The phrase 'light of Islam' appears but whether the donation was to a mosque or a saint's shrine is lost in lacunae. Other inscriptions, in Arabic, found in Ceylon during this period affirm the role of Muslims in international trade, extending as far as the Mediterranean.[18] Persian was a lingua franca, enabling Ibn Battuta to converse with the Hindu ruler of Jaffna.

A Chinese, Tamil, and Persian inscription, dated 1409, during the time of Ming maritime expansion. Colombo Museum. Courtesy Osmund Bopearachchi.

Female temple dancers, or *devadasis*, were noted in India and Ceylon by Marco Polo, Ibn Battuta and others. The institution is no longer practiced but traditional dance is taught to young girls. A Tamil mother and her daughter in Jaffna.

Perhaps Tamils at Devinuruva venerated Vishnu in a *kovil*, while Sinhalas worshiped Upulvan in a separate temple. It is possible, however, that there was one grand temple for a single deity who was perhaps known by different names to Tamils and Sinhalas. What the temple looked like in Ibn Battuta's day is unknown but it may have resembled two very different 14th-century temples from the same period near Kandy, at Lankatilaka or Gadaladeniya.

'To Rid the Imagination of the heathens ...'

The temple retained its importance throughout the colonial period, beginning with a Portuguese chronicle stating that the 'Pagode of Tanavar' was 'the most celebrated and most resorted to by pilgrims ... excepting that of Adam's Peak'; it was also likened in fame to the grand Koneshvaram temple at Trincomalee. A church document of 1551 even called it the 'chief paguode [*sic*] of Ceilao'. Europeans knew Devinuruva by various names, such as Tanauare and Tanabare, all from the Tamil Tenavarai that derived from Devinuvara. The name was thought to be taken from a 'neighbouring village in which lived the dancing girls of that Pagode' and artisans specializing in copper, silver and gold casting and producing muskets. The town was divided into sections within concentric square walls, each entered by a 'handsome gateway'. The inhabitants included 'persons of every occupation and the chief of these are women dedicated to the service of the *pagode*'.[19] This description is reminiscent of the famous temple cities of South India, such as Madurai, but these were vastly grander than Devinuvara.

The city's chief temple was 'all vaulted above ... and around it many most beautiful chapels'. It also had a gateway with a 'high and strong tower'. The main deity was not described, apart from a reference to a temple cart that 'drew him in procession'. A Portuguese Captain-major writing in 1638, Constantino de Sã de Miranda, identified the god as 'Vesnu Diuira Jurna' (Vishnu Divya Raja), or 'Vishnu, The Divine King'.[20]

The context for the oft-cited destruction of the temple in 1588 was the conflict between the Portuguese and their nemesis, Rajasimha I (1581-1593), based in Sitavaka. One version, compiled many decades later, briefly concluded that 120 soldiers in four ships 'took prizes and captives, and burnt the Pagode of Tanauare.' A more colourful Portuguese version claims that the same fleet, sailing from Colombo, was thwarted by a thunderstorm 'so furious that the ships were well-nigh lost'. Native 'heathens' on board were overheard by Sinhala Christians boasting that the unexpected tempest was proof of their god's power. The Portuguese, now wishing to 'rid the imagination of the heathens of that superstition' attacked on the morrow. They destroyed 'idols [of] more than a thousand of divers forms, some of clay, others of wood, others of copper many of the them gilt'. In this version, the temple's destruction was prompted solely by a desire to prove to the Sinhalas that there pagan gods was powerless to protect the temple. Nevertheless, the tale of the storm persisted for centuries in folklore. The storyline was turned on its head in the 1840s by the claim that the Portuguese ships were destroyed by the thunderstorm as they were sailing away, triggered by a Buddhist monk who 'called upon Buddha for vengeance'.[21]

The temple's destruction was never recorded by an eyewitness but its demolition is taken as a matter of faith by modern historians. Portuguese records from 1593, 1599 and 1614 noted that the temple's land revenues were diverted to the Portuguese, but nothing is said about the destruction of the temple. Also, it is difficult to explain why, only sixteen years after the temple's purported destruction, a drawing was prepared in 1624 by a Portuguese governor Constantino de Sã de Noronha. The Portuguese enjoyed control of this part of the coast until 1632, after which they were confined to the area of Galle. A second drawing from 1624 is a simplified city plan of Devinuvara showing the temple facing either east or west, with a street leading from the temple to the ocean.[22] Today's temple however faces south.

By 1631 Franciscans were active along this coast and recorded that the 'Deva Rajuruvu' temple 'was destroyed and razed ... and in the same place' was built a church with three naves and stone pillars. By then, 'dancing girls' and 'other servants of the temple' were few. This evidence from 1631 suggests that the destruction of the temple did not occur in 1588 but sometime after 1624 and that the temple was perhaps rebuilt when this part of the coast came under Kandyan control. Whether the temple was destroyed or spared, it was described in 1638 as the second largest temple in Ceylon, after Trincomalee.[23] None of the handful of ancient fragments at Devinuvara can be connected to the temple and this is true also for the Koneshvaram Temple in Trincomalee.

Devinuvara was later eclipsed by nearby Matara and Galle and exports from the town had shrunk to only areca nuts by 1635. Following the flight of the Portuguese in the wake of Dutch advances, a temple of some size may have sprung up. For example, a mariner noted that 'one can see from a ship … a white pagode' in the midst of a 'grove of palm trees' at 'Tanadarc'. Another observed in the early 18th century that 'the Pagoda at Dondere' marked the site of 'a well known holy city'. He then listed castes and service groups attached to the temple, such as toddy-tappers and musicians.[24]

By the end of the 18th century, the town's Buddhist and Hindu monuments were in ruin, presumably due to the suspension of royal patronage during the later phases of colonial rule. The same was true for other major temples and centres, such as Kelaniya and Trincomalee. At these places and others, such as at Ratnapura, only stone fragments have survived. Where patronage was never interrupted, such as at the Lankatilaka and Galadeniya, temples have survived in remarkably good condition.

Only sixteen years after the purported destruction of the temple in 1588, this drawing was made in 1624. *Plantas das fortalezas, pagodes & ca. Da ilha de Ceilao*, Folio 209r. Biblioteca Nacional de Madrid.

A city plan of 'Tanavare' from 1624 shows the temple ('pagode'). *Plantas das fortalezas, pagodes & ca. Da ilha de Ceilao*. Folio 210r. Biblioteca Nacional de Madrid.

The main temple from the front.

A European visitor to Devinuvara in 1796 noted nothing about a Hindu temple and referred only to the stupa's restoration, said to contain 'one of the teeth of the sacred elephant'. His sketch showed the stupa, next to the solitary stone doorway still visible in the same location. The entire area, by 1807, was scattered with ruins with 'the poor remains of a Hindoo temple ... built of mud with a thatch roof, dedicated to Vishnu'. The same 'wretched mud hut' appears in a slightly later account. Inside the temple were deities painted on cloth, and inside another shrine was a Buddha image. Above the door was the lion and unicorn adapted from the British coat of arms, prompting one missionary to fret that by this juxtaposition locals will be made to 'think that English people worship Buddha as well as God'. One account pointed to the role that Upulvan played in protecting Vijaya with a 'thread around the Prince's neck'. Another visitor noted that work was proceeding on the stupa that contained 'the bones of the Boudhou [*sic*] and a temple to the Boudhou'. He also placed the town in a cosmological context, assigning it to a cardinal direction, with other deities and commented that the Vishnu temple, known only from the pillars, expressed the 'good will' which Vishnu had 'for Boudhou, whom he accompanied to Ceylon the first time he came here'.[25]

The greatest impression made on 19th-century visitors were the hundreds of granite pillars arranged in 'a long avenue' extending from the main temple 'directly towards the sea … [and] intersected by other rows extending to the right and left', a description that differs little from the city plan of 1624. A watercolour from 1860 shows this sea of pillars.[26]

The Vishnu temple we see today was constructed during the tenure of Edmund Perera Wijetunga, the chief trustee between 1946 and 1958, according to a marble inscription. Another inscription, from 1955, records a gift of bricks, perhaps signalling the year of the groundbreaking. Outside the temple nearby are seven small modern shrines, each dedicated to a popular deity, such as Pattini

Astral deities are depicted on four horizontal registers.

Watercolour by Rev. Frederick Jobson, captioned 'Ruins of Temple to Vishnu, Dondra Ceylon'. 1860. Caroline Simpson Library and Research Collection, Syndey.

and Dadimunda. Such shrines were noted long ago and are similar to those at Kataragama. Pilgrims first make offerings in the main temple, thereby requesting permission to pay homage to the deities in the auxiliary shrines outside. The annual procession here was marred in 2014 when the reliquary atop an elephant fell to the ground, blamed on an inebriated mahout.[27]

Murals feature four parallel registers with scores of astral gods, each identified by Sinhalese captions. The top row features the Twenty-seven Lunar Mansions, (S: *nakshatras*), or constellations, revolving around the moon used in horoscopes. Each of the Lunar Mansions is divided into four steps (P: *pada*). Other deities include the Nine Planets and pan-Indian gods, such as Ganesha, but which are incorporated into an astral pantheon. In the row beneath are gods associated with the days of the week relating to the constellations, such as the lion-headed deity Doloswaka tied to the sign of Libra. These deities show much variation in Lanka and their affinities with South India have not yet been worked out. Devinuruva was known in the fifteenth century for its brahman astronomers and astrologers, described as Tenuvari Perumal brahmans.[28]

A Peacock and a Dove

A handful of poems supplement our picture of Devinuruva, with many composed in the 15th 16th centuries at the Kotte court. One poem, the *Paravi Sandesaya,* features a dove flying from Kotte to 'Devundar' that spoted a Ganesha temple near the beach. The bird then visited a stupa, a Bodhi tree, a recumbent-Buddha shrine, a temple with a seated Buddha and a three-storied monastery. The next day the dove arrived at Upulvan's temple and was delighted by the dancing women. The temple is called the King's Temple, or Raja-ge. This poem is evoked by a dove painted above the temple's side door, captioned in Sinhalese, 'Bringing a Message to Upulvan by the Dove [*paravi*]'. Over the opposite entrance is a flying peacock referring to the *Mayura Sandesaya*. A poem, the *Tisara Sandesaya* from the time of Parakramabahu V (1344-59), describes how the wives of Vishnu and Brahma deserted their spouses to run off with the irresistible Upulvan.[29] Another poem lauding Upulvan is the *Kokila Sandesaya*.

'The poor remains of a Hindoo temple'

The town's only surviving ancient temple, rebuilt completely in the 1940s, sits on a hillock less than a mile north of the main temple and was described in the 19th century as 'the poor remains of a Hindoo temple'. Two nearly equal-sized rooms make up the interior and the roof was perhaps of brick. Its modest dimensions preclude identification with any of the grand temples known from inscriptions or chronicles and its isolated location abutting an uninhabited hillock explains why it has escaped the sprawl of the modern town. It relates most closely to shrines in Tamil Nadu between the seventh and tenth centuries.[30] Many such temples from various periods probably once dotted the area. At least one temple was perched immediately overlooking the rocky coastline, directly south of the main temple, but nothing survives there.

Only this single temple remains from antiquity at Devinuvara. Reconstructed in the 1940s.

The God Moves North

Possible threats to the temple by the Portuguese may have prompted the deity's removal to a location just west of Kandy known as Alut Nuvara, or New Town. The god's identity then merged with a powerful local deity already worshipped there named Dadimunda, or 'the fearless one'. Dadimunda is today often pictured with his jungle fowl, or *Gallus lafeyettii*, an attribute shared by Vishnu in Lanka. Eventually, the deity's shrine was moved from Alut Nuvara to Kandy where the god was first known as Alut Nuvara Deviyo. The ritual paraphernalia connected to the god in Alut Nuvara was transferred to Vishnu's present shrine, the Maha Devale, or Great Shrine, next to the Kandy palace, sometime between 1614 and 1679. This deity at Kandy eventually became identified as Vishnu and is one of the major gods associated with the Temple of the Tooth. However, the Vishnu in Kandy never lost its connections with Upulvan, Devinuvara and Dadimunda of Alut Nuvara, attested by numerous hymns in Kandy and Devinuruva.[31]

Dreaming of a Log

The god Upulvan also became associated with an image made from red sandalwood (*Pterocarpu santalinus*). Upulvan came in a dream to king Dappula to say that a red sandalwood log would wash up on the coast at Devinuvara. When the log duly turned up on the beach, it was fashioned into three images, Upulvan, his consort and their son. This myth appeared first in a 15th-century poem from Kotte, the *Parakumba-sirita,* but it drew upon the *Culavamsa* to the extent that it linked Upulvan to Dappula and Devinuruva. Numerous variations on the 'sandalwood log' myth are still current in local folklore. Even as late as 1947 an English observer was told that the chief deity inside the Vishnu temple next to the palace at Kandy was a 'red sandal-wood image of the God [Vishnu] that miraculously wafted across the sea to Dondra [Devinuvara]'.[32]

The motif of a washed-up log is common to many cultures. For example, St Thomas the Apostle removed a log from Adam's Peak and caused it to drift to the coast of Tamil Nadu, a legend recorded by a 14th-century papal envoy in Lanka. Once on shore, the saint pulled the log from the beach using his miraculous belt presented to him by the mother of Christ. A Burmese legend speaks of a tree trunk that appeared on the river bank at Pagan from the Irrawaddy River; inside the tree were two brother and sister spirits, or *nats*.[33] The most well-known Asian 'floating-log-myth' however underpins the great Jaganath Temple in Puri, Orissa, where the three chief images were carved from a log recovered on the seashore, on the orders of Vishnu.

පුරාණ කිරි විහාරය

KATARAGAMA

Kataragama: 'The grievous disease of love'

Kataragama receiving his spear, or *vel*, from his mother. Sri Mahamariamman Temple, Georgetown, Penang, Malaysia.

Kataragama ranks among the island's most popular pilgrimage destinations. Indeed, few have not made at least one visit here, from fruit vendors to Prime Ministers. From a 'little more than a large clearing in the unending jungle' in the early 20th century, it is now a town of more than 20,000. The chief deity is Hindu, but Sinhala Buddhists are the majority of worshippers, reflecting the site's Sinhalicization beginning in the 19th century.[1]

The deity Kataragama is the focus, together with his two consorts, Tevani and Valli. The god's Sanskrit names include Skanda, Kumara, and Karttikeya, while his favoured Tamil name is Murugan. The god Shiva created Kataragama in order to slay a demon. His weapon was a spear (T: *vel*) that symbolizes the god's all-conquering power that devotees seek to harness for their own benefit. Such prowess has coloured his character, like Hercules and his famous Labours. In Sri Lanka, the god is usually known as Kataragama, synonymous with the location, much as St Santiago lent his name to Santiago de Compostela. The etymology is uncertain but the suffix *gama* is the Sinhalese word for village (P: *gamma).* The complex is officially named Ruhuna Maha Kataragama Devalaya, Ruhuna being an old name for the country's south and *devalaya* denoting a Hindu shrine.

Presenting offerings to the temple's ritualists, *kapuralas*, standing before the sanctum's doors.

Previous page:
The god's chief temple, right. The tree behind the temple is believed to be a descendant of the 'southern branch' of the Bodhi Tree in Bodh Gaya.

Kataragama, Valli and Teveni. The children floating on lotuses evoke Kataragama's birth in the Saravanabhava Lake.

The most widely accepted myth about the god is based on the *Kandha Puranam,* or the *History of Kandha,* compiled in about 1400 in Kanchi, Tamil Nadu. This work mostly dwells on the god's victory over demons but also offers up a classic romance, with a love-struck maiden named Valli whose parents disapprove of Kataragama, or Kandha. Valli herself sprang from 'a doe of shining beauty' that was impregnated by a sage's mere lustful glance.[2] The doe abandoned her offspring in a furrow in which grew a yam known as *valli.* The infant was soon discovered by a hunter-chief and he and his wife reared the youngster whom they named Valli, after the yam. The hunters, in the Sri Lankan version, belonged to the Vadda community. A far more famous goddess who also emerged from the ground was Rama's spouse, Sita, who was also discovered by her adoptive father and named Sita, after the Sanskrit word for furrow.

Valli and the hunters resided on Mount Valli in the versions in Tamil Nadu but in Lankan legends their residence was transposed to a mountain about six kilometres south of Kataragama known as Vadahitikanda. It was here that Valli met Kataragama before coming down the mountain to the present temple site for her marriage. The mountain was a pilgrimage spot once controlled by a Hindu ascetic which was taken over by Buddhists in the 1960s.

The god Kataragama, hearing of Valli's beauty from a sage, was immediately struck by 'the grievous disease of love'. The god then came from India to Lanka and approached Valli in the guise of a hunter. Her father came upon the two and Kataragama hid

Ganesha charges Valli who declares to Kataragama 'Save me and I will do anything you wish!'

by disguising himself as a tree. When the hunter departed, the god assumed human form and pleaded with Valli to come with him to 'where the women of heaven will worship you'.[3] Valli's father suddenly reappeared and the god transformed himself into an elderly ascetic. He requested water and was directed to a spring on the further side of seven hills; these unnamed seven peaks in the Indian Tamil version were later believed to be a range of seven hills surrounding Kataragama.

The old ascetic asked the unsuspecting Valli to 'satisfy his desire'. Horrified at the old man's advances, she ran away, leading Kataragama to ask his brother, the elephant Ganesha, to charge at Valli. (A rogue elephant also played a role in the Tamil *Manimekalai.*) The terrified girl raced into the ascetic's arms, declaring: 'Save me and I will do anything you wish!' By this ruse, Kataragama shed his disguise and took the form of a handsome hunter. Valli returned to her home but was now 'possessed' by an ecstatic love for Kataragama. Her distraught parents locked their 'love-possessed' daughter inside and local female diviners prescribed a 'dance of possession', or *veriyatal*, to rid Valli of this malevolent spirit.[4] At this point, Kataragama appeared and promised the villagers that if they worshipped him, then he would restore Valli's sanity. Valli and Kataragama quickly fled into the jungle but eventually returned to her village where the two were joined in marriage. Valli was introduced to the god's senior wife, the goddess Tevani, who welcomed her as a younger sister. This story from the *History of Kandha* blossomed into numerous variations over many centuries but the basic story-line remained remarkably stable in both India and Sri Lanka. All the myth's major characters and themes enjoyed ancient antecedents, witnessed in a Tamil poem, the *Tirumurukarruppatai*, from the first half of the first millennium.

The senior wife Tevani (T: Tevayani Amman; S: Devasena) was the daughter of Indra and her birth even figured in the *Mahabharata*. Her divine marriage with Kataragama was along predictable traditional lines. In contrast, Valli was an irrepressible village maiden and she and Kataragama could not rest until they were united in love. If Tevani represented traditional social conventions, then Valli stood for flaunting norms and impulsive sexuality. This popular god who enjoyed two wives was never a favourite of Christian missionaries whose criticism drew a rebuke from the famous Hindu Tamil reformer in Jaffna, Arumuka Navalar (1822-79). He countered in his book, *Radiant Wisdom*, that even King David had numerous wives and concubines.[5]

A boyish Kataragama with his spear, or vel. Folk art from a neighbourhood shrine in Jaffna.

Valli's miraculous birth-story finds many parallels. A goddess in Burma sprang from a fruit and later gave birth to the founder of the Shwedagon Pagoda. Other Southeast Asia parallels are children born from ascestics who impregnated deers, a theme in the *Mahabharata*, the *Ramayana* and a *Jataka* (no. 526). In one example, a sage spilled his sperm-infused urine into a 'cup in the rock' that a doe sipped and gave birth to a girl who played a role in the formation of an ancient city in Burma. A pregnant doe also gave birth to twins in the famous *Chamadevi* chronicle in Thailand. These stories from Southeast Asia were recorded only in the second millennium but how far back their origins go and their exact connection to Indian myths have yet to be established. Perhaps the best known miraculous births, however, with global consequences, occurred in Bethlehem and in the Lumbini Grove. Importantly, such births are free of the ritual pollution occasioned by human conception and birthing.[6]

The deity Kataragama has many sides to his character. His 'demonic nature' can be channeled into villainous acts, unlike other major gods with moral restraints. This facet attracts corrupt politicians and criminals seeking to destroy enemies, reminiscent of fervently religious but superstitious Sicilian Mafia bosses. For example, the widow of a crime boss donated a gold plate to the Kataragama temple in 2019 to ward off the evil machinations of her own son.[7]

Kataragama's power is so great and unpredictable that the god can even engender a sense of fear and apprehension, a feature noted as early as the seventeenth century.[8] On the other hand, the god's personality encompasses an innocent boyish nature. In this guise, he is pictured as a pre-adolescent with rosy cheeks, much like a rococo cherub or the boy-god Krishna were it not for his tiny spear, held in one hand like a child's plaything but a reminder of the god's latent power. This aspect of Kataragama evokes unconditional love, resembling a type of Hindu devotion (S: *bhakti*). Kataragama's character then has many facets and none are exclusive. This explains how a devotee can request the god to help locate an ideal marriage partner or ace an exam on one day but on another plead for him to bring down the house on an odious neighbour.

The Temple Today

The rebuilt temple follows the same design as the simple white-washed brick structure pictured in old photographs. The rear inner sanctum is preceded by a long hall and portico from which are suspended hundreds of dried *neem* tree branches. This auspicious tree, the *kohomba* (*Azadiractha indica*), is associated with a deity of the same name.[9]

Access to the temple's sanctum is zealously restricted so there are no reliable descriptions over the ages. It seems that there was never a central image within the sanctum. Instead, the chief object was likely a small metal plaque inscribed with a mystical geometric diagram (S: *yantra*) sacred to Murugan, but the plaque has never been photographed. Murugan's metal *yantra* is often inscribed with six Tamil characters, spelling out one of the deity's epithets, *sa-ra-va-na-bha-va*, after the Himalayan lake in which the god was born. The walls of the temple were in the early nineteenth century adorned with 'different gods and with historical paintings' and a 'mystically painted cloth' covered the ceiling. The deity's spear is the central object in some sanctums and the spears from seven key Sri Lankan temples were at one time taken to Kataragama and consecrated during the annual festival.[10]

The metal *yantra*, concealed in white cloth, was held by the chief ritualist who rides atop an elephant in a nightly procession during the 15-day annual festival beginning in the lunar moon of July-August, or *Asala.* The elephant leaves the main temple and proceeds to Valli's shrine some 300 metres to the south, accompanied by musicians and dancers. The object is deposited inside the goddess' temple for about 30 minutes on each night but on the last night, the plaque remains in Valli's shrine until sunrise.

The festival concludes with the 'water-cutting' ceremony in the nearby Manik Ganga river. A priest first 'cuts' a circle in the water with a 'sanctified sword or rod' into which the metal plaque is submerged and thereby cleansed. This act symbolically stands for washing the garments of the two deities, occasioned by the ritual pollution resulting from the sexual activity during the last night of the festival. In some instances, the metal plaque is placed in a special pot filled with water taken from the circle in the river and this is then returned to the temple sanctum where it remains until the next yearly ceremony. This ritual has ancient roots in Sri Lanka and was observed in 17th-century Kandy.[11]

The principal shrines within the compound today largely match descriptions left by Dr John Davy, a visitor in 1819. For example, a rebuilt Ganesha temple still stands beside the Kataragama shrine. Behind these temples were six 'empty cells' honouring the goddess

Kataragama, Valli and Tevani. From Jaffna's Saddanath Temple. Circa 18th or 19th century. Archaeological Museum, Jaffna.

Pattini and 'five demons', corresponding to the small rebuilt shrines today behind the main temple and dedicated to Pattini, Saman, Huniyam and others. In the sanctum was a throne-like seat made of dry clay draped in a leopard's skin and called Kalanamadima. It was never photographed, but was likely named after an ascetic named Kalyanakiri who was described in a 16th-century Tamil poem to have revived the site's fortunes.[12]

The head priest in the main temple was a brahman in the early 19th century who was assisted by 'twelve Kappurales' [*sic*]'.[13] Brahmans are no longer present and only white-clad Sinhala Buddhist *kapuralas* conduct rituals in the main temple. Their brahman counterparts are now restricted to the Ganesha temple next door where they chant short Sanskrit prayers and receive donations.

Posters show Kataragama astride his peacock in full plumage with his wives. The god is usually pictured with six heads since he was suckled by six women when he was an abandoned infant in the Saravanabhava Lake. Valli, often with a green hue, is on the deity's right, reflecting her superior position despite her status as 'mistress'. These two are also described in South Indian iconographic texts, with Valli holding a lotus and Tevani a blue-lotus. At least one stone image of Skanda was discovered at Polonnuruva, now in the Colombo Museum, and an unpublished sculpture set from Jaffna shows the god with his two wives. A Sri Lankan iconographic source of indeterminate age describes the god with an axe and his peacock mount.[14]

Kesopur Swami. Signed an agreement with Governor Sri Arthur Gordon in 1888 giving control of Kataragama's temples to the Dasanami sect in India. The Tevani Temple, Kataragama.

Tevani's Shrine

The complex devoted to Tevani is located off the main temple compound and is administered by *sannyasis*, or renouncers, of the Dasanami sect based in India. The Dasanamis were likely in charge of the entire Kataragama complex for some time since their role was confirmed by a Trust Deed signed in 1888 by Governor Sir Arthur Gordon and a Dasanami ascetic named Kesopur Swami. The Deed described the Dasanamis' land holdings and their rights over all of the temples in Kataragama. Since then, Dasanami control role has now been reduced to the Tevani and Ganesha temples. Dasanami priests from India continue to be appointed to Kataragama.[15]

Originally from Allahabad, Kesopur Swami came to Kataragama from Adam's Peak where he had performed austerities. His spiritual lineage continued for some years but an upstart *sannyasi* in 1933 protested in court that he had been passed over by a senior guru named Ganeshpuri. The latter won the case and a brick memorial shrine on the temple grounds bears a plaque memorializing his death in 1939.

'In Greater Esteem than the Temple at Candy'

Kataragama had attained such renown by the Dutch period that Governor Iman Willem Falck (1765-85) queried senior monks in 1765 about 'Katteregam'. The clerics described the god with six heads and listed ten objects held in his twelve hands. Those attending the annual festival included 'Budhists [*sic*], brahmin, Gentoos [Indian Hindus], Pattanies [Muslims from the Madras area], and Moors [Muslims from other locations]'. Three elephants were part of a nightly procession that included 'sixteen married women' probably drawn from the local Vaddha community. A 'gold sword from the main temple was placed on an ornamented 'bench' strapped to the back of the largest elephant at the beginning of the all-night procession. The 'gold sword' was used in the 'water-cutting' ceremony at dawn after the last night of the festival. No mention was made of separate temples for the god's two wives and there was no reference to the spectacular self-mutilations that are so associated with Kataragama today. The chief priests were likely Hindu Tamils but were assisted by 'inferior officers' that formed two classes of 'Kappuraales'. Three bowls filled with offerings were distinguished by the status and caste of the donors and the best offerings were sent to Kandy 'for the use of the temple there'. The Kandyan kings held this shrine 'in greater esteem than the temple at Candy [the Tooth-relic temple], insomuch that the king himself not only sends presents to it, but permits his subjects to visit it in great numbers'.[16]

Katarагama over the ages

The earliest notices of Kataragaram relate to a warrior clan from 'Kajaragama' that paid homage to the Bodhi tree in Anuradhapura at the time of Asoka's daughter's visit to that site. One of the original eight shoots from the tree was transplanted at Kajaragama and is now considered to be the same huge tree towering above the main shrine. (Mhv: 19. 54, 62) But the god himself makes his earliest entry into Lankan sources by the seventh century when he appeared before a prince at the port of Gokanna, an ancient name for Trincomalee. The prince conjured up the god, called Kumara, and his peacock by means of a magic incantation to wish for success in life. The peacock then sought refreshment in a coconut shell but the liquid dripped out through cracks. Enraged, the bird flew into the prince's face. To propitiate the peacock, the prince proffered one of his eyes that the peacock then slit open and 'drank thereout violently'. (Cv: 57.10) The prince proceeded to Anuradhapura where his partial blindness disqualified him from being crowned but he became a monk at the Abhayagiri monastery. This episode underscores the god's erratic violent nature and the efficaciousness of offerings. It also indicates that Buddhist chroniclers were familiar with the god and his peacock in the first millennium. The use of Kajaragama, an early name for Kataragama, suggests that the god was associated with this very place from an early time. Other references to Kajaragama appear in the chronicles but reveal little. (Cv: 58. 5)

Kataragama, among the major Sri Lankan deities within the inner corridor of the Lankantilaka Temple, near Kandy, 1344 CE. Refurbished. Courtesy: Osmund Bopearachchi.

The Chola dynasty in South India controlled much of the island in the 10th and 11th centuries, but none of the many Chola inscriptions in Lanka make reference to Shiva's son Skanda, that is, Kataragama. Skanda's great popularity, it seems, arose following Chola rule, probably augmented by a group of immigrant South Indian mendicants in the 13th century and a second wave in the 15th century. By the 14th century, however, Kataragama had achieved national acceptance, attested by his inclusion among the island's protective deities, noted in inscriptions and texts. These deities appear, with some variation, as Khanda-Kumara (Kataragama), Kihirali-Upulvan (Vishnu), Ganesha, Saman and Vibhishana. A sculpture of Kataragama, seated on his peacock mount but without his consorts, is preserved in the inner corridor of the Lankatilaka Temple near Kandy, dated to 1344. The present location of Kataragama was by this time closely associated with the deity of the same name, since the famous 15th-century Indian Tamil poet Arunagirinathar located the god Murugan at Kataragama and added that the god resided there with his Vadda damsel. Later, a Tamil chronicle from Jaffna from the 16th century, the *Takshina Kailasa Puranam*, associated the god with the location of Kataragama. Indeed, even a mythical Tamil king in India sent images of Kataragama ('Kantha-swami') and his two consorts to Ceylon, according to an 18th-century Tamil text from Jaffna.[17]

Devotees become possessed by the deity Kataragama.

Nail shoes. Some pilgrims perform austerities especially at temples dedicate to Kataragama.

A pilgrim dancing *kavadi*. Peacock feathers are associated with Kataragama's vehicle. Temple compound, Kataragama.

Kataragama was also included in the annual procession at Kandy where Robert Knox cited the deity as 'Cotteragom Dio'. Knox added that the 'name and power of this god striketh such terror' that the coastal area near Kataragama was shielded from the Portuguese and Dutch advances. But the biggest boost to Kataragama's worship was patronage from the Nayakar rulers in Kandy whose roots were in South India. These kings cleared a better track in the jungle leading to Kataragama, appointed a brahman priest to officiate rites there and were patrons of Kandy's chief Kataragama temple.[18]

Kataragama also became popular on the west coast, at Kotte, with the four national protective gods honoured by a temple at each corner of the Kotte fortress in the 15th century. There were also messenger-poems describing birds traveling to and from Kataragama. One, from 1788, had a hornbill taking a prayer from Adam's Peak to Kataragama. Another, as late as 1907, described the pilgrimage of a woman going to Kataragama from Galle.[19]

A Ceylon Lourdes and Dancing Kavadi

Pilgrims commonly travel to Kataragama seeking cures for intractable problems, often after other shrines have failed. Leonard Woolf, before his marriage to Virginia, concluded in 1910 that Kataragama was a 'Ceylon Lourdes' since so many came for healing. Offerings at the shrine may be 'retrospective offerings' honouring a vow made in the past, but can just as often be a 'prospective offering' seeking the deity's help for current problems.[20] A vow, or *baraya*, (P: *vara)* affirms a solemn reciprocal relationship between the deity and the pilgrim.

During festivals a small number engage in self-mutilation to fulfill vows. This takes many forms, such as pressing a pin through both cheeks or inserting hooks into their backs that are connected to carts. Others go about the compound on hired nail-shoes. Fire walking occurs on the last night of the annual festival when glowing embers are strewn in a narrow strip stretching nearly four metres, a practice now largely undertaken by Sinhala Buddhists.[21] Those suffering burns are taken to hospital where their scorched feet are seen as a sign that their appeals to the god have failed. Such physical acts should not be viewed as penance for sins but as supplications to Kataragama for future assistance or for fulfilling a past vow.

The much-publicized self-mutilation practices emerged only by the mid-20th century and were never noted by early visitors, such as Davy, Covington or White. Even in 1910, Woolf found that only a few pilgrims rolled 'over and over in the dust'. By the 1940s, however, sensational acts of self-mortification were not uncommon.[22]

Devotion is also expressed through the 'burden dance', or *kavadi* (T: *aattama*), enacted with a semicircular wooden frame supported on the shoulders. Its origins relate to a guru who conveyed two enormous mountains from the Himalayas to a Murugan centre in South India named Palani. The twin peaks were tied to two snakes fastened to a stick carried over his shoulders. The device itself came to symbolize overcoming adversities and the guru was offered a boon by Murugan.[23] The dance is a special feature of the Tamil festival of Thaipusam, commemorating Murugan's mother presenting him with the spear, but the dance is performed at any time in Kataragama temples and anywhere where Tamils have taken themselves, from Penang to Houston. Many replace the simple wooden frame with elaborate heavy shrines, carried over one's head and supported by sharp spikes in the torso.

A Tamil youth celebrates a festival in the Irrawaddy Delta, Burma. Such practices are not penance but done usually in connection with vow.

Pilgrims enter the temple's sandy compound in groups of between ten and twenty, gyrating to the tunes of hired bands. The 'dancing' is not festive, such as at a Brazilian carnival, but is infused with serious import. A description by a Swiss ethnologist in the 1950s is no less true today: 'Some hop from one leg to the other, others twist and turn to and fro and yet others make the most amazing leaps and behave as if they are frenzied'.[24] Some dancers are overcome with emotion and collapse, a positive sign of divine possession. Pilgrims 'dancing kavadi' are dwarfed however by the thousands of others in attendance, but the earsplitting music and ecstatic dancing blankets the compound with an infectious exhilaration.

The Kiri Vehara Stupa

A pilgrimage to Kataragama includes offerings at the Kiri Vehera Stupa some 300 metres north of the main temple. The stupa was founded by the first century BCE, attested by bricks incised with Brahmi characters. It was later enlarged, by the second century CE, with steps added to its four entrances. In the fifth century, paddy land was granted to support an unnamed ritual when it was known as the Auspicious Great Stupa, or 'Mangala Mahaceitya' at the 'Raja Mahavihara at Kajaragama'. It was one of many early Buddhist sites in the region, the most notable being the Tissamaharama Mahaviharaya stupa, some 20 kilometres south. These southeastern sites rivaled Anuradhapura, not in quantity but in quality and age.[25] Both Kataragama and Tissamaharama were included among the famous Sixteen Great Sites by the 18th century.

The stupa was in ruins for centuries but was restored, starting in the late 1940s. It conforms more or less to its original size but everything above the dome is fanciful. An octagonal stone pillar that projected originally from the top of the stupa in the centre is in the local site museum. Many such octagonal pillars are found at early sites throughout Ceylon and one larger example is seen at the Sandagiri stupa site near Kataragama. The ancient name for this pillar is unknown but it is often called today a *yupa* (Skt.), or a 'sacrificial post'.[26]

Myths blending Hindu and Buddhist traditions took many forms here over the ages but none can be traced earlier than the Dutch

Probably an eighth-century Avalokiteshvara, identified with an Anuradhapura king named Mahasena in the 20th century. Kiri Viharaya.

period. One legend noted in the 18th century claimed that the main Hindu shrine was originally a Buddhist temple and was protected by the deity Kataragama stationed 'on guard' in one of the two Bodhi trees shading the main temple. By serving the Buddha, Kataragama 'obtained the power of healing the sick', an early association between the site and physical ailments.[27]

Two relatively new myths have cemented the Sinhala Buddhist hold on Kataragama. The first places the heroic Dutthagamani (161-137 BCE) at Kataragama on the eve of his departure to drive the Tamils out of Anuradhapura. The god Kataragama appeared as an ascetic and prophesied that the king would triumph; the king then vowed that were his campaign to succeed, he would return and construct a shrine to the god. Although the myth celebrated the defeat of the Tamils, the story was, paradoxically, popular among them since it showed how a Buddhist hero-king required assistance from a Hindu god. After ever increasing numbers of Buddhists began visiting here, this basic myth took many new twists, each with the aim of confirming Sinhala claims over Kataragama in the hoary past.[28] No physical evidence associates this ancient king with the stupa here.

A second, recent myth claimed that in a previous birth Kataragama was none other than a Buddhist king in Anuradhapura named Mahasena, another Sanskrit name for Kataragama.[29] According to this view, a Hindu god was actually once a Buddhist king and by worshipping Kataragama today, one is really paying homage to a Buddhist king.[30]

An ancient stone figure found in the vicinity of the Kiri Vehera was mistakenly identified in the 1980s as this very Mahasena. The life-size sculpture is now a major devotional focus, placed inside a purpose-built glass shrine with its own *kapuralas*. However such an identification is completely fanciful and reflects Sinhala nationalist sentiments. Instead the image is likely an eighth-century Avalokitshvara.

A gilded image of Kataragama ('Khattugama') in southern Thailand. Circa 17th-18th century. Wat Phra Mahathat Woramahawihan, Nakhon Si Thammarat. Courtesy Chedha Tingsanchali.

Over the centuries, Kataragama even grew to be part of Theravada lore in Southeast Asia, probably carried from Ceylon by monks, texts and merchants. For example, a Pali chronicle from Chiang Mai, from around 1527, included 'Khattagama' among the protective gods of Sri Lanka, named as Sumana, Rama, Lakshmana. In southern Thailand, at Nakhon Si Thammarat, a two-armed seated stone sculpture is identified by an inscription as 'Khattugama', matched with a similar figure inscribed with the name 'Ramadeva'. The pair probably date to the late 17th or first half of the 18th century. These two Hindu sculptures gave rise in the 1980s to a composite deity name Jatukham Rammathep, featured on a Buddhist amulet that became a national craze for several years.[31] One suspects that Hindu merchants from Ceylon or ritualists from Ceylon introduced this deity to southern Thailand.

Spring of Eternal Life and al-Khiḍr

Muslims visited Katararagama over the centuries but it was not until the second half of the 19th century that a mosque was founded here. It is located opposite Valli's temple and is ranked among the country's important Muslim pilgrimage spots. During Kataragama's annual festival, a small number belonging to the Rifai sect engage in spectacular acts of self-mortification.

The mosque is tied to the pan-Islamic world by placing at Kataragama an important figure named al-Khiḍr, known in the Quran for discovering the Spring of Eternal Life. The special well with the 'water of eternal life' is now considered to be lost but a small replica of the well may be found in the compound. It was reported in 1888 that the 'hidden spring offering the power of rendering life immortal' was thought to be somewhere near the Manik Ganga river. A government report from the 1870s referred to a 'secret subterranean spring, the waters of which, are said to endow a person with immortality.'[32] Ibn Battuta (1304-69), also reported that al-Khidr was in Ceylon but at Adam's Peak rather than Kataragama.

The principal tomb in the compound is dedicated to Jabban Ali Shah (d. 1872) from Lucknow. A second honours Meer Sayed Alisah Bawa (d. 1945) whose death triggered litigation for control of the mosque among Muslim factions that went to the Supreme Court in 1949. Troubles lingered and a 'posse of armed constables forcibly ejected the interrenients [*sic*] to take possession.'[33]

Tomb of Jabban Ali Shah from Lucknow (d. 1872). Kataragama is believed to be the home of the Spring of Eternal Life. Kataragama Mosque, compound.

TRINCOMALEE

Trincomalee: 'The Rome of the Orient'

This temple and a second, on the west coast, were the two most sacred Hindu temples in the first millennium.

Perched at the tip of a isthmus jutting into the Indian Ocean, the temple's setting is the most dramatic of the island's sacred sites. Among the oldest and most venerated Hindu pilgrimage sites, it was named by a chronicler even in distant Goa as the 'Rome of the gentiles of the Orient'. Groundbreaking for the present temple started in 1950 and its consecration (S: *kumbha-abhisheka*) was celebrated 13 years later. The stone *lingam* in the sanctum was commissioned in Varanasi, testimony to the enduring spiritual stature of North India for Tamils in Lanka and South India.[1]

Ceremonies, or *pujas*, are scheduled six times daily, following South Indian traditions. The annual festival in March-April celebrates Shivarati, the union of Shiva and his consort (T: Matumai Amman). It once culminated in a 'water-cutting' ritual at a pond named Papanasachunai midway up the isthmus that perhaps appeared in colonial-era Dutch maps but was long ago made into a small well. This ritual has deep roots in Lanka, known from an 11th-century Tamil inscription on the opposite coast at Mannar.[2] Images of Shiva and Matumai Amman are carried in procession on feretories from the temple down into the city where Shiva is kept at the Kashi Vishvanatha Temple, known after its namesake in Varanasi, and his consort at the Sri Bhadrakali Amman Temple. From the tip of the isthmus to its base is over two kilometers.

Previous page:
Home to one of Lanka's grandest ancient temples whose precise original location is unknown. The recent temple is at the tip of the isthmus. Courtesy Dominic Sansoni.

The Koneshvaram Temple

One of the earliest names for Trincomalee was Ear-of-a-Cow (P: Gokanna), a derivation from the Sanskrit Gokarna, one of Shiva's many epithets. In the *Mahavamsa*, a third-century king constructed a monastery here named Gokanna, after destroying Hindu temples. (Mhv: 37.41) The temple's name, Koneshvaram, was a roundabout adaptation of the Sanskrit Gokarneshvara that was later replaced by the Tamil word Thiru-kona-malai. The honorific, *thiru*, is a prefix to Shaiva shrines and the word *kona* is a version of *gokarna*; the suffix *malai* is a Tamil word for hill. The word Thiru-kona-malai is found first in an 11th-century Tamil inscription just north of the city. European spellings varied, such as Tirukunamalaya, Triquilemale and Trecoenmale. Certain temples in India were also named Gokarna and one in ancient Kalinga, modern Odisha, may have been the inspiration for the one in Trincomalee.[3]

Buddhist inscriptions found in nearby caves date to before the Common Era but the most siginficant regional Buddhist site was an extensive monastery only 12 kilometres north of Trincomalee named Welgama. (Mhv: 37.40; Cv: 48. 5; 49: 15) Nearly 20 inscriptions by Tamil Buddhist donors in the 11th century were recovered amidst the ruins, some with dedications to the 'Buddha of Velkam-veram [Welgama]'. Another nearby site is Kucchaveli. Later, Nissankamalla (1187-96) included Welgama in his pilgrimage from Polonnuruva that included key sites such as Anuradhapura and Dambulla. Nissankamalla also toured a brahman settlement near Kantalai known as 'Chaturvada-brahmapura' where he enjoyed a performance of singing and dancing.[4] Kantalai is now a small town bordering the large Kantalai reservoir some 30 kilometres southwest of Trincomalee.

This region of Ceylon was known from a very early time in India, beginning with the *Mahabharata* wherein Gokarna was identified as a sacred lake in the country of 'Tamraparni', or Taprobane. This lake was probably the vast Koddiyar Bay opposite Trincomalee. In addition, an Indian Sanskrit text, the *Vayu Purana*, stated that 'on the eastern coast of that island … [there is] … a great temple of Shankara [Shiva] named Gokarna' but the date of this passage is uncertain.[5]

The temple was also included in a collection of Tamil verse known as the *Tevaram* compiled in Tamil Nadu during the seventh and eight centuries. The poems extolled 276 sacred spots, of which

The temple's bronzes, saved from the Portuguese and transferred to Tampalakaman where they are worshipped today. Koneshvaram Temple.

two were in Lanka. Ten short hymns described the 'Tirukonamalai' temple, one adding that it was 'surrounded by the roaring sea'. The second Lankan temple was the Tirukketishvara on the west coast, facing Mannar, now also completely rebuilt and also with a *lingam* from Varanasi. The *Teveram* recorded no foundation myths for these two major Lankan temples but observed that Tirukonamalai's *lingam* was 'a column of bright fire'; a much later Tamil text identified the temple with Mount Meru. That these two Sri Lankan temples were included in the *Tevaram* indicates the extent to which Ceylon was part of Indian Tamil civilization from very early times. It was also an era when rival faiths debated and disparaged each other. The *Tevaram*, for example, reveals this tension, with one passage deriding 'dirty Jain monks who walk about like rutting elephants'.[6]

The Cholas from Tamil Nadu

Trincomalee and much of northern Ceylon was controlled by the Chola dynasty, beginning with Rajaraja I (985-1014) whose capital was Tanjore, modern Thanjavur. In Chola inscriptions, Ceylon was known as Mummuti-chola-mandalam and its capital may have been Kantalai. An inscription at Tanjore's Brihideshvara Temple recorded that at least five villages in northern Sri Lanka were pledged to support the Tanjore temple with paddy, money and a special lamp-oil from a certain tree, the *Bassia longifolia*.[7] That Sri Lankan oil illuminated a royal Chola temple is further evidence for the close links between northern Ceylon and the spiritual landscape of Tamil Nadu.

Rajaraja founded the Tirukketishvara temple on the opposite coast, proved by an inscription, and so it is not surprising if he constructed the Koneshvaram temple during this period. A fragmentary inscription by Rajaraja was recovered in 1961 from the ocean bed just below the present temple and probably was tied to a temple he sponsored on the isthmus.[8] But whether both temples appeared before, during or after Chola times is guesswork.

After the Cholas withdrew from Ceylon in about 1170, patronage of the Koneshvara temple was shared by the Hindu Aryachakravati dynasty based in Jaffna and a number of petty kingdoms called Vanni located in Sri Lanka's north. These Vanni principalities were controlled by Hindu Tamil chieftains whose allegiancses shifted between Jaffna and Kandy. The period also saw Islamic merchants on this coast, known from tombstones in Trincomalee shipped over a distance of 3,000 kilometres from Cambay (Khambhat) in western India. One recorded the death of a Syrian nobel's daughter in 1329.[9]

Foundation Myths – The Southern Kailash

A handful of myths surrounding the Koneshvaram temple can be pieced together from three Tamil chronicles (T: *tala-puranams*) compiled in Jaffna. Like most temple histories, these texts are collections of multiple legends that accrued over centuries. The earliest, from the early 16th century, is the *Southern Kailash Puranam* (T. *Takshina Kailaca-puranam*; hereafter Tkp), followed by the

Koneshvaram Inscription (T: *Konechar-kalvettu),* from the 17th century and with later additions. The third was the *Tirukonachala Puranam* from the late 18th century. A leitmotif in all the histories was a parallel between the mythical mountain home of Shiva in the Himalayas, called the Northern Kailash (S: Uttara Kailasha) and the Koneshvaram Temple styled the Southern Kailash (S: Dakshina Kailasha). This linkage was the backdrop for many narratives. The temple's fame was so great that a second arose with the same name, at Kantalai, that was likely built during the reign of the Buddhist king Vijayabahu I (1058-1114). This is recorded in a Tamil inscription granting the temple gifts that included seven dancing girls. The same king gave land to a Buddha image in a monastery some 12 kilometres north of Trincomalee, a donation witnessed by the Buddha and 'Vallavar' (S: Ganesha).[10] Below are some of the most important legends.

One myth surrounding the Koneshvaram temple derived indirectly from the famous story about the Ganges River that descended from the Himalayas and whose destructive force was broken by cascading onto Shiva's matted locks. In the myth's transmutation, the river in Ceylon was identified with the mighty Mahaweli Ganga that rises from Horton Plains near Adam's Peak and debouches into Koddiyar Bay. The river, in this domesticated version, emanated from Shiva's 'pure red-lotus foot' at the spot on the isthmus associated with the Koneshvaram Temple.[11]

Another theme was that Lanka itself was created from a part of Mount Meru conveyed from the heavenly Himalayas by the wind god Vayu, recorded in the Tkp. In addition, the mountain on which the Koneshvaram Temple was situated was also described in the Tamil chronicles as three-peaked (S: *trikuta*). Other temple legends centred on Lanka's demon king, Ravana. The earliest source for this narrative is the last book of the *Ramayana* when Ravana's chariot was stymied from flying over Mount Kailash by Shiva. Enraged, Ravana tried to uproot the mountain but Shiva 'playfully pressed down the mountain with his big toe', trapping Ravana below. Much later lore focussed on Ravana's steadfast devotion to Shiva in order to gain his freedom, such as chanting praises of the god over a millennium. To prove his sincerity, Ravana severed one of his heads to use as a sound box for an instrument whose strings were made from his sinews. Finally relenting, Shiva released Ravana and presented him with a sword and a *lingam* for worship in Lanka. It is this very *lingam* that was thought to be enshrined in the primordial Koneshvara Temple. Many of these key stories are found in the Sanskrit *Shiva-purana* which spawned numerous variations in South India that in turn were adapted in Tamil Ceylon.[12] Hot springs just outside of Trincomalee celebrate the spot where Ravana conducted his mother's funerary rites, another episode formulated in Sri Lanka and woven into the *Tirukonachala Puranam.*

Just steps away from the modern temple's entrance is a massive chasm in the cliffside plunging into the treacherous waves below.

Ravana stands by his stringed instrument whose sound box was fashioned from one of his severed heads. Next to Ravana's Cut.

The fissure was integrated into the temple's mythology by the time of the 17th- or 18th-century *Tirukonachala Puranam* and is known as Ravana's Cut (T: *ravana-vettu*). The story opens with Ravana's mother at Trincomalee complaining that her infirm condition prevented her from climbing the Northern Kailash mountain to pay homage to Shiva. Ravana then tried cutting off a portion of the mountain to give to his mother in Lanka but his sword shattered.[13]

The frightful chasm was evidence of Ravana's unfinished handiwork but it symbolized his filial devotion. Ravana sang Shiva's praises with his special stringed instrument and finally the god restored the demon's body parts and consented to move the Northern Kailash temple to his ailing mother in Lanka. This myth probably arose after Chola times since Ravana does not figure in any Lankan Chola inscriptions. Ravana's brother, Vibhishana, also requested Rama to build a temple honouring Shiva at 'the place of Gokarna', according to the Tkp. The temple's foundation thus encompassed two important characters in the *Ramayana*, Rama and Vibhishana. Other major Shiva temples in northern Sri Lanka, the Munneshwaram and the Thiruketishwarama, have temple histories (T: *tala-puranam*) that tie their origins to Shiva and Rama.[14]

The three Tamil chronicles also contain a myth about a temple named Matsya-keshavaram. Matsya is the fish-*avatara* of Vishnu who rescued the Vedas from a cosmic flood, but Sri Lankan Tamils devised a myth in which the gods complained to Vishnu that their jewellery had been cast into the sea by a demon. Shiva then requested Vishnu to deploy his fish-*avatara* to recover these treasures by scouring the ocean floor This episode was likely inspired by the dramatic drop off on all sides of the isthmus, since this myth is not found in Tamil Nadu but is preserved in a lost Tamil text devoted to the episode, the *Maccacentiya-puranam,* noted in the Tkp. Two Chola inscriptions in Lanka refer to a temple named 'Matsya-keshvaram' at 'Konanamalai [*sic*]', suggesting that a temple dedicated to Matsya was once on the isthmus. Moreover, one of the two inscriptions recorded that Shiva, in his form as the 'Blue-necked One' (S: 'Nilakanta'), was enshrined on 'Konamalai', indicating perhaps another Shaiva temple. Some have argued that this fish-avatara temple and the Koneshvaram Temple are one and the same but each was probably a separate temple.[15]

Another temple legend noted in all three Tamil texts centres on a legendary Buddhist king named Kayavaku whose eyesight was restored after pledging himself to Shiva at the temple. Physical ailments or deformities cured by devotion, penance or pilgrimage are a recurrent theme in Tamil temple myths. For example, a boy cursed with the face of a mongoose (S: *nakula*) had his handsome looks restored after a dip in a hot spring named Keerimalai located next to a major Shiva temple named in his honour, Nakulesvara, north of Jaffna on the coast. Even a princess with a horse-face was cured after bathing in the same spring. Both miracles are referred to in *The Garden of Jaffna Events*, composed in Jaffna in 1736.[16]

Another legendary personnage was King Kulakkottan who appeared in all the Jaffna chronicles. He was perhaps a composite figure based on Chola kings in India of the same name, such as Kulakkottan (1070-1118) who is mentioned in a Lanka inscription. He may have also been modeled on a Chola prince appointed viceroy in Ceylon by Rajaraja I. Sources differ but most claim that his father came from Tamil Nadu to rebuild the Koneshvaram Temple but that after his death, according to the Tkp, the temple's completion fell to his son. The king imported a variety of service groups, including female singers to join the temple's dancing women. He also patronized the Shaiva Pashupata sect and constructed a Vishnu temple and a tank for ablutions on the peninsula. Many 19th-century palm-leaf manuscripts extolling his piety survive, with examples in the Nevill Collection and London's Wellcome Institute.[17] Bards probably retold his story at courts and villages and kept the king's legacy alive.

The modern Tapalakaman temple and two of the bronzes removed from the Koneshvaram Temple. Signboard coming from Trincomalee.

One Tamil chronicle from Jaffna even attributed the Koneshvaram temple to Sri Lanka's founder, Vijaya, immortalized in the *Mahavamsa* but painted as a staunch Shaiva who founded the temple at Trincomalee and three others temples.[18] A modern tradition asserted that the temple was one of five Shaiva temples (S: Pancha Ishvaram), begun by Shiva himself in Sri Lanka but this finds no support in ancient sources and seems to have been started by Paul Pieris. The formulation was probably inspired by a South Indian tradition that linked five key Indian Shaiva shrines, known as the Panch Bhoot Stala.

The Temple Icons Resettled

What exactly happened to the Koneshvara Temple and other temples on the isthmus during the colonial period is plagued by enigmatic, if not conflicting, sources and historical gaps, beginning from the 16th century. The famous temple left no trace, like the impressive Vishnu temple once at Devinuvara, the Shaiva Tirukketeshvaram Temple and the many Buddhist shrines at Kelaniya. A handful of stone fragments and sculptures have survived but these can not be reliably associated with any specific temples. One almost certain fact, however, is that the temple's bronze deities were shifted sometime in 1624 to the small town of Tampalakaman, only 15 kilometres southwest near Tambalagam Bay. The present temple at Tampalakaman, built in the 1950s, replaced an earlier one and is named the Ati Koneshvaram, or 'Original Konehsvaram', underscoring its ties to the famous temple in Trincomalee. The bronzes removed from Trincomalee are believed to be kept at this temple but have never been studied.

A structure which resembles neither a Hindu nor Buddhist temple. After Constantino de Sã de Naronha's *Plantas das fortalezas, pagodes & ca. Da ilha de Ceilao*, 1624, Biblioteque National, Madrid. Folio 199r.

The bronzes were probably transferred here because the triangular-shaped Portuguese fort built in 1624 at the base of the isthmus effectively blocked all access to the peninsula for priests and pilgrims. It was likely at this time that an agreement was forged between the Portuguese and the Koneshvaram priests to shift the temple's bronzes to Tampalakaman, a transfer recorded in two of the 18th-century chronicles from Jaffna. One stated that it was forced upon the priests 'because of the misdeeds of evil men [the Portuguese]'. The fullest description of the famous temple is but a single sentence penned by a Jesuit nine years before the transfer, in 1613, describing the temple as 'a massive structure ... of great height, constructed with wonderful skill in blackish granite, on a rock projecting in the sea, and occupying a large space on the summit [of the isthmus]'. Other Portuguese sources mentioned the fort but none referred to any destruction of temples.

More information on the transfer is found in an unpublished diary by the Dutch Governor of Trincomalee, J. F. van Senden, who visited Tampalakman in 1786 where the temple priest recounted the transfer. He was also shown two of the images, probably Shiva and his consort. The Koneshvaram temple was also known in folklore as a 'temple of a thousand pillars', recorded in Van Senden's diary. Intriguingly, Senden's tombstone was discovered in Trincomalee, the area having been designated a Dutch province in 1766 under the name of Tamblegam.[19]

The temple's purported destruction is believed to be at the hands of Constantino de Sã de Naronha in 1624. This demolition nonetheless should be questioned since a sketch prepared by De Sã himself in 1624 shows the completed fort but also a large rectangular box toward the tip of the isthmus captioned 'Pagode' that was presumably the famed temple. A year later, in 1625, a Jesuit document recorded that General Da Sã 'carried on his shoulders a great Cross' and 'placed it on the spot occupied by a *pagode*. From a hole in the cross, just above the nails of Christ's feet, 'emitted much liquid blood with which the people soaked many handkerchiefs, an event over three days in October'. Whether this cross marked the site of the grand Koneshvaram temple or was a lesser temple is hard to say. However, 12 years after the fort was established, a Captain-major in Trincomalee, Constantino de Sã de Miranda, noted in 1638 that stones from the destroyed temple were used to build the '*fortalice*' [fort] while in the same breath referring to three existing pagodas on the peninsula, the largest at the beginning of the isthmus and 'two smaller ones from which the gentiles used to jump into the sea'. These same three structures also appeared on his drawing of the peninsula, where he added that his drawing shows a village of married Porgugeuse ['*casados*'] with their church'. This description informed the chronicler Queiros in the 1660s who repeated the story of the temple's demolition. [20] His chronicle was first published in English in 1930 and became the standard version of Portuguese colonial Ceylon that has too often been accepted uncritically.

The 1624-codex by Da Sã even included a drawing of the temple, casting additional doubt about its destruction. This walled building, however, bears no resemblance to Hindu or Buddhist shrines. Perhaps it was an open-air ritual bathing structure that may have been the site of former 'water-cutting' ceremonies. More evidence unfolds in a later plan, by Pedro Barreto de Resende from 1635, which also shows the Portuguese fort together with a number of structures toward the tip, three of which appear to be temples.

The exact location of the Konehsvaram temple remains unknown, partly because the tip of the isthmus is so sharply tapered and marked by rocky outcroppings, that space for a large temple at the summit seems improbable. Overall it is difficult to envision any large temples anywhere on the isthmus since its rocky spine is narrow, with steep drop-offs into the sea on all sides, as old maps indicate. A map by C.F. Reimer, from 1790, shows the huge fort at the base, contrasted with the open ground taking up the remainder of the isthmus. A spot at the tip is labeled 'remains of the pagode from which the mountain received its name' but was this the site of the grandest temples in Lanka? What this map does prove is that no standing temple was left at the tip by the late 18th century. Several old maps show extensive structures beyond the fort up to the tip but these designs were never put into effect, presumably due to the uncooperative topography.[21] Today this large area is covered by thick vegetation inhabited by deer and monkeys. The original Koneshvaram temple may have been

The site of the fort prevented easy communication with any temples that may have been further up the sloping isthmus. After Constantino de Sa de Naronha's *Plantas das fortalezas, pagodes & ca. Da ilha de Ceilão*, 1624, Biblioteque National, Madrid. Folio 198r.

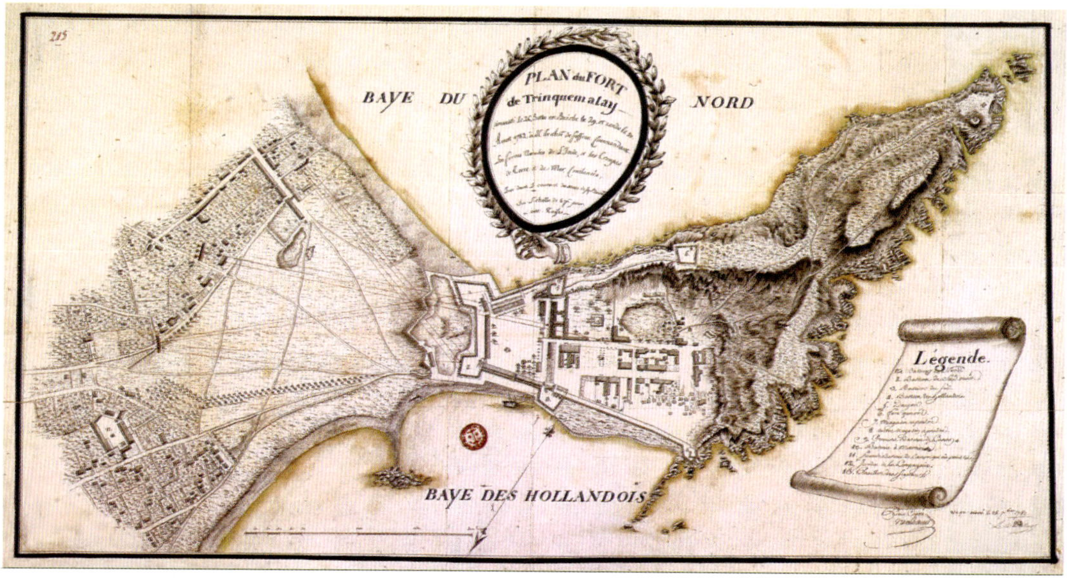

The topography suggests that little of consequence could be built beyond the fort. From 1782, when the French briefly controlled Trincomalee. Archives nationales d'outre-mer.

located on the isthmus but somewhere closer to the present Dutch Fort where a large flat space for a huge temple was more favourable.

No more than a dozen or so sculptural and architectural fragments have been recovered from the isthmus but none can be tied to the Koneshvaram Temple or any other. A few pillars were discovered that nearly match the one just outside the temple's entrance and can be dated approximately to the 12th or 13th century, after the departure of the Cholas (see below). A standing female figure and a standing Vishnu were also uncovered long ago and appear to be post-Chola in date.[22] A Nandi was also discovered in 2013. But it is impossible to connect them with the famous Koneshvaram Temple since there was certainly more than one temple on the isthmus. Ancient remains have also been found on the ocean bed just below the tip of the peninsula but the total is insufficient to account for an enormous temple and are of uncertain date. Also, if the stones of the temple were intended for the fort's construction, then why were they tossed into the sea? Perhaps the basic fabric of the temples was brick, a material that could more easily be dismantled and reused at locations outside the isthmus.

A Dutch force captured the fort from the Portuguese in 1639 and began reinforcing it. In the 1640s the Dutch and the Kandyan kingdom came to an agreement whereby the Dutch departed Trincomalee and the fort was dismantled, perhaps in 1643. The Dutch returned in the 1660s and vastly expanded the fort which also closed off the isthmus. A Dutch governor reviewed the city's defenses in 1767 and laid plans for a second fort, named Oostenberg, located at the entrance to the Koddiyar Bay.[23]

One Tamil author claimed, with no evidence, that the temple was 'blasted into the sea' with explosives by the Portuguese. Fueling this conclusion was underwater exploration undertaken in the 1950s

An ancient Nandi, discovered in 2013, can not be associated with any surviving temple. The *lingam* is modern.

with a team including the science fiction author, Sir Arthur Clarke. However, the few damaged fragments are hard to attribute to any period and are too few in number to warrant thinking that one or more major temples were hurled off the cliffside.

Another fanciful theory maintained that some priests bravely escaped with the sacred bronzes on the heels of the Portuguese attack, while others were 'mercilessly slaughtered'. Portuguese soldiers, disguised as Hindu priests, entered the temple as saboteurs and once local worshippers departed, then the 'plundering started' ... and the temple was 'destroyed and the masonry either thrown into the sea or used to construct the fort'. The discovery in 1950 of seven ancient bronze images just outside the fort falsely 'proved' that priests escaped and that these were the hidden icons.[24]

The memory of the fabled temple stayed alive over the ages. Maps from the 18th century designated part of the isthmus as Pagodeberg (Temple Hill) or La Mountaine of the Pagod (Pagoda Mountain). No temples of any significance were recorded on the isthsmus in the 19th century and one account mentions only a solitary Hindu priest who performed ceremonies overlooking Ravana's Cut.[25]

Fort Frederick and the British

The road meandering up to the isthmus passes through a gateway built into the walls of the Dutch fort now encompassing a military garrison. An inscription on the outer face reads 'Anno 1673' and another on the inner side 'Anno 1676'. The British took Trincomalee in 1795 when the fortifications were renamed Fort Frederick. The royal arms on a panel set into the entrance matches another inserted into the Dutch gateway at Galle. Both appear to be stone but were made by a special kiln-fired process invented by Eleanor Coade (1733-1821) in England. The twin panels were produced from the same mould and are Coade's only works in Ceylon. The panel here has been cut at the top to fit the gate's pediment. The original knight's helmet at the top, visible in the Galle example, has been reworked into a weathered orb. The one in Galle is inscribed with its date, 1818, beneath the coat of arms, but the lower part of the panel here has been removed.

Fort Frederick. The coat of arms matches the one in Galle, both provided by Eleanor Goade in 1813.

Lover's Leap and Poor Francina

An ancient pillar, from perhaps the 12th or 13th century, now stands upon a small rocky peak just outside the entrance of the temple. It was engraved with a Dutch inscription: 'This [pillar] has been erected on the 24th April, 1687, to commemorate Francina van Rheede, Lady of the Manor of Mydreght [Mydrecht].' Francina was the daughter of the famous Hendrik van Rheede, a Dutch officer and compiler of the *Hortus Malibaricus* devoted to the flora of Malabar and upon which Linneaus drew. Rheede's home was in Mydrecht, near Utrecht, but he was called back to Ceylon by the VOC to investigate Ceylon's rampant corruption. He inspected the fort on *'Pagoodsbereg'* (Pagoda Hill), but what prompted him to commemorate Francina's visit to the place with an inscription is unknown.[26]

The Dutch pillar spawned much British folklore from around the mid-19th century. Francina, the story goes, was set to wed a Dutch officer but he balked at the terms of the dowry at the last moment, leaving her to witness his ship sailing into the distance. Disconsolate, she ran 'like a young fawn ... and throwing her fair white arms above her head dived boldly down' into the Indian Ocean. One Englishman added that the 'mangled remains ... of the forsaken fair one' could be seen on the rocks below. One moralistic observer, however, felt that her act of 'self-murder .... [marked] by the pillar on this conspicuous situation' could be construed as condoning suicide. Her 'mournful fate' was even turned into a short story in 1901.[27]

Francina's story was in fact complete fantasy since records show that she was very much alive after her purported jump, having married for the second time in 1694. Francina was in reality a girl whom Van Rheede was forced to adopt in Malabar after losing a game of dice. The pillar was at one time placed on a stone base at the end of the peninsula but was transferred to its present natural rock outcrop when its inscription was effaced. Her jump from the cliff also piggybacked on much earlier Portuguese lore that claimed that 'idolatrous navigators' threw 'themselves down in sacrifice to their idols ... persuaded that by that leap into Hell they are lifted to Paradise'.

Inscribed in 1687 to record Francina van Rheede's visit here. She was believed to have jumped to her death in the ocean, memorialized in folklore.

Sri Bhadrakali Amman Temple

About two kilometres from the fort's entrance is a temple dedicated to Bhadrakali, one of the horrific emanations of Shiva's consort. Although constructed in the 20th century, the temple's foundation probably dates to Chola times since a Tamil inscription from the time of Rajaraja was built within the inner wall of the present temple. The deity is referred to as a 'goddess of victory' and another inscription, from Kantalai, refers to Kali.[28] Within the central sanctum is the goddess, concealed, apart from her face, by shiny silk fabric and garlands that are replaced throughout the day.

The centrepiece is an enormous seated eight-arm Bhadrakali dominating the central aisle before the sanctum's entrance. The most unique composition, however, is dedicated to Skanda, aka Kataragama, who was suckled by six mothers. Six infants are depicted joined to a single mother by umbilical cords. Each newborn is shown with a tiny metal spear (T: *vel*), Skanda's symbol. Nearby are the god's mothers, each with a giant mouth on her breast, evoking the god's suckling.

Skanda, known as Kataragama in Ceylon, was suckled by six mothers, each shown here with an umbilical cord. Bhadrakali Aman Temple.

Bhadrakali Aman Temple, dedicated to a horrific form Shiva's consort. The temple's origins may date to Chola times, according to an inscription.

Meschhed = Harun al Raschid + 808 Nadir

ISLAM

Islam: Mosques and Hermitages

Colombo's Dewatagaha Mosque honours the tomb of an Iraqi saint. From 1906, it replaced an earlier mosque from 1885.

Ceylon was known to Muslim writers in the Middle East in the first millennium but firm evidence for Islam's presence is a tombstone from Colombo inscribed with the date of 949 CE. Another of the same age, from Mantai on the west coast, is further testimony to Islam's growing role in the long distance Indian Ocean commerce until the arrival of European powers in the 16th century.[1]

The most venerated Islamic sites honoured saints who are thought to have visited Ceylon in the distant past. Among the more important today is the Dewatagaha Mosque, a stone's throw behind Colombo's City Hall and opposite Lipton Circus. A date on the facade, 1906, marks the rebuilding of the mosque we see today. A metal plate above the entrance, dated 1885, was likely salvaged from the earlier one. Old photographs taken sometime after 1906 show little has changed, apart from the adjoining worship hall added in 1983. The mosque's centrepiece is a small chamber containing the tomb of Sheik Usman Volliyullah, a saint believed to have been deputed to Ceylon in the seventh century by Islam's first caliph. Some even assert that it was Muhammad himself who sent the sheik to Ceylon. Men recite prayers beside his tomb and women worship from behind a glass screen. Also, a hair-relic of the sheik is displayed annually with thousands queuing up to view it but little is known about its history.

How the mosque came to be built in this location is explained in a myth that opens with a poor woman, in 1802, coming to the local market to sell oil from a clay pot. She stumbled, shattering the pot. A man dressed in green suddenly appeared who instructed her to return the next day with an empty vessel. The man then touched the spot where the pot broke, some say with his toe, and from there oil gushed. A wealthy local physician then spoke to the women and in a dream that night he was instructed that the lost tomb of the famous Sheik Usman Volliyullah was buried near to where the oil flowed at a spot between a large Devata tree and a fruitless date-palm. The Devata tree (*Carallia integerrima*) gave rise to the shrine's name, Dewatagaha. Another version claims that a sheik from North Africa in 1847 identified the lost tomb to a saint with a different name. No sheiks by either name are known in traditional Islamic sources so the legend likely arose in the 19th century as increasing numbers of Muslims settled in Colombo. The story may be a conflation of the spilled-oil episode and lore about the dream. Similar narratives wherein dreams lead to the discovery of hidden relics are also known to Buddhists, Hindus and Christians.

Previous page:
Cliffside shrine representing the hermitage of a famous Iraqi saint, Abdul Qadir al-Jilani. By Jan Brandes (1743–1808). Rijksmuseum.

An Iraqi Saint's Hermitage

A major pilgrimage destination is Daftar Jailani located on a remote hillside, known as Kurugala, about 70 kilometres south of Adam's Peak. It centres on an Iraqi saint named Sheik Muhiyadeen Abdul Qadir al-Jilani (d. 1166 CE) who founded the Qadiriya Sufi order that is well known in India.[2] The saint never left Iraq but Sri Lankan Muslims believe that he meditated for twelve years in a cave at Daftar Jailani after first paying respects to Adam's footprint nearby. The saint's tomb is an important monument in Baghdad but the sanctity of this Sri Lankan site rests on the belief that this was his hermitage. Worship takes place within a small open-air mosque constructed in 1922.

The site was first home for a small number of Buddhist monks living in caves from around the time of Christ, known from three inscriptions. By the late 18th century, however, the place was known for its Islamic associations, meriting a depiction by a Dutch artist named Jan Brandes. Dated to 1795, the shrine is shown below the cliff's massive stone overhang. Its whitewashed brick wall is faced with an elaborate brick and stucco entrance frame that resembled typical doorways of the age, such as at Dambulla's Cave 3. Nothing remains of this shrine wall today. Brandes never visited Kuragala but based his watercolour on a sketch made by an unknown artist. Whether this painting represents this Islamic site has been rightly questioned, but no one has yet suggested another site which this specific landscape could represent. A pencil inscription of unknown date at the top of the painting names two prominent Islamic figures with the date of their deaths, Caliph Harun al-Rashid (d. 808) and Nadir Shah (d. 1747), and a reference to a 'tomb and mosque of marble'. This perhaps reflects lost local lore that connected the site with these two venerable Islamic personalities.[3]

A tombstone, from Mantai, attests to an early Islamic presence in Ceylon by the 10th and 11th centuries. National Museum, Colombo.

Thousands come to commemorate Qadir Jailani's death in a month-long festival that opens with raising a special flag. It commences with women reciting a prayer honouring the wives of earlier prophets and Fatima, the prophet's youngest daughter. This special prayer was written expressly for the women of Ceylon by a south Indian Muslim who played an important role in the revival of Islam in Tamil Nadu in the 19th century. In the evening some men enter trances and a female healer exorcises spirits from women. Music in the evening features two rows of men opposite each other, with each playing a tambourine and chanting special songs in Arabic and Urdu. These songs are in honour of another Iraqi saint, Hazrat Ahmad Kabir Rifai (1118-81), who founded the Rifai Sufi order that bears his name. A small group of Rifai mendicants, known as Bawas, engage in self-mortification, using spikes, daggers and needles. The Bawas number no more than a hundred nationally

Muslims from throughout Sri Lanka attend Daftar Jailani's annual festival. Courtesy Dennis McGilvray.

The 'blessing' of a new banner before being hoisted on a flag pole. Daftar Jailani. Courtesy Dennis McGilvray.

and many are present at major Islamic festivals, such as at Kataragama.

Another tradition claims that the saint and his holy successors left their handprints on the cliffside in sandalwood paste. This outcrop is famous as Kaiyadi Malai, or 'handprint mountain'. That the handprints suggest a subtle echo of Adam's footprint is a tantalizing speculation. How this particular location came to be chosen for veneration is uncertain but its growth may in some ways represent a counterpoint to nearby Adam's Peak whose popularity grew in the 19th century. The site's fame may have faded at a later time since it is said that the place was rediscovered in 1875 by an Indian business man from the tiny chain of islands off Kerala named Lakshadweep.[4] The strong Muslim presence at Hindu Kataragama began only in the second half of the 19th century.

Daftar Jailani has joined the growing list of Islamic sites that are flashpoints for Buddhist nationalists. In addition to the early Buddhist inscriptions, some today claim that this is the 'hidden cave', or Divaguha (Pali), in which the Buddha rested after impressing his footprint on top of Adam's Peak. Calls for the mosque's removal began some time ago, with the complicity of the Department of Archaeology arguing that since it was first a Buddhist site then it should remain one.[5] The government provocatively granted permission to the Ministry of Cultural Affairs to construct a stupa on the hill above where the saint is believed to have meditated.

Galebandara's tomb, venerated by both Muslims and Buddhists. A tree trunk emerges from his tomb. Karunegala.

A Muslim King with a Buddhist Father: Galebandara

The occasional intersection of Islam and Buddhism is revealed in a populous town between Colombo and Kandy named Karunegala. The shrine's age is hard to say but its fame had arisen by the 19th century, if not much earlier. Its foundation myth is set in the time of King Bhuvanekabahu I in the 13th century. An astrologer prophesied that a crown prince would be born by a queen belonging to a different religion. Meanwhile, one of the king's wives was a Muslim who soon gave birth to Ismail, sometimes called Wathhimi but more commonly Galebandara. The king went off to war and his 20 wives, suspecting his death, leapt off his cliffside fortress, reminiscent of the legendary suicides of queens at Sigiriya and a later queen and daughter at Sitawaka. The only queen to survive was his Muslim wife and therefore her son Galebandara inherited the crown. In time, a golden pot floated in a nearby lake and when local Sinhalas failed to retrieve the treasure they feared their new Muslim king's wrath would spell their doom. Anticipating retribution, Buddhist monks plotted Galebandara's assassination by tricking him to ascend the hill where their agents cast him to his death below, after which he was entombed at the base of the Karunegala mountain. But the Muslim king's avenging spirit took to terrorizing the populace before the Hindu god Kataragama intervened and offered him the status of a deity if he would cease his torments.[6]

One variation claims that a Buddhist prince from the king's chief queen escaped and hid in the countryside. Upon the king's death, a blindfolded elephant was sent by the court minister to discover the exiled prince who was brought back to assume the throne and to remove the capital to Dambadeniya.[7] It is hard to say how old this myth is but it appears that diverse legends were woven together by the 18th century when increasing numbers of Muslims moved into Ceylon's interior. Although open to many interpretations, the myth clearly speaks of friction between local Muslims and Buddhists.

Galebandara's tomb is a Muslim shrine near the base of the massive stone outcrop for which Karunegala is famous. The site is unique since a tall dead tree trunk protrudes directly from the coffin covered in concrete. Local lore claims that the king's body was separated from his head at the time of his fall at the foot of the mountain. The entire body, it is believed, was later transferred to this present site and entombed; and directly from his body a banyan tree arose from a seed carried by a bird from the site of the original fall. In addition, the leaves of the banyan, known to be bitter, became sweet due to the miraculous power of Galebandara.[8] A short distance from the tomb at the base of the rock is a Buddhist monastery connected to the Islamic tomb and visited by Buddhists and Muslims where a modern statue of Galebandara is shown seated on a white horse. The king's name, Galebandara, comes from the Sinhala word for a class of local deities, called *bandaras*, and from *gala*, or rock, here referring to the mountain towering over the town of Karunegala.

A major Sufi site is a large mosque north of Matara on the south coast at Porvai, revered for a saint's tomb revealed in a dream to two Muslim merchants from Galle as an avatar of Qadir al-Jailani. Another is the Beach Mosque on the southeast coast that is affiliated with a saint named Hazrat Seyid Abdul Qadir Shahul Hamid (1490-1579) whose tomb is a major sacred site on the Tamil Nadu coast at Nagore. He is also believed to have spent 40 days meditating inside a cave at Daftar Jailani. This saint was born in north India but is considered a 13th generation descendant from Qadir al-Jailani. The annual festival marking his death is celebrated widely in Sri Lanka. Colourful street processions in his honour were described in Colombo in the 1880s.[9]

Son of a Buddhist king and a Muslim mother, Galebandara was assassinated, thrown down from Kurunegala Mountain. Galebandara's shrine, Kurunegala. Courtesy K.T. Silva.

Kandy

KANDY: THE SACRED TOOTH

Previous page:
The moat and octagonal pavilion called the *Paththirippuwa* were constructed during the reign of the last Kandyan King, Sri Vikrama Rajasimha (1798-1815).

Kandy and the tooth-relic are inseparable, like Paris and the Eiffel Tower or Agra and the Taj Mahal. Even the island's Buddhist identity is now fused with the relic and the town's annual procession. This sacred object however stands apart from other corporal relics of the Buddha, since it was never enshrined within a stupa to be forever unseen. By contrast, the tooth always enjoyed a public role and a peripatetic history that few relics can rival, beginning from the time of the Buddha's cremation in India to the tooth's final resting place in Kandy nearly 2,000 years later. The relic itself rests today within the smallest of seven stupa-shaped metal reliquaries, or *karanduva*, of diminishing sizes placed one inside the other, like wooden Russian dolls. That the relic so symbolized Sinhala identity made it a target for the Tamil Tigers whose massive truck bomb struck on 25 January 1998, nearly destroying the entrance gate and damaging the temple itself.

Our focus is the tooth-relic (P: *datha-dhatu*) and its temple, the Dalada Maligawa, or Palace of the Tooth. The temple's auxiliary shrines, dedicated to Vishnu, Nath, Pattini, and Kataragama, and the city's annual pageant are excluded, together with other landmarks such as the Asgiriya and Malwatta monasteries, the Dharmaraja College (1887) founded by H. S. Olcott, St Paul's Anglican church (1843), St Anthony's Catholic church (1874) and the Mahayyawa Grand Mosque.

The tooth itself is a tapered whitish object curved in one direction and measuring some five centimetres in length, or just

'Town of Kandy, from Castle Hill'. 'Drawn on the spot by Lieut. Wm. Lyttleton' in 1815 for an aquatint set published in 1819.

under two inches. Europeans belittled it from the beginning, such as a Portuguese chronicler who took it for a buffalo's tooth. A later English visitor concluded that it must be 'ivory' and 'discoloured by age'. Another scoffed that it belonged to either 'a boar or a crocodile'.[1] Tests could determine its true nature but it is a matter of faith that the relic came from India to Anuradhapura in the fourth century. That the venerated tooth today is the same that was brought to Anuradhapura is possible but history's vicissitudes make this unlikely. For similar reasons, the hoary pedigrees of Christian relics in Europe cannot be accepted at face value.

The tooth-relic, 'as exhibited to the Prince of Wales' in 1875. After, *Illustrated London News*, 8 January 1876, p. 34.

The outermost reliquary stands nearly two metres. A profusion of thin gold chains suspended from its top nearly conceals its underlying contour. Fixed to one chain is a spectacular bird-pendant of precious stones and a priceless diamond that was once fixed on a ring presented to the Ceylonese ambassador to Batavia (Jakarta) at the time of Kirti Sri Rajasimha (1747-82). The king himself ordered that 'this diamond shall be set in the forehead of the bird now being made for dedication to the Dalada Maligawa'. Replicas of the innermost reliquary and the tooth were displayed at Chicago's Columbian Exposition in 1893 and later in the Colombo Museum.[2]

The tooth's legendary history is an interplay between the relic and royal patrons under widely different circumstances. The context usually involved pious kings rescuing the tooth from evil-doers or the tooth performing miracles for the realm's benefit, such as ensuring rainfall. (Cv: 74. 239; 87. 3-9) The relic could also bear witness when declaring vows or affirming agreements, like the Bible in court proceedings. In several 15th-century instances, the tooth- and the bowl-relic were both invoked to honour an accord.[3] The relic was thus never a passive or static recipient of veneration but required interaction with royal votaries. Such a reciprocal relationship is no less true for the thousands of everyday pilgrims today at the temple, each bearing an offering, even if a single flower.

Monks and laymen approach the entrance to the Dalada Maligawa.

The relic's outer casket, with the bird-pendent, studded with a diamond from Batavia during the reign of Kirti Sri Rajasimha. Courtesy Igor Grunin.

The Monk Khema and the Sacred Tooth

The story of the relic begins when the Buddha's four eye-teeth were dispersed at the time of the cremation in India. One went to the god Sakka in his own heaven and a second was enshrined in Gandhara. A third went to an underworld realm of snake-kings and the fourth appeared in Kalinga, the modern Indian state of Odisha. It is the tooth taken to Kalinga that is now believed to be in Kandy. These four locations were appended to the famous Pali *Discourse on the Great Extinction,* (P: *Mahaparinibbana Sutta*), an addition made by Sri Lankan monks, according to Buddhaghosa.[4] (Da: 2) The Buddha's teeth numbered 40 and were of equal size and taken together as a set were among the 32 special physical marks that distinguished the Buddha.

Since the Buddha's cremation took place long before the start of the Common Era, many centuries elapsed before the tooth reached Anuradhapura in the fourth century. Some type of object believed to be the Buddha's tooth was likely in worship in Anuradhapura at this early stage, if evidence from the later *Culavamsa* can be accepted. In addition, the fifth-century Chinese pilgrim, Faxian, reported that the tooth 'made of the seven precious substances' resided within a temple and was taken in procession each year to the Abhayagiri monastery where it resided for three months. The seventh-century Indian monk Vajrabodhi also noted that the tooth was kept at the Abhayagiri vihara. The Chinese pilgrim Xuanzang never visited Sri Lanka but he recorded that the 'Temple of the Tooth' stood beside the palace and had 'a tower capped by a giant pearl'. Xuanzang noted other tooth-relics in India but the archaeological evidence for these examples is thin.[5]

The first notice of the tooth comes in the *Culavamsa* that stated simply that an unnamed brahman woman from Kalinga conveyed the tooth to Anuradhapura during the reign of Kit Siri Meghavanna (301-328). The tooth was placed in a reliquary within the Temple of the Tooth (P: *datha-dhatu-ghara*) and was also taken annually to the Abhayagiri monastery at Anuradhapura for a period of time. (Cv. 37. 92-98) From the beginning, the relic was vastly overshadowed by others, such as the collarbone in the Thuparama Stupa or the relics in the Ruvanvali Stupa donated by Asoka. Moreover, the tooth was also a latecomer to Anuradhapura and had no connection with the Buddha's visits to the island or to famous kings. These reasons help explain why it merited a scant ten verses in the *Culavamsa* contrasted with other relics that took up entire chapters. Also, few kings patronized the tooth in Anuradhapura. Indeed, following the reign of Aggabodhi VIII (804-15), there is a gap of nearly 200 years in references to the relic. Only in the time of Mahinda IV (956-72) did the relic begin its remarkable ascendancy, starting with the king's rebuilding a ruinous tooth-temple in the centre of Anuradhapura. (Cv: 54.45) A handful of structures at Anuradhapura have been identified as possible tooth-relic temples but with little success. In fact, the tooth-relic's paramountcy came only after it was transferred from Anuradhapura to Polonnaruva early in the second millennium. However, the relic certainly did not function as a palladium during its centuries at Anuradhapura. The tooth was only later paired with the alms bowl relic but a tenth-century inscription stating that 'the gem-set bowl used by the Buddha' was under worship indicates the bowl's growing importance.[6]

The Chronicle of the Tooth-Relic

Sri Lankan beliefs today about the relic derive largely from the early 13th-century Pali poem, *Chronicle of the Tooth Relic,* or *Datha-vamsa,* (hereafter Dath.) compiled by a monk after the relic was transferred from Anuradhapura to Polonnaruva. It drew on the *Culavamsa's* reference to a brahman woman from Kalinga but is otherwise a vast expansion. How much information was devised by the monk-author and how much reflected many centuries of story-telling is hard to say. The chronicle opens with the Buddha's disciple named Khema removing one of the Buddha's left canine teeth (P: *vama-datha-dhatu*) from the smouldering funerary ashes; whether the tooth was the upper or lower canine is unspecified. The monk then presented the relic to a king in Dantapura, or Toothville, in the country of Kalinga. The tooth was honoured for centuries until the reign of Guhasiva whose realm was plagued with heretics 'enveloped in the darkness of ignorance and hankering after gain'.[7] (Dath: 17) These disbelievers [P: '*niganthas*'] are usually interpreted as Jains. Guhasiva banished these undesirables who then migrated to Pataliputra, or modern Patna, hundreds of miles from Dantapura. One of the right canines was believed to reside in Sakka's heaven but whether it was the upper or lower tooth was not stated. (Mhv: 17.14)

Guhasiva was then ordered by his overlord to send the tooth to his capital in Pataliputra. This king, a devotee of Vishnu, connived

A Garuda retrieves the tooth-relic stolen by a snake-king. Delgamuwa Raja Maha Vihara.

The tooth-relic resisted hammering at the court of a Hindu king. A Shaiva ascetic, with his trident, looks on. By Solias Mendis, 1930s. Kelaniya Monastery.

with the banished heretics to destroy the relic. Tossed into a fire, it emerged unscathed. Placed on a chopping block, it resisted hammering. Drowning the tooth in a scented basin of water resulted only in the relic swimming 'hither and thither, like a swan dipping and rising'. (Dath: 30) The tooth was also cast into a 'moat which became loathsome on account of rotten dead bodies' but the polluted water was 'converted into a tank full of five kind of lotuses'. (Dath: 24, 30) Relics or Buddha images consigned to a putrid moat by heretics was a theme likely derived from a Pali commentary on the *Dhammapada* that enjoyed wide currency in the Theravada world; it usually featured a queen or daughter of an heretical king. (DhA: 3.46) In fact, the eight Buddha images flung into a muddy moat by a heathen king in Burma generated enough bad karma that the entire Mon kingdom became 'a desolate wilderness'.[8] The king in Pataliputra finally acknowledged the tooth's power and with the relic attached to his crown proceeded around the city before returning the relic to Kalinga.

The tooth remained in peril, since a neighbouring 'purse-proud' king demanded it. (Dath: 34) Guhasiva then instructed his daughter, Hemamala, and her husband named Danta-kumara, or Tooth-Prince, to disguise themselves as brahmans and to convey the relic to Sri Lanka to his friend, a ruler named Mahasena (274-301). The princess concealed the relic in her headdress which emitted 'rays like straight silver spokes'. In India, the couple buried the tooth in a sandy riverbank for safekeeping as they rested but an avaricious snake-king discovered the relic, swallowed the casket and absconded to Mt. Meru. Bereft, Hemamala and the prince then spotted an enlightened worthy-being, (P: *arahant*), who transformed himself into a raptor (P: *garula*; S: *garuda*), who quickly recovered the tooth. The sandy shore in which the tooth was buried later provided the foundation myth for one of Thailand's major stupas, in Nakhon Si Thammarat. In Burma the *Datha-vamsa* became the model for a major myth in the 15th-century wherein the monk Khema was replaced by a monk named Gavampati who plucked the tooth from the funeral pyre after which it it multiplied 33 times.[9]

The duo reached Sri Lanka by boat at Lanka-pattanam, thought to be on the east coast near Trincomalee; another source claimed it arrived on the opposite coast. It was then taken to the Meghagiri monastery northeast of Anuradhapura where the king walked out to welcome it. This monastery has not been traced, but some think, without justification, that it should be the ruins at Madukana, north of Trincomalee. The king named Kit Siri Meghavanna, Mahasena's successor, doubted the authenticity of the pale-coloured tooth, since the Buddha's teeth should glisten white like 'the morning star'.[10] The relic then rose up, spun around, and performed other miracles, putting all doubts to rest. Returning to the city with the tooth atop his head, the king built a relic-room inside the palace. The king eventually transferred the tooth to Anuradhapura's Abhayagiri monastery.

Sacralized replicas of Kandy's tooth-relic were acquired in Burma during the 1890s. A Burmese delegation is shown in Kandy, left, and the relic arriving in a procession to the Shwesandaw Pagoda in Prome.

Later Tooth-Relic Chronicles

The relic's growing importance in the second millennium produced a number of Sinhalese tooth-relic chronicles that that were either based on the *Datha-vamsa*, its recensions or commonly held lore that was often in disagreement. One was the *Praise of the Tooth-Relic* (P: *Dalada-sirita*) from the reign of Parakramabbahu IV (1302-26) Another from about the same time was the *Dalada-pujavaliya,* while centuries later the *Sinhala Dalada Vasay*a took the narrative forward to the reign of Kirti Sri Rajasimha. Other sources touch only briefly on the relic and often differed greatly from the *Datha-vamsa*. One text for instance does not even mention the beloved Princess Hemamala but maintained that the tooth was taken to Lanka by the son of a Kalinga king. In another, it was the Kalinga king himself who delivered the tooth to Sri Lanka. Another stated that the tooth was not one of the left canines but came from the right side.[11] These variations are proof of different traditions but all agreed that the relic came from Kalinga and was tied to kingship. The *Culavamsa* and stone inscriptions referred to the tooth-relic now and then, but a reliable chronological sequence for the relic is elusive in as much as these sources differ also.

The interaction between kings and the relic is treated in a number of texts. The earliest is the 13th-century *Kandavuru-sirita* that specified 16 kinds of offerings, a concept borrowed from South India.The king also swept the floor of the shrine with a broom made of his own hair, reminiscent of king Bayinnaung and his queen in 16th-century Pegu who sent brooms made of their own hair to the tooth-temple in Kotte. From the 14th century is the *Dalada-sarita* when the tooth- and the bowl-relic resided in the capital of Kurunegala. In the same temple was another tooth-relic, belonging to one of the Buddha's chief disciples, Mahakassapa.[12]

Untangling the legendary and 'true' history of the tooth requires sifting through chronicles, inscriptions and a skimpy archaeological record. Its trajectory is clouded by purported conflicts, usually between evil-doers who seized the relic and pious heroic rulers who reclaimed it. The protagonists are wicked Sinhala rebels or often South Indian Hindu realms, all serving as foils for strong Sinhala rulers. Evaluating these historical claims requires caution, since such fictitious dramatic dichotomies between goodness and badness were commonplace in Theravada thought. Even Emperor Asoka was plagued by a queen of rotten character who was

An oil painting by T. F. Simon, a Czech painter in Kandy in the 1920s, depicts the staircase that is now protected by a covered corridor.

contrasted with a queen of pristine virtue. Kernels of truth may be behind the purported conflicts over the tooth, but most were hyperbole and few cases can be firmly corroborated. The evidence is further distorted even by flat contradictions. For example, an invading Kalinga king named Magha is normally painted as an unredeemable anti-Buddhist, but the *Sinhahala Dalada Vamsaya* described him as a devotee of the tooth. Historians have too often blended such diverse and unreliable information and produced a muddle. However, these stories about the relic, even if fanciful, provide invaluable insights about how Buddhists conceived the past.

Tracing the Temple

The centre of power shifted by the 11th century from Anuradhapura to Polonnuruva where the tooth- and bowl-relics began their inseperable union over many centuries. A tooth-temple was constructed by Vijayabahu I (1055-1110) that is probably a ruinous temple known today as the Atagade, some of its pillars being incised with the Sinhalese word for tooth, '*dalada*'. (Cv: 60.16) Its foundation inscription, both in Tamil and Sanskrit, tells us that both the tooth- and bowl-relic (P: *dhatu-patta*) were taken from Anuradhapura where they had been under the care of the Uttaramula division of the Abhayagiri Monastery. The inscription is undated and the king instructing his minister to build the temple was unspecified but it may have been either Vijayabahu or Gajabahu II (1132-53). The care of the relics in Polonnuruva was assigned to a well-known group of Tamil mercenaries, the Valaikkaras, famous for protecting merchant guilds in Tamil Nadu. How Tamils could be entrusted with the tooth's welfare flies in the face of the virulent anti-Tamil bias in so many Sinhala religious chronicles. Later, king Nissankamalla (1187-96) 'presented' his son and daughter to the two relics and redeemed them by granting the *sangha* their own weight in gold, symbolicaly measured by the two children placed on a scale in a ceremony known as *tulabhara* or *tulya-purusa*, a tradition inherited from India.[13] Some have identified the tooth-temple as Polonnuruva's famous circular temple, called the Vatadage. Nissankamalla was credited with a stone tooth-temple ('*dalada-geya*') and a circular temple ('*vata-geya*') but neither can be safely identified. (Cv: 90. 121)

The tooth-relic rides atop a caparisoned elephant in the annual procession, accompanied by musicians. Courtesy Igor Grunin.

In time, both relics in Polonnuruva were threatened by an avaricious Sinhala king, Jayabahu I (1110-1111), and were removed for safety to the south where they fell into the hands of a renegade king. (Cv: 61.59; 70. 254) A turning point was the accession of the great king Parakramabahu I (1156-86) whose recovery of the relics was the cornerstone of his biography, like Caesar's conquest of Gaul. The king greeted the relics at Polonnuruva and carried the tooth on his head, the tooth likened to the crescent moon adorning Shiva's locks. (Cv: 74. 193) The relic was enshrined in its own temple and the bowl-relic was placed in a golden temple that 'rested on four wheels', an indication of its portable nature.

(74. 198, 210) A much later source claimed that Vijayabahu discovered the tooth and the bowl in a hidden location, together with an auspicious spear.[14]

Following Parakramabahu's reign, the two relics faced new threats from an ursurper, prompting monks from the Pumsulika group to take the two for safety to Kotmale where they were buried. Then follows a centuries-long perigrination, beginning in Dambadeniya in the 14th century and chronicled in a 16th-century Sinhala text, the *Rajaratnakaraya.* Another text, the *Pujavaliya*, added that the two relics were conveyed to Polonnuruva where a three-month festival was held. The relics were then transferred to two locations and later returned to Polonuruva before being taken for safekeeping to Yapahu. A Tamil king then captured the tooth but it was returned to Polonnuruva after negotiations and eventually removed to Kurunegala with the alms-bowl relic. (Cv: 90, 51, 66) The tooth-relic may then have gone to Gampola but there is no reference to the bowl-relic. From Gampola, the tooth-relic was removed to Kotte, near Colombo, where it was placed in a newly built three-storied temple by the beginning of the 15th century. (Cv. 91.17) Kotte was visited by missions from Thailand and the tooth-relic was removed from Kotte's palace (*'pasada'*) and displayed there to monks from Pegu in Burma. In Kotte, there seems to be no reference to the bowl-relic, but the tooth-relic was mentioned in four messenger-poems, some of which also spoke of Vishnu, Shiva, Natha and Saman. No traces remain in Kotte of the temple today but its location has been suggested.[15]

The Buddha's footprint, detail from a fabric gifted to the Tooth-Relic temple from Siam. Museum, Dalada Maligawa.

The Buddha's Alms-Bowl

The famous alms-bowl was created when Four Heavenly Kings (P: *lokapalas*) gave the Buddha four bowls that miraculously coalesced into one. This bowl, as a relic (P: *patta-dhatu*), was taken to Sri Lanka by Asoka's grandson and contained numerous unspecified corporal relics that were enshrined in the Ruvanvali Stupa. The bowl was then kept inside the palace. (Mhv: 17.12; 20.13) Said to be imbued with 'ten miraculous powers', it was captured by the Tamils by the second century BCE and taken to India. (Mhv: 33.55) How the bowl returned to Sri Lanka is nowhere stated but by the fourth century it was back in Anuradhapura and employed in a rain-making ceremony. (Cv: 37: 192) A much later tradition asserted that the bowl was recovered from India by the great Gajabahu I. In the 19th century the bowl was thought to be enshrined within either of two small stupas next to Kandy's Nath Temple. The foundations of both stupas are dated to the 14th century but have never been excavated. In the 1890s a metal bowl at the temple was thought to have belonged to the Buddha and was 'the receptacle for the coins'.[16] No early illustrations of the bowl have survived and the knowledge of this once famed bowl has faded completely.

32 body parts, such as nails, teeth and skin, subject to meditation (P. *patikkulamanasikhara*), in a wooden folding shrine. Circa 19th or early 20th century. National Museum, Kandy.

Both the tooth and bowl relics were worshipped in this temple, confirmed by a Tamil and Sanskrit inscription visible on the left.

He offered his own son and daughter to the Tooth and Bowl relics

The Buddha's sacred tooth and bowl, though never enshrined within a stupa, became major relics by the tenth and eleventh centuries, that is, toward the end of the Anuradhapura period and the capital's shift to Polonnuruva during the reign of Vijayabahu I (1055-1110). A modest temple contained the two relics, identified by a Tamil and Sanskrit inscription describing a group of Tamil mercenaries, known as the Valaikkaras, who supervised and protected the temple.

The temple was originally two-storied but the principal remains are fifty-four stone pillars, of which thirty-two were embedded in the brick walls. A small number of the pillars were incised with the word *'dalada'*, a Sinhalese word for 'tooth'. Three tall Buddhas stood at the rear of the ground floor while upstairs was reserved for the the bowl and tooth.

A major patron of the two relics was King Nissankamalla (1187-96) who constructed a tooth-temple ('*dalada-geya*') and a circular temple ('*vata-geya*') but the location of these two monuments has not been fixed. This pious ruler symbolically offered his son and daughter to the relics and redeemed them, so to speak, by ordering a stupa made of solid gold.

A few of the temple's fifty-four pillars are incised with the name '*dalada*', a Sinhalese word for tooth.

Polonnuruva's ancient name was Pulastipura, treated in many chapters in the national chronicle, the *Culavamsa*. None of the city's monuments were included in the famous Sixteen Sacred Sites of Sri Lanka, since Polonnuruva was never visited by the Buddha nor included in the Buddha's prophesies. The city's most influential king was Parakramabahu I (1156-86) who 'purified' and unified the *sangha*, at least in theory. His crowning achievement was the recovery of the bowl and tooth relics that had been seized by a king in the south. (Cv: 61.59; 70: 254) Two large stupas survive at Polonnuruva but myths attached to them from this early period are nowhere stated. Two inscriptions found at the largest stupa, known as the Rankot, record that King Nissankamalla oversaw the stupa's construction and worshipped unnamed relics inside the stupa. (Ez: vol. 2, pp. 137, 142)

Polonnuruva and its environs were also home to no less than fourteen Hindu temples constructed during the period of Tamil control and from the time of Vijayabahu and his successors. Temples were dedicated to Shiva, Ganesha, Durga, Vishnu and other deities. Some were of stone and others of brick. The largest and best preseved is called now 'Shiva Devale 2'. Among the temple's five inscriptions, one refers to Rajendra I (1012-44) of the Chola dynasty of Tamil Nadu while another names three categories of brahman priests attached to the temple, together with drummers and young women who sang and danced. (Pathmanathan 2006, p. 144)

The Rankot Stupa, one of two colossal stupas at Polonnuruva. The drum and spire are restored but the shrines encircling the base are original. King Nissankamalla worshiped in one of these shrines on the south side. Courtesy Dominic Sansoni.

Among the Hindu temples from Chola dynasty rule at Polonnuruva, this is the largest and best preserved, known today as Shiva Devale No. 2. Some Buddhist kings, such as Nissankamalla, were great patrons of Hindu temples.

This reclining Buddha and the standing image, possibly representing the disciple Ananda. Parakramabahu's reforms of the *sangha* are incised on the sloping projection to the left of the standing figure.

The tooth-relic was hidden between these two grinding stones until it was taken to Kandy. Delgamuwa Raja Maha Vihara.

Whither the Tooth Relic ? Goa, Kotte and Kandy ?

The tooth in Kotte remained there for over a hundred years until the middle of the sixteenth century when the Portuguese elevated to the throne the grandson of a king who was assassinated in 1551. The king, Dom João Dharmapala (r. 1551-1597), converted to Christianity in 1556-67 and embarked on anti-Buddhist policies, donating to the Franciscans for example the land holdings once gifted to the Kotte tooth-temple and the Kelaniya monastery. It was this tooth in Kotte that some sources say was scurried away to Jaffna in 1560 to protect it from Dharmapala but from where it was captured by the Portuguese and widely purported to be destroyed in Goa, pulverized and burnt and thrown into a river. Another version maintained that the tooth in Kotte was hidden out of harm's way in Delgamuwa, near Adam's Peak, and placed between two enormous grinding stones, according the *Sinhala Dalada Vamsa*. It was eventually brought to Kandy by Vimala Dharma Suriya I (1592-1604) where it has remained ever since. There were then possibly two tooth-relics, the one taken to Goa from Jaffna and the other taken to Kandy. The record is further muddled by a claim that the tooth was captured in Kotte by the Chinese admiral Zheng He who presented it to the emperor, recounted in a Ming period edition of Xuanzang. (Li: 1996: 353) The conflicting sources touching on this episode in Goa is a Gordian Knot that has been brilliantly unravelled recently.[17]

The Portuguese Viceroy of Goa, Afonso de Noronha (1550-54), came to Kotte, explicitly to seize the state treasury, following the death of Dharmapala's grandfather in 1551. De Noronha confessed that he failed to 'find any treasure, in spite of making a diligent search' but a number of precious objects from the treasury and the Temple of the Tooth were removed to India. Many of the valued stones and jewellery were auctioned in Goa, while others were sold to the Vijayanagara court, most of which were enumerated in a Portuguese document. De Noronha's professed failure to locate the treasury may have been a ruse to fool others about his innocence in as much as if he never found the treasure then he could never be accused of profiting. De Noronha's greed was in fact so notorious that it even ocassioned a stern warning from the king in Lisbon in 1552. Kotte's tooth-temple was not destroyed but reused as a church dedicated to St Anthony.[18]

How came the tooth to Kandy?

Several tales arose but all agree that the relic now in Kandy was originally taken from Kotte to protect it from the danger posed by Dharmapala. The most popular version begins with a Kotte nobleman named Keerawelle Hiripitiye who was instructed in a dream, in both Sinhalese and Tamil, to remove the tooth for safety to the neighbouring realm of Sitavaka, then controlled by the staunch anti-Portuguese ruler named Mayadunne (1521-1581).

In the cover of darkness, he mounted his steed for Sitavaka. The tooth was then transferred for its protection to the remote village of Delgamuwa near Adam's Peak. This is confirmed by a poem, *Savul Sandesaya*, dated to 1580, that refers to the relic in Delgamuwa. By about 1600, Kandy's new ruler, Vimala Dharma Suriya I (1591-1604), sent for the relic in Delgamuwa and the tooth has remained in Kandy ever since. The tooth in Kandy, taken from Delgamuwa, fits the scenario that there were two tooth-relics at the time, one in Jaffna in about 1560 and another in Kotte that was taken later to Kandy, a conclusion also reached by a Portuguese chronicler. The role Kotte and Delgamuwa played was recorded in at least two later Sinhalese sources and was also told to John Davy in Kandy in 1817. Two fourteenth-century stone inscriptions refer to the tooth-relic and a third to both the tooth and bowl but their locations are unstated.[19]

The episode in Goa occurred during the reign of Burma's powerful Bayinnaung (r. 1550-1581), whose reign in Pegu overlapped with Dharmapala's. One of his inscriptions, from 1557, speaks about two brooms made with his hair and his queen's being sent to Lanka for sweeping the floor of the tooth relic temple that was almost certainly in Kotte. Later, when news that the tooth was being ransomed in Goa, a Pegu delegation was sent to Goa to purchase the relic but the offer was rejected. This caper first appears in Couto but has been repeated endlessly ever since and fits into a long tradition of mocking Asian gullibility, duplicity and 'the superstitions of these barbarous heathen'.[20] This reaction matched European disparaging response to witnessing the devotion to white elephants in Burma and Thailand.

Burmese sources tell a different story. One chronicle recorded that a tooth-relic, set within a stupa-shaped gold reliquary, was sent by Dharmapala to enlist Bayannaung's support against his unnamed enemies. The tooth was greeted by the king himself at Bassein on 13 July 1576 and then taken to Pegu and eventually to Upper Burma where it was enshrined in 1636 in the present Kaung-hmu-daw stupa, just southwest of Mandalay. An inscription there, dated to 1650, recorded that now lost murals depicted both the tooth and bowl.[21] This stupa was compared in the inscription to Anuradhapura's Thuparama, though the size and shapes are entirely different. This stupa in Burma is today a major sacred site but the bowl-relic has been forgotten.

Monk Khema fetching a tooth-relic from the funeral pyre and presenting it to the king of Toothville (Dantapura). Khaung Muh Daw Pagoda, near Mandalay.

A blindfolded man and woman picking their spouses from a basket, from *Emblematum Secularium*, woodcut by Theodor de Bry (1528-1598).

How Fate is Blind

Perhaps the sole surviving art work from this age to represent the tooth-relic is an ivory box probably made in Kotte. The tooth is pictured with its two roots, unlike nearly all later depictions showing the relic as conical shaped with a curved contour. This sacred and 'famous temple' was given over to the Franciscans who removed 'all of the idols' and 'consecrated' it as a church named St Anthony's. The box has been attributed to the reign of Bhuvanekabahu VII (r. 1521-1551) but more likely belonged to the time of his grandson Dharmapala. The key to understanding the box is Dharmapala's turn from Gotama to the Gospels and the implications for Portuguese-Sinhala realpolitik relations. The context was the yearlong seige of Kotte in 1557-58 by the neighbouring Sitavaka realm controlled by the Portuguese nemesis named Mayadunne. Security concerns eventually forced the court to abandon Kotte in 1565 and shift to the more easily defendable Colombo. The land revenues that once belonged to the tooth temple ('Pagoda Deladasde') were now transferred to the Portuguese.[22]

The Portuguese royal arms are on the sides of the box, together with biblical scenes based on Northern European woodcuts available to the Kotte ivory carvers, despite Catholic orthodoxy prevailing in Portuguese overseas communities. Three adjacent scenes were probably designed to be read from left to right, setting the stage for the last panel highlighting the tooth-relic. The first features two charging horsemen. The next shows a man-of-arms beneath an arch who may be Afonso de Noronha, the Viceroy of India (r. 1550-54) who came to Ceylon to seize Kotte's treasures.[23]
A crowned figure on the right looking down on the scene is perhaps the Portuguese king Joao III (1521-57), together with his queen on the left. The third panel perhaps shows a Portuguese war casualty.

The last panel shows a crowned figure, probably Dharmapala, on a balcony looking down upon the tooth-temple. The man next

Ivory box from the Portuguese era, probably made in Kotte. c. 16th century. State Museum, Berlin.

to the temple is possibly João de Villa Conde, the Franciscan who baptized Dharmapala. His right hand is placed on top of the temple while his other hand directs attention to the temple, the chief subject of the panel. On the other side is a soldier with a drawn sword. The peculiar woman with her face fully concealed by striated fabric perhaps unlocks the panel's purport, her size and position in the composition underscoring her importance.

In European art from this age, men and women whose faces were fully covered in cloth demonstrated a proverb about by how our choice of a spouse is left to blind faith. The Latin expression, *Heu nimium caecis errant counubia fatis,* or 'Alas, too many marriages go wrong because of blind fate', expressed the proverb's message: that marriages are blind to the unexpected, like ships sailing over invisible shoals. Many artists at the time revelled in depictions of these proverbs and maxims. Most of the 16th-century books featuring 'emblems' are from northern Europe but the ateliers in Kotte were familiar with woodcuts from Northern Europe.

A European foreman in a Kotte atelier probably sketched out the subjects for the box, purposely inserting this woman whose concealed face relates to the above-mentioned proverb. A woodcut by the sixteenth-century Flemish artist brings this adage to life in a collection titled *Emblematum Secularium.*[24] This blindfolded woman on the Kotte ivory casket is then perhaps an 'emblem' that relates not to marital choices but to the kingdom of Kotte's unexpected fate relating to its unanticipated new status under Dharmapala, created by the military conflicts depicted in the preceding panels.

This mysterious woman on the casket demonstrates that events are too often unforseen, even when our eyes are wide open. That the celebrated and cherished tooth-temple of Kotte, which enjoyed regional fame as far as Burma and Siam, should pass into Portuguese hands by the flourish of a pen and become St Anthony's furnished dramatic proof of this axiom for all to see in the 1550s. This identification is somewhat speculative, but this peculiar woman with her face concealed and standing so prominently by the tooth-temple finds no other ready explanation.

'How fate is blind', expressed by the blindfolded women, in disbelief about the Kotte tooth-temple passing into Portuguese hands.

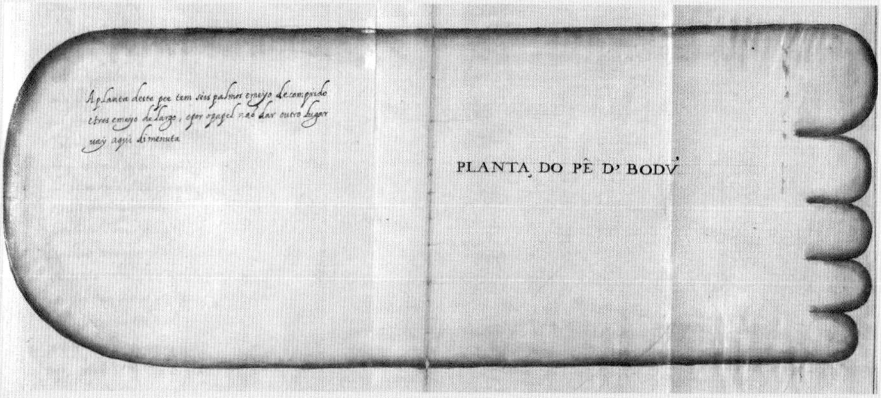

Drawing of a stone replica of the Sri Pada in Kandy, now lost. *Plantas das fortalezas, pagodes & ca. Da ilha de Ceilao*, 1638. Biblioteca National, Madrid. Folio 36r.

The Missing Footprint

King Vimala Dharma Suriya visited the 'mountain of Adam' and 'set up the dimensions of the footstep in Kandy' where 'much offerings are made' during a festival, according to the first Dutch envoy to Kandy, in 1602, Joris van Spilbergen.[25] In 1638, the footprint was sketched by a Portuguese captain named Constanino de Sã de Miranda. Miranda's drawing runs over two pages, with the following caption: 'the sole of the foot is six and half palms in length and three and half in width, and since this paper is limited in size, there is no rendering here [that is, a true facsimile]'. Six and one half palms is 1.32 metre, or 4 feet 3 inches. Later Portuguese and Dutch sources also refer to this replica. By 1862, it was described as 'a huge impression, in granite, of the Buddhu's [sic] foot', and was found in the 'grounds and grove around the Temple of the Tooth'. This was likely the wooded area behind the Temple of the Tooth that later became the site of the British Kachcheri (1880) that subsequently became the High Court and is now the International Buddhist Museum. By the late 1860s, the 'The rock bearing the impress was a few years ago conveyed to .... the Natha dewale .... where it is now seen'.[26] The stone impression has long gone missing but may turn up with a diligent search.

The Temple through the ages

In Kandy, Vimala Dharma Suriya I is credited with constructing a two-storey temple for the newly arrived tooth-relic from Delgamuwa. (Cv: 94.14) Several drawings of the palace and its surroundings from this age survive but matching such visual evidence with indigenous sources and descriptions by foreigners has been elusive. Moreover, the structures shown on the various plans are depicted inaccurately, further adding to the uncertainty. The earliest plan was drawn during Spilbergen's visit in 1602 but the legend identifying the principal structures has been lost and so the identifications are guesswork. Moreover, the short captions on Spilbergen's plan make no reference to a temple of any sort. A later plan, made by Miranda in 1638, shows a domed octagonal building that may have been the tooth-relic temple, depicted within the

A detail from a Dutch parchment painting dated 1753, captioned as 'a highly named Pagoda [temple]'. Perhaps this was the tooth-temple in Kandy. Lund University Museum.

enclosure containing the palace. Miranda also included two structures, labelled 'Pagodes', that should be identified as the Nath and Pattini temples.[27] One clearly shows a damaged roof, explained by Miranda: 'Constantino de Sã blew up half of the roof of one pagoda'. This was almost certainly the Pattini temple, since the Nath temple retains its ancient form. A 100 years following Miranda, a German named J.W. Heydt visited in 1736 and sketched only the palace exterior. Heydt also made no mention of the tooth-temple but a tower appears in the drawing, labelled 'tower as it appears resting on the pagoda [temple]'. This was probably the tooth-relic temple. An English envoy attended court in 1762 but made no reference to a tooth-temple. A two-storied circular temple shown on a parchment painting from 1753 perhaps gives some idea of how the famed temple in Kandy would have appeared. It is captioned, 'Here above is shown the figure of a highly named

Mural fragment, second floor of Dalada Maliqawa, the Twenty-Four Buddhas, dated 1924. Dalada Maligawa Museum.

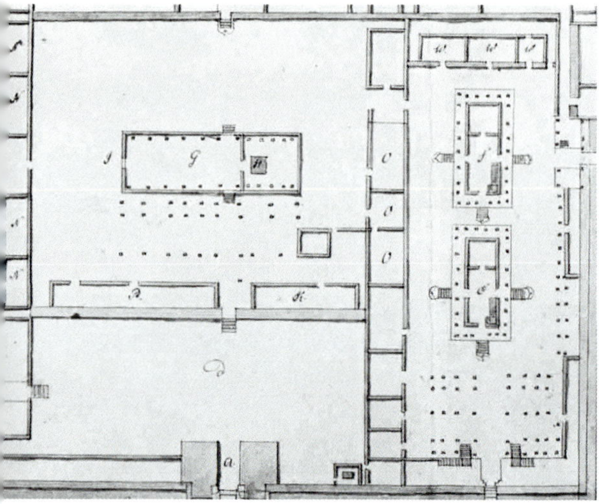

Detail from plan of Kandy Palace, dated 1765, showing old and new tooth-temple, back-to-back. National Archives of the Netherlands.

Pagood, or chapel, in which the Singaleesen keep their idols and to these come to bring their offering'.

It was only during the occupation of Kandy by Governor Lubbert Jan van Eck, in 1765, that accurate plans were prepared. One drawing encompassed the entire palace area that included two back-to-back tooth-relic temples on an east-west axis, one labeled old ('*oude*') and the other new ('*nieuwe*').[28] The 'old' temple, on the top in the east, was probably built by Narendrasimha (1707-39) whose 'heart was grieved' when he saw the temple 'fallen into decay' constructed by his father, Vimala Dharma Suriya II (1687-1707). The *Culavamsa* credited Narendrasimha with a two-storied tooth-relic temple with a 'graceful roof'. (Cv: 97. 37) Narendrasimha's successor, Vijaya Rajasimha (1739-1747), is said to have made extensive changes to the entire palace area but no mention is made of a new tooth-temple.(Cv: 98: 69) Nowhere is Kirti Sri Rajasimha mentioned as the founder of the present temple; he is thought to have only had it 'beautifully decorated'. (Cv: 99. 142)

Narendrasimha commissioned 32 *Jataka* paintings for the 'the two walls of the courtyard' that were removed long ago. (Cv: 97. 39) The *Jatakas* were individually named and included only four from the famous last ten tales (P: *mahanipata*). One Jataka in the list, the Dhamosodha, was never part of the canonical series of 548 but was popular in Lanka. It was also the only *Jataka* represented in a royal manuscript dated to 1811, preserved in Kandy's Malwatta monastery, a measure of its popularity. Also from the early 19th century were 15 unpublished painted hell-scenes that were recorded in a watercolour. These were probably the murals that A. M. Hocart noted in the early twentieth-century as 'recent pictures of hell', located to the left of the stone entrance leading to the covered corridor leading to the tooth-temple.[29]

The Pattini and Nath temples, foreground, one damaged by Portuguese cannon. *Plantas das fortalezas, pagodes & ca. Da ilha de Ceilão*, 1638, Biblioteca National, Madrid. Folio 40r.

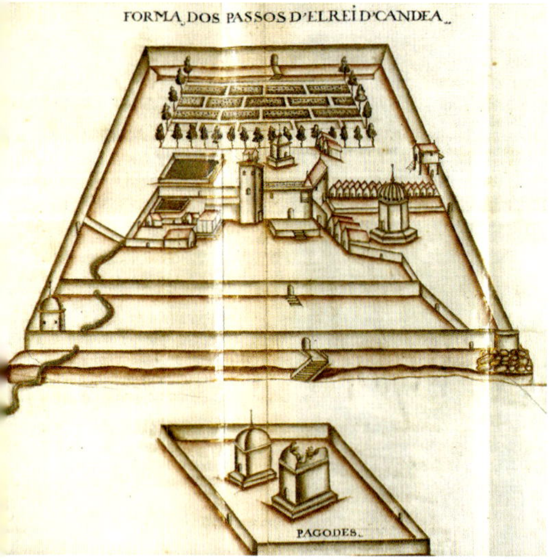

Restoration of the temple after the bomb blast revealed three layers of painting inside the upper story. The earliest were *Jatakas* arranged in seven horizontal rows. Only one has been identified, based on an ink inscription, the *Rajavodi*. Two tales share this name, nos. 151 and 334, but too little painting survives to determine which the painting depicts. These fragmentary *Jatakas* likely belong to the reign of the original temple's founder who is probably Narendrasimha. The layer placed over this was too obliterated to make out.[30] The outermost layer was added in 1924 and shows the Twenty-four Buddhas, each numbered and captioned and appearing in a clockwise direction. The donor's painted inscription on the south wall provided the 1924-date. There were also rows of standing *arahants*. Original fragments and reproductions of some of these murals are displayed in the temple museum.

It is hard to know how exactly the temple was 'beautifully decorated' by Kirti Sri Rajasimha but he may have ordered painters to adorn the bare wooden brackets supporting the upper floor of Narendrasimha's temple. No underpainting on the brackets has been detected, so the painting is original, albeit refreshed. The king's portrait on the temple's facade, together with Vimala Dharma Suriya I, lends weight to the suggestion that this wave of patronage occurred during Kirti Sri Rajasimha's reign. Above the entrance is a seated image of the Buddha of the Future, identified by a Sinhalese inscription, 'Maitri Bosatanan'. Other deities, shown in recessed niches on the sides of the temple, include Brahma and Sakka. The subjects of the paintings vary widely, including rabbits, horses, men wrestling boars and processions. A single episode from a *Jataka* appears, showing the hunter with his dogs threatening the hunchbacked brahman Jujaka from the Vessantara tale.

The Kandy Palace, a detail from Spilbergen's *Historical Journal*, 1604. The Dalada Maligawa is perhaps the small circular domed structure on the right within the walled enclosure on the left.

'Fifteen different kinds of hell at Maligawa's wall'. Watercolour, Wellcome Institute, London. c. Nineteenth century.

A Sinhalese inscription above one of the temple's side doors relates that in the 'year of the Sri Buddha 2450, AD 1907 .... the paintings of the canopy which were in ruins in the downstairs of the palace of the tooth-relic, in Kandy' were restored by gentlemen 'belonging to the higher caste, both from the upper and lower countries'. How extensive these restorations were is unknown but some original panels were destroyed and the wood replaced with some of the works we see today, judging by comments by Ananda Coomarswamy who illustrated one of the destroyed panels, a floral composition, that he captioned as 'destroyed'. He bemoaned that the 'verandah ceiling' painting was 'now altered, and for the worse'.[31] How extensive these renovations were in 1907 is hard to say but the survivng painting on the brackets are masterpieces of Kandyan art and consistent with murals at the Ridhi Vihara and at Degaldoruva that are tied to Kirti Sri Rajasimha's reign.

The Dalada Maligawa is now overshadowed by modern buildings on three sides, though for hundreds of years it stood isolated in an otherwise empty courtyard visible in old photographs. The two matching structures on the north and south sides went up in 1956 to celebrate 2,500 years following the Buddha's death. The plans came from the Colombo firm, Edwards Reid and Begg,

Facade detail, Kandy Museum, 1930s.

the same group that designed the Kelaniya temple in the 1930s.

A wide, elevated, viewing hall joined to the upper floor of the temple was in place by the early 1920s. The floor of the wooden building is supported by rows of stone columns crisscrossing the Drumming Hall below. This upper floor was designed originally as a space for monks to recite protective verses, or *pirit mandape*, but is now for pilgrims proceeding in front of the opened shrine doors upstairs. English and Sinhalese inscriptions on some of the pillars record donations, each pillar costing 500 rupees. Several donors were from Burma. For example, one was gifted on January 7 1914 by the 'high priest U Kelatha' and a 'pleader' and his wife and others from 'Kyaikalat', a town near old Rangoon. Another inscription mentions a 'broker' on Crisp Street, Rangoon.

The Entrance Gate and Museum

The temple's main entrance suffered the full impact of the truck bomb in 1987. Four stone panels depicting elephants and female acrobats were so pockmarked that they were replaced with copies, with the scarred originals now in a sculpture garden just above the Audience Hall. The damaged slabs with female acrobats are identical to an example at Hanguranketa, about 30 kilometres southeast of Kandy. This entrance gate was probably built at the beginning of the 19th century. Visitors first pass over the moat and turn right to ascend a covered staircase leading to the main shrine added sometime after about 1917, judging from a much earlier sketch that shows the same doorway exposed to the open air. The spectacular stone doorway, probably from the time of Sri Kirti Rajasimha, leads through a narrow corridor to the Drumming Hall. The covered hallway was once painted with Kandyan nobles framed in individual niches but has been entirely repainted.[32]

The temple's three-storied museum was built in 1936-37 and is just steps behind the temple. It was designed by Tom Neville Wynne-Jones, the same architect who headed the group responsible for Colombo's Independence Memorial Hall in 1953. The architects meshed together many different pre-modern Sri Lankan sculptural idioms, similar to the Kelaniya temple built during the same decade. Visitors today enter through steps off the temple courtyard but its spectacular formal entrance is on the opposite side, facing the hillside, and shown in *The Buddhist Annual of Ceylon* (1937).

The temple museum design by Tom Nevill Wynne-Jones, 1936-1937, was altered. After *The Buddhist Annual of Ceylon*, 1937.

The two upper stories showcase hundreds of objects connected to the temple's history. A major donation was an ancient bone fragment excavated from a stupa at Taxila in ancient Gandhara. It was hand-delivered in 1917 by India's Director of Archaeology, John Marshall, who was close to the reformer Anagarika Dharmapala. The relic came in a metal reliquary in the shape of a Gandharan stupa that was once kept in the main shrine of the tooth-temple. Its inscription relates that it was presented to Ceylon by the Viceroy and Governor General of India in the seventh year of King George V's reign. The bone relic is said to be now in a small reliquary within the inner sanctum. The British also made a similar gift from Gandhara to Burma, now worshipped in a hall at the foot of Mandalay Hill. A seated silver Buddha image taken from Burma was given to the temple by Governor Barnes in 1827. Its Sinhalese inscription recorded that it was from 'the Dagoba [stupa] and Wihara [monastery] at Rakkaduwa'. The image's whereabouts is unknown but Rakkaduwa was probably Rakhine, since this region came under British control in the 1820s.[33] There is also a silver plaque offered to the temple by Governor Barnes. Two lamps were donated by Governor Gregory (1872-1877) but they are not on display.

Among the oldest offerings is a silver pot gifted by Kirti Sri Rajasimha on a full moon day, inscribed with a date in the Sakka era, 1688, or 1766. One spectacular metal fan from Burma bears an inscription, 'For the merit of Mg Aung Kyaw Zan and Ma Hnin Ye at Pyay [Prome] city, 1898'. Many objects were donated from Thailand, the most spectacular being a yellow fabric featuring the Buddha's footprint, about two metres in length. It is labeled as a gift brought to Kandy by the Siamese monk Upali in the mid-1750s but there is no corroborating documentation. Its purpose-built lacquered wooden base made in Thailand suggests that the fabric dates to the late 19th or 20th century. More recent royal offerings include a silver bowl presented by Cambodia's King Sihanuk in 1962. The temple's godowns must be a cornucopia of treasures from Asia and Europe.

Monks and lay folk from Burma presenting a reliquary, at the rear of the Dalada Maligawa. Circa 1900.

'In the Old Palace, Kandy, Ceylon', 1880. By Marianne North. Oil on paper. Royal Botanic Gardens, Kew.

Duke and Duchess of Cornwall, 1901. By H. M. Paget, after a sketch by S.P. Hall. Wellcome Institute, London.

DAMBULLA

DAMBULLA: A VOW FULFILLED

Portico built in stages, between 1915 and 1923. Monks lived in caves here for over two thousand years.

Dambulla is associated with neither relics nor famous ancient Buddhist legends. Its sacredness rests instead on ties to ancient kings celebrated for their fervent Buddhist patronage. Its history is pieced together from chronicles, inscriptions, and a handful of Kandyan-era manuscripts.

The story begins when a king was forced into exile from Anuradhapura by invading Tamils, recorded first in the *Dipavamsa*. (20. 18) The ruler was Vattagamani Tissa (29-17 BCE), or Valagamba, who plotted his comeback under the protection of a monk in an unidentified location. (Mhv: 33. 53) The king's 14-year exile, which is also recounted in the *Mahavamsa,* grew into an elastic legend wherein the king sought refuge in numerous caves up and down the land, one of which was Dambulla. Miraculously, it was a hunter who guided the king to the Dambulla caves, according to a manuscript from 1726. The connection between Valagamba and Dambulla probably arose no earlier than the 13th century.[1] By the 16th century, however, Valagamba became forever linked to the site's founding. One twist in folklore, noted in the 19th century, was that the king vowed that if he were to retake his kingdom, then he would 'embellish his former rocky asylum'.[2]

Caves Two and Three were once a single cavern until its partition in the eighteenth century. Cave One was created about the same time, followed by Caves Four and Five.

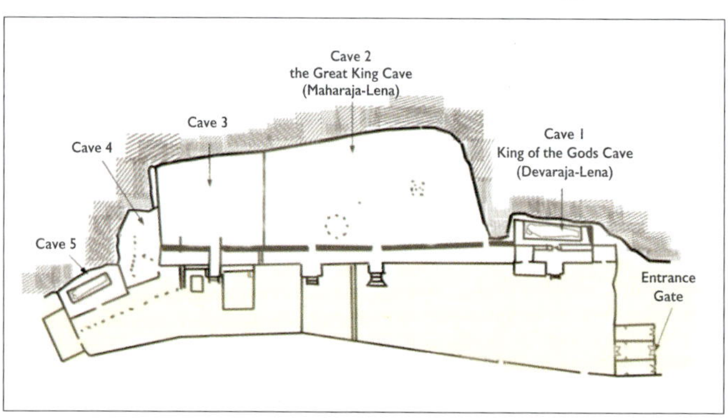

Valagamba is today overshadowed by the nationalist hero Dutthagamani but his legendary biography resonated over the centuries. The great Parakramabahu I (1153-86), for example, opened his famous schism edict at Polonnuruva by singling out Valagamba for homage. And later, Kandy's Kirti Sri Rajasimha (1747-82) (hereafter, Kirti Sri), likened himself directly to Valagamba since both were forced from their capitals by foreign invaders.[3] Valagamba's tenacity in the face of adversity is what likely made him so compelling to later generations.

The five Caves

The principal caves are located high up on the southern face of a massive gneiss outcropping and were part of a large monastic community encompassing over 80 caves at the bottom of the escarpment's southern base. These small caves were donated by nuns, monks, local chiefs and lay folk, known from more than 30 short inscriptions dated between the third century BCE and the second century CE. During this early period, there was a single long cavern that was partitioned into Caves 2 and 3 in the 18th century. An inscription found just above Cave 3 reads: 'The Great Cave ('*maha-lena*') of the great king Gamani Tissa [is given] to the Sangha of the Four Quarters'. Another donor-king was Gamani Abhaya but how these monarchs fit into Anuradhapura's history is uncertain.[4] Such an enormous cave may have been used for collective ceremonies. There is a similar large cavern at the Buddhist site of Kanheri, near Mumbai.

Ancient steps, chiselled into the cliff on the western side and still in use today, were once described in the 19th century as a 'toilsome path' leading to a 'miserable gateway' near Cave 1. An inscription recorded the donation of 13 stone steps while another donor gave 11. Even a single step was gifted by a pilgrim from as far away as the Jaffna Peninsula, known as 'Nak'.[5]

Centuries later, a major patron was Nissankamalla (1189-98) whose Sinhalese inscription on the rock face is beside Cave 1. He sponsored a ceremony (S: '*puja*') and named the location the Golden Mountain Cave (S: 'Suvarna-giri Guha'), that is now Rangiri, or Golden Mountain. The site was also named 'Dambulla-lena', or Dambulla Cave, a word perhaps derived from the Sinhalese *Jambukola*, meaning Rose-Apple Garden. (Cv: 60.60) That Nissankamalla included only the country's most sacred sites on his pilgrimage suggests Dambulla's fame by this time. However, this rock inscription of 25 lines is silent about Valagamba, a strong indication that this king's ties to the site arose only later. Also, Dambulla was close to a regional trading centre named Galevela administered by two Hindu Tamil merchant guilds in the 12th century.[6]

The caves were once protected by a 'rude verandah' indicated in a drawing from 1847. Later, a long whitewashed verandah in front of the cave entrances was built between 1915 and 1923.[7] One of its porticos was gifted in the Buddha Era 2464 (1920) by W. Bandaranaike who boasted of his 'grand manor house' ('*maha walauwa*') that was later renovated by Geoffrey Bawa.

The earliest surviving painting are tiny patches above Cave 3 that were once part of a massive fresco covering a large section of the cliffside. The fragments show only geometric patterns and date between the fifth and eighth centuries.[8] Along the top of the escarpment are many small shallow holes probably used for ancient scaffolding.

Nissankamala established here 73 gilded statues in the seated, standing and recumbent positions, according to two inscriptions from Polonnuruwa.[9] None of these can be identified today but his patronage of the seventy-three sculptures became wedded to Dambulla's enduring lore. (Cv: 80. 23)

Three 18th-century palm-leaf manuscripts recording grants (*tudapata)* furnish extensive information about royal patronage over the ages. The earliest is the *Dambulla Vihara Tudapata,* from 1726 and the reign of Narendra-simha (1707-39) but was purportedly a copy of a copper-plate grant from the time of Senarat (1604-35). This text refers to the partitioning of the single large cavern into Caves 2 and 3 by an external and an internal wall. The second manuscript, from 1780, dates toward the end of Kirti Sri's reign. The third, the *Nilagama Tudapata*, belongs to the reign of Sri Vikrama Rajasimha (1796-1815) and attributed the major work at Dambulla to Kirti Sri.[10] Many royal patrons appear in these manuscripts but only three are highlighted, Valagamba, Nissankamalla and Kirti Sri. This trio of texts present ambiguous, if not conflicting, information, making a credible history of Dambulla still illusive.

From Kandy, Kirti Sri traveled in 1755 to Dambulla for an eye-opening ceremony for the numerous images that he restored. It was probably during this visit that the king's major renovations and mural painting began. The sculptures he refurbished in 1755 are described in detail, such as 'three Buddha images, each two cubits high and seated upon lotus thrones'.[11] The majority of the images restored by Kirti Sri probably survive in their original locations, albeit refurbished. The king's activities at Dambulla were surprisingly omitted in the *Culavamsa*, whereas his other cave projects, at Degaldoruwa and the Ridhi Viharaya, are described in detail. This omission is probably because he did not sponsor a completely new project but rather only a refurbishment.

The artists chiefly responsible for the murals belonged to a family based in a nearby village named Nilagama that traced its roots to craftsmen who accompanied Asoka's daughter from India. Its members enjoyed key commissions from Kandyan kings and its masters were awarded land grants. A handful of different painting styles have been identified here but whether these styles reflect diverse artists' hands or belonged to different generations of the Nilagama family is hard to tell. Most of the painting in Caves 2 and Cave 3 are thought to date to the 1770s.[12]

Gongalegoda Banda, the leader of a rebellion against the British, awaiting his prison term in Malacca. After *Illustrated London News*, June 7 1851.

Cave 1 The rebellion of 1848

This cave is described in the 1726-manuscript but exactly when it was excavated is uncertain. The current whitewashed porch replaced a simple structure known from a photograph by Clara and Alfred Plâté based in Colombo. The portico's donors were Dambulla's chief monk and his assistant, referred to in a stone inscription above the portico, dated to the Buddhist Era 2467

(1923). A large reclining Buddha, cut from the living rock, dominates the narrow interior.

A key part for Buddhist pilgrims today is paying homage to Vishnu in a separate shrine next to Cave 1 that belonged to the portico built in 1923. A ritualist, or *kapurala*, sits next to the entrance and ties protective strings on visitors' wrists for small cash donations. The chamber inside is blocked from view by a modern cloth painting featuring a seated Vishnu.

A *kapurala*, with protective strings (*pirit nula*), inside Cave 1's portico.

The association between Vishnu and Cave 1 began in the 18th century when a wooden Vishnu image once stood next to the feet of this reclining Buddha, according to the 1726-manuscript. This sculpture was long ago called the God King, or 'Devaraja', an epithet of Vishnu. Later, it was moved from next to the feet to near the Buddha's head at the time of Kirti Sri's renovations. The Vishnu was ascribed to Valagamba in one manuscript and Kirti Sri is said to have restored it in another manuscript. This image today is enclosed inside a 20th-century locked wooden tabernacle near the head of the recumbent Buddha.[13] When the portico went up in 1923, the sacred wooden image remained in Cave 1 but worship likely shifted to the new small shrine next door.

This wooden Vishnu image assumed major significance by the 19th century when it enjoyed 'superior sanctity' over the Buddhist images. It served as a 'witness' before which 'the most serious oaths were often sworn'. Accused criminals were taken to Cave 1 to face 'the ordeal by oath, and even by hot oil'. The images's power however failed to protect the shrine's *kapurala* who was trampled by a rogue elephant in 1835. But little has changed since 1983 when pilgrims 'flocked to this place [the Vishnu shrine] for the redress of their suffering and for divine intervention'.[14] Placing Vishnu images next to reclining Buddha images was commonplace in the Kandyan period and later, as seen at the Kelaniya temple and the 'Thai Temple' in Colombo. (Cv: 100. 249)

An anti-British insurrection in 1848 was launched at Cave 1, drawing its strength from the Vishnu image. Its leader assembled at Dambulla with over 700 followers, claiming descent from the Kandyan royal household. A head monk conducted a makeshift coronation with the Vishnu sculpture as a

A wooden Vishnu, once the focus of a revolt against the British in 1817. It is inside a locked tabernacle only rarely opened. Cave 1. Courtesy Ulrich von Schroeder.

backdrop. The insurgency fizzled and its leader died en route to a prison in Malacca. The Dambulla monk pleaded at an inquest that he was forced to perform the coronation and therefore guiltless of treason. The monk then spent 'many years in hiding' before becoming a 'loyal though perhaps regretful subject of the English Government'. A parallel instance in Burma centred on a Hindu sculpture used in an aborted assault on British Bodh Gaya.[15]

This Vishnu figure was also linked in lore to the major Vishnu site on the south coast, Devinuvara. It was here that a beached sandalwood log was thought to have been carved into this very Vishnu image that was taken from the south to Dambulla. The core myth of the beached image myth began by the 15th century in Sri Lanka but was expanded to include the Dambulla Vishnu probably only in the 19th century. These legends even claimed that the sandalwood Vishnu was taken to a temple west of Kandy, known as Alu Viharaya, and then to the Maha Saman Devale in Ratnapura before its final repose at Dambulla. The Vishnu in Cave 1 has never been tested, but sandalwood (*Santalum album*), was prized in Sri Lanka. A Dutch governor for example gifted a sandalwood log weighing over ninty kilos to a Kandyan king.[16]

The original identity of this wooden image is uncertain, since Vishnu normally has four arms and a distinctive crown. Its hand-gestures however are the same as the two-arm Vishnu sculpture in Cave 2. Its hairstyle resembles that of bodhisattas, with an oval motif above the forehead that may have been once painted with a seated Buddha. A short garment below the waist was painted at some stage to resemble a tiger skin, an attribute of Avalokiteshvara. A painted halo on the wall conforms to the profile of the image, suggesting that the sculpture was moved to this side of the chamber at the time of Kirti Sri's refurbishments. The original context of this wooden figure is uncertain but it may belong to the late Anuradhapura period when it was worshipped as a bodhisatta. Perhaps the sculpture was moved to Cave 1 when the large cavern was partitioned into two caves.

Cave 2 His Virtue As Deep as the Ocean

The Great King Cave, or Maharaja-lena, figures in the manuscript of 1726 but a step-by-step chronology for the cave has yet to be worked out. An enormous amount of stone was removed to fashion the cave, evinced by figures carved from deep inside. A 'door of communication'which once existed between this cave and Cave 3 is now filled with rubble but its original wooden jambs and lintel remain. The cave's embellishment, including the murals, is conventionally attributed to Kirti Sri whose 'virtue was as deep as the ocean', according to the *Nilagama Tudapata*.[17]

The murals celebrate the life of the Buddha and legendary events recorded in the Pali *Mahavamsa*. The majority of scenes are identified by Sinhalese captions. Work began with smoothing the ceiling's surface, but the stone is uneven in many places and explains the shadows made by modern lighting. Painters first prepped the surface with plaster, followed by a light-coloured primer on which the compositions were sketched with fine lines before colour was applied. Numerous visible preparatory lines indicate how artists altered their designs slightly as work proceeded. In a small number of spots on the rear wall the present murals seem to be covering earlier painting but how much time separates the two phases is uncertain.[18]

The Life of the Buddha

The ceiling murals highlight scenes from the Buddha's life organized in a loose chronological sequence. It begins on the cave's left side with a vertical panel divided into rows. The narrative zigzags from left to right, from the top, and then from right to left in the row below. This format mirrors hanging cloth scrolls, or *petikadas,* three of which from the Kandyan period are on view in the Colombo Museum. Other cloth paintings had a horizontal format.

The two topmost rows show the Twenty-four Buddhas. Below is Gotama in Tusita Heaven followed by Anotatta Lake and queen Maya. The white-elephant is shown ascending the 'silver mountain' before entering Maya's womb. Such a small detail like this mountain suggests that artists relied on sketches closely following the Pali *Nidanakatha* or more likely Sinhalese recensions. The next row shows Maya's procession to her natal village and grasping the

Interior, Cave 2. Only four snake-hooded images encircled the stupa in the early 19th century.

The God Sakka, left, instructs Vishnu to protect Buddhism in Sri Lanka. Vishnu, shown again, kneeling before the Buddha. Cave 2. Circa 1770s.

flowering tree. Other familiar subjects are the Ploughing Ceremony, the Four Omens, the Great Departure and the Anoma River. Many of these same episodes are ascribed to the murals commissioned by Kirti Sri in the Nilagama Tudapata.

One register features the Ten Bodhisattas who succeeded the historical Buddha Gotama. The first is Metteyya and the last two are elephants, described in the Pali text *Dasabodhisattuppatt-katha*. This representation is perhaps the earliest-known depiction of the theme.[19] Later examples are found among the ceiling panels at the Malwatta ordination hall in Kandy and at the Talava Maharaja Vihara at Marassana, near Kandy.

Below the Ten Bodhisattas are eight stupas representing the Buddha's bodily relics divided among Indian kingdoms, each with a caption. One reads: 'The great *dagoba*, [stupa], erected by the great king of Licchavi of Vesali'. The last scene shows the Buddha's demise between two flowering trees with the disciple Kassapa worshipping the Buddha's feet protruding from the pyre. Below is Ananda and Kassapa at the First Buddhist Council. This long panel concludes with two kings paying homage to a reliquary at the site of the cremation, Kusinagara.

Adjacent ceiling scenes are largely drawn from the *Mahavamsa*. In one, the Buddha is seated, with the god Sakka standing before Upulvan, identified by the inscription: 'Sakka grants the protection of Buddhism in Sri Lanka to Upulvan'. Upulvan is then shown again with four arms, kneeling before the Buddha and holding a conch.

Two merchants made food-offerings to the Buddha and were given hair-relics. The last of the Seven Weeks at Bodh Gaya. Cave Two. Circa 1770s.

The Seven Weeks and the Retreats

Dambulla's largest panels focus on the Buddha's Seven Weeks at Bodh Gaya and his First Sermon at the Deer Park. These two themes are paired since without the enlightenment there would be nothing to teach. The demon Mara is shown falling topsy-turvy off his elephant, like a rodeo cowboy, concluding the Buddha's first week at Bodh Gaya. The sequence and many details follow the *Nidanakatha*.

The panel showing the fifth week, in which Mara's daughters tempt the Buddha is far greater in size. The largest dancers are the demon's three daughters who multiplied themselves 'in a hundred different guises … since varied are the expectations of men; some are attracted by women in the prime of youth … and some others by older women'.[20] The dejected Mara in the lower corner is consoled by one of his offspring. His lowered index finger indicates the moment when Mara scratched sixteen lines on the ground that symbolized the same number of virtues that the demon rejected.

The last in the sequence shows the seated Brahma Sahampati requesting the Buddha to pass on his teachings, a prelude to an enormous panel on the right dedicated to the Deer Park scene that included his five disciples and deities such as Brahma and Vishnu and Shiva.

The Buddha spent some 45 years travelling in northeastern India during the three-month rainy season (P: *vassa*). These scenes unfold in a long row and include the Vulture Peak, labelled 'Gijjhakuta'. In Vesali, Mara, shown with eight arms, urged the Buddha to end

Mara scratched sixteen lines on the ground, each a virtue that he rejected. Consoled by one of his daughters. Cave 2. Circas 1770s.

Vijaya's men held hostage in a lotus pond by the demoness Kuveni.

his life soon. Rows of small seated Buddha figures take up much of the ceiling on the right. A total of 1,300 Buddhas was recorded in the 1780-manuscript but no one has mustered the patience to count.

On the rear wall is a seated Ganesha, Kataragama and Vibhishana. This wall also features Anuradhapura's Ruvanvali Stupa founded by Dutthagamani who holds the stupa's reliquary. Scenes below include a recumbent Buddha captioned, 'The Buddha prophesied that his sacred relics .... will be placed inside the Suvanamala Cheity [Ruvanvali stupa] and will remain 5,000 years'. Other scenes show the Buddha Dipankara, the *Temi Jataka*, prince Vessantara gifting his elephant, the defeat of Mara, the *bodhisatta* severing his hair, and the infant bodhisatta placing his feet on the head of Kaladeva. A rare scene shows the Buddha plucking hair relics, with his left hand, for the deity Sumana. A row of elephants below copies the elephants around the base of the Ruvanvali Stupa. On this wall also is the Maricavatti Stupa at Anuradhapura and Dutthagamani, his queen and others shown paying homage.

Further along is the defeat of the Tamil king, Elara, at the hands of Dutthagamani, their two elephants going head-to-head. Elara is shown struck by a fatal arrow but it was a blow from a lance, according to the *Mahavamsa*. (Mhv: 25. 70). Below the elephant is perhaps Elara's slain general, Dighajantu.

Murals showcasing the conversion of Ceylon cover the reverse side of a huge seated Buddha carved from the rock in one corner of the hall. The scenes are based on the *Mahavasma* and unfold in loose zig-zag fashion, from top to bottom. At the top is Kassapa Buddha, who preceeded Gotama and who visited a land called Mandadipa to save its inhabitants from an internecine war. He stands on a hill, as described in the *Mahavamsa*. (15. 125-59) The king, with his bow on the ground, pays homage to Kassapa, presaging the scene of Mahinda below. This episode was rarely, if ever, depicted.

King Kit Siri Mevan (301-328) is perhaps worshipping the tooth-relic and displaying the relic from a viewing platform.

Buddha Kassapa averting a war and converting a kingdom. Below is Devanampiya Tissa's conversion. Both episodes in the *Mahavamsa*. Cave 2.

Below is Devanampiya Tissa hunting deer and a cart conveying Mahinda to Anuradhapura. Scenes below are the elephant harnessed to a plough laying out the Mahavihara's boundaries and the arrival of the Bodhi Tree from India. The last scene shows the king holding a reliquary, perhaps containing the collarbone intended for the Thuparama stupa. The bottom-most register may show king Kit Siri Mevan (301-328) worshipping the tooth-relic inside a reliquary and then displaying the reliquary from a viewing platform. This panel concludes with a three-storied temple which is often associated with the tooth-relic.

The nearby cave wall shows a scene from Sri Lanka's first settler, Vijaya, whose men are shown being held hostage in a lotus pond by the demoness Kuveni. (Mhv: 7.17) Close by on the ceiling are the Sixteen Sacred Sites and the Seven Weeks, tucked away in the corner of the cave, almost as an afterthought.

King Dutthagamani, his queen consort and retinue paying homage at Anuradhapura's Maricavatti Stupa. Circa 1770s.

The Demoness Neighed Full Loudly

Before Anuradhapura's founding, a prince named Pandukabhaya needed to foil his murderous uncles. Fortune favoured the prince since he happened upon a wild mare with 'a white body and red feet' and magical powers. In reality, she was a demoness (P: *yakkhini*) but with a kind heart. Together, the duo slayed his uncles, the prince wielding a sword. The mare 'neighed full loudly', striking terror among the kinsmen before the prince 'raised a pyramid of skulls', these grisly decapitations shown in the mural. (Mhv: 10: 69, 72) The battle site was thought to be Buddhist cave site of Ritigala.[21] (10: 63) When the prince finally came to rule in Anuradhapura, the mare was rewarded with a place in the palace. She is shown in the mural with an equine face and the seated king on the left. The register above shows the prince's men visiting the uncles, bearing weapons as gifts. The uncles, feigning friendship, believed they had lulled the prince into believing a truce was in force. But it was at that instant that the prince and mare launched their attack. This subject matter is rare, perhaps unique, and it also sets the stage for nearby murals focused on Anuradhapura.

Sculpture

The principal sculpture is the Buddha facing one of the entrances, carved from the living rock. Flanking the standing Buddha are tall wooden images identified as Natha and Metteyya in the 1726-manuscript. Both have a seated Buddha in their headdress. Metteyya, on the Buddha's right side, has one hand in the teaching-gesture and the left in the gesture of removing obstacles**.** (The hands of Natha appear to be restored.) The pairing of Natha and Metteyya was not uncommon during this age, both deities residing together in Tusita Heaven.[22] Behind this ensemble are standing images of Sumana and Vishnu painted in their traditional colours, white and blue, respectively, their hands posed in the same way as Metteyya.

Scene showing the horse-faced demoness, on the right.

All four sculptures are identified in the 1726-manuscript and so it is likely that Kirti Sri refurbished them sometime after 1750. These are wooden images, with details in repainted plaster.[23] Hands or arms were made entirely of plaster fitted around wooden or metal armatures. Over the principal images are ceiling murals mimicking cloth hangings placed over images in temples. Original woodwork from the Kandyan period is a window frame on the exterior wall of Cave 3.

Ranged along both sides of the hall are four large seated Buddhas, likely representing Gotama and the three preceding Buddhas. At the end is a larger Buddha, perhaps Metteyya. The dated manuscripts also mention a sculpture of the cave's founder, Valagamba, and another of Nissankamalla, but they are not described nor their locations in the cave specified. Valagamba is conventionally identified as the figure on the left near the entrance. This may originally have been an image of Shiva since it was noted in 1817 as having a 'double-headed snake about the neck, the body of which serves as a necklace, and the heads as ear-pendants'. The right hand is in the teaching-gesture but the lowered left is probably restored. In the opposite corner is a huge standing image identified in lore as King Nissankamalla.[24] This figure is unlike any others, since its the only large sculpture in the cave with a degree of contrapposto. His right hand is in the teaching-gesture, his left at his side. He is dressed regally, with a tapered crown.

Identified today as Nissankamalla, the royal patron whose incription is incised next to Cave I. River Books.

The cave's large stupa is encircled by eight seated Buddhas, two with snake-hoods. Only four images were present in the early 19th century and all were snake-hooded.

'Sacred as the Water of the Ganges'

A metal pot on the floor collects water dripping from a long fissure in the ceiling that appeared in the reign of Vimala Dharma Surya II (1687-1707), according to the 1726 manuscript. To staunch the drip, a soft malleable amalgam of '4,000 *palamas* of lead and 200 *palamas* of quicksilver' was pressed into the crack. The hardened substance became impermeable, much like the amalgam pressed into a tooth cavity. This solution eventually failed and the drip resumed. Artists during the time of Kirti Sri then cleverely turned the ceiling crack into a river enlivened with fish. The water was believed to be 'sacred as the water of the Ganges'.[25]

A fissure in the ceiling appeared by the 17th century. Plugged by an amalgam, it later failed and artists made the crack look like a river with fish.

Cave 3

This cave was embellished by Kirti Sri, with the encouragement of the Asgiriya monastery's chief in Kandy, according to the 1780-manuscript. A large arch made of plaster embellishes the single entrance to the cave. Two snake-hooded figures stand at the sides, while celestials float above in clouds. Some figures have retained bits of original painting and the arms of several figures have broken off, exposing metal armatures

King Kirti Sri, left. The mural illustrates a cosmological theme, the Anotatta Lake in the Himavan Mountains.

Facing the entrance is a seated Buddha. On one side of the hall is a large reclining Buddha and on the other a life-size portrait sculpture of Kirti Sri. On the ceiling is the Buddha forecasting the coming of Metteyya and another composition showing Metteyya himself in the Tusita Heaven. A caption identifies the kneeling figure as Ajita, Metteyya's previous name. The rows of small Buddhas on the ceiling are referred to in the 1780-manuscript as a thousand in number.

'... to rid her of human stains'

The Anotatta Lake from where the Buddha set off for Sri Lanka.

Next to the standing image of Kirti Sri is a large mural featuring the mythical Anotatta Lake that enjoyed a special position in Sri Lanka since the Buddha set off from this lake before his first visit to the island. (Mhv: 1. 19) This mythical lake in the Himavan mountains weaves in and out of Buddhist literature and descriptions of the lake also appear in cosmological texts, notably in the 14th-century *Traibhumi-katha* from Sukhothai. Its bountiful waters even refreshed Asoka's subjects and Sri Lankan notices of the lake conform largely to the Pali and Thai texts.[26] (Mhv: 5. 24)

Lake Anototta is the most famous of seven lakes in the Himavan mountains. Light from the sun and moon never shone on it directly and so its waters were forever cool. Even the Buddha's mother found herself at the Anotatta Lake where its waters 'rid of her human stains' in preparation for her miraculous conception.[27]

From the lake flow four rivers from the mouths of animals, a lion, elephant, horse and a cow. The rivers encircle the lake three times. The

The Anatotta Lake, Maya's lustration and the elephant on the 'silver mountain', from the *Nidanakatha*. The preparatory sketch is visible beneath the elephant.

South River flows beneath a huge rock named Vijjha from which it divides into five rivers, two being the Ganges and Jumna. Three white elephants in the upper right refer to Jataka 514 featuring the elephant named Chaddanta and his two wives, known in Pali literature and in cosmology and associated with Chaddanta Lake. The banyan tree above appears in this birth-tale while nearby are flowering Shala trees, marking the grove where the grudge-match between his two wives began. Even Buddhaghosa remarked that the elephant named Chaddanta preferred the peaceful forest and lakes of Himavan to cities.[28]

Three seated figures toward the top are perhaps *pacceka* Buddhas to whom one elephant-queen made an offer in exchange for a boon to be reborn as a human queen in Varanasi. Pacceka Buddhas also visited the Anotatta Lake before their flight to the Deer Park, known from a commentary on the *Majjhima Nikaya*. A monk named Sumana stands before a stingy serpent named Pannaka who refused to allow him to draw water from the lake, reminiscent of the Buddha's disciple, Mogallana, who faced off with a snake-king among the murals of the Mahamuni Temple in Mandalay.[29] A lion, two geese and an ascetic also inhabit the landscape, all included in the descriptions found in the Pali Commentaries. As the universe comes to its end, the Anotatta is among the last lakes to dry up.

Why the theme received such prominence at Dambulla is hard to say, since it enjoyed few important depictions in Sri Lanka. What models did the artists rely on or was their composition guided by learned monks ? Or perhaps the focus on Anottata Lake reflects the well-known influence from Siam during this period where the theme was more popular. The earliest depiction of this lake in Southeast Asia is found among Pagan's murals in Burma (temple 475), where the lake is also pictured with the elephant king and his two wives. The same is true for a painted wooden panel in Bangkok at Wat Rakhang.

Preparatory drawings made by Dambulla's muralists are easily visible in Cave 4.

Cave 4

This cave is often called the Western Cave, or Pacchima, since it was the most westerly from the main entrance until the addition of Cave 5. It was probably excavated between 1725 and 1780 and an inscription on one wall is dated to 1918.

The ceiling scene shows the Buddha preaching before the ascent to the Tavatisma Heaven, marked by three staircases with the Buddha accompanied by Sakka, Brahma and Vishnu. Another panel shows the Buddha teaching amidst a group of royal figures, probably at Savatthi. On one wall is a row of *arahants* bearing lotuses, led in procession by Mogallana. Traces of the preparatory line drawings can be seen where work was never completed. Many areas show restored patches made between the 1890s and 1930s.

The cave's large brick stupa was thought to contain jewellery belonging to Valagamba's second Queen, Somadevi. Robbers broke into the stupa in 1983 but departed with only indelible stains on their karma. Discovered inside later was a small stone relic chamber that included small Buddha images, bones and beads.[30]

Cave 5

This cave is lowest on the cliffside and is Dambulla's last addition, created between 1817 and 1847, with a reclining Buddha as the focus. On the rear wall is painted a twelve-arm Kataragama, with his peacock, and a dark two-arm figure usually identified as Vishnu. Both are formal icons, appearing frontally, contrasting to the third smaller figure who is poised at an angle and who holds a short sword and a cane. He may represent the deity Dadimunda, who also holds a cane and is associated with Vishnu.[31] The cave was renovated in 1915 by a nobleman whose portrait is just inside the doorway, noted in a caption above his head.

Three deities behind the reclining Buddha in Cave 5. Possibly Dadimunda, left, Vishnu, centre, and Kataragama.

Odium Theologicum and the Golden Hill

Controversy has recently dogged Dambulla, like so many World Heritage sites where tourism, piety and riches all collide in ungodly ways. Control over Dambulla is shared between Kandy's Asgiriya monastery and the Central Cultural Fund, unlike Sigiriya that is administered by the government.This powerful monastery enjoys jurisdiction over seven temples but Dambulla is the jewel in its crown. This control began when Kirti Sri removed local monks at Dambulla for not performing the 'rituals of the temple satisfactorily', probably a lame excuse for Dambulla's rising importance (and revenues) and the king's desire to place such an important temple more closely under royal control.[32]

The site is now so lucrative that a Sri Lankan colleague jested that Dambulla is a 'solid cash cow'. But tourism's corrosive impact started over a century ago when guides demanded 'fresh sums' to open the doors to each cave and showed themselves 'no less greedy than any guide to a catacomb or church'.[33]

Dambulla's recent abbot, Inamaluwe Sumangala, even provoked a turf war with his Asgiriya brethren in Kandy by reversing a policy about ordinations that were required to be performed in Kandy. He flaunted these rules by not only performing the ceremony at Dambulla but also for nuns. Moreover, he launched in 1997 the Sri Lanka Bhikkhuni Re-awakening Organization, another salvo in his dispute with his seniors down the road in Kandy. Sumangala also headed a violent Buddhist demonstration in 2012 against a mosque and Hindu temple. The powers of this contentious monk have been recently reduced and much of the money collected by the monastery is now used for professional conservation.[34]

Corruption is scarcely restricted to our current age since the chief monk at Dambulla in 1869 sold 'to a low-country carpenter all the valuable timber belonging to one of the forests' owned by the monastery. The monk pocketed the money and the '*vihara* chest' was left with nought. An exasperated English official wished that such infractions 'could be dealt with as a matter of good government, untrammeled by *odium theologicum*', a 19th-century expression for religious discord. The government requested the Asgiriya chief monk in Kandy to discipline the Dambulla monk but he admitted that all control had been lost over the Dambulla monks. Such complaints pushed the government to enact the Buddhist Temporalities Ordinance that placed temple property under trustees.[35]

But the *sangha* was never free from discord. Even during the Buddha's lifetime two groups actually came to blows over a disciplinary dispute at the Kosambi monastery. Unable to reconcile the opposing parties, the Buddha was eventually asked to leave Kosambi. The proven resilience of religious strife, or *odium theologicum,* ensures that there will be future unattractive chapters in Dambulla's history.

Around Dambulla

A ruinous Buddhist monastery complex is not far from the foot of the mountain on the south side. A brick stupa begun here in the second century was then enlarged 200 years later. Rituals may have been performed here by the monks inhabiting the many nearby small caves. This ancient site has been recently named Somavati, after Valagamba's queen.

A much larger Buddhist complex nearby is at Manikdena, about ten kilomtres south of Dambula. A 10th century stupa, a circular Bodhi Tree shrine, and a temple are dated to the eight or ninth-century; a second stupa there is thought to be from the 10th century. Several stone Buddha figures from here are on display in the Sigiriya museum.

GALLE

Previous page:
The Galle Fort. Courtesy Dominic Sansoni.

Galle: A Rooster on a Rock

The great tsunami in 2004 was especially cruel to the south coast but Galle's fort held fast and so saved an irreplaceable colonial township dotted with religious sites. Although first a Portuguese fortress, Galle was no match for a Dutch fleet that prevailed after only four days in 1640; by contrast, the Dutch siege of Colombo took over seven months. Before the Portuguese, this coast lay within the realm of the Kotte dynasty, centred near Colombo, but the chief commercial and religious hub in the south at that time was coastal Devinuvara further east. It was Devinuvara for example that was visited by the 14th-century Arab traveller Ibn Battuta who made only a brief mention of Galle, or 'Quali'. It is commonplace to attribute the name of Galle to the Portuguese but the name was probably adopted directly from the Sinhalese Gala, derived from rock, known from 14th-century Sinhalese poems. The word Gala also resembled the Portuguese *galo*, or rooster, and hence a rooster perched atop a rock became the city's emblem. The rooster is also the national bird of Portugal. Many variants grew up, such as Puncto Galle or Point de Galle. Little survives from Portuguese Galle, or what was called Santa Cruz de Gale, but archives and old maps furnish much detail.[1]

The Dutch capture of Galle was celebrated annually by a 'public Thanksgiving to God our Lord', once conducted by the famous cleric Phillipus Baldaeus. Inside the fort the Dutch found some 250 Portuguese families and about '600 hundred of various handicraftsmen, all Christian'.[2] Galle, Colombo and Jaffna were the chief Dutch centres, their municipal arms accorded special crests. Four Portuguese churches were within the walls, the largest designated a cathedral and located near today's Meera Mosque

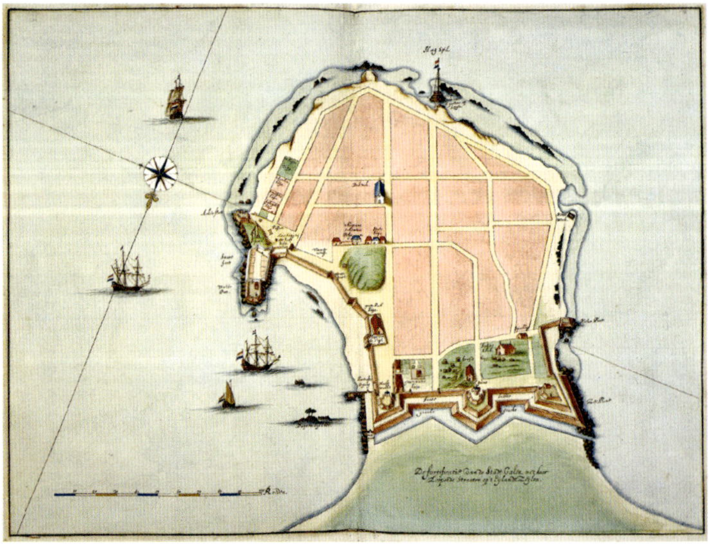

Galle, by Joannes Vingboors, 1663, before the construction of the VOC warehouse in 1668-1669. Austrian National Library.

bordering the seawall. None have survived but the Dutch adapted these churches for their own use even into the 1660s. All of Ceylon passed from Dutch to English control in 1802 with the Treaty of Amiens.

The initial design for the fort was made in 1659 by Adriaan de Leeuw with later improvements by Johannes Vingboons in the early 1660s. However, it was not until 1668-69 that the long and narrow VOC warehouse was incorporated within the city walls, with a wide covered entrance in the middle immediately opposite the quayside. The VOC monogram is featured on a large stone panel set into the gateway. The central oval is supported by two lions, arranged *rampant guardant*, with the date, 'Anno MCCLXIX' (1669). On the top is Galle's symbol, a rooster on a rock, set amidst turbulent seas. Important sites within the walls at the time were the 'Groote Kerk', a mosque, a gunpowder mill and a Javanese encampment. The perimeter walls were partially made of coral blocks, called *klipsteen*, a material favoured over stone since 'coral stone' is of 'a meally nature and cannot be shivered into pieces by the stroke of a cannon-ball'.[3]

Glazed jars from Lower Burma, known as Martabans, were exported widely in Southeast Asia. This example, found in the Penal Palace's kitchen in Sintra, Portugal, is among the many found in Europe.

Hundreds of objects from this era were recovered from the *Avondster*, a shipwreck in the bay in 1659. Many are on view in the fort's Maritime Museum. Ceramic storage jars from China and Thailand were found, together with one or two glazed Martaban jars, named after the port in Lower Burma from where these jars were exported throughout Southeast Asia and even into Europe. The Dutch called these special jars Martavandes or Martavanas and used them in various ways, such as for storing gunpowder, sealing the openings with wooden covers covered by lead. Over fifty of these jars 'ordered from the coast [India]' were even used to build earthenworks on Hammenhiel Island near Jaffna.[4]

Many Muslims lived within the fort and outside and the Dutch appointed a Chief of the Moors for Galle. The centre of Islamic life during the British period was the Meera Mosque, established in the early 1900s, with patronage from Sir Mohamed Macan Markar (1887-1952). Muslims in Galle excelled as jewellers and the Markar family owned a shop in the Grand Oriental Hotel, Colombo, with branches in Cairo and Jerusalem.

A German, Johann Wolfgang Heydt, was in Ceylon for over two years and employed by the VOC beginning in 1733. His draftsman and painter, Arent Jansen, contributed illustrations to Heydt's book on Ceylon published in 1744 that featured six of Galle. The fort's population was comprised of 'Costizos, Mestizos, Moors, Malabars, Sinhalese and Chitties, mostly mixed together'. A Mestizo was one born from a caucasian parent and anyone from another race, and a Costizo was a product of a caucasian and a Mestizo. Heydt found that the 'streets are not ordered symmetrically but run now crooked, now straight'. The lanes were pocked

The VOC monogram, 1699, within the inner wall of the Dutch warehouse. A rooster, the symbol of Galle, above.

with many shallow ditches serving as overnight homes for drunkards 'to sleep off their befuddlement'. There was even a name for these ditches, 'Home-goers-bed'.[5] The Dutch gentry mainly lived outside the walls.

The National Maritime Museum now occupies the Dutch warehouse built in the 1660s for the tons of goods shipped in and out of Galle. A plan of the warehouse made in 1717 indicates exactly where exported products were stored. The cavernous upper floor was reserved for the precious cinnamon stock, while the lower was portioned out to various products, such as a special wood for ship construction. Conch shells were traded to India where they were 'sawed into rings of various sizes, and worn on the arms, legs, fingers and toes of the Hindoos, both male and female'.[6]

Eleanor Coade and her 'Twice-fired-Stone

On the outer face of the old Dutch entranceway is a beige panel containing the British Royal arms before its design changed slightly in 1837. The panel appears to be made of stone but is actually a clay substance resembling stone developed by Eleanor Coade (1733-1821). Artificial stone was in use for some time but Coade perfected a new formula for the clay that was kiln fired twice for four days at more than 1,000 degrees centigrade. She coined the word, *lithodipyra*, meaning 'twice-fired-stone' in Greek, to describe her creations. John Sealy was her cousin and business partner until his death in 1813 and a weathered inscription near the panel's bottom reads 'Coade & Sealy London 1813'. Coade enjoyed commissions at Windsor and Buckingham Palace. Another panel made from the same mould is above the entrance to Fort Frederick in Trincomalee. These two panels are the only works by Coade known in Sri Lanka.[7] Below the panel's stone frame is a date, 1668, and a small keystone in the brick arch below bears the VOC monogram.

Britain's royal arms, 1813, from clay fired in a technique invented by Eleanor Coade, matches one at Trincomalee's fort. Outer wall of Dutch warehouse.

The Groote Church, 1752-1755, designed by Abraham Anthonisz. All Saints Anglican church, further along the same street.

The Groote Kerk

Groundbreaking for the church was on 4 July 1752 and was presided over by Galle's Commandeur Casparus de Jong. Two years later the walls were 'raised to their appropriate height' and the roof was begun. The architect was Abraham Anthonisz who supervised local carpenters making ships and houses. Anthonisz was the first of his family to come to Ceylon from Amsterdam in 1736. The roof was completed in time for his third marriage that was performed after the church's consecration in 1755.

The church is often said to have replaced a Portuguese convent but Heydt's town plan indicates that this spot was vacant in the early 1730s. An earlier Dutch church was, however, across the street where part of its façade survives as the entrance to the Maritime Museum, still with its keystone, dated to 1672. The church's original belfry still stands nearby on top of the city wall, shown in a lithograph.[8] A stone block at its base is inscribed 'Anno 1701'.

The plan of the Groote Kerk is a Greek Cross but the transepts are far shorter than the nave, unlike the Wolvendaal church and the destroyed church in Jaffna in which the nave and transepts were of equal length. The original ironwood ceiling, painted blue with gold stars representing heaven, was replaced in 1925. The origin of the wood used for the pulpit and its soundboard is uncertain but the example once in Jaffna, in ebony, came from either from the Indian coast or from the Vanni area south of Jaffna.[9]

The Latin phrase *Spes set Regerminat* ('Again there is hope that it will sprout'), the motto of the Dutch Reformed Church of Sri Lanka. This wooden panel is attached to the elevated choir stall above the church entrance.

Transept and nave of different dimensions, unlike the cruciform plan of Colombo's Wolvandaal church and Jaffna's Kruys church.

A 19th-century stained glass window at the rear depicts the symbol of the Dutch Reformed Church of Ceylon, a tree stump from which new green shoots sprout. Above is the Latin, *Spes set regerminat* (Job 14:7), or 'Again there is a hope that it will sprout again'. The remaining stained glass has been restored, based on original designs, but their garish colours mar otherwise chaste walls. The only significant change to the original Dutch interior was the removal of some pews in order to accommodate the Anglican service in which the host is administered.

The majority of the Dutch tombstones embedded in the floor were removed from various locations in and around Galle. Over 70 stones are found on the floor and walls and more are placed outside. The earliest dates from 1662. Many were shifted here in 1853 from a cemetery within the fort begun in 1710. A new cemetery outside the fort was started, with some coffins 'laid one over the other' and 'the pestiferous stench that is diffused by this abominable custom is indescribable', noted in 1786.[10]

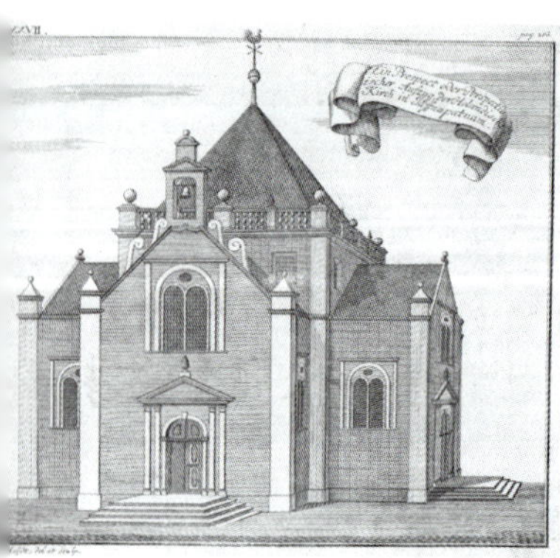

Jaffna's Kruys church, 1706. destroyed during the recent civil war. Johann Wolfgang Heydt (1744), National Library of the Netherlands.

The wall plaques are mostly from the English era. One commemorates a 20-year old soldier who fell during the 1857 Indian Mutiny and was erected 'by his old comrades left in garrison at Galle'. One marble memorial on the rear wall is for John Joachim Vanderspar, the Consul in Ceylon for His Majesty the King of the Netherlands. For some plaques, the name of the sculptor or atelier was engraved along the bottom edge. One was commissioned from Llewellyn and Company, a firm based in Calcutta that sent stones throughout neighbouring British colonies. Another was commissioned in London from Samuel Manning, a sculptor who exhibited in the Great Exhibition of Industry of all Nations in 1851. At least two memorials came from the workshop of Thomas Bedford on Oxford Street, London.

Four wooden hatchments, or *wapenbords*, pay tribute to former church notables. The earliest, from 1758, belongs to Ras Macquet,

'Commandeur of Galle'. Another, dated to 1800, honoured Theobald von Hugel, a captain in the Wurttemberg Regiment, a German military unit in South Africa employed by the VOC. The most recent is from 1903, for a local physician P.D. Anthonsz. Surviving wills and testaments in archives fill out the picture of colonial life. A Dutch couple mused in one document that 'there is nothing more certain than death, yet nothing more uncertain than the time or hour thereof'. The couple added that our 'immortal souls' are destined to 'the merciful hands of Almighty God' while 'our perishing bodies enter into the bosom of the earth'.[11]

Angels and the Grim Reaper

The most outstanding hatchment in all of Sri Lanka commemorates Abraham Samlant, a former Galle Commandeur who expired on 3 May 1766. His family history illustrates the wide reach of the VOC, stretching from the Netherlands to Indonesia. The four shields represent the Samlants and related families, going clockwise from the upper left: the Samlant, Emanns, Martien and Lemmens. The tattered white tunic is thought to be his own but it has never been scientifically tested. The Samlant's armorial bearings were three columns confined to a square box. The commander's accouterments appear on the sides, sculpted in wood, such as a sabre, lance, halberd, rifle, drum, bugle and cannon. He was originally buried in the former Dutch cemetery within the fort where a large monument was erected but demolished in 1853 when the tombstones were transferred here.

On the floor opposite the hatchment lies his tombstone, with his prone figure resting atop a coffin.[12] The Grim Reaper balances nimbly on his scythe, beneath the winged angel playing two trumpets. His bony right hand emerges out of the sealed coffin, adding a whimsical touch to his macabre vocation of 'harvesting' souls with his scythe. The Reaper enjoyed many names in Holland but perhaps 'Bone-man' (*Beenderman*) best fits this depiction. The smiling cherub above is a reminder of the soul's serene afterlife that cannot commence until a reckoning with Mr Reaper.

Commandeur Samlant's hatchment (*Wapenbord*), with the accouterments of his office. The white tunic is probably original.

Tombstone of Abraham Samlant, Galle Commandeur. 1766. The Grim Reaper enjoys the tunes from a pair of trumpets as he dips his hand into the coffin.

All Saints Church designed by James G. Smither, the architect of the National Museum, Colombo. Work began in 1868.

All Saints Church

This Anglican church was designed by James G. Smither, an architect responsible for major projects, such as the National Museum in Colombo. Anglicans first worshipped in the Groote Church before All Saints' completion. The foundation was laid in 1868 by the Bishop of Colombo, with its consecration in 1871.

The stained glass was sent out from London at different times. One in the transept commemorates two young sisters who drowned near Matara in 1890. The inscription above, beginning 'Suffer Little Children .... ', echoed the tragedy. In the corner is 'Cox. Edgley, artists, 69 Berners Street, London'. The rose window was dedicated by the parents of a son who died in 'Formosa' in 1934. The floor tiles are made with different coloured clays by the encaustic technique invented by English Gothic Revival artists. Such tiles were mass produced in England and covered floors in all British colonies. One fine example is in the charming Warleigh church in the tea country.

Suddhamalaya

An important Buddhist site within the fort was founded some fifteen years after All Saints. The temple's chequered history is known principally from a seven-page Supreme Court filing summarizing a dispute in 1918 between the temple's trustees and its chief monk. The trustees demanded the monk's immediate removal but he refused to budge. Reasons for the trustees' disapproval are nowhere stated but the monk had served here for over ten years. The case moved up the legal ladder with the district judge ruling in favour of the trustees. The monk then appealed to the Supreme Court in 1921. He rested his case on the principal of pupillary succession, since his superior at a different temple had appointed him to the Galle temple. The case was decided however on the finding that the temple and the adjacent monastic residence were

Suddhamalaya. The Pali canon was invoked in a conflict between the trustees and a monk in a ruling by the Supreme Court in 1921.

never properly gifted by a donor, with a formal ceremony, to the local Buddhist community, or *sangha*; a section from the *Chulavagga* in the *Vinaya-pitaka* of the Pali canon was invoked by the trustees, together with other arguments. Since no formal Buddhist ceremony bestowed the property to the *sangha*, then the premises should be treated as 'lay property' for which the rule of pupillary succession was moot. The temple, according to the judge, never became '*sanghika*, that is to say, it never belonged to the priesthood or *sangha*, with all of the incidents applicable to ecclesiastical property of that description'.[13] The appellant monk was therefore forced to leave. The judge contributing the opinion was Sir Thomas Edward de Sampayo, KC, Cambridge-trained and the first President of the Catholic Union of Ceylon. That a case revolved on a Buddhist point of law was decided by a Catholic judge in a British court is a reminder of Sri Lanka's pluralism.

The published ruling provided other information about the temple that is otherwise lost. The trustees sought to purchase a suitable building in the late 1880s and selected what was probably an existing Christian church. This church is likely the large building still visible from the main street. Its original entrance faced the nearby city walls but is now bricked up and whitewashed. The church survives in three parallel sections, each with its own tiled roof. A truncated section of the ornamented roof cornice is all that remains on the front. A row of neo-Gothic stone arches faces the side street with a date in the Buddhist era, 2430 (1887). The temple now houses a recumbent Buddha, flanked with modern posters of Hindu deities. The small stupa in the compound was constructed in about 1908.

Galle also enjoyed a special place in the nation's recent Buddhist history, for it was here that Henry Steel Olcott and Elene Petrovna Blavatsky recited the Five Precepts (P: *pancasila*) and so became Buddhists.[14] This ceremony took place at the Vijayananda Temple on May 19 1880. The temple, about three kilometers northeast of the fort, was once in the country but is now lost in Galle's lanes. The chief monk at the temple was Akmimana Dhammarama who belonged to the Ramanna division that advocated a return to 'pure' Buddhism.

COLOMBO

COLOMBO: 'SUCH A MIXTURE OF NATIONS, MANNERS AND RELIGIONS'

Previous page:
Portuguese Colombo encompassed the Fort and Pettah before the Dutch reduced the city's perimeter to include only the Fort. *Atlas Major*, 1662-1672. Austrian National Library.

The 14th-century traveler from Tangier, Ibn Batutta, lauded Colombo, or 'Kalanbu', as 'one the finest and largest towns in Serendib', yet the origin and meaning of the name Colombo is still debated.[1] Centuries later, the Dutch knew the city as Colombo and adopted a tree with a perched bird as the capital's coat of arms. British rule in the nineteenth century inagurated a wave of new Buddhist monasteries, churches and mosques sponsored by new urban elites.

Buddhists were in the Colombo area from as early as the third-century BCE, known from inscriptions in caves. The closest site was Koratota that was once a tourist attraction. The region also was within Anuradhapura's orbit, known from two 10th-century inscriptions from the nearby Kelaniya monastery.[2] However, Colombo's history comes into sharper focus only when Muslim traders controlled commerce along the west coast at the turn of the first millennium. The earliest evidence is a tombstone, found in Colombo in the 18th century, marking a death in 949 CE. A fourteenth-century Papal legate in Ceylon found a certain 'tyrant, an eunuch ... an accursed Saracen' who dominated the coastline. Ibn Battuta echoed this when he found Colombo in the hands of 'the Wazir and ruler of the Sea, Jalasti', who commanded some 500 Abyssinian retainers. In the same century, Muslim and Jewish merchants were shipping cinnamon and fabrics to the Mediterranean.[3]

The Portuguese arrived in the early sixteenth century and came into conflict with the Kotte dynasty whose centre, Jayawardanapura, was some 12 kilometres southeast of Colombo's fort. This dynasty once controlled nearly all of Ceylon and received Buddhist embassies from Siam and Lower Burma. Its most sacred shrine held a tooth-relic of the Buddha that is the one now believed to be in Kandy. The Kotte court culture blended Hindu and Buddhist rituals, with kings patronizing popular Hindu temples, such as Munneshvaram in 1438. In this period arose the most important temple dedicated to the demon Ravana's brother, located at the the Kelaniya monastery. Nearby at Nawagamuwa, a major temple arose honouring the goddess Pattini. The Kotte kingdom eventually forfeited its autonomy to the Portuguese following the conversion of a Kotte king who was renamed Dom João Dharmapala (1541-1597).

Begun in 1873 by the monk Hikkaduwa Sri Sumangala, the Vidyodaya Oriental College was a centre for Buddhism's revival. The two horseshoe-shaped arches above the entrance are modeled on the façades of early Buddhist cave temples in western India.

The Portuguese presence

The earliest tangible signs of Portuguese presence is the country's heraldic arms incised on a boulder near the President's House within the Fort but its date, either 1505 or 1506, is still debated. The Portuguese also likely established a small stone cross, or padrao, in its vicinity. This standard, or *padrao*, had on one side the arms of Portugal and on the other a sphere representing Portugal's global empire. This very stone cross in Colombo was even mentioned in a letter from Goa's Viceroy to King Manuel in Lisbon: 'the cross of Christos and the royal arms and the device [the sphere] have been left in Ceilam on a *padram*'. Similar crosses were erected at a number of Portuguese landfalls, with none surviving in India or Ceylon but eight found in Africa. One document suggests that the cross in Colombo was perhaps prepared in Cochin.[4]

The Portuguese coat of arms incised on a boulder facing the harbour, in 1505 or 1506. Nearby was probably a stone cross, or *padrao*, front and reverse. After Ferguson (1907).

The small triangular-shaped fortress from 1518, named *Fortaleza de Santa Bárbara,* was soon abandoned but the Portuguese returned from Goa in the 1550s and a far larger fort was completed by the 1560s that included modern Pettah. A bastion was destroyed by an earthquake in 1614, according to an account published in Lisbon by an eye-witness.[5] Colombo was then the second largest walled city in Portuguese Asia, after Goa, with a population of about 60, 000. Few places boasted 'such a mixture of nations, manners and religions' that included 'Moors, Malabars [Tamils], Travancorians, Malays, Hindoos, Gentoos [Buddhists], Chinese, Persians, Arabians, Turks, Maldivians, Javians and Parsees'. These various groups were also never strictly segregated as they were in Indian Portuguese walled communities, fostering a hybrid, or *mestizo*, culture. Two

Amsterdam's coat of arms likely belonged to the Amsterdam bastion. Discovered in 1901, now at the YMCA within the Fort area.

broad divisions emerged. One comprised offspring from European and Asian unions labeled 'mixed', or *mestico* in Portuguese, or *mestiezen* or *mixties* in Dutch, with many variants. This group, also called Burghers, was never fully accepted in colonial society but were given preferential treatment over Sinhalas. Burghers are now thought of as Dutch-Sinhala descendants but its original meaning encompassed those of mixed Portuguese descent also. The children of mestizos were classified as *toepasses* or *topazes,* a term stemming from the old Hindustani *do-basha*, or 'two languages', since the children often spoke the languages of both parents. Dutch descendants formed the Dutch Burgher Union of Ceylon in 1907. Little survives in Colombo from the Portuguese era, apart from stone inscriptions in the National Museum and a few gravestones, such as at St Thomas Church near the harbour.[6] Other survivals include carved ivory boxes and precious metalwork.

The Portuguese lost Colombo to the Dutch after a seventh-month siege in 1656, with help from Kandyan forces and Javanese troops. The Dutch victors then reduced the city's exposure to attack by greatly drawing in the city's walls to exclude the Pettah area. The leading city planners were a military surveyor named Adriaan de Leeuw and an engineer, Jan Christiensz Toorzee. The redesigned city walls measured little more than two kilometres, with seven bastions bearing Dutch names, such as Delft. A stone once embedded in the Amsterdam bastion turned up in 1901. Another that may have been set into the Hoorn bastion, dated 1698, is in the National Museum.

The Dutch, by virtue of the Kew Letter of 1788, gave Britain the mandate to protect Dutch Asian possessions. The English therefore took possession of the fort. The walled city, with 'three hundred piece of heavy cannon', would have looked more or less like the forts today in Galle and Jaffna. The walls were eventually reduced to a few meagre sections, a casualty of urban development between 1869 and 1871. Capturing the flavour of elite Dutch domestic life is now the Dutch Museum in Pettah, the former residence of Governor Thomas van Rhee (1692-1697).

The nave of St Peter's was originally the ground floor of the Dutch Governor's residence.

The Treaty of Amiens in 1802 forfeited all Dutch possessions in Ceylon to Britain. The Fort area then became inhabited 'chiefly by English' and the Pettah area by tradesmen of Dutch and Portuguese descent who intermarried with locals. Indigenous Sinhalas lived largely beyond the walls. English rule brought Christian missionaries who actively challenged Buddhism, and Colombo assumed a leading role in the push back against the missionaries. For example, the Vidyodaya Oriental College was founded in 1837 by a leading monk named Hikkaduwe Sumangala.[7] Later, another key centre was a monastery headed by a Thai prince, treated in a following chapter.

Saint Peter's

A banquet for Kandyan envoys hosted by Governor Iman Falck, 1772. The lost original oil painting by C.F. Reimer was nearly two metres long but several copies exist. Rijksmuseum, Amsterdam.

This Anglican church located in the old Fort area was once the two-storied Dutch Governor's residence facing the harbour, seen in old drawings and watercolours. The best known shows a banquet for the annual mission from Kandy in 1772 hosted by Governor Iman Willem Falck. By 1804, the roof was in 'so shattered a state to admit the rain' that the upper storey was ordered to be removed. The upper floor, which had been the private residence of the governor, was taken away and the ground floor converted into a house of worship. It was known as the Fort Church until its consecration in 1821 and thereafter St Peter's. It was also used for 'the most gay and festive amusements … and for serious and solemn duties'. The ceiling was raised by extending the height of the nave walls, with visible metal trusses supporting the tile roof. The present portico and verandah were likely added in 1832.[8]

Memorial plaques lining the walls tell the story of British colonial life. The earliest, commemorates a young Lieutenant who fell in the war with Kandy in 1803. So many British perished in this war that a special cemetery was created in Pettah. One plaque is dedicated to John D'Oyly who played a role in the capture of Kandy in 1815 but whose actual tomb is in Kandy's Garrison Cemetery. Another stone inscription, from 1817, honours William Tolfrey who devoted his 'oriental learning to the propagation of the Gospel by rendering the Holy Scriptures in the Sinhalese and Pali languages'. Tolfrey sought to remove the 'Dutch idiom' out of earlier translations.[9] Another important Anglican landmark was Christ Church, from 1853, near the Galle Face Green.

Marriages took place at St Peter's even before the church's consecration in 1821. One union became the talk of the town. The Dutch wife was accused by her English husband of having illicit relations with the ship's doctor while returning from England with her five children. The cuckolded husband sued for a divorce and £7,000 from the doctor 'who seduced, debauched, and carnally knew

The Wesleyan Mission House by the Burgher artist Peter P. van Houten, 1816. It was the first Methodist chapel in Asia. Simpson Collection, Sydney.

H. Pedris faced a British firing squad following the Buddhist-Muslim riot of that year in 1915. A memorial temple built by his father is the Isipathanaramaya Monastery, with murals by H. Sarlis.

Mara's defeat, 1939-1940, by the Burgher painter George Keyt in a temple designed by Andrew Boyd. Gotami Monastery.

her' even after her return to Colombo. The husband won the case but was soon thrown from his horse, fatally.[10]

The early 20th century saw a handful of temples and monasteries funded by well-to-do locals. One was named Isipathanaramaya and founded in 1916 by the mining magnate D. D. Pedris. The project memorialized his son, Henry, who faced a British firing squad for 'treason by levying war against Our Lord, the King' in the Buddhist-Muslim riot of 1915. Its murals, from 1920-21, were by H. Sarlis (1880-1955) who cast Buddhist characters in Western garb. Life-size portraits of Pedris and his two sons are on one wall. Nearby is a similar temple, the Asokaramaya, from the 1930s. Colombo's most innovative religious painting was by the Burgher artist George Keyt (1901-1993) in the Gotami monastery where he spent six months filling the walls of a temple designed by Andrew Boyd. Keyt's Mara's demons are made somehow even more diabolical in a style reminiscent of Picasso's *Guernica*.[11] Traditional Buddhist murals in Colombo are in Kotte, circa 1880, and at Sapuskandha from 1886.

Navroz Baug, established in 1927, and its Parsi priest.

A tiny but influential minority were the Parsis. Most came from Bombay but many returned to India after independence in 1948 and with the rise of Buddhist nationalism in the 1950s. Their numbers peaked by the 1930s, totalling about 450, but by 2015 only thirty-four Parsis were registered in the community's association, or Anjuman.[12] A fire-temple, from 1927, is located about five kilometres south of the Fort on Galle Face Road. Parsi temples are ranked according to their ritual fires, the two highest described as *atash behrams* and *atash adarans*. The Colombo temple is the least sacred, known as a *dadgah*, or a heath fire, in which the fire is lit only during ceremonies. The priest today is Mr Sarosh Sidhwa whose training was in Mumbai.

Gangaramaya

Ranked among the most sacred Buddhist sites in Colombo, it is venerated neither for ancient relics nor for a visit from the Buddha. Instead, its sanctity is based on its early association with highly venerated monks, notably Hikkaduwe Sumangala (1827-1911) who founded the temple in 1885. Another factor was prestigious lay patronage, since such sponsors, like pre-modern royalty, lend auspicious lustre to sites. For Gangaramaya, it was the same family that sponsored the Kelaniya temple, the Wijewardanas. Its recent fame is enhanced by its annual street procession, or *perahera*, begun in the 1980s and now second in popularity only to Kandy's procession.

Another factor explaining the temple's sanctity are the thousands of diverse objects donated over decades, ranging from an antique MG motorcar in the compound to scores of old wrist watches displayed in dusty glass cases. Other cabinets contain ivory pieces, metal bangles and old cameras. The most valuable item is a stone panel from the 9th- or 10th-century Pala dynasty in India. How this museum-quality object came to reside amidst such oddities is a mystery but similar stone reliefs found their way to Burma, also under unknown circumstances.[13] Several damaged Anuradhapura-period standing Buddhas are also placed about the complex. These were likely found locally and resemble the standing images at the nearby Kelaniya monastery.

This ancient stone sculpture from India was donated to the Gangaramaya temple under unknown circumstances.

Founded by Hikkaduwe Sumangala in 1875, the Gangaramaya was patronized by the same family that sponsored the Kelaniya monastery.

These thousands of peculiar odds and ends may be misconstrued as a museum of kitsch, but such 'museums' serve as repositories of donations throughout the Theravada world. The objects are not relics in a strict sense but they function, like relics, in augmenting the auspicious character of sites. In many instances, the precious offerings by devotees to stupas proved more important than the relics enshrined inside, judging from inscriptions and chronicles that often minutely described donated precious objects at the expense of the relics themselves.

The site's large temple bordering the street was founded in the 1930s. The impish frolicking figures encircling the exterior base were probably modeled on the Kelaniya and Bellavila temples. In the foyer are images of Ganesha and Kataragama and Vishnu with his special junglefowl, *Gallus lafayettii,* framed by an arch dated to 1930. The temple hall is dominated by several enormous tableaux, the central one showing the Buddha at the time of his defeat of the demon Mara. The wooden ceiling panels depict the Sixteen Sacred Sites of Lanka.

St Anthony's

The church's founding legend reflects the period when Catholics were an oppressed minority in Dutch Ceylon. A purge of Catholic 'heretics' began once Dutch rule began but small groups of Indian priests recruited in Goa crossed over to Ceylon to minister to the island's Catholics and to missionize illegally. The semi-legendary founder of the church, Father Anthony, was part of this narrative, living clandestinely in a fishing village. The Dutch were tipped off to his presence and he fled along the coast to Colombo where he found fisherman unable to launch their craft because the sea was fast encroaching. Meanwhile, the Dutch were hot on his trail to deport him back to India, or worse. The Dutch caught up with the priest by the shore and issued a challenge: he would be left to preach in Ceylon, if he could control the rising ocean. Planting his cross on the beach, the sea receded. Exactly where this cross stood became the home of the future St Anthony's church. Another legend involved a sculpture of St Anthony that washed up on shore north of Colombo in 1730. Another centred on a fishing craft blessed by an image of St Anthony that miraculously netted fish to fill the boat's hold. Even a Kandyan king kept in his palace an image of this saint that had helped recover money stolen from the treasury.[14]

St. Anthony standing on the shore where he caused the sea to recede.

It was the Dutch governor, Willem Maurits Bruynick (1739-1742), who allowed St Anthony's church to be built in its present location. There was by then a fragile understanding that the Indian Catholic missionaries were allowed to preach. The

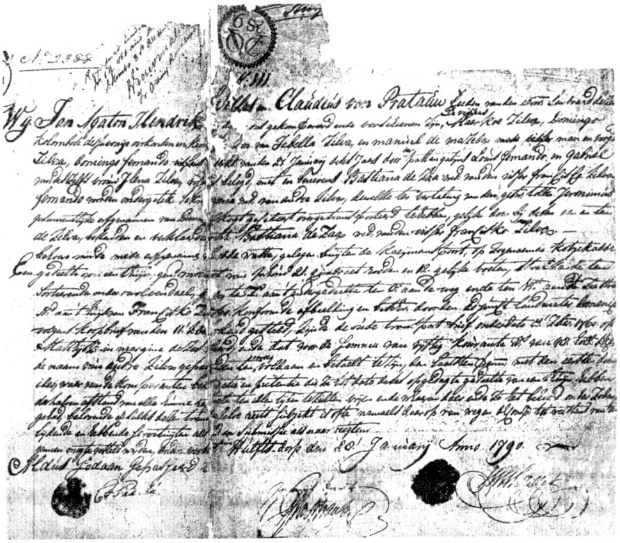

Title deed for St. Anthony's dated 20 January 1790.

church grounds were later officially awarded to the church on 20 January 1790. A new church went up in 1822 but was dismantled and the current church built in 1939, with an Italianate Renaissance facade popular both in South India and Sri Lanka in the 19th century. The church's present fame probably started sometime in the 1950s since St Anthony's did not merit a mention in early guidebooks that included other Catholic churches, like Ste Lucia.

A sacred image in the church is a small statue of the saint from Goa taken to Colombo in 1822 and protected by a bulletproof glass shrine. A model of St Anthony, at the time of his death, is placed in a glass case at the rear of the church, based on the one in Padua, Italy. The tomb of St Anthony (1195-1231) in Padua is especially venerated by Catholic pilgrims from India and Sri Lanka. Beside it is a tall gilded reliquary containing a fragment of St Anthony's tongue that was taken from the full-body relic of St Anthony in Padua; the reliquary is an exact replica of the one in Italy. [15] Additional relics from Padua were displayed in the church in 2010 and taken around the island. This urban church has become a popular place for Buddhists and Hindus to recite vows in order to receive divine assistance.

Another major sacred site is Ste Lucia's located in the nearby Kotahena district and is the seat of the archbishop. The Dutch permitted its construction in 1779 and it rivals St Anthony's in popularity. The present church was completed in 1902. It is famous for its statue of Ste Lucia who was martyred in Roman times. In the 1790s the church's vestments were considered so auspicious that they were lent out to other churches, prompting complaints from the vestments' donors who demanded the articles remain at St Lucia's. The lending out was stopped and violators were threatened with excommunication.[16] The miraculous powers believed to be tied to vestments underscores beliefs about the role sacred objects play.

Wolvendaal Kirch: '... Carnal Indulgence Their Happiness'

Today's entrance is on the west. Services are conducted in Sinhalese, Tamil and English and the church is also popular for weddings.

If stones could talk, then Colombo's Wolvendaal church would have a lot to say. Its floor, embedded with a sea of inscribed gravestones, is a Who's Who of Dutch Ceylon. Indeed, the bones of five governors are entombed here together with over a score of their spouses and offspring. Treading on these massive memorials is a sober reminder not only of life's transience but the ebb and flow of the Dutch mercantile empire in which Ceylon played no small part.

Colombo was wrested from the Portuguese in 1656 in a seven-month siege and Dutch rule continued until the surrender to the British in 1796. Inside the fort was the Portuguese church named São Francisco that was converted to Calvinist use, much like St Anthony's in Cochin. New construction in Colombo, as a visitor noted in 1681, was 'after the Dutch manner'. So it is no surprise that a Dutch gable went up above the refurbished Portuguese church, seen in a painting from 1710.[1] This Fort Church, or Kasteel Kirch, was next to the Dutch Governor's residence facing the harbour. Nothing remains today.

The Fort Church was eventually 'damaged badly by long rains' and 'half of it fell in with a terrifying noise', probably in 1735. New beams for the roof were 'ready for a long time but could not be brought here from Galle' since ships with 'a gangway for heavy cargo' were unavailable.[2] The Governor petitioned the Dutch East India Company (*Vereenigde Oostindische Compagnie,* or VOC), to dismantle the crumbling walls and establish a replacement on the same spot. The request was denied but the church was later repaired

The Dutch Kasteel Kirch inside the Fort. The gravestones from here were taken to the Wolvandaal church in 1813. Pen & Ink drawing. C. 1765-1775. Attributed to Johannes Rach or A. de Nelly. A detail. Rijksmuseum.

during the governorship of Gustaaf Willem Baron van Imhoff (1736-1739). It was during this refurbishment that an imposing tower was erected, pictured by a Dutch artist in circa 1765-75. The tower was later partially dismantled, however, shown in a drawing by Jan Brandes from 1785.[3]

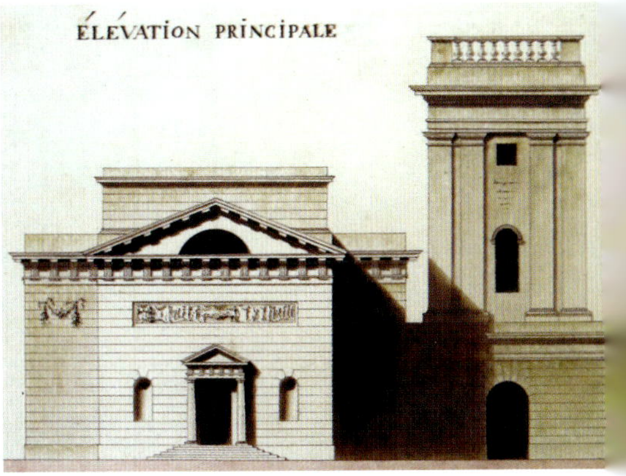

Architectural drawings for a replacement for the Fort Church were prepared by Chevalier La Groupillier. National Archives, The Hague

The Wolvendaal Church was begun during the tenure of Governor Julius Valentijn Stein van Gollenesse (1743-51). It was set on a hill overlooking the harbour and a mixed commercial and residential district known as Pettah. The church was intended mainly for the growing number of Tamil and Sinhala Christians while the Dutch elite continued to attend the crumbling Fort Church. A design for its replacement was prepared by Chevalier La Goupilliere in the French classical style but never put into effect.[4]

The only prominent Dutch figure to be buried in the Fort Church after the surrender to the British was Governor Jan Gerard van Anglebeek (1794-96). His coffin was lowered into the family vault next to his wife 'whose skeleton was seen through a glass in the cover of the coffin'. The ceremony was followed by a procession to the deceased's home where there there was 'a mixture of all nations, who spent the evening in drinking various liquors and smoking tobacco'. Dutch funerals, like marriages, were opportunities to compete in ostentatious opulence, prompting rules in 1658 restricting excesses. Other VOC directives even regulated the social composition of mourners in funeral processions in order to avert conflicts in this status driven society.[5] Detailed descriptions of prominent funerals were published in Holland.

Above the church's southern entrance are Gollenesse's initials, along with the year of groundbreaking, 1749. The church was later pictured in watercolours by the Burgher artist, J.K.L. van Dort (1831-98). Construction took eight years, the consecration being on 6 March 1757 with Tamil, Sinhala and Dutch representatives. The day's sermon was from Genesis 28:22: 'And this stone, which I have set for a pillar, shall be God's House'. Two new pastors, or *predicants*, were assigned to the church, one a former Sinhala Buddhist and the other a Tamil named Willem Ondaatje whose descendants included the famous author Michael Ondaatje.

The formal entrance, south side. A crowned lion representing the Netherlands, visible on the roof, was destroyed by lightning in 1856. By J.K. L. van Dort, a Burgher artist. 1888. KITLV

On the Wolvendaal site was originally a small Dutch parish church used as a schoolroom and nearby was a modest Portuguese church known to the Dutch as 'Kerck Agoa de Loepo', translated into Dutch as Wolvendaalsche Kirch, or Church of the Dale of the Wolves. The Portuguese were long familiar with wolves in Europe but not Asian jackals, hence the present name of the church and even the surrounding district. This Portuguese church, though altered, still stood in the Dutch period when it was used by visiting Kandyan ambassadors who were 'made as comfortable as possible ... [and]... presented with such trifles as snuff, tea, etc.' The church was also used earlier as a Dutch headquarters for the siege

The Dutch church at Jaffna, Kruys Kerk, completed in 1706, fifty years before the Wolvendaal in Colombo. Both churches were based on the Greek Cross plan. By Cornelis Steiger. c. 1710. Watercolour. Rijksmuseum.

of Colombo, noted in a *Description of the East Indian Countries,* by the missionary Philippus Baldaeus.[6]

The new church's ground plan was based on the Greek Cross, with four intersecting barrel-vaulted naves of equal size. The Greek Cross plan was popular among Calvinists since 'all the people may see as well as hear the minister', as an English visitor to Holland reflected on this 'new fashion' in 1634. Catholic churches, built in the shape of a cross, isolated the priest toward the end of a long nave. Also, Catholic churches often enshrined relics in crypts toward the nave's end but relics were eschewed among Calvinists. The architect is unknown but the basic design had antecedents in Holland, such as the Nieuwe Kerk in Haarlem from 1645. A more likely immediate model was Jaffna's Kruys Kerk, completed about 50 years earlier, in 1706. The Jaffna church's design is usually given to Martinus Leusekam but he more likely had only a supervisory role.[7] This priceless church was a casualty in the recent civil war. Another similar church is the Grotte Kerk in Galle, finished in 1755, but the intersecting naves are of unequal size. These three metropolitan churches are now the most well known but hundreds of quite modest churches once dotted the landscape throughout Dutch Ceylon. A score or more were in the Jaffna Peninsula alone, many illustrated by Baldaeus.

The wide central interior space was capped by an eight-sided brick dome supported by brick arches. In 1856, the roof came crashing down after a lightning strike and was replaced by the present wooden ceiling. One of the arches bears a date, Anno 1783, suggesting that perhaps the arches were strengthened long after the consecration of 1757. The roof was topped by a metal weathervane in the shape of a crowned lion grasping a sword in one hand and seven arrows in the other, each arrow representing one of the Seven United Provinces of the Netherlands. No trace of the weathervane has survived but the crowned lion has remained a symbol of the church.

The church walls are nearly two metres thick and made up of small laterite blocks, rubble, and brick bonded with thick mortar, exposed in spots where the plaster has chipped off. Laterite is a special 'stiff clay' that becomes rock hard after exposure to sun light. Laterite stone of 'very poor durability' was used in the Fort Church and it may have been taken from nearby Kotte where quarries still exist. The local name for the stone was *cabook* and varied in quality. The word cabook perhaps derived from the Portuguese word for quarry, *cavouco*.[8] Many bricks were imported from a brickworks near Arnhem, though the bricks for the Jaffna church were made locally. As the walls of the Jaffna church reached over two metres in height, a million more bricks were estimated to complete the project.

Other bricks were imported from the 'Fatherland' [Holland] to Jaffna and sent to Colombo. Kilns supplying bricks and tiles were established by the Dutch along the Kelani River near the famous monastery. In some cases, the clay was made ready by 'walking oxen over it in a circle'. Even after the completion of the Wolvendaal church, there were '300,000 bricks in readiness' for other projects.[9] Metal drain pipes still in use were ordered in the nineteenth century from the Saracen Company, Glasgow.

An elevated wooden pulpit is capped with a wide sounding-board for enhanced acoustics. The wood for the Jaffna pulpit was ebony and possibly imported from Malabar in India or perhaps from northern Ceylon. Opposite the pulpit was the King's Gallery, or royal pew. Two smaller pews placed in the remaining corners were reserved for Elders and Deacons. A number of chairs remaining in the King's Gallery are from the mid-18th century. These were special church chairs, or *kerkstoel*, kept at home and carried to church by slaves for weekly services; women saw that their chair was 'provided with a stately cushion', both in Jaffna and Batavia.[10]

Kayman's Gate Belfry, still standing, is located on the street coming from Pettah. Van Dort. 1888. KITLV

The church's old belfry is on the street coming up the hill from the Pettah district. It was called Kayman's Gate Belfry, perhaps after a Dutch officer named Keuneman. The bell, dated by a 16th-century inscription, belonged first to Kotte's Franciscan church before it was shifted to the Dutch church in Colombo's Borella district. It was only later installed here. Even in 1906, the bell was rung at 8 pm to alert 'tavern-keepers to close their doors by 9 o'clock'.[11] The last time the bell rang marked Japan's surrender in 1945.

Low church attendance was a problem from the outset. A Dutch governor complained that residents 'are rather negligent regarding attendance and weekly sermons'. Indeed, priests 'had not unfrequently to preach, as it were, to empty seats'. The reasons were put down to the congregants 'being destitute of inward piety' or, worse still, who 'made luxury a virtue, carnal indulgence their happiness and pride their glory'.[12]

The raised puplit with it's sounding-board, diagonally facing the King's Gallery.

The local Burgher community, whose members descended from mixed Dutch and Sinhala unions, were closely associated with the church from the beginning. (Burghers also included those of mixed Portuguese and Sinhala descent.) Burghers and others in Colombo founded the Wolvendaal Foundation in 2005, with support from the Dutch government. Church archives number close to 37,000 pages bound in 140 volumes, a portion of which, from 1735 to 1797, is now translated into English.[13] The name, Dutch Reformed Church, was changed to the Christian Reformed Church in 2008. There are now some 30 affiliated churches nationwide with about five thousand adherents.

Henrietta Tugendreich's tombstone, 16 June 1778. The eight-spoked wheel and two unicorns are repeated on her father's hatchment in the destroyed Dutch church at Jaffna (*Journal of the Ceylon Branch of the Royal Asiatic Society*, 1903, vol. 18, pl. IV).

One of three small oval hatchments present in the choir loft. This unidentified example includes a rare contemporaneous reference, a Sinhala bowman. The three hatchments appear in a single watercolour by J.K.L. van Dort, dated 1889.

The Tombstones

'Grudge not the tribute of a Tear'

Most of the floor's massive memorial tablets were originally embedded in the floor of the Dutch Fort Church. Their removal to the Wolvandaal in 1813 began by first prying the gravestones from the floor and then lifting up hundreds, if not thousands, of brittle bones below. A torchlit procession led by the English Governor on 4 September 1813 transported the remains from the Fort to the Wolvendaal church and then lowered into freshly dug vaults beneath the floor and then sealed by their massive tombstones taken from the Fort Church. The average gravestone measured some 2.5 metres in length (just over 8 feet). An Armenian gravestone from South India dated 1754 with similar dimensions weighed 1,135 kilograms. The deceased were placed into 'a soldered copper coffin tinned over … and placed in a good water-tight wooden case'.[14] Whether the memorials were placed over the correct bones will never be known, though the gravity of mismatching gravestones over the wrong bones is too dreadful to ponder.

The practice of church floor burials at the Wolvendaal differed from Dutch traditions in South India where the gravestones were generally laid flat in outdoor cemeteries. In Galle, burials also took place in the church floor as well as in two crypts beneath the church. Major Dutch cemeteries are found within the coastal strip to the north and south of Chennai, the most important being at Pulicat, Nagapattanam and Sadras.

The gravestones included the deceased's armorial bearings and often the arms of families connected by marriage. The gravestone of Governor Imhoff's only child displays sixteen family crests representing marital alliances going back generations. Families of the deceased must have supplied the stone cutting ateliers with the information incised on stones, such as birth and death dates and the names of spouses. Many English-period grave markers are set into the interior walls. Memorials are frequently white marble tablets silhouetted against a flat black stone backing, a specialty of Edward and Thomas Gaffin whose London shop address, 63 Regent Street, appears beneath one of the plaques.

Tombstones were exported from South India to Dutch communities abroad but information is scanty. One example from Sadras was shipped to distant Batavia, so the distance to Ceylon was in easy range. At least some of the Fort Church's flooring stones were sent from the Coromandel coast, according to the Dutch Political Minutes of 27 June 1749. However, the majority of stones at the Wolvendaal appear to have been carved locally since they differ in style from those in South India. Gravestones from Colombo and the Coromandel coast share certain affinities indicating that artists' pattern-books were used in common. For example, one tombstone set out outside the church and dated to 1664 resembles many from the Coromandel coast. Another example at the Church is based on the same pattern-book responsible for a gravestone from Pulicat.[15] Common motifs are cherubs, winged angels, skulls and hourglasses.

Sculptors used identical pattern-books in Ceylon and India or moved between locations with the books. A tombstone, 1792, at the Wolvendaal Church, left, and a second at Pulicat, Tamil Nadu, 1777. After Rea, pl. 37.

The elaborate funeral of Governor Isaac Augustin Rumpf (1716-1723) in the old Fort Church began with eight days of bell ringing at intervals. The governor purportedly died from shock on 'hearing of the assassination of Barent van der Swaan and his wife by their slaves'. Rumpf's interment followed a procession with hundreds, starting off beside the bastion named Amsterdam. Behind the coffin marched Dutch, Burghers, and indigenous soldiers known as *lascarins* and the deceased's bodyguards. Drummers, trumpeters and *houtboyists* (a type of oboe) lent a somber tone. The drummers even had a distinctive beat, 'the so-called Sinhalese march', noted in the procession for Governor Van Eck. The coffin was draped in a black cloth showing the family's eight coats of arms, or quarterings (eight more were added to his son's tombstone at the Wolvandaal). The coffin was finally 'lowered on to iron staves in a vault'. The procession then proceeded to the 'house of mourning to offer their condolence to the Lady of the late Governor'. No mention is made of Van Eck's tombstone, but it was probably being made ready. A Latin poem inscribed on the stone concludes with 'Grudge not the tribute of a Tear'.[16]

In some instances the carved motifs on the gravestones were reversed from those of the genuine arms. For example, the heads of animals facing one way in the real arms were turned the opposite way in the sculpted version. These mistakes can be explained by immagining the local sculptors basing their designs on the actual family seals and not on the impressions stamped on paper.[17] The pedantry of Dutch heraldry in Ceylon was a lifelong interest of the great Burgher scholar and former national archivist, R.G. Anthonisz, whose research appeared in the *Journal of the Dutch Burgher Union*. Historical events depicted on the stones are rare. A single case is known in Ceylon, a tombstone showing a fallen soldier, evoking the deceased, Governor Lubbert Jan Baron van Eck (1736-1785). He led an assault on 'Candia', or Kandy, in 1765 but his triumph was a melancholy one since upon his return 'he shrank from seeing anyone' and in eight days was 'in extremis'. At the top is a fallen soldier during the siege of Kandy, together with a mortar, cannon balls and two hand-grenades, or 'granadoes'. Grenades were also used in the Dutch assault on Colombo. In another tombstone a soldier who was the first to scale the walls during the siege of Colombo derided the 'haughty Lusitanians [Portuguese]', another rare historical reference. Frequently mentioned locations include Tutucoryn (Tuticorin), Malabaer (Malabar), Madure (Madurai), and Cochim (Cochin) and

Governor Rijckloff van Goens and his second wife presented this silver basin for the baptism of their daughter named Celonia. The couple's initials appear on the rim. The shell motif is symbol of the VOC. The dish in the upper left commemorates the 'spiritual home' that the church pro-vided for Dutch troops in the Second World War. Courtesy Dominic Sansoni.

Rijckloff Van Goen's first wife, their two children and a servant. The original oil painting, from 1656, was destroyed in a fire 1864 but survives in this copy. Museum Boijmans Van Beuningen, Rotterdam.

Governor Lubbert Jan BaronVan Eck's assault on Kandy was evoked on his tombstone. Fallen soldier, cannon and greanade ('*granadoes*') and a captured lion-standard.

This memorial, between two tombstones, was for Governor Rijckloff van Goens and his first and second wife. It was originally set into the wall of the Fort Church.

Batavia.[18] The causes of death are rarely mentioned but cholera, malaria and dysentery took the greatest toll.

Some ten large memorial stones were placed upright against the church wall in 1908, having been taken here at the same time as the others but remaining outside as the bones were never located. The grandest commemorates two successive wives of Governor Rijckloff van Goens (d. 1675) who were buried in the old Fort Church. This memorial, complete with flanking pilasters, was not placed into the floor of the Fort Church but set upright in an interior wall. The family arms of both wives are joined together in a composite circular frame on the right, while the governor's arms are on the left. Women's arms were usually set within oval or lozenge-shaped shields. Governor Van Goens, his first wife Jacomina and their two children were painted in 1656. Other early tombstones can be seen in the Dutch Museum on Prince Street, the former residence of Governor Van Rhee. A handful of Portuguese-era stones are in St Thomas' church compound near the Ponnambaleshvara Temple, as well as some in the National Museum. An example from 1536 marks the island's first archbishop who was connected to the church of São Lourenço near the Batenberg bastion.[19]

The most important tombstones are described in Leopold Ludovici's *Lapidarium Zeylanicum*, issued in Colombo in 1877, with line drawings and lithographs by the two best artists of the day, J.L.K van Dort and Richard Henricus. The former was married in the church in 1861. The church's history was compiled in 1938 by R. L. Brohier, illustrated with photographs by the famous Lionel Wendt, with a new edition including photographs by Dominic Sansoni.

The Hatchments, or Wapenbords

High on one wall is a triangular wooden hatchment, or *wapenbord* ('weapon board'), dedicated to Iman Willem Falck (1765-1785), the governor who negotiated a treaty with the Kandyan king. Over a red shield is a golden falcon evoking his namesake, Falck, the old name for falcon in Dutch. The falcon in his coat of arms reflects a special type of wordplay or punning known in heraldry as *armes parlantes*, or 'canting heraldry'. A well-known example is the family arms of the poet Shelley that included sea shells, the shells repeating the first syllable of Shelley's family name.

A copy of the wooden hatchment, or *wapenbord* ('weapon board') for Governor Iman Willem Falck. By J. K. L. Van Dort. 1889. KITLV

The two hatchments on the opposite wall were commissioned in 1805 by Jacomina Gertruida van de Graaf (maiden name). The one on the right is in honour of her mother who married Governor Van de Graaf; the matching hatchment on the left was dedicated to her grandmother who married Governor Van Angelbeek. The name Angelbeek, or 'angle-streamlet' in English, is indicated by three fish hooks; '*angel*' can mean hook, or *haak* in Dutch, and relates to the English word 'angling', for fishing; the three wavy lines represent a stream, or *beek.*

Hatchment honouring the Christina Elizabeth van de Graaff, the wife of Governor van de Graaf, the second to the last Dutch Governor of Ceylon. Established by her daughter in 1805.

The tombstone of Jacomina's mother, Christina Elizabeth van de Graaff, was set into the floor facing her hatchment but her grandmother's stone has never been found. Jacomina remained in Colombo after the Dutch capitulation and married the British Paymaster, an earl's son, when she was fifteen. Such a union, between a member of the Dutch elite and an English official, is a reminder that the clean breaks in history books are the exceptions. Such a 'mixed marriage' was not unusual. In one case, five Dutch sisters 'accompanied five English officers to the altar'.[20] Three small painted wooden roundels were placed in the old organ loft above the modern entrance and recorded in a painting by Van Dort. One represent the Anglebeeks, with fishhooks. Another belongs to the Levers family, while the third is unidentified.

Ponnambaleshvara Temple

Colombo saw a wave of new Hindu temples, Buddhist monasteries, churches and mosques at the end of the 19th century.

Shiva's Courtesans and a Hindu Revival

Colombo has no shortage of Hindu shrines but none better reflects the colonial religious milieu than the Ponnambaleshvara Temple. Its founder, Sir Ponnambalam Ramanathan (1851-1930), was a Tamil politician and mystic with one foot in the past and the other in the modern world. No foundation myths underpin this temple and so it differs from famous ancient Hindu temples, such as South India's Minakshi complex in South India or Trincomalee's Koneshvaram in Sri Lanka.

The temple's name, Ponnambaleshvara, comes from the Tamil *pon-ambalam*, or 'golden hall', in which Shiva, known as the Lord (S: *ishvara*), performed his 'dance of bliss' (S: *ananda tandava*). This dance signals the dissolution and creation of the universe and is often associated with Tamil Nadu's Chidambaram Temple.[1] The focus of worship is Shiva's stone *lingam* enshrined within the sanctum.

In awe of Shiva's cosmic dance stood two devotees. Patanjali, started life as a snake but was rewarded for his devotion by being reborn from a mother married to a sage. Astonished that her newborn son was half-snake-half-child, she dropped him from her folded hands (S: *pata-anjali*), and his namesake was borne. The second figure, Vyagrahpada, was so dedicated to Shiva that he gathered flowers for the deity that had never been touched by honeybees. Thorns on the ground, however, pierced his feet so Shiva gave him tiger paws (S: *vyagra-pada*) that enabled him to roam over any terrain. Life-size images of these two acolytes stand facing the temple's five-storied brick tower (S: *gopuram*), adorned with 100s of painted deities.

Sir Ponnambalam with the gold medal presented to him by Queen Victoria at her Diamond Jubillee in London, 1897. Modern painting by S. Gnanakuruparan, based on a portrait photograph. Ponnambaleshvar Temple.

The temple's builders relied on ancient Sanskrit architectural manuals (S: *shilpa shastras*) and other texts (*agamas*) associated with the Shaiva Siddhantas of Tamil Nadu. Its architectural style conforms to temples of the Nayaka period (16th-18th centuries) in Tamil Nadu.[2] Festivals mark the annual lunar calendar, each with its own rituals celebrated among Tamil communities worldwide. Each month is divided into twenty-seven periods (S: *nakshatras*) during which certain constellations are associated with different lunar phases tied to auspicious times for rituals.

The sanctum faces east and is enclosed by a wide gallery. Devotees stand before the shrine door, waiting in turn to give offerings to priests who then present them to the *lingam* inside. Five deities are arranged around the sanctum's outer walls. On the south side are Ganesha and the Teacher of Divine Knowledge (S: Dakshinamurti) while an image of Shiva emerging from a *lingam* (S: Lingodbhavamurti) is at the rear. Brahma and Durga appear on the north. In the encircling gallery are separate shrines for individual deities, including Ganesha, Vishnu and Kataragama, together with wooden images carried in street processions, such as the bull Nandi, Garuda and Skanda's Peacock (P: Paravani). A separate shrine devoted to Shiva's consort is also on the south side.

Half-snake-half man devotee of Shiva. Ponnambaleshvaram Compound.

Ceremonies (S: *pujas*) occur six times daily, based on a ritual cycle found in Shaiva temples in Tamil Nadu. The first is at 5:30 a.m. when Shiva's bull Nandi and the door guardians are honoured. This ritual awakens the deity with offerings of milk, betel leaves and fruit. The most important daytime *puja* occurs at the day's zenith, followed by three hours or so during which activities are suspended. Evening sessions end at about 8:00 p.m. with worship to Shiva in his role as Lord of the Dance. Images of the god and his consort are borne on a palanquin by temple servants in a clockwise fashion within the temple. Rituals are accompanied by a musician on the double-reed *nagasvaram* and another who strikes a steady beat on a drum known as a *tavil*. The *nagasvaram* was even the subject of a poem by the famous painter, George Keyt.[3]

A wide corridor encircles the central sanctum.

Temple employees include priests, watchmen, gardeners and sweepers. Over 20 brahman ritualists are supported by income from temple properties and interest accrued in banks. Such service groups attached to temples are well-known from ancient South Indian stone inscriptions. Fresh milk required for certain rituals is supplied from a handful of cows housed in a shed at the rear of the compound.

Auspicious times for performing a specific ritual at the temple are in the 90-minute period before sunrise or after sunset every fortnight on the 13th day of the waxing and waning of the moon. This ritual (S: *pradosham*), or 'removal of sins', requires a special circumambulation (S: *somasutra pradakshina)*, beginning in a counter-clockwise direction and then reversing in the other direction. The major deities invoked are a special four-armed Shiva known as Chandrashekera and Nandi.

Durga, one of five gods on the sanctum's exterior wall.

'.... straying into other folds'

The present temple was begun in 1907 and cost two million rupees before its completion and consecration in 1912. The prime mover was Sir Ponnambalam whose aristocratic family came from Jaffna, with ties to the British Empire. This led to him and his first wife being invited for an audience with Queen Victoria in 1886. Construction of the Colombo temple began when Ramanathan was approaching the peak of his career.[4]

Colombo's rapidly expanding population after the 1850s produced an urban culture divorced from traditional roots in the countryside. A growing anomie among all religious communities set in, heightened by zealous missionary activity from Britain and the United States. Hindus in Colombo probably felt especially vulnerable since they numbered only 19% of the population in 1919, trailing behind Buddhists, 31%, Christians, 28%, and Muslims, 22%. In addtion, Hindus in Colombo were 'becoming oblivious of the ancestral faith … and straying into other folds', as Ramanathan's biographer lamented. Many of these same social factors fostered a Hindu revival in South India and Ceylon, led by reformers like Jaffna's Arumuka Navalar (1822-79) and prompted a wave of temple building and refurbishing in the early twentieth century.[5] Three impressive Nayaka-style temples alone were founded in nearby Sea Street and still function.

The present stone temple replaced a brick shrine founded in 1856 by Ramanathan's father on land purchased from John Foulstone, a captain whose marriage vows were recited in the nearby Wolvendaal Church. Local lore maintains that the granite blocks were imported from India but in fact the quarries were in Veyangoda, between Colombo and Karunegala. Although architects and workmen imported from South India emulated the conventions of Tamil Nadu, the temple competes poorly with the far older famous and grander Hindu temple complexes of South India, such as Madurai's Minakshi Temple.

Skanda's mount, a peackock named Paravani. Such wooden figures are carried in street processions.

Ramanathan was highly Westernized but like so many of his social class he advocated a return to perceived traditional Asian values. He promoted Asian faiths in the West, lecturing abroad. His cousin was Ananda K. Coomaraswamy, the art historian at Boston's Museum of Fine Arts. Also in Ramanathan's circle was the eccentric English actress, Florence Farr, a former lover of George Bernard Shaw before she moved to Jaffna for a teaching post at Ramanathan's invitation. Ramanathan also taught yoga to Allan Bennett who became a guru to the occultist, Aleister Crowley.[6] His impact therefore went well beyond his family's temple in Colombo. His second wife was an Australian-born English woman who died in Jaffna in 1953. Ramanathan also knew H. S. Olcott who founded the Theosophical Society. Others in his orbit included Swami Vivekananda whose visit to the earlier brick temple in 1897 is memorialized with a portrait statue in the temple's compound. The Swami was no friend of the Theosophists whom he accused of diluting Buddhism.

A modern dance school meets in the temple compound on the weekend.

'… a legally married wife'

Attached to the Ponnambaleshvara Temple was a dancer, or *devadasi,* named Ancukam whose 240-page Tamil memoir was published in 1911. A single surviving copy of her book was recently uncovered in the British Library. She belonged to a family of *devadasis* based in the old Madras Presidency where her

Indian Temple dancers cast in nun's habits, from Marco Polo's *Travels*, in the fifteenth-century *Livre des Merveilles du Monde*. Bibliotheque Nationale, Paris. Ms. 2810, folio 80.

grandmother was 'discovered' by a prominent Hindu visiting from Ceylon. He invited her to settle and perform in Jaffna and she agreed 'only because of her longing' to see 'Katirkamam' (Kataragama).[7] In Jaffna, she and her daughter came to the attention of Ramanathan's father who requested them to perform in Colombo. The young girl began vocal and dance training at the age of six in Jaffna and was a recognized performer at twelve when the 'consecration necklace' (T: *tiruppottu*), was placed around her neck at the Ponnambaleshvara Temple. Receiving this necklace was a rite-of-passage for dancers who were henceforth wedded to the temple. She styled herself as one of 'Shiva's Courtesans' (S: *rudraganika)*, a term used first in South India as early as the 12th-century. Ancukam soon became the companion-lover of a well-to-do Colombo Tamil businessman named K. C. Pillai who was also a temple trustee, a relationship that endured for 25 years until his death. In her memoir, she concluded that 'He treated me as he would have treated a legally wedded wife'.[8]

The institution of temple dancers became controversial in later colonial times for its perceived associations with prostitution, becoming a *cause célèbre* for Christian and Hindu reformers who sought to ban the institution. *Devadasis* were then pejoratively styled 'nautch girls'. On the other side were those, including Ancukam, who hoped to revive genuine dance traditions of South India as part of a rebirth of ancient Hindu culture, a movement coupled with emerging nationalism. Temple dancers caught the attention of Europeans long ago and an imaginary troupe was featured in a Marco Polo manuscript from circa 1400, drawing on his *Travels*.[9] No dancers are now attached to the Ponnambaleshvara Temple but school girls study traditional dance here on the weekends.

A poem describing the dancers at the Kelaniya Buddhist monastery captures the enchantement that these divine dancers inspired:

Like divine maidens come down from heaven
Beguile they the gods with their dances
When the dancing girls finish their dance
Drenching the floor with sweat[11]
(Hamsa-sandesaya)

No longer are we able to savour Ancukam's performances inside this Colombo temple but our bare feet tread today on the same floor that she danced upon at the turn of the century.

Temple dancers in Ceylon juxtaposed with the north gateway of the Rameshvaram Temple in Tamil Nadu. Postcard from Ceylon, circa 1915.

Dipaduttama Monastery

Constructed in 1871, the temple was a focus for a resurgence of Sinhalese Buddhism at the turn of the 20th century under the leadership of the Sri Lankan monk, M. Gunananda, and later by a Thai prince named Prisdang. This Mahabodhi Temple replicca was constructed between 1908 and 1910.

The Thai Priest-Prince

Tucked away in Colombo's Kotahena neighbourhood is a modest Buddhist monastery that was once centre stage for a national Buddhist pushback against Christian missionizing. It was also home to a Siamese prince whose self-exile in Colombo has forever linked the temple to Thailand. Indeed, many in Colombo know it as the 'Thai temple' but its formal name is the Dipaduttamarama Thai Raja Maha Viharaya, or simply Dipaduttama. Visiting Thai royal family members have dedicated trees here, beginning with a red sandalwood in 1939. The last was an ironwood tree, planted by Princess Sirindhorn in 2013.

When the British took control of Colombo in 1796, only two major Buddhist centres existed and both were outside the city's perimeter, at Kelaniya and Kotte. However, by the 1830s private funds financed a temple in the Kotahena district in Colombo. Nothing survives from then and today's temple, finished by 1872, was the 'largest modern temple in Ceylon'.[1] The walls are made of laterite blocks, covered with whitewashed plaster. The facade follows European conventions with its Ionic columns but its surviving original roof is modeled on Sri Lankan stupas.

At the apex of this *retablo* are the English coat of arms and a Buddhist Era date of 2416 [1872], the year the temple was founded. Marble reclining Buddha from Burma, lower right.

One wall is dominated by a wooden backdrop, with an oval frame set between the British lion and unicorn, with an inscription listing a date in the Buddhist Era 2416, or 1872. The inscription also mentions an 'auspicious *chaitya*', or stupa, and an 'auspicious Buddha image' ('*sadhathuka chaitya sadhathuka Buddha*). The '*chaitya*' is the stupa in the compound and the image is the recumbent Buddha, made of brick and covered with painted plaster. This baroque-style backdrop resembles gilded *retablos* produced at that time for Catholic churches. Before 1872, this wall featured a reclining marble Buddha from Burma set within a glass coffin-like niche that appeared in a rare lithograph in the German *Die Katholischen Missionen* from October 1890 and is reminiscent of saints on view in Catholic churches. The entrance foyer was formerly named the 'Burmese Chapel' because of this marble Buddha and its murals reportedly painted by Burmese artists. Reclining Burmese marble Buddhas were not uncommon in Ceylon during this period. An old postcard shows one inside the Kelaniya temple and another is in the Ridhi Viharaya near Kandy.

The shrine's entrance is gained by two doorways, capped with elaborate arches ubiquitous in this period. The sculpture has been repainted many times but is largely original from the temple's completion in the 1870s. Over one door are images of Brahma, holding an umbrella and a palm-leaf manuscript, and a four-arm Shiva.

Near the feet of the reclining Buddha inside the long sanctum is a colossal four-arm standing Vishnu that 'both Hindus and Buddhist alike come to worship…[since]…Vishnu offers greater promise of worldly blessing, and by means of offerings …[he is] … propitiated and made merciful'. This description agrees with the continuing importance of a Vishnu sculpture at Dambulla. (see Dambulla chapter) Opposite Vishnu is the two-arm Saman, the deity of Adam's Peak. Surrounding the central chamber are life-size plaster images of 'the Four-and-Twenty Perfect Buddhas that have come and gone'. Tableaus on the side walls illustrate scenes from the Buddha's life and popular *Jatakas*, probably added in the recent past. In the late 19th century, a 'shrine, dedicated to a Hindu deity' was added to the compound but no longer exists.[2] But its presence indicates that even during that age of self-conscious Buddhist orthodoxy there was nevertheless room for a Hindu deity.

Two doorways to the chamber with the recumbent Buddha. These original figures have been repainted many times.

An enormous figure of Saman, the god of Adam's Peak, stands near the head of the recumbent Buddha. Vishnu stands on the opposite side.

The temple's chief monk, M. Gunananda, played a pivotal role in the Panadura Debate in 1873 that pitted Buddhism against Christianity. Gunananda belonged to the Amarapura Buddhist division (P: *nikaya*) that formed as a protest to the dominant Syam Nikaya based in Kandy.[3] Gunananda was also a senior member in the Theosophical Society, begun by H. S. Olcott and H. P. Blavatsky.

The Kotahena monastery was among a handful of institutions in Colombo following similar paths. Only blocks away is the Paramananda Purana monastery where the famous monk, H. Sri Sumanagala, was invited in the 1870s for a rainy season retreat. Its bell tower was donated by a widow from the influential Bandaranayke family, recorded on a metal plaque dated 1906. The temple murals and sculpture are in a Westernized style but a small mural above the entrance represents the last phase of 19th-century work. Other important Colombo temples at this time were the Dhammodayaramaya, established in 1903, and the Vajiraramaya c. 1901 and headed by the prelate of the Amarapura school. Other major institutions in Colombo were the Vidyodaya Pirivena under Sumangala and the Parama Dhammacetiya Pirivena, started in 1841.[4]

The Opening of the Eyes and Easter Sunday, 1883

The reclining Buddha at the temple was consecrated at a special festival lasting over a month in 1883, culminating in an 'opening-of-the-eyes' ceremony, or *netra pinkama*, on March 20. The eyes were fitted with semi-precious stones costing 'about a thousand rupees', recorded by the head of India's Brahmo Samaj Hindu movement who was in attendance. 100s were present, 'gaily dressed' and 'brilliantly ornamented'. Five days later a religious procession through the streets coincided with an Easter Sunday parade from nearby Ste Lucia's Cathedral. Tensions between the two communities ran high and the police arranged for Christians to march in the morning and Buddhists in the afternoon. Rumors broke out that the Buddhist procession featured a crucified monkey and that a Buddhist monk had been struck by a Catholic. All hell broke loose quickly, resulting in two deaths, with many injured. A British commission later concluded that all parties shared the blame, including the police. A Buddhist Defense Committee arose and Olcott presented the temple's grievances to the Colonial Office in London. Ethnic politics played no role since the rioters were largely Sinhalas and the different communities during this period directed their wrath at each other and not yet against their colonial masters. However, this 1883-riot planted the seeds of 'early Sinhala Buddhist nationalism' and was also a harbinger of the far deadlier Muslim-Buddhist Riots of 1915.[5]

Prisdang, kneeling before his spiritual guide, Waskaduwe Subhuti. Modern mural at the monastery, based on an antique photograph.

The Priest-Prince

The temple today is known for its associations with Thailand's Prince Prisdang Jumsai (1851-1935) who was 15 years in Ceylon, from 1896 to 1911. He served as the monastery's incumbent for five years, beginning in 1905. He was an offspring of a non-royal consort and King Rama III and so belonged to a minor branch of the royal family. After his degree from King's College, he served as a roving ambassador to European courts. On his return to Bangkok his proposed reforms of the monarchy, including abolishing polygamy, attracted royal censure. It was also rumoured that he had an inappropriate relationship with a widow of the noble class. He eventually fled Siam, sailing first to Hong Kong. His falling out of favour with the royal family was a black cloud that he could never dispel.[6]

The prince arrived in Colombo in 1896 and was ordained by a famous monk named Waskaduwe Subhuti whose hermitage was in Waskaduwa, on the coast below Colombo. The prince then became known as P.C. Jinawarawansa but was nicknamed the Prince Priest. Much was made of this prince who gave up the luxuries of court life for the austere regime of a monk, with parallels to Gotama Buddha for all to see. However, his self-exile in Ceylon was a melancholic one, since he remained plagued by his treatment in Siam and his desire to gain approval from King Chulalongkorn in Bangkok. He vainly tried to unify the fractious Ceylon *sangha* and the Buddhists in Burma under the leadership of the Siamese king, a factor behind the insult that the visiting king suffered at the Temple of the Tooth in Kandy.[7]

Prisdang made a pilgrimage to India in the 1898 and while there news reached him that relics of the Buddha had been recently excavated in the village of Piprahwa near ancient Kapilavastu, the Buddha's birthplace. The prince visited the area and met William Peppé, the landowner on whose property the excavated mound was found. Visiting Peppé's estate, Prisdang exchanged a valuable stamp album (now missing) for three small bone relics.

The remainder of the bodily relics were eventually given by Peppé to the British government. Prisdang then successfully lobbied the British to have these presented to King Chulalongkorn for distribution among Buddhist nations, evoking memories of

Emperor Asoka. The Siamese king presented some relics to deputations in Bangkok sent from Rangoon, Mandalay, Anuradhapura, the Malwatta and Asgiriya monasteries in Kandy and three monasteries in Colombo. Some relics came to reside at Subhuti's hermitage in Waskaduwa but it is not clear if these were given to Subhuti by Prisdang directly or came from Siam. The relics at Subhuti's hermitage are now in a modern reliquary within a colonial age octagonal structure marking the site of Prisdang's ordination there. The relics that went to Burma have left no trace and this is true for the relics sent to Colombo from Bangkok. Many of these relics are enshrined in Bangkok's Golden Temple, or Wat Saket.[8]

Once the manuscript library at Waskaduwa, it now houses a reliquary with relics given to Subhuti by Prisdang.

Meanwhile, a Siamese official in Bangkok claimed that Prisdang had confessed to him in Calcutta that he had stolen the three relics from Peppé's collection, a transgression triggering expulsion from the *sangha*. As a result, Prisdang received a telegram in Colombo from the court in Bangkok stating that he would be defrocked should he return to Siam. This alleged theft was likely a fabricated charge made by a Siamese officer who was Prisdang's long-standing nemesis. Under the pressure of such bad news, the prince's health failed and he retreated to an islet near Matara which he called Little Lanka, or Chulalanka. It was home to a number of Europeans who had taken the tonsure, such as a German named Anton Guth. This island was visited by a stream of European notables, such as Queen Victoria's granddaughter.[9] An invitation in 1905 to become head monk at the Diputtarama in Colombo put him back in the centre of the island's religious affairs.

The prince attended the cremation of King Chulalongkorn in Bangkok in 1910 where he found himself disrobed and forbidden to take the tonsure again. Stripped of his status and shunned by many of his former friends, he got by in Bangkok with small translation jobs, teaching English and a modest court stipend. He even came to sell a small wood carving from Thailand or Cambodia to his friend, Ananda Coomaraswamy, the famous curator then at the Museum of Fine Arts, Boston.[10] His life slowly slipped away without notice until his death at eighty-three.

Two small shrines in the compound are devoted to Hindu gods. The goddess Kali, centre, with Shiva, Kataragama and Vishnu. Sri Lankan deities here include Dadimunda and Huniyam.

Although Prince Prisdang was treated poorly upon his return to Siam, his reputation is now fully rehabilitated. Thais of all persuasions now praise his accomplishments. The prince even merited a special postage stamp in Thailand in 2010. The prince established a museum next to the temple but it was replaced long ago. The museum's eclectic collection included plaster casts of ancient Bodh Gaya stone railings and a replica of the Kandy

The monastery's modern museum displays a plaster copy of the emaciated Buddha in the Lahore Museum, based on one given to Prince Damrung Rajanubhab that eventually was enshrined at the Temple of the Emerald Buddha.

Tooth relic. One room included a piece of the original Bodhi Tree and a fragment of what was taken to be the Buddha's alms bowl recovered from the ancient Sopara Stupa in India. Another prize was a fragment from an Ashokan capital. It all amounted to a 'strange congeries of things'. The only important surviving item from the old museum is a plaster sculpture of the famous 'starving Buddha' in the Lahore museum, brought from Bangkok.[11] A plaster copy of this Lahore image was gifted in 1891 by the Government of India to Prince Damrung Rajanubhab who presented the image to Rama V who enshrined it at the Temple of the Emerald Buddha. This image inspired numerous copies, such as this one in Colombo, and replicas that are still produced both in Thailand and Burma.

The Mahabodhi Temple

A replica of the Mahabodhi temple in India was built within the compound by the Priest Prince. A booklet describing the temple by Prisdang was published in 1910 just as the replica's base was completed. It was republished in 2013 by the great-great nephew of the prince, the well-known architect, Sumet Jumsai.[12] Construction began in 1908 and probably finished late in 1910. Prisdang invited King Chulalongkorn to lay the foundation stone when he was in Colombo in 1907 but the king declined to even visit the temple, a deep disappointment for the prince. A wealthy Buddhist from Penang soon arrived who agreed to provide funds but only if she was able to lay the foundation stone, a ceremony concluded on 20 March 1908 and conducted by Mrs Bandaranayake, whose husband had been associated with the nearby Paramananda monastery.

Many relics were interred but the most valuable were an unspecified number of 'true Relics of the Buddha' which the Prince 'brought back from India'. These relics were probably the 'three relics' that he received from Peppé in India, in exchange for the stamp album. These relics are among the oldest relics in Sri Lanka, rivaling a relic from Taxila presented to the Temple of the Tooth in 1917 by the Government of India. Two additional Buddha relics interred in this monument once belonged to Sampson Rajapaksa, a leader of the Salagama caste.

The replica follows the basic elevation of the Mahabodhi temple in India but with clear differences. Prisdang's original idea called for numerous individualized images placed in hundreds of small niches that included Metteyya, Mahakassapa, and the Buddha's mother and father. An an old photo suggests that these were never installed.[13] In the niches today are identical small seated Buddhas donated by an officer of the Bank of Thailand in 2004. The new spire was donated by the King of Thailand in 2010. The prince was never able to see his completed Mahabodhi Temple, since he was forbidden to visit Ceylon after returning to Bangkok.

Subodharama Viharaya

'The Buddha saw me'

The most famous visitor here was the Russian mystic, P.D. Ouspensky (1878-1947), who wandered into the monastery's grounds from his seaside Hotel Lavinia in 1913. Standing before the enshrined Buddha, Ouspensky had a revelation: 'The Buddha saw me ... all that was hidden in the most secret recesses of my soul'. The mystic was also struck by the Buddha's glistening 'sapphire eyes', echoing an ancient tradition of inserting precious stones, such as rubies and saphires (P: '*nila mani-ratana*'), into the eyes of sculptures.[1] The Subodharama has no major relics or foundation legends but it is among the few temples that has escaped extensive refurbishment in the Colombo area, some 15 kilometres south of the Fort.

Overlooking the compound is a shrine whose facade is embedded with thousands of tiny English and Chinese porcelain bits. A Sinhalese inscription records that an 'artistic image house' and a shrine dedicated to 'Sri Pada' were built by local donors in the Buddhist Era 2441, or 1897, a date also incised on the central pilaster. A footprint of the Buddha painted within its original 1897-plaster frame is inside a nearby domed octagonal shrine.

Ceramics were embedded into floor of the sanctum with the reclining Buddha in 1898 (2442 Buddhist Era).

An inscription from donors in 1897 identifies this as an 'artistic image house'. Thousands of Chinese and English porcelain fragments are embedded in the facade.

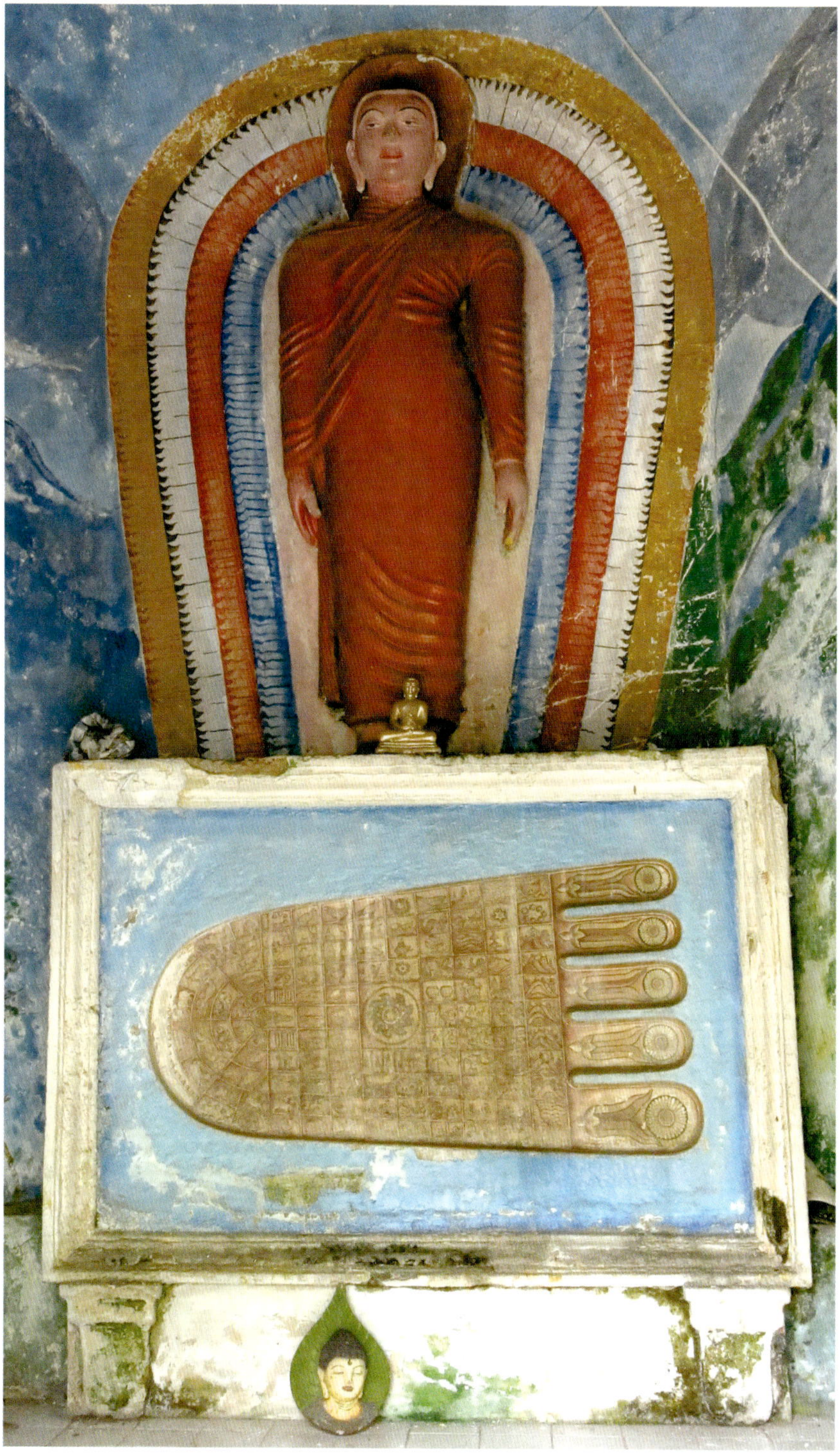

The Buddha and his footprint on Adam's Peak, a mural inside a small shrine referred to in an inscription from 1897.

The monastery's Dhamma Hall, with a raised wooden preaching platform, circa 1894. Murals illustrate scenes from the Buddha's life and the Sixteen Sacred Sites, circa 1898.

The Dhamma Hall

This tile-roofed hall, constructed probably around 1889, is used on full-moon days, or *poyas*, and festivals, when *dhamma* is disseminated by earsplitting loudspeakers. The murals are confined to two bands below the ceiling, unlike most temples from this age where compositions extended to the floor. The lower row shows the Sixteen Sacred Sites while the upper row has events in the Buddha's life. The sequence for both series moves clockwise, beginning on the right as one enters.

The Sixteen Sacred Sites (P: *Solosmasthana*) is a common theme in this period but this series is distinguished by unusual narrative details. Scenes juxtapose the mythical past with contemporary life, such as ancient stupas illuminated by street lamps and a pilgrim climbing Adam's Peak sporting a British jacket. The series begins with the deity Sumana at Mahiyangana holding an open reliquary to receive the Buddha's hair-relics. Next is the god Samiddhisumana who sheltered the Buddha during his second visit to Lanka, to Nagadipa, with his umbrella in the form of the kingstead tree (P: *rajayatana*). (Mhv: 1. 53) This rarely represented espisode is also found above the doorway at the Kelaniya Viharaya.

Beneath the sacred sites are identifying Pali verses, an unusual if not unprecedented feature. The verses were taken from a recent influential book, the *Buddhist Beliefs,* or *Bauddha Adahilla,* written by M. Gunananda (1823-90), a prominent monk based at Colombo's Dipaduttaramaya ('Thai') monastery. For example, one poem reads:

The god Samiddhisumana shielding the Buddha with a kingstead tree on Snake-Island, or Nagadipa, during the Buddha's second visit to Sri Lanka. Nagadipa is one of the Sixteen Sacred Sites. The Dhamma Hall.

'I pay homage to the Kataragama stupa where the Chief Sage [the Buddha] preached *dhamma* for united deities and which was honoured by the god Mahasena'. The murals in the hall have been assigned to the late nineteenth century by Senake Bandaranayake but the painting can now be dated more precisely, that is, probably soon after the first publication of *Buddhist Beliefs* in 1889.[2]

The Buddha's Rainy Seasons

The top register illustrates scenes from the Buddha's life organized around the three-month annual rainy season retreats (P: *vassas*). Generally, monks were expected to keep on the move, apart from the monsoon period when it was permitted to enter a monastery or remain in a single location. The first retreat was at the Deer Park at Sarnath, after which the Buddha moved throughout northeastern India for some 45 years. Some spots were monasteries while others were caves, forest-groves or even a brahmin village. (MA: 4) The retreats are identified by Sinhalese captions and English numerals that indicate their sequential position. The more familiar Pali names are listed here below. The retreats provided a chronological scaffold for attaching biographical events that in most cases were unconnected to the retreats. A recurring figure is the Buddha's disciple Moggallana, recognized by his dark complexion. His hue is based on a Pali source in which he resembled a 'dark blue water lily' or a 'dark storm cloud' but a belief in folkore is that his dark colour was a result of bad karma in a previous life. (MA: 74)[3]

Front Wall For the first retreat, at Sarnath, the Buddha is addressing his five former ascetic companions. The next shows Yasa's conversion, followed by one of the five ascetics at Sarnath. Next comes the episode with the Kassapa heretics at Uruvela who threatened the Buddha with a snake, the scene labeled, the 'subjugation of the snake' ('*nagadamanaya*').

The caption for the Bamboo Grove Monastery donated by King Bimbisara, records that the Buddha spent the second, third and fourth rainy seasons here. A bowl filled with food is delivered by the monk Kaludayi hovering in the clouds. The Buddha then moves to Kapilavatthu, with 20,000 monks in tow here telescoped to eight standing figures. Many in the Buddha's clan snubbed him but he replicated himself in the air, the 'twin miracle', causing his snooty kinsmen to change their tune and convert. The wall's last scene shows the Buddha's visit to his ancestral home. Inside is the Buddha's step-mother, one hand pointing toward her returning stepson and the other toward her husband. The events on this wall occurred within the first year after the retreat at Sarnath but are not included in the standard description of the retreats.

Side Wall The Buddha's return to his hometown begins with the visit to his wife, Yasodhara. The Buddha's emotionally charged homecoming after abandoning Yasodhara and their son for seven years is treated in canonical Pali texts. Later, popular Sinhalese poems also took up the theme from different angles.[4] The Buddha's son Rahula reclining in an armchair, awaits the reunion with his father. After this visit, the Buddha did not return to Kapilavatthu until his father's death during the retreat numbered 15. The next scene shows the donation to the Buddha of a monastery in the Great Forest (P: '*Mahavana*'), marked number five. The last episode is the Buddha recumbent in a cave on Mount Mankula, identified by the number six.

The Buddha's son, Rahula, reclines in an armchair under a clock and awaits his father's return.

The charged moment when the Buddha meets his wife Yashoda, after his seven-year absence. The Dhamma Hall.

Rear Wall The opening scene centres on a mango seed that instantly became a flowering tree and the Buddha's second performance of the 'twin miracle' in the sky. Next is the Buddha stepping up to the summit of Mount Meru in the Tavatisma Heaven during the seventh retreat, identified by the number seven. The next is a teaching scene, with the Buddha shielded by the famous night-flowering jasmine tree (P: *parijata*), with a lake nearby. The Buddha's descent from this heaven comes next. Next in the series is Sankassa, followed by a preaching scene in a monastery on Mt. Sumsumargiri, the name of which, together with the number eight, appears in the caption.

The next two scenes occur at Kosambi, in the ninth and tenth years. The first shows a preaching episode in the Ghosita Monastery followeed by the Parileyyaka Forest where an elephant and a monkey present offerings to the Buddha. The next concerns a disrespectful brahmin farmer named Bharadvaja who eventually became a monk in the village of Ekanala, followed by the conversion of a brahman in the village of Veranja. The captions contain the names of these places, together with the retreat numbers, 11 and 12. The last scene, with the numbers 13 and 18 below, shows the Buddha recumbent in a cave located on Mount Caliya, fanned by a monk named Meghiya. The Buddha returned to this location for the eighteenth retreat and conversed with a weaver's daughter who is not depicted.

Side wall The Buddha's defeat of the demon Alavaka in the sixteenth retreat is the subject of three segments. (SnA: i.217) Alavaka was the subject of several Sinhalese poems from the Kandyan period, such as the *Alavakadamanaya,* 1681. This work may have been based on a thirteenth-century text, the *Amavatura.* The tale was also a favorite of much contemporary folklore.[5]

The Buddha is then shown teaching in the Jetavana monastery, the caption referring to nineteen retreats there. The next scene depicts the Eastern Monastery, or Pubbarama, the site of six rainy seasons. The caption of the next scene gives the name of the mountain (P: 'Gijjhakutta') from which the wicked Devadatta is shown tipping boulders down on the Buddha. The remaining scenes are identified by inscriptions. The first shows the Buddha's physician, Jivaka, donating a monastery in a Mango Grove in Rajagaha. The next shows the courtesan, Ambapali, presenting a monastery, an event toward the end of the Buddha's life. The last is the merchant Kalaka dedicating a monastery in Saketa. These three culminating scenes are not associated with retreats and are the only episodes without numbers, suggesting perhaps that the artists needed to fill up empty space.

Among the earliest lists of retreats is the Pali Commentary on the *Buddhavamsa*, known as the *Madhuratthavilasini,* perhaps from the eighth century. (MA: 4). Its sequence of retreats remained largely consistent over the centuries and is the one adopted here. In later Buddhist literature, the retreats were used to structure a continuous biography but episodes were sometimes added that were not associated with the retreats themselves. For example, a sixteenth-century northern Thai chronicle cited the retreats in the standard order but inserted his three visits to Sri Lanka that were never part of the Pali canon.[6] The first twenty rainy seasons were spent in many places, but all subsequent retreats were at the Jetavana monastery at Savatthi and in the nearby Eastern Monastery 'because there was a constant supply of requisites'. (MA: 5) Since the Jetavana towered above the others, it has sometimes been indiscriminately substituted for other retreats. For example, the *Mahavamsa* placed the Buddha's visits to Lanka during his retreats at the Jetavana monastery in the fifth and eighth year whereas these seasons were actually spent at Vesali and in a mountain monastery, respectively. (Mhv. 1. 45. 72)

The 'retreats' are known in nineteenth-century murals in Lanka but the theme is not ubiquitous, say, like the Twenty-four Buddhas or the Sixteen Sacred Sites. The retreats appear with some frequency among eighteenth-century murals in Upper Burma. The best known is at the Upali Thein ordination-hall at Pagan in which

Twelve Signs of the Zodiac within a ceiling panel in the Dhamma Hall. A second panel features the Nine Planets.

Acrobats in a procession of over 100 figures encircling the base of the wooden pavilion, 1894.

the Buddha is shown within various Indian monasteries but with no extra biographical episodes. The retreats also appear in illustrated manuscripts in Burma but within the context of an expanded biography of the Buddha.[7]

What sources did artists turn to for these compositions in Colombo? The mural's impressive detail, together with extensive captioning, indicates that the painters did not rely on memory or folklore. The models then were probably artist-copybooks that adhered closely to popular Sinhalese biographies of the Buddha but no specific literary or artistic models for the murals have yet come to light.

Hundreds of thin wooden panels forming the ceiling are filled with symmetrical designs and four large roundels. One highlights the Nine Planets and another the Twelve Signs of the Zodiac, identified with inscriptions. The third roundel shows male acrobats, while the fourth contains a circle of geese.

A police band in the procession. A date, 1894, is written on their helmets.

Ceremonial processions

The base of the preaching platform features over one hundred figures silhouetted against a red background. The subject is a procession, or *perahera*, with two elephants, musicians, a police band and others. This platform has been dated to 1894, some five years after the probable date for the wall painting.[8]

The characters on the front and on the two sides proceed in two groups toward the entrance. The figures on the rear panels move in no particular direction, as if the pageant paused mid-course. Such acrobats and jugglers were hired at weddings and festivals and even entertained Governor North in 1803.[9] Similar processions are found sometimes among murals elsewhere, usually on the lowermost

One of the few surviving wooden preaching pavilions. Ariyakra Viharaya at Mihripenna, southeast of Galle, circa 1890s.

wall register, such as at the Sapugoda monastery and the Rankot monastery at Panadura. Identical motifs among these three locations suggest that the same group of artists traveled between the sites, or, alternatively, similar sketchbooks were held in common by different groups of painters. For example, at all three sites a female performer tosses a clay pot in the air in nearly identical fashion.

Similar wooden platforms from the 19th century must have been common but few have survived. A rare example is at the Ariyakra Viharaya at Mihripenna, southeast of Galle.[10] The panels do not depict a procession but show separate individual scenes. One may be the Golden Crab Jataka (no. 389), about a snake, a crow and a crab, and perhaps these scenes represent *Jataka*-dramas staged in villages.

Minstrels and costumed figures were among the procession.

The Image Hall: The Man with a Pipe

The Image Hall shares a raised section of the compound with a stupa and a belfry. Painted Sinhalese inscriptions above the paired doorways provide two dates in the Buddhist Era. On the right is a female portrait, probably the donor, framed by two unicorns, with the inscription: 'the 10th day of the month of Vesak in the year 2339 [1795]'. This date likely signifies the temple's founding but is too early to be associated with any of the surviving painting. The second inscription, below the Buddha of the Future (P: Metteyya) reads: 'Second ceremony of fixing [opening] the eyes, 2435 [1891], on the 26 day …' The inscriptions imply that the first eye-opening

The 24 Buddhas, *Jatakas*, episodes from the Buddha's life, and morality-tales drawn from the Buddhist canon, its Commentaries and Sinhalese adaptations are featured in the murals, circa 1890-1891. Image Hall.

The murals were probably finished in 1890, judging from the date painted on this man's pipe. The temple's eye-opening ceremony was in the following year. Image Hall.

The dated pipe

A bearded man near the top of the wall on the left holds a Dutch-style clay pipe whose bowl bears the date 1890, suggesting the murals were finished in the same year. He does not belong to the neighbouring narrative and his clothing does not fit the context, so perhaps the artist has devilishly snuck his portrait into his composition. Once the painters completed the murals in 1890, then the eye-opening ceremony took place in 1891, according to the inscription above one of the doors.

ceremony occurred in 1795 but that the temple's murals date from about 1890-91. This conclusion is confirmed by a man holding a pipe painted with the year '1890'. Another painted inscription near the reclining Buddha recorded the dedication of floor mosaics in 2442 Buddhist Era [1898], probably part of the campaign that included the neighbouring temple dated a year earlier and described above.[11] Perhaps the monastery was begun in 1795 but extensively refurbished in the last decades of the nineteenth century.

The two doors leading to the inner sanctum are framed by two arches, the one on the right with two *makaras* and the other with heads of lions. Above on the right appear Shiva and Vishnu. On the other side is Brahma and possibly Sakka. Hovering over both doorways is an unusual crowned female. Painted between the doors is a two-arm Shiva, identified by his third-eye.

'... terrify them with your goblin power'

The murals on the two side walls stress the rewards for charity and the hell to pay for miserliness. Three of the five narratives are *jatakas* while two are from Pali Commentaries. The murals are also reminders that the immutable law of karma are gender-blind. The

Perhaps the single example in Sri Lankan art where artists depicted the preamble to a *jataka*, or the 'story of the present' (P: *paccupanna-vatthu*). The *Khadirangara Jataka* (no. 40). Image Hall.

topmost of the wall's five registers features the 24 Buddhas, each with a Sinhalese caption, beginning to the right of the entrance and proceeding counter-clockwise.

The artists chose an extremely rare way of depicting a *jataka* by focussing on the tale's preamble, called the 'story of the present' (P: *paccupanna-vatthu*). Such preambles accompany every *jataka* and set the stage for the main story by sketching the circumstances in which the story is told. The tale itself is called the 'story of the past' (P: *atita-vatthu*). There is usually a thematic connection between the preamble and the *jataka* story that follows. Only one example of this type of depiction has been found in Burma, a 12th-century painted textile at Pagan.[12] The example in Colombo appears to be the sole surviving instance in Sri Lanka.

The preamble here, for the *Khadirangara Jataka*, focusses on the most famous legendary merchant patron, Ananthapindika. Outside his mansion was a gateway inhabited by a female heretic with supernatural powers. She and her kids were constantly disturbed by monks coming and going to the house for alms. Meanwhile, the kind-hearted merchant 'sank by degrees into poverty' due to unpaid loans to his friends. (no. 40: 100) The heretic pleaded that he should cease donating his dwindling funds to the *sangha*, a suggestion that prompted the infuriated Anathapindika to drive her and her children from her gateway home. Cast out, she wandered 'homeless, leading … [her] … children by the hand'. The god Sakka then advised her to restore her master's fortune, since this would lead to her being welcomed back to her comfy gateway.

The king refused to confess to the paternity of the child tossed in the air by his mother until the boy levitated. His mother was then appointed queen.

Sakka advised her then to visit the town's tradesmen who owed money to Ananthapindaka and to 'terrify them with your goblin power' so they would make good on their loans. This terrorist-tactic worked wonders and Ananthapindika's fortunes soon revived. Anathapindika then introduced the she-goblin to the Buddha, after which she entered a higher spiritual plane. The key events go from right to left. The demoness is shown as a young woman with her kids, but a real demon shadows her as she puts the squeeze on debtors. She also received help from four-arm Vishnu. The last scene shows her before the seated Buddha.

The long *jataka* story attached to this preamble was restricted to a narrow frame on the left, labelled '*Khadirangara Jataka*', wherein the Buddha-to-be was a state treasurer in Varanasi who wished to give alms to a special Buddha (P: *pacceka*). Mara, in order to block people from making offerings, created a fire pit filled with embers of the acacia tree (*khadira*). The story culminates on the left when the treasurer himself stepped into the pit of coals that turned into lotuses. The story also figures in the Commentary to the *Dhammapada*. (DhA.1. 447) Why the artists concentrated on the preamble is impossible to say but the painters perhaps read the tale in a Sinhalese version and found the preamble more compelling than the *Jataka* itself.

The greater part of this wall is taken up with the *Nimi Jataka* (no. 541), one of the last ten tales. The Buddha-to-be accompanies the god Matali in a chariot, first viewing the torments of hell contrasted with life in heaven. It starts at the bottom, on the left, and then reverses direction in the row above. In the next register the action is reversed again in zigzag fashion. Sinhalese inscriptions record the immoral acts and the corresponding gruesome retributions. The caption speaks of those who slayed animals like mongoose, stags and boars and those who hunted deer with dogs and went fishing. The hell is labelled 'Verala' (P: Vetarani), the name of the river along which these punishments are witnessed.

The top row tells the Jataka story of a king whose understanding of *noblesse oblige* took an ignoble turn with a peasant woman whom he met in the forest by chance (no. 7) The contemptible king presented his signet ring to her so that the boy could later prove his paternity. Later, the mother and her infant came to the palace but the king insulted her by calling the boy a 'nobody's son', that is, a bastard, or *nullius filius*. The mother then tossed the infant into the air, declaring if the king's son should fall then her claim was false. When the child levitated, his mother was elevated to queen and the son later inherited the throne. A single caption identifies the mural ('*Kattahari Jataka*'), the action moving from left to right. This *jataka* is also found at the Raja Mahavihara at Kotte.

Unfolding below is the story of Mr Kosiya, a business man whose miserliness contrasted with his wife's generosity. He craved a certain type of cake that his wife offered to bake not only for him but for the whole town! Furious with her largess, Kosiya ordered her to the seventh floor of their mansion to bake only one cake, using cheap broken rice grains. Meanwhile, the Buddha's disciple, Moggallana, hovered outside, indicating his wish for something to eat but Mr Kosiya refused. Meanwhile, the single cake upstairs magically multiplied. Moggallana then transported this mismatched couple to the Jetavana Monastery where they donated the cakes to five hundred monks. The story appears in the Commentary on the *Dhammapada*. (Dh.A: I. 367) An inscription on the left identifies the story, '*Macchikosiya katha*', while on the right is found the caption '*Jetavana*'. The action moves from left to right. Banishment of women to the 'seventh floor' was a common theme, in some cases to ensure their virginity.[13]

The lowest register relates the cautionary tale of the miserly Revati whose rich husband, Nandiya, gave generously to all. Once her husband left on a business trip, shown driving away on an ox cart, she put a speedy end to the family's altruism. The story starts on the right, showing a monastery that her husband donated at Sarnath, captioned '*Isipatanam*'. Another label reads *Revati's Mansion* (P: '*Revati vimana*') and shows Revati berating four monks. The tale continues on the bottom register with Revati standing seductively with two men outside. Her husband returns and is shown inside the house and also standing before three seated monks. The next scene depicts the blue-hued Moggallanna speaking to three women, but he played no role in the known Pali versions of the story. Revati is shown standing before her sleeping husband before she sets off to torch an alms house, a scene identified by an inscription at the Purvarama monastery where the same *jataka* is found.[14] This arson is nowhere found in the Pali texts but was a Sinhala addition. The next scene contrasts Nandiya, shown in a mansion captioned 'Tusita', with hapless Revati being snatched from home by ogres and escorted to the Gutha Hell ('*Guthanam-narakaya*'), also repeated in a caption at the Purvarama. At the end is a four-line inscription mentioning Revati and Nandiya and reminding us that giving ('*dana*') produces goodness all around.

Nandiya performs good works, doling out food, as his miserly wife watches in dismay.

Revati's story weaves in and out of early Pali literature, with slight variations, beginning with the *Vimmana-vatthu* and *Peta-vatthu*; her story also appears in at least two Pali Commentaries. (DhAiii. 290; VvA.220) Many of the tales were reworked in a popular Sinhalese version in the reign of Kirti Sri Rajasimha (1747-1782). Numerous *Vimana-vatthu* stories are also found among the murals of Pagan, Burma, circa 1113.[15]

Rear Wall

'... both eyes serve only to distract...'

The popular *Mahajanaka Jataka* (539) takes up the lower register, the action going from left to right with a single caption, '*Mahajanaka Jataka*'. The tale ends with Mahajanaka refusing his wife's request to join him in a reclusive life. Recovering from this rejection, she built stupas marking the various spots of his spiritual journey. He then spotted a fletcher fashioning an arrow, with one eye closed to guage the arrow's straightness. Seeing the fletcher triggered a profound realization for Mahajanaka, like a Zen riddle, who concluded that 'the wide horizon of both eyes serves only to distract the view. But if you get a single line, your aim is fixed, your vision true'. (no. 539: 36)

The remaining three registers above are scenes from the Buddha's early life, in zigzag fashion starting at the top on the left with the Buddha in Tusita Heaven. The action below starts on the right and ends with Sujata presenting food to the Buddha prior to the enlightenment. The lowermost row begins on the left with the Buddha tossing his bowl into the river. This register has Mara's defeat, followed by the Seven Weeks and finishes with the 'first-sermon' at Sarnath.

Facing the sanctum on all sides of the outer wall is a wide band depicting the *Ummagga Jataka* (546), a tale among the last ten. These paintings, on wooden slats, are thought to date to 1897 and are executed in a totally different style and palette than the temple's other murals. Above, on the sloping ceiling encircling the sanctum are twenty heavens belonging to the 31 Realms of Existence, a cosmic ordering described in the earliest Pali texts and numerous Commentaries. (M: 1.326; Vsm: 415) These cosmic Realms of Existence were treated in the *Story of the Three Worlds* (P: *Traibhumikatha),* composed in Sukhothai in circa 1345, and the *Lokapannatti*, often associated with Burma; much of the material derived from Sanskrit sources, such as the *Mahavastu*. The heavens are represented as European-style mansions, each inhabited by its principal deity and two or more flanking figures. These ceiling

This fletcher, from the famous *Mahajanaka Jataka* (no. 539), illustrates the axiom, 'if you get a single line, your aim is fixed, your vision true'.

panels have been dated to the 1890s, probably painted at the same time as the *Ummaga Jataka* mural.[16]

Each heavenly mansion is captioned according to its sequence in the Pali sources, here with European numerals and the number of eons (P: *kappas*; S: *kalpas*). Nearly identical murals are found at Panadura's Rankot monastery, circa 1897, and at Colombo's Isipathanama monastery from about 1915. No surviving visual examples of these heavens have survived from the ancient period nor in 18th-century Kandyan painting. Its rise to popularity seems to be no earlier than the second half of the 19th century, perhaps a response to Christian critics who argued that Buddhism lacked a coherent cosmology.

Twenty heavens in the Thirty-one Realms of Existance form part of ancient Buddhist cosmology. Each of these four heavens are shown as European style mansions, with its principal deity. Circa 1890s.

Endnotes
Further Reading
Index

Endnotes

Introduction

1. C. Brito, trans., *Yalpana-Vaipava-Mailai* (New Delhi: Asian Educational Services, 1999), p. 9.
2. R. L. Stirrat, *Power and Religiosity in a Post-Colonial Setting: Sinhala Catholics in Contemporary Sri Lanka* (Cambridge: Cambridge University Press, 1992), p. 32.
3. *Sunday Leader*, 4 May 2017; personal interview, Reyyaz Salley, Board Chairman, Dewatagah Mosque.
4. Richard Gombrich & Gananath Obeyesekere, *Buddhism Transformed: Religious Change in Sri Lanka* (Princeton: Princeton University Press, 1988), p. 411.
5. K.D. Paranavitana, trans., *Memoir of Librecht Hooreman: Commandeur of Jaffna, 1748*, (Colombo: Department of National Archives, 2009), pp. 40,47 and V. Perniola, *The Catholic Church in Sri Lanka (The Dutch Period, 1747-1795)* (Dehiwala: Tisara Prakasakayo Ltd., 1985), vol. 3, pp. 3, 7.
6. Timothy J. Coates, trans., *Diogo do Couto, Dialogue of a Veteran Soldier: Discussing the Frauds and Realities of Portuguese India*. (Dartmouth: University of Massachusetts Press, 2016). Portuguese echoing similar themes include Joao Ribeiro, *The Historic Tragedy of the Island of Ceilao*, trans., P.E. Pieris (New Delhi: Asian Educational Services, 1999).
7. *Pubbakammapiloti, apadana* 387. See Oskar von Hinuber, *A Handbook of Pali Literature* (New Delhi: Munshiram Manoharlal, 1996), p. 61.
8. *Epigraphia Zeylanica*, vol. 2, pp. 281; Hinuber, *Handbook*, p. 9
9. Ranjini Obeyesekere, trans., *Jewels of the Doctrine: Stories of the Saddhama Ratnavaliya* (Albany: State University of New York Press: 1991), p. x. See also Anne A. Hazlewood's *Saddhammopayan* (M.A. Thesis, Australian National University, 1983) and Junko Matsumura's *The Rasavahini of Vedeha Thera* (Osaka: Toho Shuppan, 1992).
10. James de Alvis, trans., *The Attanagalu-vansa or The History of the Temple of Attanagalla*. (London: Williams & Mrg., 1866) and C. E. Godakumbura, ed. *Hatthava-nagallaviharavamsa*. (London: Pali Text Society, 1956)
11. Robert Knox, *An Historical Relation of Ceylon* (Dehiwala: Tisara Prakasakayo, 1981), p. 230.
12. V. Perniola, *The Catholic Church in Sri Lanka: The Dutch Period, 1658-1711* (Dehiwala: Tisara Prakasakayo, 1985), vol. 1, p. 182.
13. Donald K. Swearer *The Buddhist World of Southeast Asia*. (Albany: State University of New York Press), p. 95.
14. Jonathan Forbes *Eleven Years in Ceylon Comprising Sketches of the Field Sports and Natural History of that Colony, and an Account of its History and Antiquities* (London: Richard Bentley, 1841), vol. 2, p. 174.
15. R.A.L.H. Gunawardana, 'The Kinsmen of the Buddha: Myths as Political Charter in the Ancient and Medieval Kingdoms of Sri Lanka' in *Religion and Legitimation of Power in Sri Lanka*, Bardwell L. Smith, ed. (Chambersburg: Anima Books, 1978), pp. 96-106.
16. *Epigraphia Zeylanica*, vol. 1, p. 225 and vol. 2, p. 148.
17. Donald Ferguson, trans., 'The History of Ceylon, from the Earliest times to 1600 A.D., As Related by Joao de Barros and Diogo do Couto', *Journal of the Ceylon Branch of the Royal Asiatic Society,* 1908, vol. 20, no. 60, p. 85. J. Penry Lewis, *List of Inscriptions on Tombstones and Monuments in Ceylon* (Colombo: H.C. Cottle, Government Printer, 1913), p. 1.
18. Dennis McGilvray and Mirak Raheem 'Origins of the Sri Lankan Muslims and Varieties of the Muslim Identity' in *The Sri Lanka Reader,* John Holt, ed. (Durham and London: Duke University Press, 2011), p. 417.
19. L. Kalus and C. Guillot, 'Reinterpretation des plus anciennes steles funeraires islamique nousantariennes: 3. Sri Lanka', *Archipel,* 2006, vol. 72, pp. 15-68. See also Elizabeth A. Lambourn, 'Carving and Communities: Marble Carving for Muslim Patrons at Khambhat and around the Indian Ocean Rim, Late Thirteenth-Mid-fifteenth Centuries", *Ars Orientalis,* vol. 34, pp. 99-133.
20. S.D. Goiten, *Letters of Medieval Jewish Traders* (Princeton: Princeton University Press, 1973), pp. 183, 185.
21. S.G. Perera, trans., *Fernao de Queyroz* [Queiros], *The Temporal and Spiritual Conquest of Ceylon* (New Delhi: Asian Educational Services, 1992), vol. 2, p. 742.
22. Sophie Pieters, trans., *Rycklof van Goens, Instructions from the Governor-General and Council of India to the Governor of Ceylon, 1656-1665* (Colombo: H.C. Cottle, Government Printer, 1908), p. 64.
23. *Epigraphia Zeylanica*, vol. 1, p. 249 and vol. 3, p. 242 for Pollonuruva. For Kelaniya, see *Epigraphia Zeylanica*, vol. 1, p. 170. For Nissankamalla, see *Epigraphia Zeylanica*, vol. 2, p. 120.
24. *Epigraphia Tamilica*, vol. 1, p. 43 and *Epigraphia Zeylanica*, vol. 6, p. 89.
25. Personal Communication, Chandra Richard de Silva.
26. V. Perniola, trans., *The Catholic Church in Sri Lanka: The Portuguese Period, 1658-1711*. (Dehiwala: Tisara Prakasakayo, 1985), vol 1, p. 123
27. Ibid., p. 157.
28. R. G. Anthonisz, *Report on the Dutch Records in the Government Archives at Colombo* (1907; Colombo: H.C. Cottle, Government Printer, 2015), p. 131

29. Perera, *The Temporal and Spiritual Conquest of Ceylon*, vol. 1, p. 195.
30. K. Karunaratne, trans., *Rajaratnakaraya (The Gem Mine of Kings)* (Colombo: Central Cultural Fund, 2009), p. 71.
31. N.A. Jayawickrama, trans. & ed., *The Chronicle of the Thupa and the Thupavamsa: Being a Translation and Edition of Vacissaratthera's Thupavamsa* (London: Luzac, 1971) and Stephen Berkwitz, trans., *The History of the Buddha's Relic Shrine: A Translation of the Sinhala Thupavamsa* (Oxford: Oxford University Press, 2007). For *Samantakuta-vannana,* see Ann A. Hazlewood, trans., *In Praise of Mount Samanta by Vedeha Thera* (London: Pali Text Society, 1986).
32. *Epigraphia Zeylanica.*, vol. 4, p. 258.
33. N.A. Jayawickrama, trans., *The Sheaf of Garlands of the Epochs of the Conqueror, being a Translation of Jinakalamalipakaranam* (London: Luzac, 1968).
34. Donald M. Stadtner, *The Sacred Sites of Burma: Myths and Folklore in an Evolving Spiritual Realm* (Bangkok: River Books, 2015), p. 36.
35. John C. Holt, *The Buddhist Vishnu: Religious Transformation, Politics and Culture* (New York: Columbia University Press, 2004), p. 57. Gananath Obeyesekera, *The Cult of the Goddess Pattini* (Chicago: University of Chicago Press, 1984), p. 315.
36. *Epigraphia Birmanica*, vol. 1. pt. 2, p. 141
37. *Epigraphia Zeylanica*, vol. 1, p. 132.
38. A.J. Suraweera, trans., *Rajavilaya* (Ratmalana: Savodaya Vishva Lekha, 2000), p. 19.
39. Gananath Obeyesekere, 'Where have All the Vaddas Gone' in Buddhism and Aboriginals in Sri Lanka' in *The Hybrid Island: culture crossing and the invention of identify in Sri Lanka*, Neluka Silva, ed. (Colombo: Social Scientists Association, 2002), p. 17.
40. *Epigraphia Zeylanica*, vol. 2, p. 115
41. Rongxi Li, trans., *The Great Tang Dynasty Record of the Western Regions* (Berkeley: Numata Center, 1996), pp. 323, 328.
42. Andy Rotman, trans., *Divine Stories: Divyavadana* (Somerville, Mass: Wisdom Publications), Part 2, p. 252, and Joel Tatelman, trans., *The Heavenly Exploits of Buddhist Biographies from the Divyavadana*, vol. 1. (New York: New York University Press, 2005), p. 422
43. Brito, *Yalpana-Vaipava-Mailai*, pp. 1-3.
44. Paul Halliday, pers. comm. See also his 'Envisioning Law's Empire in Ceylon' in *Centre for History and Economics*, University of Cambridge (online journal).
45. James Cordiner, *A Description of Ceylon Containing an Account of the Country, Inhabitants and Natural Productions with Narratives of a Tour round the Island in 1800, the Campaign in Candy in 1803, and a Journey to Ramisseram in 1804* (London: Longman, Hurst, Rees, and Ormer, 1807), p. 41
46. Edward Upham, *The Mahavansi, The Raja-ratnacari, and the Raja-Vali, forming the sacred and historical Books of Ceylon. A Collection of Tracts. In Three Voumes. Vol* (London: Parbury, Allen, and Co., 1833), vol. 2, pp. 318-322.
47. Karunaratne, *Rajaratnakaraya, p. 15.*
48. John C. Holt, *The Religious World of Kirti Sri: Buddhsim, Art and Politics in late Medieval Sri Lanka* (New York: Columbia University Press, 1996). Kevin Trainor, 'A Textualized Landscape: *Diva-guhava* and the Sri Lankan Tradition of the Sixteen Great Pilgrimage Sites (*Solosmasthana*)' in *Mudita: Deshabandhu Sirisumana Godage Abhinandana Shastriya Sangrahaya*, Ven. Induragare Dharmaratana et al. (Colombo: S. Godage Saha Sahodarayo, 2012), p. 649 and K.D. Somadasa, *Catalogue of the Hugh Nevill Collection of Sinhalese Manuscripts in the British Library* (London: The British Library, 1995), p. 203
49. Carol S. Anderson, " 'For Those Who are Ignorant' " : A Study of the *Bauddha Adahilla*' in *Constituting Communities: Theravada Buddhism and the Religious Cultures of South and Southeast Asia, John Holt et al.* (Albany: Albany: State University of New York Press, 2003), pp. 171-188.
50. *Epigraphia Zeylanica*, vol. 2, p. 832

Chapter 1: Anuradhapura

1. *Manorathapurani, Anguttara Commentary*, 1. 90. A. B. Griswold & Prasert Na Nagara, 'The Epigraphy of Mahadharmaraja I of Sukhodaya', *Journal of the Siam Society,* 1973, vol. 60, p. 101.
2. B. Gunasekara, trans., *A Contribution to the History of Ceylon, translated from Pujavaliya* (Colombo: H.C. Cottle, 1895), p. 4.
3. *Inscriptions of Ceylon* (Colombo: Department of Archaeology, 1970), vol. 1, p. 6 and vol. 2, pt. 1, 1983, p. 34.
4. A.J. Suraweera, trans., *Rajavilaya* (Ratmalana: Savodaya Vishva Lekha, 2000), p. 36.
5. *Epigraphia Zeylanica*, vol. 1, p. 34. R.A.L.H. Gunawardana,'The Kinsmen of the Buddha: Myths as Political Charter in the Ancient and Medieval Kingdom of Sri Lanka' in *Religion and Legitimation of Power in Sri Lanka*, Bardwell L. Smith, ed. (Chambersburg, PA: Anima Books, 1978), p. 100.
6. Jonathan Forbes, *Eleven Years in Ceylon*. (London: Richard Bentley, 1841), vol. 2, p. 226.
7. S.G. Perera, trans., *Fernao de Queyroz* [Queiros], *The Temporal and Spiritual Conquest of Ceylon*, vol. 2, (New Delhi: Asian Educational Services, 1992), p. 742 and vol. 3, p. 1155.
8. Ibid., vol. 1, pp. vi & 16. P.E. Pieris, trans., *The Historic Tragedy of the Island of Ceilao* (New Delhi, Asian Educational Services, 1999), p. 79.

9. Anne E. Monius. *Imagining a place for Buddhism: Literary Culture and Religious Community in Tamil-Speaking South India* (New Delhi: Navayana Publishing, 2001). Osmund Bopearachchi, *Roots of Sri Lankan Art*, (Colombo: Department of Archaeology, 2021).
10. *Epigraphia Zeylanica*, vol. 1, p. 256.
11. Senake Bandaranayake, *Sinhalese Monastic Architecture: The Viharas of Anuradhapura* (Hyderabad: Orient Blackswan Private, 2009), p. 46.
12. *Epigraphia Zeylanica*, vol. 1, pp. 8, 69, 73, 112.
13. Ibid., p. 229.
14. Bandaranayake, *Sinhalese Architecture*, p. 48.
15. Rongxi Li, *Lives of Great Monks and Nuns* (Berkeley: Numata Center, 2002), p. 207.
16. Monika Zin, *The Kanaganahalli Stupa: An analysis of the 60 Massive Slabs Covering the Dome* (New Delhi: Aryan Books International, 2018), pp. 5, 120. *Epigraphia Zeylanica*, vol. 1, p. 255.
17. J.G. Smither, *Archaeological Remains, Anuradhapura, Ceylon: comprising the Dagabas and certain other ancient ruined structures* (London: Cooper and Budd, 1894), p. 38. Hema Ratnayake. 'Jetavana: Stupa and Monastery Complex' in *The Cultural Triangle of Sri Lanka*, Ananda Guruge et al. ed. (Colombo: Unesco and Central Cultural Fund, 2006), pp. 64-85. *Inscriptions of Ceylon*, vol. 3, p. 9.
18. Bopearachchi, *Roots*, p. 3. *Epigragphia Zeylanica*, vol. 4, p. 274. Monika Zin, 'Buddhist narratives and Amaravati' in *Amaravati: the art of an early Buddhist Monument in Context*, Akira Shimad and Michael Willis. ed. (London: The British Museum, 2016), p. 48. Pers. comm., Naomi Appleton.
19. *Epigraphia Indica*, vol. 20, p. 23.
20. Gunawardana, *Robe and Plough*, p. 30.
21. *Epigraphia Zeylanica*, vol. 1, 99ff.
22. Li, *Lives of Great Monks, p. 206.* Kate Crosby, 'History versus modern myth: the Abhayagirivihara, the "Vimuttimagga" and "Yogavacara" Meditation" ', *Journal of Indian Philosophy,* 1999, vol. 27, pp. 507-550. John M. Seneviratne, 'Chino-Sinhalese Relations in the Early and Middle Ages by M. Sylvain Levi: translated from the French', *Journal of the Ceylon Branch of the Royal Asiatic Society*, 1915-16, vol. 24, pp. 74-105. Anuradha Seneviratne, 'The Buddhist Monastic Law in Sri Lanka', *The Jurist,* 2000, vol. 60, 162-203
23. Peter Skilling, 'Vaidalya, Mahayana, and Bodhisatva in India; An Essay towards Historical Understanding' in *The Bodhisattva Ideal: Essays on the Emergence of Mahayana* (Kandy: Buddhist Publications Society, 2013), pp. 69-239. Jeffrey Sundberg and Rolf Giebel, 'The Life of the Tang Court Monk Vajrabodhi as Chronicled by Lu Xiang', *Pacific World*, 2011, no. 13, pp. 129-220. Kellie Powell , 'Rituals and Ruins: Recovering the History of Vajrayana Buddhism in Sri Lanka'. (M.A. Thesis, University of California, Berkeley, 2018).
24. M.H.F. Jayasura, *The Jetavanarama Gold Plates* (Kelaniya: University of Kelaniya, 1988). *Epigraphia Zeylanica*, vol. 3, p. 199; Gregory Schopen, 'The Text on the "Dharani Stones from Abayagiriya": A minor Contribution to the Study of Mahayana Literature in Ceylon', *Journal of the International Association of Buddhist Studies*, 1982, vol. 5. no. 1, pp. 100-08. *Epigraphia Zeylanica,* vol. 1, p. 40 and vol. 3, p. 170.
25. Li, *Lives of Great Monks, p. 204.*
26. K. Karunaratne, trans., *Rajaratnakaya (The Gem Mine of Kings)* (Colombo: Central Cultural Fund: 2009), p. 43. Suraweera, *Rajavilaya, p. 51.*
27. *Epigraphia Zeylanica*, vol. 1. p 228 and vol. 2, pp. 25, 38. Gunawardana, *Robe and Plough*, pp. 37, 39, 107.
28. Osmund Bopearachchi, *From Bactria to Taprobane: Selected Works of Osmund Bopearachchi*, New Delhi: Manohar, 2015) vol. 2, p. 190. Ananda Abeyderra, 'The Geographical Perceptions of India and Ceylon in the *Periplus Maris Erythraei* and in Ptolomy's *Geography'*, *Terrae Incognitae*, 1998, vol. 30, no. 1, pp. 1-23. Prabho Mahindukulasuriya, 'Persian Christians in the Anuradhapura Period' in *A Cultured Faith: Essays in Honour of Prof. G.P.V. Somaratna on His Seventieth Birthday*, Prabo Mahindulasuriya et al. ed.(Colombo: Colombo Theological Seminary, 2011), p. 12. John Carswell, *Mantai: City by the Sea,* John Carswell et al. (Aichwald, Germany: London Soft Verlag, 2013). Rika Gyselen, pers. comm.
29. Keir Magalie Strickland, *A Time of Change: Questioning the 'Collaspse' of Anuradhapura, Sri Lanka* (Oxford: Archaeopress, 2017). Gunawardana, *Robe and Plough*, p. 86.
30. S. Pathmanathan, *Tamil Inscription in the Colombo National Museum* (Colombo: Department of National Museums, 2005), p. 34. *Epigraphia Zeylanica*, vol. 1, p. 249. *Epigraphia Indica*, vol. 36, p. 23.
31. S. Pathmanathan, *Hindu Temples of Sri Lanka* (Colombo & Chennai: Kumara Book House, 2006), p. 192.
32. *Epigraphia Zeylanica*, vol. 1, 109.
33. J. I. Chapman, 'Some Additional Remarks on the ancient city of Anarajapura or Anaradhepura', *Transactions of the Royal Asiatic Society of Great Britain and Ireland,* 1833, vol. 3, pp. 164-178. Walisinghe Harischandra, *The Sacred city of Anuradhapura.* (New Delhi: Asia Educational Services, 1985). S.M. Burrows, *The Buried Cities of Ceylon.* (Colombo: A.M. & J. Ferguson, 1894).
34. *Sunday Observer*, 3 July 2011. A. Cunningham, *Mahabodhi or The Great Buddhist temple under the Bodhi Tree at Buddha-Gaya* (London: W.H. Allen & Co., 1892), p. 30

35. H.E. Weerasooriya *Historical Guide to Anuradhapura* (Colombo: W.E. Bastion,1939), p. 9. Wilhelm Geiger, *Culture of Ceylon in Medieval Times,* Heinz Bechert, ed. (Stuttgart: Franz Steiner Verlarg, 1986). p. 187. Ulrich von Schroeder, 'The Principal Buddha of the Sri Maha Bodhi Shrine at the Mahavihara in Anuradhapura' in *Gerd Mevissen Felicitation Volume,* (forthcoming), Claudine Bautze, ed.

36. G.E. Mitton, *Old Ceylon: The Lost Cities of Ceylon.* (London: John Murray, 1916), p. 5.

37. Robin Coningham, pers. comm.

38. *Epigraphia Zeylanica*, vol.1, p.p. 55, 108, vol. 2, p. 281 and vol. 5, p. 340.

39. Bandaranayake, *Sinhalese Monastic Architecture*, pp. 164, 189.

40. K.S. Manilal, *Van Rheede's Hortus Malabaricus (*English edition) (Thiruvanathapuram: University of Kerala, 2003), vol. 1, p. 97. Lodewijk Wagenaar, 'The Euro-centric Outlook of the Dutch Toward Sri Lanka' in *Four Hundred Years of Dutch-Sri Lanka Relations: 1602-2002*, Saman Klegama & Rosshan Madawela, ed. (Colombo: Institute of Policy Studies of Sri Lanka, 2002), p. 100.

41. Robert Knox, *An Historical Relation of Ceyl*on (Dehiwala: Tisara Prakasakayo, 1981), Giovanni dei Marignolli, 'Marignolli's Recollection of Eastern travels' in *Cathay and the Way Thither: being a Collection of Medieval Notices of China*, Henry Yule, trans. (London: The Haklyut Society, 1866), vol. 2, p. 245.

42. Karunaratne, *Rajaratnakaya*, p. 74.

43. Ibid., 75. *Epigraphia Zeylanica*, vol. 2, p. 32 and vol. 4, p. 9.

44. Jonathan Forbes, *Eleven Years in Ceylon* (London: Richard Bentley, 1840), vol. 1., 229. James Emerson Tennent, *Ceylon: An Account of the Island* (London: Longman, Green, and Roberts, 1859), p. 625.

45. Oskar von Hinuber, *A Handbook of Pali Literature*, (New Delhi: Munshiram Manoharlal Publishers, 1996), p. 94. G.P. Malalasekera, *The Pali Literature of Ceylon* (Colombo: M.D. Gunasena & Co. 1958), p. 158. Somapala Jayawardana, 'A Survey of Literature on the Sacred Bodhi Tree at Anuradhapura', *Journal of the Royal Asiatic Society of Sri Lank*a, 1990-91, vol. 35, pp. 23-52. A translation of a fourteenth-century Sinhalese version, the *Bodhivamsa*, is under preparation by Stephen C. Berkwitz.

46. A. B. Griswold & Prasert Na Nagara, 'The Epigraphy of Mahadharmaraja I of Sukhodaya', *Journal of the Siam Society,* 1973, vol. 60, pt 1. p. 117. N.A. Jayawickrama, trans., *The Sheaf of Garlands of the Epochs of the Conqueror, being a Translation of Jinakalamalipakaranam* (London: Luzac, 1968), p. 139. Taw Sein Ko, 'A Preliminary Study of the Kalyani Inscription of Dhammacheti, 1476', *Indian Antiquary,* vol. 22, p. 46. *The Glass Palace Chronicle of the Kings of Burma,* trans., Pe Maung Tin & G.H. Luce. (Rangoon, Rangoon University Press, 1923) p. 116. Than Tun, trans., *Royal Orders of Burma* (Kyoto: Center for Southeast Asian Studies, 1986), vol. 5, pp. 213, 216, 221.

47. Sophie Pieters, trans., *Rycklof van Goens, Instructions from the Governor-General and Council of India to the Governor of Ceylon, 1656-1665* (Colombo: H.C. Cottle, Government Printer, 1908), p. 119.

48. Bandaranayake, *Sinhalese Monastic Architecture*, p. 18. Mohan Abeyratne, 1994, 'TL Dating of Sri Lankan Archaeological Sites', *Quarternary Science Reviews,* 1994, vol. 13, pp. 585-588. Ian Bailiff et al., 'Luminescence dating of brick stupas: an application to the hinterland of Anuradhapura, Sri Lanka', *Antiquity.* 2013, vol. 87, pp. 189-201.

49. Hans Ruelius, 'The Stupa in the *Silpasastras* and the Rituals of the Sinhalese" in *The Stupa: Its Religious, Historical and Architectural Significance,* Anna L. Dallapiccola, ed. (Wiesbaden: Franz Steinber Verlag 1980), pp. 267-275).

50. N.A. Jayawickrama, *The Chronicle of the Thupa and the Thupavamsa: Being a Translation and Edition of Vacissaratthera's Thupamsa.* (London: Pali Text Society, 1971). Stephen C. Berkwitz, *The History of the Buddha's Relic Shrine: A Tranlsation of the Sinhala Thupavamsa.* (Oxford: Oxford University Press, 2007).

51. *Epigraphia Zeylanica*, vol. 2, p. 71.

52. S. Paranavitana, *The Stupa in Ceylon*. (1946; Colombo: State Printing Corporation, 1989) pl. 5. Anna A Slaczka, *Temple Consecration Rituals in Ancient India: Text and Archaeology.* (Leiden: E.J. Brill, 2007)

53. K. Peiris, et al., 'Engineering Features of Ancient Stupa Structure: A Review Based on Jethavana Vihara', *Engineeer,* 2019, vol. 43, pp. 59-69.

54. N.A. Jayawickrama, *The Sheaf of Garlands of the Epochs of the Conqueror, being a Translation of Jinakalamalipakraranam*, (London: Pali Text Society, 1968), p. 134.

55. Jonathan Forbes, *Eleven Years in Ceylon*, vol. 1. p. 222. Bruno Dagens, trans., *Architecture in the Ajitagama and the Rauravagama* (New Delhi. Sitaram Bhartia Institute, 1984, 28.

56. Bruno Dagens, trans., *Mayamata: An Indian Treatise on Housing Architecture and Iconography*, Sitaram Bhartia Insitute, 1983), p. 80

57. Smither: *Archaeological Remains*, p. 33. Paranavitana, *The Stupa in Ceylon*, p. 5

58. Ibid., p. 36. F.B.J. Kuiper, 1959, '*Yupayasti* (*Divy*. 244, 11)', *Indo-Iranian Journal,* vol. 3, pp. 204-205. Adalbert Gail, 'Cosmical Symbolism in the Spire of the Ceylon Dagoba" in Dallapiccola, *The Stupa: Its Religious, Historical and Architectural Significance,* pp. 260-265.

59. Donald M. Stadtner, 'Rajadhiraj's Rangoon Relics and a Mon Funerary Stupa", *Journal of the Siam Society*, 2015, pp, 63-88.
60. Than Tun, 'History of Buddhism in Burma, A.D. 100-1300', *Journal of the Burma Research Society*, 1978, vol. 61. Pts. 1 & 2. p. 225.
61. Elizabeth Nissan,'Polity and Pilgrimage Centres in Sri Lanka', *Man*. n.s. vol. 23, no. 2, p. 261. Steven Kempers, *The Presence of the Past: Chronicles, Politics and Culture in Sinhala Life* (Ithica: Cornell University Press), p. 142
62. U.B. Karunananda, 'The Administration of the Atamasthana at Anuradhapura', *Rohana Research Journal*, 1993, vol. 4, pp. 137-156. W.R. Ievers, *Manual of the North Central Province*, (Colombo: G.J.A. Skeen, 1899), pp. 42-43. BC. Law, *The Dathavamsa (A History of the Tooth-relic of the Buddha* (Lahore: Motilal Banarsidas, 1925), p. 34.

Chapter 2: Sigiriya

1. Gananath Obeyesekera, 'Sigiriya Narratives: Tellers of Stories, Writers of History' in *The Buddha in Sri Lanka*, ed. Gananath Obeyesekere (New York: Routledge, 2018), p.127
2. B. Gunasekara, trans., *A Contribution to the History of Ceylon, translated from Pujavaliya* (Colombo: H.C. Cottle, 1895), p.27.
3. Ibid., p. 27. S. Paranavitana, 'The Significance of the Paintings of Sigiri', *Artibus Asiae*, 1961, vol. 24. nos. 3 & 4, pp. 382-387. *Epigraphia Zeylanica*, vol. 1, pp.35
4. Ibid., *Epigraphia Zeylanica*, vol. 1. p. 225 and vol. 2. pp.215, 288.
5. Senake Bandaranayake, *Sigiriya* (Colombo: Central Cultural Fund, 2005). Nilan Cooray, *The Sigiriya Royal Gardens* (Delft: Deflt University of Technology, 2012).
6. Obeyesekera, *Sigiriya Narratives*, p.142.
7. *Epigraphia Zeylanica*, vol. 1, p.228
8. Ibid., p.106
9. C. Ellepola, 'Conjecture Hydralics of Sigiriya', *Ancient Ceylon*, vol. 5, no. 11, 72-227. Mats Mogren, 'Seven Years in Sihagiri Bim : an account of a Sri Lankan-Swedish Collaboration in Settlement Archaeolgiy in Sigiriya 1988-1995', *Current Swedish Archaeology*, 1999, vol. 7, p.118.
10. Osmund Bopearachchi, *From Bactria to Taprobane: Selected Works of Osmund Bopearachchi*, vol. 2 (New Delhi: Manohar, 2015), p.184. Nilan Cooray, *Sigiriya Royal Gardens*, p. 206. A. Bauer and K Morrison, 'Water Management and Reservoirs in India and Sri Lanka' in *Encyclopedia of the History of Science, Techology and Medicine in Non-Western Cultures*, Helaine Selin, vol. 1 (Berlin: Springer, 2008), pp.2207-2214.
11. Akira Shimada, 'The Use of Garden Imagery in Early Indian Buddhism' in *Garden and Landscape Practices in Pre-colonial India*, ed. Ali Daud & Emma Flatt (NY & London: Routledge: 2012). *Sutta Nipata*,1. 11. N.A. Jayawickrama, trans. *The Story of Gotama Buddha: the Nidana-katha of the Jatakatthakatha* (Oxford: The Pali Text Society, 2000), p.66.
12. *Epigraphia Zeylanica*, vo. 1, p.29 and vol. 2, p.134.
13. Robert Goldman and Sally J. Sutherland Goldman, trans. *The Ramayana of Valmiki: the Complete English Translation* (Princeton: Princeton University Press, 2021), pp.228, 405.
14. L. Corneille Wijesinha, 'Kasyapa the Parricide', *The Orientalist, A Monthly Journal.* 1884, vol. 1, p.178.
15. Jagath Weerasinghe, *Sigiriya: Managing Heritage with Community* (Colombo: Neptune Press, 2025), p.15.
16. *Epigraphia Zeylanica*, vol. 3, p.152.
17. S. Paranivitana, *Sigiri Graffiti,* 2 vols. (Oxford: Oxford University Press, 1956), pp. 2, 113, 118, 309, and Benille, Priyanka, 'Readings of hitherto unread graffiti on the miror wall and the Guhava at Sigiri' in *The Settlement Archaeology in the Sigiriya-Dambula Region*, ed. Senake Bandaranayake et. al. (Colombo: University of Kelaniya, 1990), pp.201-18.
18. H.C.P. Bell, 'Interim Report on the Operations of the Archaeological Survey at Sigiriya, 1897', *Journal of the Ceylon Branch of the Royal Asiatic Society*, 1897, vol. 15, no. 48, p.109.
19. Ibid., pp.110-112.
20. Ibid., 94. *Paintings of Sri Lanka: Sigiriya,* ed. Nandana Chutiwongs et al. (Colombo: Central Cultural Fund, 1990), p.35.
21. T. W. Rhys Davids, 'Sigiriya, the Lion Rock, near Pulastipura, Ceylon', *Journal of the Royal Asiatic Society of Great ritain and Ireland*, 1875. n.s. vol. 7, p.193
22. *Majjima Nikaya, sutta* 84. A. Foucher, 1896 'Note sur les fresques de Sigiriya (Ceylan)', *Comptes rendus des seanaces de l'Academie des Inscriptions et Belles-Lettres,* 1896, vol. 40, no. 1, p. 23. R.A.L. H. Gunawardana,'The people of the lion: the Sinhala identity and ideology in history and historiography', in *Sri Lanka: History and the Roots of Conflicts*, ed. Jonathan Spencer (New Yro: Taylor and Francis, 1990), pp.60-61.
23. Ananda K. Coomarasway, *Medieval Sinhalese Art* (Broad Campden, Gloucestershire: Essex House Press, 1908), p. 178. Senake Bandaranayake, 'Sigiriya: City, Palace and Royal Gardens' in *Cultural Triangle of Sri Lanka,* (Colombo: Central Cultural Fund, 2006), p.119. Weerasinghe, *Sigiriya*, p.55.
24. Christopher Reynolds, ed., *An Anthology of Sinhalese Literature up to 1815* (London: George Allen and Unwin Ltd. 1970), p.259. Weerasinghe, *Sigiriya*, p.64.
25. *Dhammapada-atthakatha*, 1. 273. Frank E. Reynolds & Mani B. Reynolds, *Three Worlds According to King*

Ruang: A Thai Buddhist Cosmology (Berkeley: Asian Humanities Press, 1982), p.227.

26. Obeyesekera, 'Sigiriya Narratives'.
27. Paranavitana, *Sigiriya Graffiti*, no.18.
28. C. Ernest Fayle, ed. *Voyages to the East Indies: Christopher Fryke & Christopher Schweitzer*, (London: Cassell & Company Ltd. 1929), p.245.
29. Gunasekara, trans., *A Contribution to the History, p.27.*
30. *Wijesinha, 'Kasyapa the Parricide', 178.*
31. Senake Bandaranayake, 'Notes on the Conjectural Reconstruction of the Palace and the Lion Staircase' in *Sirinimal Lakdusinghe Felicitation Volume*, ed. P. Gunawardhana et al. (Colombo: Nepture Press, 2010), p.38.
32. Senake Bandaranayake, 'Sigiriya: The Lion Mountain and the palace in the sky: notes on the the identity of the royal complex at Sigiriya' in *Abhinandamala: Nandana Chutiwongs Felicitation Volume,* ed. L. Prematillake (Bangkok: SPAFA Regional Center of Archaeology and Fine Arts, 2010) p.117. Obeyesekere, *Sigiriya Narratives*, p.145.
33. *Vinaya-pitaka*, 2. 146. Ibid., *Inscriptions of Ceylon*, vol. 1, p.67.
34. K. Karunaratne, trans. *Rajaratnakaraya (The Gem Mine of Kings)* (Colombo: Central Cultural Fund, 2009), p.30.
35. Bhikkhu Nanomoli, trans. *Visuddhimagga: The Path of Purification*. (Kandy: Buddhist Publications Society, 2010), p.70.
36. Marijke Klokke, 2008. 'The Buddhist Temples of the Sailendra Dynasty in Central Java', *Arts Asiatique*, 2008, vol. 63, pp.154-167. James Emerson Tennent, *Ceylon: An Account of the Island* (London: Longman, Green, and Roberts, 1859), vol. 2, p.380.

Chapter 3: Kelaniya

1. *Inscriptions of Ceylon* (Colombo: Department of Archaeology, 1970), vol. 1, p. 86.
2. Pe Maung Tin & Luce, G.H., 'Inscriptions of Burma', *Bulletin of the Burma Historical Commission,* 1960, vol. 1, 1960, p. 20. N.A. Jayawickrama, trans., *The Sheaf of Garlands of the Epochs of the Conqueror, being a Translation of Jinakalamalipakaranam* (London: Luzac, 1968), p. 47.
3. Bijoya Goswami, trans., *Lalitavistara* (Kolkata: The Asiatic Society, 2001), p. 251.
4. Junko Matsumura, *The Rasavahini of Vedeha Thera* (Osaka: Toho Shuppan, 1992), p. cxxxix.
5. *Manorathapurani, Anguttara Commentary*, 1. 9. Frank E. Reynolds & Mani B. Reynolds, *Three Worlds According to King Ruang: A Thai Buddhist Cosmology* (Berkeley: Asian Humanities Press, 1982), p. 330.
6. Paula Richman, *Women, Branch Stories, and Religious Rhetoric in a Tamil Buddhist Text* (New York: Syracuse University, 1988), p. 7. Anne E. Monius, *Imagining a place for Buddhism: Literary Culture and religious Community in Tamil-speaking South India* (New Delhi: Navayana Publishing, 2001), p. 14.
7. K. Karunaratne, trans., *Rajaratnakara (The Gem Mine of Kings)* (Colombo: Central Cultural Fund, 2009), p. 25. B. Gunasekara, trans., *A Contribution to the History of Ceylon, translated from Pujavaliya* (Colombo: H.C. Cottle, Government Printer, 1895), 46.
8. *Vamsatthappakasini*, p. 431. Jonathan S. Walters, *The History of the Kelaniya* (Colombo: Social Scientists' Association, 1996), p. 35.
9. *Epigraphia Zeylanica*, vol. 6, p. 5. R.A.L.H. Gunawardana, *The Robe and the Plough* (Phoenix: The University of Arizona Press, 1979), p. 67.
10. Jayawickrama, *The Sheaf of Garlands,* p. 130. Anne M. Blackburn, *Locations of Buddhism: Colonialism & Modernity in Sri Lanka* (Chicago: University of Chicago Press, 2010), p. 149. H.C.P. Bell & M. A. Gunasekara,'Kelani Vihara and Its Inscriptions', *Ceylon Antiquary and Literary Register*, 1916, vol. 1, no. 3, p. 16.
11. Jonathan Forbes, *Eleven Years in Ceylon* (London: R. Bentley, 1840), vol. 1, p. 153.
12. U.P. Meddegama, trans., *Amavatura (The Flood of Nectar) by Gurujugomi* (Colombo: Central Cultural Fund, 2006), p. 191. Pali sources treating these two footprints are found in Charles Duroiselle, 'Note on the Ancient Geography of Burma (Rangoon: Government Printing Office, 1906). For the Burmese site commemorating the two footprints, see Donald M. Stadtner, *Sacred Sites of Burma: Myths and Folkore in an Evolving Spiritual Realm* (Bangkok: River Books, 2015), pp. 190-197.
13. Ann A. Hazlewood, trans., *In Praise of Mount Samanta (Samantakutavannana) by Vedeha* (London: Pali Text Society Society, 1986). Oskar von Hinuber, *A Handbook of Pali Literature* (New Delhi: Munshiram Manoharlal, 1996), p. 97
14. *Epigraphia Zeylanica*, vol 1, p. 135, and vol. 2, pp. 119, 141, 144, 147, 165.
15. Gunasekara, *Contribution to the History,* pp. 39, 46.
16. *Inscriptions of Ceylon*, vol. 7, 26. Gunawardana, *Robe and the Plough*, p. 304
17. W. F Gunawardhana, trans., *The Nikaya Sangrahaya* (Colombo: H.C. Cottle, Government Printer, 1908), p. 25. Vesak Nanayakkara, *The Temple of Kelaniya.* (Colombo: Academy of Sri Lankan Culture, 1994), p. 15. Christopher Reynolds, ed., *An Anthology of Sinhalese Literature up to 1815* (London: George Allen and Unwin Ltd. 1970), p. 291.
18. *Inscriptions of Ceylon*, vol. 8, p. 91. Bell & Gunasekara, 'Kelani Vihara', p. 157. R. Raven-Hart, trans., *Heydt's Ceylon*. (Colombo: Government Press, 1952), p. 12.

19. John C. Holt, *Buddha in the Crown: Avalokitesvara in the Buddhist Traditions of Sri Lanka*. (Oxford University Press, 1991). *Inscriptions of Ceylon*, p. 91. Bell & Gunasekara, *Kelani Vihara*, p. 157.
20. V. Perniola, *The Catholic Church in Sri Lanka. The Portuguese Period* (Dehiwala: Tisara Press, 1989), vol. 1, p. 353. S.G. Perera, trans., *Fernao de Queyroz* [Queiros], *The Temporal and Spiritual Conquest of Ceylon*, (New Delhi: Asian Educational Services, 1992), vol. 2, 425. P.E. Pieris, *Ceylon: The Portuguese Era, being a History of the Island for the Period 1505-1658* (Colombo: Colombo Apothecaries Co., 1913), vol. 1, p. 197.
21. A.V. Suraweera, trans., *The Rajavilaya and the first ever translation of the Alakesvara Yuddhaya* (Ratmalan: Vishva Lekha, 2000), p.78.
22. Perniola, *The Catholic Church*, 130.
23. Queiros, *The Temporal*, p. 29.
24. Perniola, *The Catholic Church,* p. 296. Donald Ferguson, trans., 'The History of Ceylon, from the earliest times to 1600, as Related by Joao de Barros and Diogo do Couto', *Journal of the Ceylon Branch of the Royal Asiatic Society,* 1909, vol. 20, no. 60, pp. 1-445. Perera, *The Temporal*, p. 293. Sinnappah Arasaratnam, trans., *Francois Valentijn's Description of Ceylon* (London: Hakluyt Society, 1978), p. 236. Suraweera, *Rajavilaya*, p. 14.
25. Raven-Hart, *Travels*, p. 14. For the Dutch decision to remove the monks from the monastery, see J.D. Palm, 'An Account of the Dutch Church in Ceylon', *Journal of the Ceylon Branch of the Royal Asiatic Society*, vol 1. no. 3, pp. 32, 37-38 and Kitsiri Malalgoda, *Buddhism in Sinhalese Society 1750-1900* (Berkeley: University of California Press, 1976).
26. Raven-Hart, *Travels*, p. 14. Clements Markham, trans., *Garcia da Orta, Colloquies on the Simples & Drugs of India* (London: Henry Sotheran and Co. 1913), p. 55. Arthur C. Burnell & P.A. Tiele, *The Voyage of John Huyghen van Linschoten to the East Indies: From the Old English Translation of 1598*) (Delhi: Munshiram Manoharla Publishers Ltd. 1997), vol. 2, p. 115. G.P.V. Somaratna, *History of Christianity in Sri Lanka up to* 1800 (Colombo Theological Seminary, 2016), p. 228. Sophie Pieters, trans., *Rycklof van Goens, Instructions from the Governor-General and Council of India to the Governor of Ceylon, 1656-1665* (Colombo: H.C. Cottle, Government Printer, 1908), p. 64.
27. Robert Hooke, 'An Account of the Plant, call'd Bangue, Before the Royal Society, Dec 18, 1689', *Philosophical Experiments and Observations of the late Eminent Dr. Robert Hooke*, W. Derham, ed. (London: W. J. Innys, 1726), p. 211.
28. Raven-Hart, *Travels,* p. 12.
29. Bell & Gunasekara, '*Kelani Vihara*', pp. 149-150. F.H. de Vos, 'A Short History of the Principal Events that Occurred in the Island of Ceilon', *Journal of the Ceylon Branch of the Royal Asiatic Society*, 1889-90), vol. 11, no. 3, p. 140.
30. Bell & Gunasekara, '*Kelani Vihara* ', p. 161.
31. *Inscriptions of Ceylon*, vol. 9, p. 60. Bell & Gunasekara, '*Kelani Vihara',* pp. 161.
32. Max de Bruijn & Remco Raben et. al., *The World of Jan Brandes, 1743-1808*. (Amsterdam: Rijksmuseum, 2004), pp. 327, 330.
33. Colin McKenzie, 'Remark on Some Antiquities On the West and South Coasts of Ceylon: written in the year 1796', *Asiatick Researches*, 1801, vol. 6, p. 449. Bell & Gunasekara, '*Kelani Vihara*', p. 151.
34. Bell & Gunasekara, '*Kelani Vihara',* p. 151. John Deschamps, *Scenery and Reminiscences of Ceylon* (London: Ackermannn and Co., 1845).
35. D.B. Dhanapala, *Among Those Present* (Colombo: M.D Gunasena, 1962), p. 181.
36. Translation provided by Osmund Bopearachchi. Kitsiri Malalgoda, *Buddhism in Sinhalese Society,* (Berkeley: University of California Press, 1976) p. *136*.
38. Ananda K. Coomaraswamy, *Medieval Sinhalese Art* (Gloucestershire: Essex House Press, 1908), pl. viii.
39. Donald M. Stadtner, " 'If you spill a single drop': Innovation in the Jataka Traditions of Pagan", *Orientations*, 2015, vol. 46, no. 1, pp. 2-11.
40. Junko Matsumura, *The Rasavahini of Vedeha Thera* (Osaka: Toho Shuppan, 1992), vol. 1, p. 2 Chris Baker and Pasuk Phongpaichit, *From the Fifty Jataka: Seclections from the Thai Pannasa Jataka* (Chiang Mai: Silkworm Books, 2019), p. 175. P. S. Jaini, *Pannasa-Jatakas or Zimme Pannasa (in the Burmese recension)*, 2 vols. (London: Pali Text Society, 1981, 1983).
41. Pers. comm., Leedom Lefferts. *Epigraphia Zeylanica*, vol. 2, p. 287.
42. Edward Upham, *The History and Doctrine of Buddhism, Popularly Illustrated* (London: R. Ackermann, 1829). Marie Gatellier, 'Les peintures du temple de Kelaniya a Sri Lanka', *Arts Asiatiques.* 1983, vol. 38, pp. 49-70.
43. Sophie Anthonisz, trans., *Memoir of Thomas van Rheee*, 1697 (Colombo: H.C. Cottle, Government Printer, 1915), p. 37. Sophie Pieters, trans., *Memoir of Hendrick Zwaardecroon, 1697* (Colombo: Government Printer, 1911), p. 13. Ananda K. Coomaraswamy, 'Painted Ceiling at Kelaniya Vihara,Ceylon', *Journal of Indian Art*, 1914, vol. 16, p. 113.
44. Senake Bandaranayake, *The Rock and Wall Paintings of Sri Lanka* (Colombo: Lake House, 1986), p. 204. Marie Gatellier, *Peintures murales du Sri Lanka: l'ecole Kandyenne, eighteenth-nineteenth Centuries.* 2 vols. (Paris: L'ecole Francaise d'Extreme-Orient, 1991).
45. Edward W. Perera, *Sinhalese Banners and Standards* (Colombo: H.C. Cottle, Goverment Printer, 1916), p. 16.

46. Don Martino de Zilva Wickremasinghe, *Catalogue of the Sinhalese Printed Books in the Library of the British Museum* (London: British Library, 1901), p. 168.
47. Vajira Nalinda Jayathilaka, 'Kalaniya Rajamaha Viharaya Reconstructured in the mid-20th Century: Inspirations and Politics' in *Evolving Traditions of Buddhist Image Houses*, Asoka de Zoysa et al., (Colombo: Samkathana Research Centre, University of Kelaniya, 2018), pp. 177-196. For the most complete photographic survey of the Kelaniya murals, see Arjuna Samaravira, *Urumayak Arumaya*, 2 vols. (Colombo: Department of Archaeology, 2016).
48. Pers. comm., V. Mahinda Sangharakkhita.
49. A.V. Suraweera, *The Rajavilaya and the first ever translation of the Alakesvara Yuddhaya* (Ratmalan: Vishva Lekha, 2000), p. 26. Stephen Berkwitz, trans., *The History of the Buddha's Relic Shrine: A Translation of the Sinhala Thupavamsa* (Oxford: Oxford University Press, 2007), p. 160.
50. Suraweera, *Rajavilaya*, p. 27.
51. Anthonisz, *Memoir of Thomas van Rheee,* p. 58.
52. Dhanapala, *Among Those Present*, p. 180.
53. Gunasekkara, *Contribution*, p. 3.
54. Frank E. Reynolds & Mani B. Reynolds, *Three Worlds According to King Ruang: A Thai Buddhist Cosmology* (Berkeley: Asian Humanities Press, 1982), p. 172. John S. Strong, 'Asoka's Wives and the Ambiguities of Buddhist Kingship', *Cahiers d'Extreme-Asie,* 2002-2003, vol. 13, pp. 35-54.
55. Jayawickrama, *Chronicle*, p. 160. G.P. Malalsekera, *The Pali Literature of Ceylon* (Colombo: M.D. Gunasena & Co., 1958). p. 162. E. R. Gooneratne, '*Tela-kataha-gatha*', *Journal of the Pali Text Society*, 1894, pp. 49-68. Hinuber, *Handbook*, p. 186. Nicolas Revire, "Compte rendu de 'Research Report on: The Establishment of Sri Lankan Buddhism in Thailand during the Dvaravati Period', *Aseanie*, 2002, no. 29, p. 153.
56. Rongxi Li, *Lives of Great Monks and Nuns* (Berkeley: Numata Center, 2002), 198 and *The Great Tang Dynasty Record of the Western Regions* (Berkeley Numata Center, 1996), p. 224 and *The Biographical Scriptures of King Asoka*, (Berkeley: Numata Center, 1993), p. 16. John S. Strong, *The Legend of King Asoka: A Study and Translation of the Asokavadana* (Princeton: Princeton University Press, 1983), p. 73.
57. E. Jayasuriya, trans. *Salalihini Sanddesa of Totagamuve Sri Rahula Thera* (Colombo: Central Cultural Fund, 2002), p. 49. Bell and Gunasekera, *Kelani Vihara*, p. 157.
58. Perera, *Fernao de Queyroz,* p. 30. *Merlin Peris,* 'King Kelanitissa's Crime'. *Journal of the Royal Asiatic Society of Sri Lanka*, 1997-98, ns., vol. 32, pp. 91-116. Forbes, *Eleven Years*, vol. 1, p. 152. A.B. Griswold & Prasert na Nagara, 'The Inscription of Vat Jan Lom (1349)', *Journal of the Siam Society,* 1971, vol. 59, pp. 189-208. *The Grand Tour of the British Princes: the visit of Prince Albert Victor and Prince George to Ceylon* (Colombo: Ceylon Observer Press, 1882), p. 9.
59. Jayawickrama, *Story of Gotama Buddha*, p. 64.
60. Dhanapala, *Access*, p. 184
61. *Ceylon Independent*, 30 January 1930, p. 6. Vesak Nanayakkara, *The Temple of Kelaniya*, p.113. Kumari Jaywardena, *The White Woman's Other Burden: Western Women and South Asia During British Rule*.(New York: Routledge, 1995), 287. Pers. comm., Rohan de Soysa and Jean Arasanayagam.
62. E. Jayasuriya, trans., *Salalihini Sandesa of Totagamuve Sri Rahula Thera* (Colombo: Central Cultural Fund, 2002), p. 54.
63. Nanayakkara, *Temple*, p. 52.

Chapter 4: Sri Pada (Adam's Peak)

1. John M. Senaveratne & Sylvain Levi, 'Chino-Sinhalese relations in the early and Middle Ages', *Journal of the Ceylon Branch of the Royal Asiatic Society*, 1915-1916, vol. 24, no. 68, p. 88. Alexander B. Griswold & Prasert Na Nagara, 1978. 'The Buddhapada of Vat Pavaranivesa and its Inscription', *Journal of the Siam Society*, 1978, vol. 60, no. 2, p. 121. For a summary of the legendary footprints in India and Sri Pada, see John S. Strong, *Relics of the Buddha* (Princeton: Princeton University Press, 2004), pp. 90-94.
2. Simon Sawers and Henry Marshall, 'Recollection of a Journey from Kandy to Calatura, by way of Adam's Peak, made in the Year 1819', *Memoirs of the Wernerian Natural History Society*, 1823, vol. 4., pt. 2, p. 408. Jorge Manuel Flores, *Os Olhos do Rei: Desenhos e Descricoes Portuguesas de Ilha de Ceilao (1624, 1638)* (Lisbon: Comissao National para as Comemoracoes Dos Descobrument Portugueses, 2001), p. 149, folio 35r. R. Raven-Hart, *Ceylon: History in Stone* (Colombo: Associated Newspapers of Ceylon Ltd., 1964), p. 103.
3. Anne E. Hazlewood, trans., *In Praise of Mount Samantu (Samantakutavannana)* by Vedeha Thera (London: Pali Text Society, 1986), p. 94. A Theravada tradition arose in Thailand by the sixteenth century that the Buddha impressed his footprint on a mountain named Pasanaka, near Rajagaha; see N.A. Jayawickrama, *The Sheaf of Garlands of the Epochs of the Conqueror, being a translation of Jinkalamalipakaranam* (London: Luzac, 1968), p. 54.
4. For the Pali textual traditions, see Charles Duroiselle, *Note on the Ancient Geography of Burma* (Rangoon: Government Printing Office, 1906). For a related Sanskrit source, see Andy Rotman, *Divine Stories: Divyavadana*, pts. 1-2 (Boston: Wisdom Publications, 2008), pt.1, p. 71. Buddhaghosa's

reference to the two footprints appears in the *Samantapasadika*. For the legendary locations, Yonaka and Sunaparanta, see G.P. Malalasekera, *A Dictionary of Pali Proper Names*, 2 vols. (London: Pali Text Society, 1960).

5. Hazlewood, *In Praise*, p. 94-95. Udaya Prasanta Meddegama, trans., *Amavatura (The Flood of Nectar) by Gurujugomi* (Colombo: Central Cultural Fund, 2006), p. 191. Bijoya Goswami, trans., *Lalitavistara* (Kolkata, The Asiatic Society, 2001), p. 251.
6. Kayoko Kusumoto, 'Aspects of Sri Lanka's Footprints of the Buddha' in *Critical Gaze*, Kulatilaka Kumarasinghe, ed. (Colombo. Godage & Brothers, Ltd., 2014), pp. 765-787. Peter Skilling 'Symbols on the Body, Hand, and Feet of a Buddha', *Journal of the Siam Society*, 1992, vol. 80. pt. 2, pp. 67-80. Claudio Cicussa, *The Pali Buddhapadamangala or Auspicious Signs on the Buddha's Feet* (Bangkok: Fragile Palm Leaves Foundation, 2011). Alexander B. Griswold and Prasert Na Nagara, 'The Inscription of Vat Traban Jan Phoak', *Journal of the Siam Society*, 1971, vol. 59, no. 1., p. 174.
7. Strong, *Relics*, p. 85. Christiane Gruber, 'The Prophet Muhammad's Footprint' in *Ferdowsi, the Mongols and the History of Iran,* R. Hillenbrand et al., ed. (London: I.B. Tauris, 2013), p. 297. Ranjini Obeyesekere, trans., *Portraits of Buddhist Women: Stories from the Saddharmaratnavaliya* (Albany: State University of New York Press, 2001), p. 17. Rotman, *Divine Stories*, vol. 2, p. 248. Hazlewood, *In Praise*, p. 94.
8. Anne E. Monius, *Imagining a Place for Buddhism: Literary Culture and Religious Community in Tamil-speaking South India* (New Delhi: Navayana Publishing, 2001), p. 103. Paula Richman, *Women, Branch Stories, and Religious Rhetoric in a Tamil Buddhist Text* (New York: Syracuse University, 1988), p. 21. S. Krishnaswamy Aiyangar, *Manimekhalai in its Historical Setting* (London: Luzac, 1928), pp. 136, 200.
9. Rongxi Li, *Lives of Great Monks and Nuns* (Berkeley: Numata Center, 2002), p. 204. Rongxi Li, *The Great Tang Dynasty Record of the Western Regions*. (Berkeley: Numata Center, 1996), p. 333. For Malaya, see Malalasekera, *Dictionary*. Senaveratne & Levi, *Chino-Sinhalese*, p. 88. Vincent Tournier, 'Mahakasyapa, His Lineage, and the Wish for Buddhahood: Reading Anew the Bodhgaya Inscriptions of Mahanaman', *Indo-Iranian Journal*, 2014, vol. 57, pp. 1-60.
10. *Epigraphia Zeylanica*, vol. 2, p. 217. *Inscriptions of Ceylon* (Colombo: Department of Archaeology, 2007), vol. 6, p. 10.
11. Senerat Paranavitana, *The God of Adam's Peak* (Ascona: Artibus Asiae Publishers, 1958), p. 15. *Epigraphia Zeylanica*, vol. 2, p. 95.
12. K. Karunaratne, trans,, *Rajaratnakaraya: The Gem Mine of Kings* (Colombo: Central Cultural Fund, 2009), p. 63.
13. *Epigraphia Zeylanica*, vol. 3, p. 337. Senaveratne & Levi, *Chino-Sinhalese*, p. 101.
14. A. H. Mirando, *Buddhism in Sri Lanka in the Seventeenth and Eighteenth Centuries* (Colombo: Tisara Prakasakayo Press, 2010), pp. 3, 27. Alexander McKinley, *Mountain at a Center of the World: Pilgrimage and Plurarlism in Sri Lanka* (Chicago: University of Chicago Press, 2024), p. 66. For other kings who made donations at the footprint, see K. Karunaratne, trans., *Rajaratnakaraya: The Gem Mine of Kings* (Colombo: Central Cultural Fund, 2009), pp. 63, 81.
15. C.F. Beckingham, trans., *The Travels of Ibn Battuta* (London: The Haklyut Society, 1994), p. 853. J. Still, 'Notes on Adam's Peak and some of the Paths in the Range', *Spolia Zeylanica*, 1908, vol. 8, no. 5. pt. 8, pp. 80-86. Archibald Campbell Lawrie, *A Gazetteer of the Central Province of Ceylon* (Colombo: G. Skeen, Government Printer, 1896), vol. 1, p. xi. *Scientific American*, July 1902, vol. 54, pp. 2164-2165.
16. William Skeen, *Adam's Peak: Legendary, Traditional and Historic Notices of the Samanala and Sri-Pada*. (Colombo: W.L.H. Skeen & Co., 1870), p. 339. Anna Marie Walker, 'Journal of an ascent to the Summit of Adam's Peak, Ceylon', *Companion to the Botanical Magazine, 1835, vol. 1,* pp. 3-14. Sawers and Marshall, *Recollection*, p. 413. *Great Temples of India, Ceylon and Burma*, anonymous author (Madras: Christian Literature Society for India, 1904), p. 70.
17. Nigel Bryant provided a translation of the Middle French text accompanying the illustration in this unpublished Marco Polo manuscript, ms-5219, in the Bibliotheque de l'Arsenal, Paris. For the different versions of Marco Polo manuscripts, see Sharon Kinoshita, *Marco Polo: The Description of the World* (London: Hackett Publishing, 2016).
18. Donald Ferguson, 'Mulgiri-Gala', *Journal of the Ceylon Branch of the Royal Asiatic Society*, 1911, vol. 22, no. 64, pp. 197-244. John Strong, *The Buddha's Tooth: Western Tales of a Sri Lanka Relic* (Chicago: University of Chicago Press, 2021), p. 60;
19. The Dutch text on this Lund University museum painting has not yet been translated. The parchment was likely donated to the university by Kilian Stobaeus in 1735. John Strong brought to my attention how the depiction conformed to at least two written descriptions, see my 'Whose Footprint? Tracing Sri Pada through the Ages', *The Ceylon Journal*, vol. 1, no. 2, pp. 1-10.
20. Kinoshita, *Description*, p. 168. Ananda Abeydeera, 'Paths of Faith: Following the Blessed Footsteps of Adam to Ceylon', *Diogenes*, no. 159, 1992, p. 81. Minoo S Southgate, trans., *Iskandarnamah, A Persian*

Medieval Alexander-Romance (New York: Columbia Universtiy Press, 1978), p. 31. Duarte Barbosa, *A Description of the Coasts of east Africa and Malabar by Duarte Barbosa* (London: The Hakluyt Society, 1866), 169. J. Harward, 'Fra Mauro's Map', *Journal of the Ceylon Branch of the Royal Asiatic Society of Great Britain and Ireland*, 1915-1916, vol. 24, no. 68, pt. 1, p. 15. Beckingham, *Travels*, p. 853. Mirando, *Buddhism*, p. 3.

21. J. Still, 'Notes on Adam's Peak and some of the Paths in the Range', *Spolia Zeylanica*, 1908, vol. 8, no. 5. pt. 8, p. 83. Davy, *Account*, p. 341. Alexander McKinley, 'The Spacing of Pilgrimage: Two Journeys to Sri Pada in Sinhalase Verse', *Sagar*, 2017, vol. 25, p. 99.
22. Hazlewood, *In Praise*, p. 94. Kevin Trainor, "The Buddha's 'cave of midday rest' and Buddhist Relic Practices in Sri Lanka', *Material Religion*, vol. 9, no. 4, pp. 516-521. Don Martino de Zilva Wickremasinghe, *Catalogue of the Sinhalese Printed Books in the Library of the British Museum* (London: British Museum, 1901), p. 152.
23. McKinley, *Mountain*, p. 163ff. Jonathan Duncan, 'An account of two Fakeers, with their portraits', *Asiatic Researches,* 1799, vol. 5, p. 39.
24. Ryuiji Okudaira provided the translation. Fabio Rembelli, 'In the Footprints of the Buddha: Ceylon and the Quest for the Origin of Buddhism in Early Modern Japan – A Minor Episode in the History of the Japanese Imagination of India' in *Buddhism and the Dynamics of Transculturarlity,* Birgit Kellner, ed. (Berlin: De Gruyter, 2019), p. 155.
25. Pers. comm., Alexander McKinley. Skeen, *Adam's Peak*, p. 183. Marcus Aksland, *The Sacred Footprint: A Cultural History of Adam's Peak* (Bangkok, Orchid Press, 2001), p. 111. Edward Upham, *The Mahavansi, The Raja-ratnacari, and the Raja-Vali, forming the sacred and historical Books of Ceylon, A Collection of Tracts. 3 vols.* (London: Parbury, Allen, and Co., 1833), p. 222. Justin Henry, *Ravana's Kingdom: the Ramayana and Sri Lankan History from Below* (Oxford: Oxford University Press, 2023), p. 91.
26. Lawrie, *Gazetteer*, vol. 1, p. xi. Skeen, *Adam's Peak*, p. 356. Anne M. Blackburn, *Locations of Buddhism: Colonialism & Modernity in Sri Lanka* (Chicago: University of Chicago Press, 2010) pp. 21-32. Kitsiri Malalgoda, *Buddhism in Sinhalese Society 1750-1900.* (Berkeley: University of California Press, 1976), p. 140.
27. Lawrie, *Gazetteer*, vol. 1, x. Blackburn, *Locations*, p. 21ff. Premakumara de Silva, 'Kings, Monks and Pre-Colonial States: Patron of the Temple of the Sacred Footprint' in *Asian Art and Culture: A Research Volume in Honour of Ananda Coomaraswamy,* ed. Sachee Raneweera et al., 2012, pp. 41-53.

Chapter 5: Ratnapura

1. Bruce Kapferer, *A Celebration of Demons: Exorcism and the Aesthetics of Healing in Sri Lanka* (Bloomington: Indiana University Press, 1983), p. 158. Gananath Obeysekere, *The Cult of the Goddess Pattini* (Chicago: University of Chicago Press, 1984), p. 64.
2. Hans-Dieter Evers, *Monks, Priests and Peasants: A Study of Buddhism and Social Structure in Central Ceylon* (Leiden: E.J. Brill, 1972), p. 28. *Inscriptions of Ceylon*, (Colombo: Department of Archaeology, 2014), vol. 7, p. 36.
3. John D'Oyle, *The Diary of Mr. John D'Oyle* (Colombo: Lake House, 1995), pp. 96, 123.
4. James Cordiner, *A Description of Ceylon* (Colombo: K.V.G. de Silva, 1983), vol. 2, p. 431.
5. H.C.P. Bell, 'Maha Saman Devale and its Sannasa', *Journal of the Ceylon Branch of the Royal Asiatic Society*, 1916-1917, vol. 2, pt. 1, p. 37. Jonathan Forbes, *Eleven Years in Ceylon,* (London: Richard Bentley), vol. 1, p. 185. P.L. Simmonds, 'Notes on an Excursion to the Summit of Adam's Peak', *Simmon's Colonial Magazine and Foreign Miscellany*, 1848, vol 15, p. 15.
6. *Illustrated London News*, 25 October 1852, p. 322. Charles Pridham, *An Historical, Political and Statistical Account of Ceylon and Its Dependencies,* (London: T. and W. Boone: 1849), vol. 2, p. 609.
7. Tharaka Ananda and Charmalie Nahallage, 'The Present Status of Traditional Mahabamb Kolama in the Saparagamu Maha Saman Devalaya Perahera', Colombo: Eighth Research Conference of the Royal Asiatic Society, 2015.
8. A.H. Mirando, *Buddhism in Sri Lanka in the Seventeenth and Eighteenth Centuries.* (Colombo: Tisara Prakasakayo: 2010), p. 27. Pers. comm., Tharaka Ananda. John S. Strong, *The Buddha's Tooth: Western Tales of a Sri Lankan Relic* (Chicago: University of Chicago Press, 2021), p. 54.
9. 1961. P.E.P. Deraniyagal. 'The Saman Sirita, A Hymn to the Presiding Deity of Mount Saman', *Spoila Zeylanica,* 1961, vol. 29, pt. 2 , p. 303.
10. Pridham, *Historical*, p. 609.
11. Pers. comm., Alexander McKinley
12. V. Perniola, *The Catholic Church in Sri Lanka: The Dutch Period* (Dehiwala: Tisara Prakasakayo Ltd., 2005), vol. 1, pp. 163, 212.
13. Jorge Manuel Flores, *Os Olhos do Rei: Desenhos e Desclricoes Portuguesas de Ilha de Ceilao (1624, 1638)* (Lisbon: Comissao National para as Comemoracoes Dos Descobrument Portugueses, 2001), pp. 42, 99. Pers. comm., Chryshane Mendis.
14. John Davy, *An Account of the Interior of Ceylon, and of its Inhabitan*ts (London: Longman, Hurst, Rees, Orme and Brown, 1821), p. 338.

15. K. D. Paranavitana, *Journal of Spilbergen: The First Dutch Envoy to Ceylon, 1602* (Dehiwala: Sridevi Publishing, 1997), p. 44.
16. Gananath Obeyesekere, 'Representation of the Wild Man in Sri Lanka' in *Beyond Primitivism: Indigenous Religious Traditions and Modernity,* Jacob K Olupona, ed. (New York: Routledge: 2004), p. 274. Obeyesekera, *Cult of the Goddess*, pp. 304, 311.
17. Archibald Campbell Lawrie, *A Gazatteer of the Central Province of Ceylon*,(Colombo: G. Skeen, 1896, 1896), vol. 1, p. 125. Edward Upham, *The History and Doctrine of Buddhism, Popularly Illustrated* (London: R. Ackermann, 1829.), fig. 24. Davy, *Account*, p. 198.
18. Senarat Paranavitan, *The God of Adam's Peak* (Ascona: Artibus Asiae Publishers, 1958), p. 47. Pers. comm., Alexander McKinley.
19. John Callaway, *Yakkun Nattannawa, A Cingalese Poem Descriptive of the Ceylon System of Demonology to which is appended the Practices of a capua or Devil Priest and Kolan Nattannawa* (London: Oriental Translation Fund, 1829), p 5. L.D. Barnett, *Alphabetical Guide to Sinhalese Folklore from Ballad Sources* (Bombay: British India Press, 1917), pp. 88, 92, 99. Upham, *History*, p. 51. Alexander McKinley, 'The Apotheosis of Emptiness: God Suniyan and the Soteriological Necessity of Negativity in Sinhala Buddhism" in *The Meaning and Power of Negativity*, Ingolf U. Dalferth and Trevor W. Kimball, ed. (Tubingen: Mohr Siebeck, 2021), p. 353.
20. D.W. Ferguson, 'The Inscribed Mural Stone at Saman Devale, Ratnapura', *Journal of the Ceylon Branch of the Royal Asiatic Society*, 1899, vol. 16, no. 50, p. 85.
21. Maria Manuela Mota, 'Codice Casanatlense: an Indo-Porltuguese Portrait of Life in 16th-Cebntury India' in *Indian and Portugal: Cultural Interactions*, Jose Pereira and Pratapaditya Pal, ed. (Bombay: Marg Publications, 2001), pp. 34 -45.
22. A.B. Griswold and Prasert Na Nagara, 'The Buddhapada of Vat Pavaranivesa and its Inscription', *Journal of the Siam Society*, 1978, vol. 60, no. 2, pp. 112-122. Michel Lorrillard, 'Aux origines du bouddhisme siamois [Le cas des buddhapada], *Bulletin de l'Ecole francaise d'Extreme-Orient*, 2000, vol. 87, no. 1, pp. 23-55.
23. R. K. de Silva, *Early Prints of Ceylon (Sri Lanka), 1800-1900* (London: Serendib Publications, 1985), p. 192. Anne M. Blackburn, *Locations of Buddhism: Colonialism & Modernity in Sri Lanka* (Chicago: University of Chicago Press, 2010), p. 2.
24. Sophie Anthonisz, trans., *Memoir of Cornelis Joan Simon for his Successor, Hendrick Becker, 1707* (Colombo: Government Printer, 1914), p. 8. Davy, *Account*, p. 343. D'Oyle, *Diary*, p. 96.
25. Simmonds, *Notes*, pp. 15, 21-22. William Skeen *Adam's Peak: Legendary, Traditional and Historic Notices of the Samanala and Sri-Pada*. (Colombo: W.L.H. Skeen & Co.,1870), p. 155.
26. De Silva, *Early Prints*, pp. 192, 202.
27. Philippus Baldaeus, *A Description of the East India Coasts of Malabar and Coromandel with their Adjacent Kingdoms and Provinces & of the Empire of Ceylon*. [1703], trans., anonymous. (New Delhi: Asian Educational Services, 2000), p. 650.
28. Ananda K. Coomaraswamy, *Medieval Sinhalese Art* (Gloucestershire: Essex House Press, 1908), pl. xxii.

Chapter 6: Seruvila-Somavathiya

1. N.A. Jayawickrama, *The Chronicle of the Thupa and the Thupavamsa, Being a Translation and Edition of Vaccissaratthera's Thupavamsa* (London: Luzac, 1971), p. 54. Commentary on the *Dighna Nikaya* (*Sumangalavilasini*), 2. 614. Archibald Campbell Lawrie, *A Gazatteer of the Central Province of Ceylon*, (Colombo: G. Skeen, 1896), vol. 1, p. 125. Richard D. Cushman, *The Royal Chronicles of Ayutthaya*, David K. Wyatt, ed. (Bangkok: The Siam Society, 2000) p. 209. Pe Maung Tin, 'The Shwe Dagon Pagoda', *Journal of the Burma Research Soceity*, 1934, vol. 24. no. 1, p. 20.
2. Senake Bandaranayake, *Sinhalese Monastic Architecture: The Viharas of Anuradhapura* (Hyderabad: Orient Blackswan Publishers, 2009), pp. 147, 202. Steven Kemper, *The Presence of the Past: Chronicles, Politics and Culture in Sinhala Life* (Ithaca: Cornell University Press), p. 152. *The Buddhist Annual of Ceylon*, 1920, p. 32. Kevin Trainor, 'A Textualized Landscape: *Diva-guhava* and the Sri Lankan Tradition of the Sixteen Great Pilgrimage Sites (*Solosmasthana*)' in *Mudita: Deshabandhu Sirisumana Godage Abhinandlana Shastriya Sangrahaya*, Ven. Induragare Dhamaratana et al. (Colombo: S. Godage saha Sahodarayo, 2012), p. 650.
3. Kevin Trainor, *Relics, Ritual, and Representation in Buddhism* (Cambridge: Cambridge University Press, 1997), p. 25. S. Vijitha Kumara, ed., *A Critical Edition of the Nalata Dhatuvamsa*, (Gangodawila: Magadhi Publication, 2016) Oskar von Hinuber, *A Handbook of Pali Literature* (New Delhi: Munshiram Manoharlal Publishers, 1996), p. 95.
4. Pe Maung Tin, *Shwe Dagon*. N.A. Jayawickrama, trans., *Jinakalamali, The Sheaf of Garlands of the Epochs of the Conqueror, being a Translation of Jinakalamalipakaranam* (London: Luzac, 1968). *Inscriptions of Ceylon* (Colombo: Department of Archaeology 1970), vol. 1, p. lvii and vol. 2. pt. 1 (1983), p. 52. Kamburupitie Nandaratana Thera, ed., with a Forward by N.A. Jayawickrama, *Dhatuvamsa* (Colombo: Cultural Publication Co., 1984), p. xi.
5. *Epigraphia Zeylanica*, vol. 5, p. 269. Kamburupitie Nandaratana Thera, *Dhatuvamsa*, p. x.
6. Keven Trainor kindly shared parts of his translation of

the *Dhatu-vamsa*. Trainor: *Relics, Ritual*, p. 150. Pe Maung Tin, *Shwe Dagon*, p. 32.

7. Jonathan Forbes, *Eleven Years in Ceylon,* 2 vols. (London: Richard Bentley, 1841) v. 2, p. 222. *Inscriptions of Ceylon*, vol. 2, pt. 1, p. 39.
8. R.M.M. Chandraratne & Dilan Chathuranga Ranaweera, 'Historical Archaeology at the Somawathiya Sacred Area in North Central Province, Sri Lanka' in *Archaeology of Buddhism,* Sanjay Garg, ed. (New Delhi: Manohar, 2017), pp. 547.
9. *Epigraphia Zeylanica*, vol. 5, p. 279. K. Indrapala, 'Epigraphical Discoveries in the Last Decade (1959-1969): a Brief Survey', *Ancient Ceylon*, 1979, vol. 3. 155.
10. Pe Maung Tin, *Shwe Dagon*, pp. 9, 19, 29. Jayawickrama, *Jinakalamali,* pp. *71-76.* Pe Maung Tin & G.H. Luce, trans., *The Glass Palace Chronicle of the Kings of Burma,* (Rangoon: Rangoon University Press, 1923), pp. 17, 94.
11. Kemper, *Presence*, p. 152. Trainor, *Relics*, p. 191.

Chapter 7: Attanagalla

1. John Clifford Holt, *Buddha in the Crown: Avalokitesvara in the Buddhist Traditions of Sri Lanka* (New York: Oxford University Press, 1991), p. 59. Steven Collins, *Nirvana and Other Buddhist Felicities: Utopia of the Pali Imaginaire* (Cambridge: Cambridge University Press, 1998), p. 459. *Epigraphia Zeylanica*, vol. 1, p. 240. *Wilhelm Geiger: Culture of Ceylon in Medieval Times,* Heinz Bechert, ed. (Stuttgart: Franz Steiner Verlarg, 1986), p. 117. For other kings who took their own lives, see Merlin Peris, 'Five Royal Suicides', *The Sri Lanka Journal of the Humanities*, 2003-2004, vol. 29-30, pp. 167-177.
2. Andy Rotman, *Divine Stories: Divyavadana* (Boston: Wisdom Publications, 2008), pt. 2, p. 130. John S. Strong, *The Legend of King Asoka* (Princeton: Princeton University Press, 1983), p. 233. Rongxi Li, *The Great Tang Dynasty Record of the Western Regions* (Berkeley: Numata Center, 1996), p. 310. Victor H. Mair, 'The Linguistic and Textual Antecedents of *The Sutra of the Wise and the Foolish*', *Sino-Platonic Papers*, 1993, no. 38, pp. 1 95. For the Dunhuang murals, see *Dunhuang Art Throughh the Eyes of Duan Wenjie*, Tan Chung, ed. (New Delhi: Abhivan Publications, 1994), p. 100.
3. C.E. Godakumbura, *Hatthavanagallaviharavamsa* (London: The Pali Text Society, 1956). Oskar von Hinuber, *A Handbook of Pali Literature* (New Delhi: Munshiram Manoharlal Publishers, 1996), p. 96. James D'Alwis, *The Attanagalu-vansa or the history of the Temple of Attanagalla, translated from the Pali* (Colombo: Williams and Mrg., 1866). Anne M. Blackburn, *Buddhist-inflected Sovereignties Across the Indian Ocean: The Pali Arena, 1200-1550* (Honolulu: University of Hawai'i Press, 2024), pp. 31, 180.
4. Senake Bandaranayake, *Sinhalese Monastic Architecture: The Viharas of Anuradhapura*, (Hyderabad: Orient Blackswan Publishers, 2009), p. 152.
5. D'Alwis, *Attanagalu-vansa*, pp. 76, 112.
6. Godukumbara, *Hatthavanagallaviharavamsa,* p. xi, 121. K.D. Somadasa, *Catalogue of the Hugh Nevill Collection of Sinhalese Manuscripts in the Britisih Library*, (London: The British Library, 1955), vol. 7, p. 202. K. Karunaratne, trans., *Rajaratnakaraya: The Gem Mine of Kings* (Colombo: Central Cultural Fund, 2009), p. 40.
7. D'Alwis, *Attanagulu-vansa*, p. 111.
8. Bandaranayake, *Sinhalese Monastic*, p. 152.
9. B. Gunasekara, trans., *A Contribution to the History of Ceylon, translated from Pujavaliya* (Colombo: H.C. Cottle, Government Printer, 1895), p. 23. Godukumbura, *Hatthavanagallaviharavamsa,p. xii.*
10. A.M. Hocart, ed., *Ceylon Journal of Science, Section G., Archaeology, Ethnology, etc.,* 1928, vol. 2, pt. 1, pl. 30.
11. Gunasekara, *A Contribution, p. 23.*
12. Translation provided by K.D. Paranavitana.
13. N.A. Jaywawickrama, trans., *The Story of Gotama Buddha: the Nidana-katha of the Jatakattakatha* (Oxford: The Pali Text Society, 2000), p. 107.
14. A.V. Suraweera, *The Rajavilaya and the first ever translation of the Alakesvara Yuddhaya* (Ratmalan: Vishva Lekha, 2000), p. 50.
15. *Daily News*, 3 November 1980.

Chapter 8: Devinuvara

1. John Clifford Holt, *The Buddhist Vishnu: Religious Transformation, Politics and Culture* (New York: Columbia University Press, 2004). Gananath Obeyesekere, *The Cult of the Goddess Pattini* (Chicago: University of Chicago Press, 1984), pp. 309ff.
2. Senerat Paranavitana, *The Shrine of Upulvan at Devundara* (Oxford: Oxford University Press, 1953), p. 61. R.A.L.H. Gunawardana. *The Robe and the Plough* (Phoenix: The University of Arizona Press, 1979), p 222.
3. Heinz Bechert, ed., *Wilhelm Geiger: Culture of Ceylon in Medieval Times* (Stuttgart: Franz Steiner Verlarg, 1986), p. 13. Jonathan Forbes, *Eleven Years in Ceylon,* (London: Richard Bentley, 1841) vol. 2, p. 174. Joinville, 'On the Religion and Manners of the People of Ceylon', *Asiatic Researches,* 1801, vol. 7, pp. 397-444. Joinville does not mention Dappula but associates Vishnu with Devinuvara ('De-undere'); see p. 408.
4. Senake Bandaranayake, *Sinhalese Monastic Architecture: The Viharas of Anuradhapura* (Hyderabad: Orient Blackswan Publishers, 2009), p. 152. Paranavitana, *Shrine of Upulvan.*

5. Paranavitana, *Shrine of Upulvan,* p. 69. *Inscriptions of Ceylon* (Colombo: Department of Archaeology, 2014), p. 5.
6. B. Gunasekara, trans., *A Contribution to the History of Ceylon, translated from Pujavaliya* (Colombo: H.C. Cottle, Government Printer, 1895), p. 47. W. F. Gunawardhana, *The Nikaya Sangrahawa, being a History of Buddhism in India and Ceylon* (Colombo: H.C. Cottle, Government Printer, 1908), p. 24.
7. *Inscriptions of Ceylon*, vol. 7, pp. 36, 54. *Epigraphia Zeylanica*, vol. 4, pp. 15, 27.
8. Hans-Dieter Evers, *Monks, Priests and Peasants: A Study of Buddhism and Social Structure in Central Ceylon* (Leiden: E.J. Brill, 1972), p. 28.
9. *Inscriptions of Ceylon*, vol. 8, p. 22. Paranavitana, *Shrine of Upulvan,* p. 78. *Epigraphia Zeylanica,* vol. 3, p. 67. *Inscriptions of Ceylon,* vol. 8, p. 118. Holt, *Buddhist Vishnu,* p. 57. Obeyesekere, *Cult of the Goddess,* p. 315. Gunawardhana, *Nikaya*, p. 26.
10. *Inscriptions of Ceylon*, vol. 8, p. 10. Paranavitana, *Shrine of Upulvan*, pp. 13, 76, pl. 17. The concept of the Pancha Ishvaram was first proposed by P.E. Pieris at a meeting of the Ceylon Branch of the Royal Asiatic Society in 1917. *Epigraphia Zeylanica*, vol. 3, p. 58.
11. Obeyesekere, *Cult of the Goddess,* p. 318. James Cordiner, *A Description of Ceylon,* (Colombo: K.V.G. de Silva, 1983), vol. 1, p. 116.
12. L.D. Barnett, *Alphabetical Guide to Sinhalese Folklore from Ballad Sources* (Bombay: British India Press; 1917), p. 117.
13. C.F. Beckingham, trans. *The Travels of Ibn Battuta* (London: The Hakluyt Society, 1994), p. 855. E. Hultzsch, *South-Indian Inscriptions, Tamil and Sanskrit, Archaeological Survey of India* (Madras: Government Press, 1890), vol. 1, p. 259. V. Perniola, *The Catholic Church in Sri Lanka: The Portuguese Period* (Dehiwala: Tisara Prakasakayo Ltd., 2003), vol. 3, p. 212.
14. T.K. Nimal P. de Silva, 'Sri Lankan Architecture: the Transitional Period' in *The Art and Architecture of Sri Lanka*, Leelananda Prematilleka, ed. (Colombo: Central Cultural Fund, 2007), vol. 2, p. 444. Colin McKenzie, 'Remark on Some Antiquities On the West and South Coasts of Ceylon, written in the year 1796', *Asiatick Researches*, 1801, vol. 6, 440. Cordiner, *Description,* p. 195. J.W. Bennett, *Ceylon and its Capabilities* (London: W.H. Allen & Co., 1843), p. 325. Paranavitana, *Shrine of Upulvan,* pl. 15.
15. S. Pathmanathan, ed., *Tamil Inscriptions in the Colombo National Museum* (Colombo: Department of National Museums, 2005), pp. 53, 57. S.G. Perera, trans., *Fernao de Queyroz [Queiros], The Temporal and Spiritual Conquest of Ceylon* (Colombo: Government Press, 1930), p. 35. Tansen Sen, 'Diplomacy, Trade and the Quest for the Buddha's Tooth: The Yongle Emperor and Ming China's South Asian Frontier' in *Ming China: Court and Contacts, 1400-1450,* Craig Clunas et al. (London: British Museum, 2016), pp. 26-36. Perera, *Fernao de Queyroz*, p. 35.
16. *Epigraphia Zeylanica*, vol. 3, p. 330; Pathmanathan, *Tamil Inscriptions*, p. 53. M.L Pattaratorn Chiapravati, 'Wat Rachaburan: Deposits of History, Art, and Culture of the Early Ayutthaya Period' in *The Kingdom of Siam, The Art of Central Thailand, 1350-1800,* Forrest McGill and M.L. Pattaratorn Chirapravati, ed. (San Francisco: Asian Art Museum, 2005), p. 83.
17. *Epigraphia Zeylanica*, vol. 3, p. 337. Bhikkhu Nanamoli, trans., *Visuddhimagga, The Path of Purification* (Colombo: Buddhist Publication Society, 1975), p. 569. Pathmanathan, *Tamil Inscriptions*, p. 53ff.
18. Elizabeth A. Lambourn, 'Carving and Communities: Marble Carving for Muslim Patrons at Khambhat and around the Indian Ocean Rim, Late Thirteenth-Mid-fifteenth Centuries", *Ars Orientalis,* 2004, vol. 34, pp. 99-133.
19. Donald Ferguson, trans., 'The History of Ceylon from the Earliest Times to 1600 A.D., as related by Joao de Barros and Diogo do Couto', *Journal of the Ceylon Branch of the Royal Asiatic Society*, 1908, vol. 20, no. 60, p. 373. Perera, *Fernao de Queyroz,* p. 35. V. Perniola, *The Catholic Church in Sri Lanka, The Portuguese Period, 1505-1565* (Dehiwala: Tisara Prakasakayo Ltd., 1989), vol. 1, p. 278.
20. Jorge Manuel Flores, *Os Olhos do Rei: Desenhos e Desclricoes Portuguesas de Ilha de Ceilao (1624, 1638)*, (Lisbon: Comissao National para as Comemoracoes Dos Descobrument Portugueses, 2001), p. 165. Perera, *Fernao de Queyroz*, p. 335.
21. Ibid, p. 441. Ferguson, *History*, p. 374. Elizabeth J. Harris, *Theravada Buddhism and the British Encounter* (London: Routledge, 2006), p. 83. Henry Charles Sirr, *Ceylon and the Cingalese; their History, Government and Religion; the Antiquities, Institutions, Produce, Revenues, and Capabilities of the Island; with Anecdotes Illustrating the Manners and Customs of the People* (London: William Shoberl, 1850), vol. 2, p. 324.
22. Pers. comm., Chandra R. de Silva. Flores, *Os Olhos*, p. 86.
23. Perniola, *Catholic Church*, vol. 3, p. 212.
24. T.B.H. Abeyasinghe, trans., 'Antonio Bocarro's *Description of Ceylon'*, *Journal of the Royal Asiatic Society of Sri Lanka,* 1995-2001, vol. 39, p. 46. Perera, *Fernao de Queyroz,* vol. 2, p. 715. Donald Ferguson, 'The Earliest Dutch Visits to Ceylon', *Journal of the Ceylon Branch of the Royal Asiatic Society*, 1927, vol. 30, nos. 1-4, p. 360. Sinnappah Arasaratnam, *Francois Valentijn's Description of Ceylon* (London: Hakluyt

Society, 1978), pp. 73, 85, 138.

25. Colin McKenzie, 'Remark', pp. 431, 439. Cordiner, *Description,* pp. 115-16. Jonathan Forbes, *Eleven Years in Ceylon,* (London: Richard Bentley, 1841), vol 1, p. 177. Mary (no family name), 'Buddhist Temple at Dondra', *The Wesleyan Juvenile Offering,* 1868, p. 54. Captain Mahony, 'On Singhala, or Ceylon, and the Doctrines of Bhooddha', *Asiatic Researches,* 1803, vol. 7, p. 50. Joinville, *On the Religion*, p. 408.
26. Cordiner, *Description*, p. 115. Bennett, *Ceylon and its Capabilities*, p. 325. Frederick Jobson, *Australia With Notes by the Way, on Egypt, Ceylon, Bombay, and the Holy Land.* (London: Hamilton, Adams and Co., 1862), p. 72.
27. Bennett, *Ceylon and its Capabilities*, p. 326. Personal communication, John C. Holt. *Sri Lanka Mirror,* 15 August 2014.
28. Fred W. Clothey, 'Chronometry, Cosmology, and the Festival Calendar in the Murukan Cult' in *Religious Festivals in South India and Sri Lanka*, Guy Welbon & Glenn Yocum, ed. (New Delhi: Manohar, 1982), p. 158. Pathmananthan, *Tamil Inscriptions*, p. 62.
29. Paranavitana, *Upulvan Temple*, p. 12. Obeyesekere, *Cult of the Goddess*, p. 315.
30. Cordiner, *Description*, p. 115. Bandaranayake, *Sinhalese Monastic*, p. 352.Personal communication, Crispin Branfoot.
31. Obeyesekere, *Cult of the Goddess*, pp. 317, 320. Holt, *Buddhist Vishnu*, pp. 217-223, 247. *Robert Knox, An Historical Relation of Ceylo*n (Dehiwala: Tisara Prakasakayo, 1981), p. 224.
32. David Scott, *Formation of Ritual: Colonial and Anthropological Discourse on Sinhala Yaktovil*, (Minneapolis: University of Minnesotta Press, 1994), p. 41. Josiah Crosby, 'Buddhism in Ceylon', *Journal of the Ceylon Branch of the Royal Asiatic Society*, 1947, vol. 79, nos. 1-2, p. 51.
33. Henry Yule, trans. 'Marignolli's Recollection of Eastern Travels' in *Cathay and the Way Thither, being a Collection of Medieval Notices of China* (London: The Hakluyt Society, 1866), p. 250. Pe Maung Tin & G.H. Luce, trans., *The Glass Palace Chronicle of the Kings of Burma,*(Rangoon: Rangoon University Press, 1923), p. 46.

Chapter 9: Katargama

1. Leonard Woolf, *Growing: an Autobiography of the years 1904 to 1911* (London: The Hogarth Press, 1964), p. 227. Richard Gombrich & Gananath Obeyesekere, *Buddhism Transformed: Religious Change in Sri Lanka* (Princeton: Princeton University Press, 1988), p. 165.
2. Kamil V. Zwelebil, *The Tamil Skandapuranam* (The Oriental Institute, Prague, 1992). David D. Schulman, *Tamil Temple Myths: Sacrifice and Divine Marriage in the South Indian Saiva Tradition* (Princeton: Princeton University Press, 1980), p. 276.
3. Shulman, *Tamil Temple Myths*, pp. 276, 277.
4. Ibid., p. 277. Zwelebil, *Tamil Skandapuranam,* p. 11. Heinze Bechert, 'Skandakumara and Kataragama', *Proceedings of the Third International Conference Semina*r (Pari: International Association of Tamil Research, 1970), pp. 199-220.
5. Stephen Kaplan, ed., *Indigenous Responses to Western Christianity* (New York: New York University Press, 1994), p. 105.
6. Donald Stadtner, *Sacred Sites of Burma: Myth and Folklore in an Evolving Spritual Realm,* (Bangkok: River Books, 2015) p. 50. Donald K. Swearer and Sommai Premchit, *The Legend of Queen Cama* (Albany: State University of New York Press, 1998), p. 42. Pe Maung Tin & G.H. Luce, trans., *The Glass Palace Chronicle of the Kings of Burma* (Rangoon: Rangoon University Press, 1923), p. 8. Gananath Obeyesekere, 'The Death of the Buddha' in *The Buddha in Sri Lanka,* Gananath Obeyesekere, ed. (New York: Routledge, 2018), p. 42.
7. Ibid., *Buddhism Transforme*d, p. 185. *Mawrata News*, 23 December 2023.
8. Robert Knox, *An Historical Relation of Ceylo*n (Colombo: Tisara Prakasakayo, 1981), p. 101. John Davy, *An Account of the Interior of Ceylon, and of its Inhabitants* (London: Longman, Hurst, Rees, Orme and Brown, 1821), p. 422.
9. K.D. Somadasa, ed., *Catalogue of the Hugh Nevill Collection of Sinhalese Manuscripts in the British Library* (London: The British Library, 1995), vol. 7, pp. 96, 171.
10. Paul Wirz, *Kataragama: the holiest place in Ceylon* (Colombo: Lake House, 1966), p, 46. Davy, *Account*, pp. 420-23. M. Covington, 'Hindu Kataragama', *The Orientalist,* 1888, vol. 3, nos. 7-8. pp. 149-156. Festivals celebrating the god's spear, or *vel*, are found among Tamils worldwide. A *vel*-festival in Colombo in the 1930s is described in C. Brooke Eliot, *The Real Ceylon* (Colombo: HW. Cave & Co., 1938), p. 132.
11. Covington, *Hindu Kataragama*, p. 50. Gombrich & Obeyesekere, *Buddhism Transformed*, p. 166. Wirz, *Kataragama*, p. 55. Knox, *Historical*, p. 225. S. Pathmanathan, *Hindu Temples of Sri Lanka* (Colombo: Kumaran Book House, 2006), p. 11.
12. Davy, *Account*, pp. 420-21. Pathmanantha, *Hindu Temples*, 332.
13. Davy, *Account*, p. 423.
14. T. A. Gopinatha Rao, *Elements of Hindu Iconography* (Delhi: Motilal Banarsidass, 1985), vol. 2, pt. 2, p. 445. Edmund Rowland Gooneratne, *The Rupa Mala in Sanskrit verse with an English Translation* (Colombo: Department of National Museums, 1995), p. 8.
15. Selvam Kalyanadunderam, *A History of Kataragama* (Colombo: Vishva Hindu Parishad, Sri Lanka

Branch, 1980), pp. 22-42. *Ceylon Daily News*, 7 July 2000.

16. Edward Upham, *The Mahavansi, The Raja-ratnacari, and the Raja-Vali, forming the sacred and historical books of Ceylon, A Collection of Tracts* (London: Parbury, Allen, and Co., 1833), vol. 3, pp. 146-151. Wirz, *Kataragama*, p. 49.
17. Gananath Obeyeseker, 'Social Change and the Deities: Rise of the Kataragama Cult in Modern Sri Lanka', *Man*, 1977, n.s., vol. 12, nos. 3-4, p. 385. *Inscriptions of Ceylon* (Colombo: Department of Archaeology, 2014), p. 46. W.F. Gunawardhana, *The Nikaya Sangrahawa, being a History of Buddhism in India and Ceylon* (Colombo: H.C.Cottle, Government Printer, 1908), p. 26. Hans-Dieter Evers, *Monks, Priests and Peasants: A Study of Buddhism and Social Structure in Central Ceylon* (Leiden: E.J. Brill, 1972), p. 28. Pathmanantha, *Hindu Temple*s, p. 325. C. Brito, trans., *Yalpana-Vaipava-Mailai* (New Delhi: Asian Educational Services, 1999), p. 11.
18. Knox, *Historical*, pp. 101,224. H. L. Seneviratna, *Rituals of the Kandyan State*, (Cambridge: Cambridge University Press, 1978), p. 78.
19. G.P.V. Somaratna, *Political History of the Kingdom of Kotte* (ca. *A.D. 1400-1521)*, Unpublished Ph.D. thesis, University of London, 1969, p. 80. C. E. Godakumbura, *Literature of Sri Lanka* (Colombo: Department of Cultural Affairs, 1976), p. 50.
20. Gombrich & Obeyesekere, *Buddhism Transformed*, p. 164.
21. Ibid., p. 170.
22. Woolf, *Growing*, p. 227. Wirz, *Kataragama*, p. 42.
23. P.V. Jagdisa Ayyar, *South Indian Shrines* (Madras: Madras Times Printing, 1920), p. 158.
24. Wirz, *Kataragama*, p. 42.
25. *Epigraphia Zeylanica*, vol. 3., 214ff. Osmund Bopearachchi. *Roots of Sri Lankan Art* (Colombo: Department of Archaeology, 2020)
26. Senerat Paranavitana, *The Stupa in Ceylon*. Colombo: Government Press, 1946). F. B. J. Kuiper, '*Yupayasti (Divy. 244.11)*', *Indo-Iranian Journal*, 1959, vol. 3. no. 3. pp. 204-05.
27. Upham, *Mahavansi*, vol. 3, p. 147.
28. Gombrich & Obeyesekere, *Buddhism Transformed*, p. 425.
29. Gananath Obeyesekere, 'Myth and Political Legitimacy at the Sacred Centre in Kataragama, Sri Lanka' in *The Sacred Centre as the Focus of Political Interes*t, Hans Bakker, ed. (Groningen: Egbert Forsten, 1992), p. 221.
30. Ulrich von Schroeder, *Buddhist Sculptures of Sri Lank*a (Hong Kong: Visual Dharma Publications, 1990), p. 224. Personal communication, Osmund Bopearachchi.
31. N.A. Jayawickrama, trans., *The Sheaf of Garlands of the Epochs of the Conqueror, being a Translation of Jinakalamalipakaranam* (London: Luzac, 1968), p.122. Chedha Tinsganchali kindly provided an approximate date for the two sculptures. Craig Reynolds, 'Power, Protection and Magic in Thailand: The Cosmos of a Southern Policeman' in *Peninsular Siam and Its Neighborhood',* Wannasarn Noonshuk, ed. (Nakhon Si Thammnarat: Cultural Council, 2017), pp. 125-148.
32. Dennis B. McGilvray, 'Islamic and Buddhist impacts on the shrine at Daftar Jailani, Sri Lanka' in *Islam, Sufism and Everyday Politics of Belonging in South Asia,* D. Dandekar & T. Tschacher, ed. (London: Routledge, 2016). Covington, *Hindu Kataragam* , p. 50. M.C. A. Hassan T*he Story of the Kataragama Mosque and Shrine* (Colombo: S.A.M. Thauoos Publisher, 1968) (no pagination).
33. Hassan, *Story of the Kataragama Mosque*.

Chapter 10: Trincomalee

1. S.G. Perera, trans., *Fernao de Queyroz* [Queiros], *The Temporal and Spiritual Conquest of Ceylon* (New Delhi: Asian Educational Services, 1992), vol. 2, p. 236. David D. Schulman, *Tamil Temple Myths: Sacrifice and Divine Marriage in the South Indian Saiva Tradition* (Princeton: Princeton University Press, 1980), p. 5.
2. *Grote Atlas van de Verenigde Oost-Indische Compgnie (Comprehensive Atlas of the Dutch United East India Company*, vols. 7 (Atlas Maior, Koninklijk, Voorburg, 2011), vol. 4 (Ceylon). S. Pathmanathan, *Tamil Inscriptions in the Colombo National Museum* (Colombo: Department of National Museums, 2005), p. 11.
3. *Epigraphia Zeylanica*, vol. 4, p. 14. S. Pathmanathan, *Hindu Temples of Sri Lanka* (Colombo: Kumaran Book House, 2006), p. 11. S. Gunasingam, 'A Tamil Slab-Inscription at Nalaveli', *The Sri Lanka Journal of the Humanities*, 1975, vol. 1. no. 1, p. 71
4. *Inscriptions of Ceylon* (Colombo: Department of Archaeology, 1970), vol. 1, p. 29. *Epigraphia Tamilica*, vol. 1, p. 43. *Epigraphia Zeylanica*, vol. 2, pp. 177, 290 and vol. 3, p. 158.
5. S. Pathmanantan, *Hindu Temples*, p. 59. The reference in the *Mahabharata* appears in book 3. 88. In the *Vayu Purana*, the passage occurs in chapter 48. 3.
6. Personal communication, Indira Peterson. The *Tevaram* hymn is found in *Patikam* 3. 123. Shulman, *Tamil Temple*, p. 42. Anne E. Monius, *Imagining a Place for Buddhism: Literary Culture and Religious Community in Tamil-speaking South India* (New Delhi: Navayana Publishing, 2001), p. 84.
7. *Epigraphia Zeylanica*, vol. 4, p. 196 and vol. 6, 160. V. Venkayya, *South Indian Inscriptions*, vol. 2, pt. 4, (Madras: Superintendent, Government Press, 1913), p. 424.

8. S. Pathmanathan, *Tamil Inscriptions in the Colombo National Museum* (Colombo: Department of National Museums, 2005), p. 11. S. Gunasingam, 'Three Cola Inscriptions from Trincomalee', *Trincomalee Inscription Series*, 1979, no. 2, p. 2.
9. Elizabeth A. Lambourn, 'Carving and Communities: Marble Carving for Muslim Patrons at Khambhat and around the Indian Ocean Rim, Late Thirteenth-Mid-fifteenth Centuries", *Ars Orientalis,* 2004, vol. 34, p.108. L. Kalus & C. Guillot, 'Reinterpretation des plus anciennes steles funeraires islamique nousantariennes: 3. Sri Lanka'. *Archipel,* vol. 72, pp. 15-68.
10. Pathmanathan, *Hindu Temples*, p. 53. Alexander McKinley, *Mountain at a Center of the World: Pilgrimage and Pluralism in Sri Lanka* (Chicago: University of Chicago Press, 2024), p. 160. S. Pathmanathan, 'The Tamil Pillar Inscription from Mankanay',Sri Lanka Journal of the Humanities', 1995, vol. 21, no. 1-2, p. 41.
11. Alexander McKinley, *Mountain,* p. 160. Justin Henry, 'Lankapura: The Legacy of the *Ramayana* in Sri Lanka', *Journal of South Asian Studies*, 2019, vol. 42, no. 4, pp. 26-731.
12. Alexander McKinley, 'Making Lanka the Tamil way: a temple history at the crossroads of landscapes and watersheds,' *South Asian History and Culture*, 2020, vol. 11, no. 3. p. 257. Shulman, *Temple Myths*, p. 322-232. The relevant passages in the *Ramayana* are found in section 30. 752.
13. McKinley, *Mountain*, p. 163. Justin Henry, *Lankapura*, p. 739.
14. Henry, *Lankapura*, p. 738.
15. Padmanathan, *Hindu Temples*, 66, 68. S. Gunasingam, 'Two Inscriptions of Chola Ilankeswara Deva', *Trincomalee Inscriptions Series*, no. 1. 1974, p. 21. Gunasingam, *A Tamil Slab-Inscription*, 71. Gunasingam, *Three Cola Inscriptions*, 71.
16. Pathmanathan, *Hindu Temples*, p. 72. C. Brito, trans. *Yalpana-Vaipava-Mailai* (Asian Educational Services, New Delhi, 1999), p. 11.
17. *Epigraphia Zeylanica*, vol. 3, p. 311. S. Gunasingam, *Two Inscriptions*, p. 71. S. Gunasingam, 'Catalogue of Tamil Manuscripts in the Library of the Wellcome Insitute for the History of Medicine, *Journal of the Royal Asiatic Society of Great Britain and Ireland*, 1990, no. 2, p. 363. Pathamanathan, *Hindu Temples*, 69, 72. D.G.B. de Silva, 'New Light on Vanniyas and their Chieftaincies based on Folk Historical Tradition as found in Palm-leaf mss. in the Hugh Nevill Collection', *Journal of the Royal Asiatic Society of Sri Lanka*, 1996, n.s., vol. 41, pp. 153-204.
18. Brito, *Yalpana-Vaipava-Mailai,* p. 3.
19. Alicia Schrikker, *Dutch and British Colonial Intervention in Sri Lanka: 1780-1815*: Expansion and Reform (Leiden: E. J. Brill, 2007), p. 231. Pathmanathan, *Hindu Temples*, 103. F. H. de Vos, 'Second Supplementary Paper on the Monumental Remains of the Ducth East Indian Company of Ceylon', *Journal of the Ceylon Branch of the Royal Asiatic Society*, 1903, vol. 18 no. 54, p. 66. V. Perniola, *The Catholic Church in Sri Lanka: The Portuguese Period* (Dehiwala: Tisara Press, 1989), vol. 2, p. 414. T.B.H. Abeyasinghe, trans., 'Antonio Bocarro's Description of Ceylon translated into English', *Journal of the Royal Asiatic Society of Sri Lanka,* 1995-01, vol. 39, pp. 1 – 84. Bocarro's map dates to 1635. P.E. Pieris, *Joan Ribiero, The Historic Tragedy of the Island of Ceilao* (New Delhi: Asian Educational Services, 1999), p. 36.
20. Jorge Manuel Flores, *Os Olhos do Rei: Desenhos e Desclricoes Portuguesas de Ilha de Ceilao, (1624, 1638)* (Lisbon: Comissao National para as Comemoracoes Dos Descobrument Portugueses, 2001), p. 76. A translation of the relevant section from Flores was provided by Joaquim R. Santos. *The Catholic Church in Sri Lanka: The Portuguese Period* (Dehiwala: Tisara Press, 1991) vol. 3, p. 105. Perera, *Fernao de Queyroz,* vol. 2, p. 66.
21. *Grote Atlas*, p. 343-45, 352. Saskia van Veen provided a translation of the map's key.
22. Personal communication, Crispin Branfoot. W. Balendra, *Trincomalee Bronzes, an inquiry into their origins and their impact on Ceylon History* (Colombo: Konesar Building Fund, 1953).
23. Iman Willem Falck, 'Diary of a Tour on the East and West Coasts in 1767' in *Travels in Ceylon, 1700-1800*, R. Raven-Hart, ed. (Colombo: Lake House, 1963), p. 65. Marco Ramerini, *The History of Trincomalee during Portuguese and Dutch Rule* (Lesmo, Italy: Eta-beta Publishing, 2024). Personal communication, Marco Ramerini.
24. Sanmugam Arumugam, *Hundred Hindu Temples of Sri Lanka: Ancient Medieval and Modern* (London: Ohm Books, 2014), p. 85. Arthur C. Clarke, *The Reefs of Taprobane* (New York: Harper, 1957), p. 143-44. W. Balendra, 'Trincomalee Bronzes', *Tamil Culture*, 1953, vol. 2, no. 2, p. 190.
25. *Grote Atlas*, pp. 335, 341. Jonathan Forbes, *Eleven Years in Ceylon,* 2 vols. (London: Richard Bentley, 1841) vol. 2, p. 44.
26. Crispin Branfoot suggested to me the approximate age of the pillar. J. Penry Lewis, *List of Inscriptions on Tombstones and Monuments in Ceylon, of Historical or Local Interest* (Colombo: H.C. Cottle, Government Printer, 1913), p. 258. M.W. Jurriaanse, 'The Story of Francina van Reede', *Journal of the Dutch Burger Union,* 1942, vol. 32. no. 1, pp. 1-11.
27. A.S. Moss Blundell, 'Francina van Reede: A legend of Trincomalee', *Blackwood's Edinburgh Magazine*, 1901, no. 170, pp. 649-65. Forbes, *Eleven Years*, vol.

2, p. 46. Henry Charles Sirr, *Ceylon and the Cingalese: their history, government, and religion* (London: William Shoberl, 1850), p. 113. Perera, *Fernao de Queyroz,* p. 66.

28. Gunasingam, *Three Cola Inscriptions*, p. 6. Pathmanatha, *Hindu Temples*, p. 206. Much of the basic myths can be traced to the Tamil *Kanta Puranam*; see Kamil V Zwelebil, *The Tamil Skandapuranam* (Prague: The Oriental Institute, 1992).

Chapter 11: Islam

1. L. Kalus & C. Guillot, 'Reinterpretation des plus anciennes steles funeraires islamique nousantariennes: 3. Sri Lanka', *Archipel,* vol. 72, pp. 33, 43.
2. Dennis B. McGilvray and Mirak Raheem, 'Origins of the Sri Lankan Muslims and Varieties of the Muslim Identity' in *The Sri Lanka Reader: History, Culture, Politics.* John C. Holt, ed. (Durham: Duke University Press, 2011), pp. 410-19. Lorna Dewaraja, *The Muslims of Sri Lanka: One thousand Years of Ethnic Harmony, 900-1915.* (Colombo: the Lanka Islamic Foundation, 1994).
3. *Inscriptions of Ceylon* (Colombo: Department of Archaeology, 1970), vol. 1, p. 59. Max de Bruijn & Remco Raben, ed., *The World of Jan Brandes, 1743-1808* (Amsterdam: Rijksmuseum, 2004), p. 332-334. This entry was contributed by Nandana Chutiwongs. Pers. comm., Remco Raben.
4. Dennis B. McGilvray, 'Jailani: A Sufi Shrine in Sri Lanka' in *Lived Islam in South Asia: Adaptation, Accommodation and Conflict*, Imtiaz Ahmad & Helmut Reifeld, ed. (Delhi: Social Science Press, 2004), pp. 273 – 289. Dennis B. McGilvray, *Islamic and Buddhist impacts on the shrine at Daftar Jailani, Sri Lanka* in *Islam, Sufism and Everyday Politics of Belonging in South Asia* D. Dandekar & T. Tschacher, ed. (London: Routledge, 2016), pp. 62-76. Dennis B. McGilvray, *Crucible of Conflict: Tamil and Muslim Society on the East Coast of Sri Lanka.* (Durham: Duke University Press, 2008).
5. Bruijn & Raben, *The World of Jan Brandes*, p. 332. *The Sunday Leader*, 30 May 2015.
6. H. Parker, *Ancient Ceylon* (London: Luzac, 1909), p. 144. Jonathan Forbes, *Eleven Years in Ceylon* (London: Richard Bentley, 1841) vol. 1, p. 195. Kalinga Tudor Silva et al., *Religious Interface and Contestations between Buddhists and Muslims in Sri Lanka* (Colombo: International Centre for Ethnic Studies, 2016), p. 20. Christopher Fryke & Christopher Schweitzer, *Voyages to the Easter Indies* (London: Cassell & Company, 1929), p. 244. Heinze Bechert, 'Contradictions in Sinhalese Buddhism' in *Religion and Legitmation of Power in Sri Lanka*, Bardwell L. Smith, ed. (Chambersburg: Anima Books, 1978) p. 196.
7. Simon Casie Chetty, *Ceylon Gazetteer* (Colombo: Cotta Church Mission Press, 1834), p. 146.
8. Pers. comm., Kalinga Tudor Silva.
9. A.T. Shams-ud-di'n, 'Note on the Mi'ra Kantiri Festival of the Muhammadans', *Journal of the Ceylon Branch of the Royal Asiatic Society*, 1881, vol. 7, no. 24, pp. 125-136.

Chapter 12: Kandy

1. S.G. Perera, trans., *Fernao de Queyroz* [Queiros], *The Temporal and Spiritual Conquest of Ceylon*, (New Delhi: Asian Educational Services, 1992), vol. 1, p. 60. John Davy, *An Account of the Interior of Ceylon, and of its Inhabitants* (London: Longman, Hurst, Rees, Orme and Brown, 1821), p. 368. *The Graphic*, 8 January 1876. The most comprehensive discussion of European understandings of the relic is John S. Strong's, *The Buddha's Tooth: Western Tales of a Sri Lankan Relic* (Chicago: University of Chicago Press, 2021).
2. Archibald Campbell Lawrie, *A Gazetteer of the Central Province of Ceylon* (Colombo: G. Skeen, Government Printer, 1896), vol. 1, p. 419. Davy, *Account*, p. 367. Arthur Willey, *Colombo Museum: Guide to the Collections* (Colombo: Government Press, 1905), p. 11.
3. *Epigraphia Zeylanica*, vol. 4, 14, 25, 270.
4. John S. Strong, *Relics of the Buddha* (Princeton: Princeton University Press, 2004), pp. 179-210. Hajime Nakamura, *Gotama Buddha: A Biography Based on the Most Reliable Texts* (Tokyo: Kosei Publishing Co., 2000), vol. 2, p. 191.
5. John M. Seneviratne & Sylvain Levi, 'Chino-Sinhalese relations in the early and Middle Ages', *Journal of the Ceylon Branch of the Royal Asiatic Society*, 1915-1916, vol. 24, no. 68, p. 88. Rongxi Li, *Lives of Great Monks and Nuns* (Berkeley: Numata Center, 2002), p. 207. Rongxi Li, *A Biography of the Tripitaka Master of the Great Ci'en Monastery of the great Tang Dynasty* (Berkeley: Numata Center, 1995), p. 119. Rongxi Li, *The Great Tang Dynasty Record of the Western Regions* (Berkeley: Numata Center, 1996), pp. 35, 108, 150.
6. Dharmaratna Herath, *The Tooth Relic and the Crown* (Colombo: unidentified publisher, 1994), p. 49. Anuradha Seneviratna, *The Temple of the Sacred Tooth: History and Architecture of the Temples* (Colombo: Vijitha Yapa Publications, 2010), vol. 1, p. 23. Senake Bandaranayake, *Sinhalese Monastic Architecture: The Viharas of Anuradhapura* (Hyderabad: Orient Blackswan Publishers, 2009), p. 206. *Epigraphia Zeylanica*, vol. 1, pp. 120, 237.
7. B.C. Law, trans.,*The Dathavamsa, A History of the Tooth-relic of the Buddha* (Lahore: Motilal Banarsidas, 1925), p. 17.

8. Law, *Dathavamsa*, pp. 24, 30. N.A. Jayawickrama, *The Sheaf of Garlands of the Epochs of the Conqueror, being a translation of Jinkalamalipakaranam* (London: Luzac, Ltd.) 1968), p. 90. Angela S. Chiu, *The Buddha in Lanna: Art Lineage Power, and Place in Northern Thailand* (Honolulu: University of Hawai'i Press, 2017), p. 62. For the Mon text, dated to 1766, see Robert Halliday, trans., *The Mons of Burma and Thailand* (Bangkok: White Lotus, 2000), p. 96.

9. Law, *Dathavamsa*, pp. 34, 41. David K. Wyatt, trans., *The Crystal Sands: The Chronicles of Nagara Sri Dharmaraja* (Ithaca: Cornell University, 1975). For the Mon adaptation of the myth in Lower Burma, see my *Sacred Sites of Burma: Myth & Folklore in an Evolving Spiritual Realm* (Bangkok: River Books, 2015), pp. 147, 168.

10. Herath, *Tooth Relic*, p. 12. Law, *Dathavamsa*, p. 45.

11. John C. Holt, *Theravada Traditions: Buddhist Ritual Cultures in Contemporary Southeast Asia and Sri Lanka* (Honolulu: University of Hawai'i Press, 2017), p. 309. A. H. Mirando, *Buddhism in Sri Lanka in the Seventeenth and Eighteenth Centuries* (Colombo: Tisara Prakasakayo Press, 2010), p. 109. K. Karunaratne, trans., *Rajaratnakaraya: The Gem Mine of Kings* (Colombo: Central Cultural Fund, 2009), p. 44. A.V. Suraweera, *The Rajavilaya and the first ever translation of the Alakesvara Yuddhaya* (Ratmalan: Vishva Lekha, 2000), p. 52.

12. Tun Aung Chain, 'Bayinnaung in the Shwezigon Bell Inscription' in *Selected Writings of Tun Aung Chain* (Yangon: Myanmar Historical Commission, 2004), p. 108. Herath, *Tooth Relic*, pp. 139, 141, 161.

13. R.A.L.H. Gunawardana, *The Robe and the Plough* (Phoenix: The University of Arizona Press, 1979), p. 288. *Epigraphia Zeylanica*, vol. 2, pp. 90, 121, 250, 254. S. Pathmanathan, 'The Velaikkarar in Medieval South India and Sri Lanka', Sri Lanka Journal of the Humanities, 1976, vol. 2, no. 2, pp. 20-37.

14. Suraweera, *Rajavilaya*, p. 62.

15. Karunaratne, *Rajaratnakaraya,* p. 58, 68. Anne M. Blackburn, *Locations of Buddhism: Colonialism & Modernity in Sri Lanka* (Chicago: University of Chicago Press, 2010), p. 59. Jayawickrama, *Sheaf of Garlands,* p. 130. Taw Sein Ko, 'A Preliminary Study of the Kalyani Inscriptions of Dhammacheti, 1476', *Indian Antiquary*, vol. 22, p. 43. John S. Strong, *Buddha's Tooth,* p. 51. Prasad Fonseka, *Kotte, the Fortress* (Colombo, the National Trust, 2015), p. 76.

16. Karunaratne, *Rajaratnakaraya,* p. 38. Gananath Obeyesekere, 'Gajabahu and the Gajabahu Synchronism: An inquiry into the relationship between Myth and History' in *Religion and the Legitimation of Power in Sri Lanka*, Bardwell L. Smith, ed. (Chambersburg: Anima Books, 1978) p.164. Marturin M. Ballou, *The Pearl of India* (Boston: Houghton, Mifflin & Co., 1894), p. 232.

17. Seneviratne, *Temple of the Sacred Tooth,* vol. 1, p. 70. Li, *Great Tang Dynasty,* p. 353. Strong, *Buddha's Tooth*.

18. V. Perniola, *The Catholic Church in Sri Lanka. The Portuguese Period* (Dehiwala: Tisara Press, 1989), vol. 1, pp. 308, 310, 314, 351, 353. Hugo Miguel Crespo, 'The Plundering of the Ceylonese Royal Treasury, 1551-1553: Its Character, Cost, and Dispersal' in *Gems in the Early Modern World*, M. Bycroft and S. Dupre, ed. (Cham, Switzerland: Palgrave Macmillan, 2019), pp. 35-64.

19. Strong, *Buddha's Tooth*, p. 54. Stephen Berkwitz, *Buddhist Poetry and Colonialism, Alagiyavanna and the Portuguese in Sri Lanka* (Oxford: Oxford University Press, 2013), p. 56. Perera, *Fernao de Queyroz*, p. 60. Davy, *Account*, p. 369. Senaviratna, *Temple of the Sacred Tooth*, vol. 1, pp. 73, 75. *Inscriptions of Ceylon* (Colombo: Department of Archaeology, 2014), pp. 18, 55, 68

20. Tun Aung Chain, 'Bayinnaung in the Shwezigon Bell Inscription' in *Selected Writings of Tun Aung Chain* (Yangon: Myanmar Historical Commission, 2004), p. 108. Donald Ferguson, trans., 'The History of Ceylon from the Earliest Times to 1600 A.D., as related by Joao de Barros and Diogo do Couto', *Journal of the Ceylon Branch of the Royal Asiatic Society*, 1908, vol. 20, no. 60, 212, 243.

21. Pers. comm., Tun Aung Chain. A copy of the tooth relic was sent to Siam during the reign of Kirti Sri, recorded in a Pali text; see *Religious Intercourse between Ceylon and Siam in the Eighteenth Century, Syamupadasampada* (Bangkok: American Presbyterian Mission Press, 1914), p. 65.

22. Perniola, *Catholic Church*, vol. 1., p. 351. Hugo Miguel Crespo & Annemmarie Jordan Gschwend, *The 'Pangolin Fan': An Imperial Ivory Fan from Ceylon* (Buenos Aires: Jaime Eguigiuren, 2022), p. 127. Amin Jaffer & Melanie Anne Scwabe, 'A Group of Sixteenth Century Caskets from Ceylon', *Apollo*, March, 1999, pp. 3-14. Perera, *Fernao de Queyroz*, p. 330. Pers. comm., Hugo Miguel Crespo. Alberto Saviello has most plausibly dated the box to c. 1580 in his 'Hybrid Identity, A Sinhalese Portuguese Coat of; Arms on a Sixteenth-Century Ivory Casket from Sri Lanka' in *Heraldry in Contact: Perspectives and Challenges of a Connective Image Form,* Urte Krass & Miguel Metelo de Seixas, ed. (Ostfildern: Thorbecke Verlag, 2023), pp/ 143-148. Pers. comm., Alberto Saviello.

23. Pers. comm., Chandra R. de Silva.

24. Walter S. Gibson, *Figures of Speech: Picturing Proverbs in Renaiasance Netherlands* (Berkeley: University of California Press, 2010), p. 112.

25. K. D. Paranavitana, *Journal of Spilbergen: The First Dutch Envoy to Ceylon, 1602* (Dehiwala: Sridevi Publishing, 1997), p. 36. Donald M. Stadtner, 'A

Lost Copy of the Buddha's Footprint' in *Transcending Boundaries-Premodern Cultural Transactions across Asia: Essays in Honour of Osmund Bopearachchi*, Susmita Basu Majumdar, ed. (New Delhi: Primus Books, 2024), pp. 497-510.

26. Jorge Manuel Flores, *Os Olhos do Rei: Desenhos e Desclricoes Portuguesas de Ilha de Ceilao (1624, 1638)*, (Lisbon: Comissao National para as Comemoracoes Dos Descobrument Portugueses, 2001), p. 153. K. David Jackson supplied the translation for the text written on the footprint by Miranda. Perera, *Fernao de Queyroz*, p. 38. Ferguson, *History of Ceylon*, p. 400. Donald Ferguson, 'The Earliest Dutch Visits to Ceylon', *Journal of the Ceylon Branch of the Royal Asiatic Society*, 1928, vol. 31, no. 81, p. 118. Philippus Baldaeus, *A Description of the East India Coasts of Malabar and Coromandel with their Adjacent Kingdoms and Provinces & of the Empire of Ceylon*, Anonymous translation into English, 1671 (New Delhi Educational Services, 2000), p. 38. Frederick Jobson, *Australia With Notes by the Way, on Egypt, Ceylon, Bombay, and the Holy Land* (London: Hamilton, Adams and Co., 1862), p. 82. William Skeen, *Adam's Peak: Legendary, Traditional and Historic Notices of the Samanala and Sri-Pada* (Colombo: W.L.H. Skeen & Co., 1870), p. 269.
27. Flores, *Os Olhos*, p 158. R. Raven-Hart, trans., *Heydt's Ceylon* (Colombo: Government Press, 1952), p. 91. For a translation from the Portuguese, I thank Chandra R. de Silva. John Pybus, *Account of Mr. Mr. Pybus's Mission to the King of Kandy, in 1762* (Colombo: W. Skeen, 1862).
28. *Grote atlas van de Verenigde Oost-Indische Compagnie (Comprehensive atlas of the Dutch United East India Company* (Atlas Maior, Koninklijk, Voorburg, 2011), vol. 4 (Ceylon), p. 387.
29. Ananda K. Coomaraswamy, *Medieval Sinhalese Art* (Gloucestershire: Essex House Press, 1908), p. 179. A.M. Hocart, *The Temple of the Tooth in Kandy* (London: Luzac, 1931), p. 7.
30. Leelananda Prematilleke & Ananda Colobage, *Dalada Maligava, Recent Disvoveries, Ancient Murals* (Kandy: Dalada Maligava Publication 2000), p. 7.
31. Coomaraswamy, *Medieval*, p. 118, pl. 8. I thank the Ven. Panaval Dhammadharaja Thero for the translation.
32. Davy, *Account*, 367. Hocart, *Temple,* p. 7
33. *Times of Ceylon,* 2 February 1917. Herbert White, 'The Barnes Buddha', *Ceylon Antiquary and Literary Register*, 1918-1919, pt. 3, 169-170.

Chapter 13: Dambulla

1. Archibald Campbell Lawrie, *A Gazetteer of the Central Province of Ceylon* (Colombo: G. Skeen, Government Printer, 1896). vol. 1. p. 125. B. Gunasekara, trans., *A Contribution to the History of Ceylon, translated from Pujavaliya* (Colombo: H.C. Cottle, 1895), p. 18.
2. K. Karunaratne, trans., *Rajaratnakaraya: the Gem Mine of Kings* (Colombo: Central Cultural Fund, 2009). John Davy, *An Account of the Interior of Ceylon, and of its Inhabitants*. (London: Longman, Hurst, Rees, Orme and Brown, 1821), p. 472. S.M. Burrows, *The Buried Cities of Ceylon* (Colombo: A.M. & J. Ferguson, 1894). p. 24.
3. *Epigrphia Zeylanica*, vol. 2, p. 273. *Epigraphia Zeylanica*, vol. 5, p. 475.
4. *Inscriptions of Ceylon* (Colombo: Department of Archaeology, 1970), vol. 1, pp. 64-66 and vol. 2, pt. 2 (2001), p. 5.
5. Jonathan Forbes, *Eleven Years in Ceylon* (London: Richard Bentley, 1841), vol. 1, p. 368. *Inscriptions of Ceylon*, vol. 2, pt. 1, p. 6 and vol. 2, pt. 2, p. 276.
6. *Epigraphia Zeylanica*, vol. 1, p. 135. S. Pathmanathan, 'The Nakaram of the Nanadesin in Sri Lanka', *The Sri Lanka Journal of the Humanities*, vol. 14-15, nos. 1-2, 1998-1999, p. 112.
7. William Knighton, 'The Rock Temples of Dambool, Ceylon', *Journal of the Royal Asiatic Society of Bengal,* 1847, vol. 16, pt. 1, fig. 7. A translation of the portico inscription was provided by Chryshane Mendis.
8. Senake Bandaranayake, *The Rock and Wall Paintings of Sri Lanka* (Colombo: Lake House, 1986), p. 141.
9. *Epigraphia Zeylanica*, vol. 2, pp. 119, 177).
10. Nandana Chutiwongs et. al., *Paintings of Sri Lanka: Dambulla* (Colombo: Archaeological Survey of Sri Lanka & Central Cultural Fund, 1990), p. 51. Lawrie, *Gazetteer*, vol. 1, p. 127. Kitsiri Malalgoda, *Buddhism in Sinhalese Society 1750-1900* (Berkeley: University of California Press, 1976), p. 54. Anuradha Seneviratna, *The Golden Rock Temple of Dambulla: Caves of Infinite Buddhas* (Colombo: Vijitha Yapa Publications, 2009), p. 110.
11. Seneviratna, *Golden Rock*, p. 115.
12. Ananda K. Coomaraswamy, *Medieval Sinhalese Art*, (Gloucestershire: Essex House Press, 1908), p. 168. Bandaranayake, *Rock and Wall Paintings*, p. 158.
13. Lawrie, *Gazetteer*, vol. 1, p. 125. Chutiwongs, *Painting of Sri Lanka*, p. 52. Ulrich von Schroeder, *Buddhist Sculptures of Sri Lank*a (Hong Kong: Visual Dharma Publications, 1990), p.382. Ulrich von Schroeder kindly provided me with a photograph of this image.
14. Knighton, *Rock Temples of Dambool*, p. 345. Forbes, *Eleven Years*, vol. 1, p. 368. Anuradha Seneviratna,*Golden Rock Temple of Dambulla* (Colombo: Central Cultural Fund, 1983), p. 51.
15. Lawrie, *Gazetteer*, vol. 1, p. 128. John Clifford Holt, *The Buddhist Visnu: Religious Transformation, Politics and Culture* (New York: Columbia, University Press,

2004), p. 70. T.W. Rhys Davids, 'The Cave of the Golden Rock, Dambula, Ceylon', *Indian Antiquary*, 1872, p. 141. Donald M. Stadtner, 'The Hindu Sage Kapila, the Liberation of Bodh Gaya and Burma on the Eve of the Modern Era', *Journal of the Siam Society*, 2021, vol. 109, pt. 2, pp. 103-130.

16. Gananath Obeyesekere, *The Cult of the Goddess Pattini* (Chicago: University of Chicago Press, 1984), p. 318-19. Holt, *Buddhist Visnu*, p. 66. David Scott, *Formation of Ritual: Colonial and Anthropological Discourse on Sinhala Yaktovil* (Minneapolis:University of Minnesota Press, 1994), p. 41. C. Ernest Fayle, ed., *Voyages to the East Indies: Christopher Fryke & Christopher Schweitzer* (London: Cassell & Company, 1929), p. 242.
17. Davy, *Account*, p 468. Senaviratna, *Golden Rock Temple, Caves of Infinite Buddha*, p. 111.
18. Personal communication, Osmund Bopearachchi.
19. Nicolas Revire, 'Buddhas of the Past and of the Future: Southeast Asia' in *Brill's Encyclopedia of Buddhism*, vol. 2, Jonathan A. Silk et al. (Leiden: E. J. Brill, 2019).
20. N.A. Jaywawickrama, trans., *The Story of Gotama Buddha: the Nidana-katha of the Jatakattakatha* (Oxford: The Pali Text Society, 2000), p. 106.
21. *Epigraphia Zeylanica*, vol. 1, p. 136.
22. Holt, *Buddhist Visnu*, p. 71. *Inscriptions of Ceylon*, vol. 9, p. 51.
23. Schroeder, *Buddhist Sculptures*, p. 382.
24. Davy, *Account*, p. 47. Burrows, *Buried Cities*, p. 26
25. Lawrie, *Gazetteer*, vol. 1, p. 127. R.J. Farrer, *In Old Ceylon* (London: Edward Arnold, 1908), p. 122.
26. Frank E. Reynolds & Mani B. Reynolds, *Three Worlds According to King Ruang: A Thai Buddhist Cosmology* (Berkeley: Asian Humanities Press, 1982), pp. 292-96. A.V. Suraweera, A.V. Suraweera, *The Rajavilaya and the first ever translation of the Alakesvara Yuddhaya* (Ratmalan: Vishva Lekha, 2000), p. 2.
27. Jayawickrama, *Story of Gotama*, p. 67
28. Reynolds & Reynolds, *Three Worlds*, p. 299. Nanamoli Bhikkhu, trans., *Visuddhimagga, The Path of Purification* (Colombo: Buddhist Publication Society, 1975), p. 678.
29. *Papancasudani*, Book 1. 386. Donald M. Stadtner, *Sacred Sites of Burma: Myths and Folklore in an Evolving Spiritual Realm* (Bangkok: River Books, 2015, p. 272).
30. H.T. Basnayake, *Dambulla Project: First Archaeological and Research Report* (Colombo: Central Cultural Fund, 1988), p. 102.
31. Obeyesekere, *Cult of the Goddess*, p. 312.
32. Ananda Abeysekara, *Colors of the Robe: Religion, Identity, and Differences* (Colombia: University of South Carolina Press, 2002), p. 190.
33. Ferrar, *In Old Ceylon*, p. 123.
34. Nirmala Salgado, *Buddhist Nuns and Gendered Practice: in search of the female renunciant* (New York: Oxford Press, 2014). Stephen C. Berkwitz, 'Buddhism in Sri Lanka: practice, protest and preservation' in *Buddhism in World Cultures: Comparative Perspectives*, Stephen C. Berkwitz, ed. (Santa Barbara, abc-clio Press, 2006) p. 63. *Sunday Observer*, 23 July 2017.
35. The quotation concerning the corruption at Dambulla is is taken from the Report of the Temple Lands Commissioners for 1871 found in Coomaraswamy, *Medieval Sinhalese Art*, p. 16. Kitsiri Malalgoda, *Buddhism in Sinhalese Society 1750-1900* (Berkeley: University of California Press, 1976), p. 127.
36. For the incident at Kosambi, see G.P. Malalsekere, *Dictionary of Pali Proper Names* under the entry Kosambi and *Jataka* number 423.

Chapter 14: Galle

1. K.D. Paranavitana, *Galle Fort: The Heritage City* (Moratuwa: United Printers, 2005). An outstanding source for colonial era maps and plans of the major Dutch cities in Ceylon is *Grote atlas van de Verenigde Oost-Indische Compgnie* (*Comprehensive atlas of the Dutch United East India Company*, (Atlas Maior, Koninklijk, Voorburg, 2011), vol. 4 (Ceylon). A parallel text in Dutch and English accompanies the illustrations. Two important Portuguese codices, with maps and plans from 1624 and 1638, are fully treated in Jorge Manuel Flores, *Os Olhos do Rei: Desenhos e Desclricoes Portuguesas de Ilha de Ceilao (1624, 1638)* (Lisboa: Comissao National para as Comemoracoes Dos Descobrument Portugueses, 2001). For an excellent overview of Portuguese Galle, see C.R de Silva, 'Galle Four Hundred Years ago,' *The Ceylon Journal*, 2024, vol. 1, no. 1. pp. 1-6.
2. P.E. Pieris, trans., *Captain Joao Ribeiro, The Historic Tragedy of the Island of Ceilao* (New Delhi: Asian Educational Services, 1999), p. 35.
3. *Grote atlas*, pp. 171-173, 176 77. R. Raven-Hart, trans., *Heydt's Ceylon* (Colombo: Government Press, 1952), p. 46. John Christopher Wolf, *The Life and Adventures of John Christopher Wolf, Late Principal Secretary of State at Jaffanapatnam, in Ceylon* (London: G.G. J. and J. Robinson, 1785), p. 207.
4 Robert Parthesius, ed., *Excavation Report of the VOC Ship Avondster (1659)*. (Amsterdam: Centre for International Heritage Activities, 2007). Brigitte Borrell, 'A True Martaban Jar: A Burmese Ceramic Jar in the Ethnological Museum in Heidelberg, Germany', *Artibus Asiae,* 2014, vol. 74, no. 2, pp. 257-297. R. Raven-Hart, trans., *Travels in Ceylon: 1700-1800* (Colombo: Lake House, 1963), p. 21. Sophie Anthonisz, trans., *Joan Cornelis Simons 1707, a Memoir for his successor, Hendrick Becker*

(Colombo: Government Printer, 1914), p. 26. Sophie Pieters, trans., *Rycklof van Goens, Instructions from the Governor-General and Council of India to the Governor of Ceylon, 1656-1665* (Colombo: H.C. Cottle, Government Printer, 1908), p. 73.

5. Raven-Hart, *Heydt's Ceylon*, pp. 43, 46.
6. James Cordiner, *A Description of Ceylon*, (Colombo: K.V.G. de Silva, 1983), vol. 1, p. 10.
7. Caroline Stanford, 'Revisiting the Origins of Coade Stone', *The Georgian Group Journal,* 2016, vol. 24, pp. 95-116.
8. Raven-Hart, *Heydt's Ceylon*, pp. 42, 46.
9. Sophie Pieters, trans., *Hendrick Zwaardecroon, a memoir for the Council of Jaffnapatam, 1697* (Colombo: Government Printer, 1911), p. 77. F. H. de Vos, 'Supplementary Paper on the Monumental Remain of the Dutch East India Company in Ceylon', *Journal of the Ceylon Branch of the Royal Asiatic Society*, vol. 16, no. 51, p. 137.
10. All the important tombstones in Galle and its environs are briefly described in J. Penry Lewis, *List of Inscriptions on Tombstones and Monuments in Ceylon, of Historical and Local Interest* (Colombo: H.C. Cottle, Government Printer, 1913).
11. R.G. Antonisz, *Report on the Dutch Records in the Government Archives at Colombo* (Colombo: H.C. Cottle, Government Printer, 1907), pp. 64-65. M.W. Jurriaanse, *Catalogue of the Archives of the Dutch Central Government of Coastal Ceylon, 1640-1796* (Colombo: Department of National Archives, 1943).
12. Lewis, *List of Inscriptions*, p. 163.
13. *The New Law Reports*, 1922, p. 241.
14. Stephan Prothero, *The White Buddhist: the Asian Odyssey of Henry Steel Olcott* (Bloomington: Indiana University Press, 2011).

Chapter 15: Colombo

1. C.F. Beckingham, trans., *The Travels of Ibn Battuta* (London: the Haklyut Society, 1994), p. 856.
2. *Inscriptions of Ceylon* (Colombo: Department of Archaeology, 1970), p. 86. George J.A. Skeen, *Guide to Colombo* (Colombo: A.M. and J. Ferguson, 1898), p. *vi. Epigraphia Zeylanica*, vol. 6, p. 5.
3. L. Kalus & C. Guillot, 'Reinterpretation des plus anciennes steles funeraires islamique nousantariennes: 3. Sri Lanka'. *Archipel,* vol. 72, p. 33. Hentry Yule, trans., *Cathay and the Way Thither, being a Collection of Medieval Notices of China* (London: The Haklyut Society, 1866), vol. 2., p. 231. Ibn Battua, *Travels*, p. 856. S.D Goitein, *Letters of Medieval Jewish Traders* (Princeton: Princeton University Press, 1973), pp. 183-85.
4. Donald Ferguson, 'The Discovery of Ceylon by the Portuguese in 1506', *Journal of the Ceylon Branch of the Royal Asiatic Society,* 1907, vol. 19, pp. 338.
5. Jorge Manuel Flores, *Os Olhos do Rei: Desenhos e Desclricoes Portuguesas de Ilha de Ceilao (1624, 1638)*, (Lisboa: Comissao National para as Comemoracoes Dos Descobrument Portugueses, 2001), p. 107. Chryshane Mendis, 'The Fortess of Colombo: from the Portuguese and Dutch to the British,' *Fort*, 2017, vol. 45 p. 58. H.N. Seneviratne et. al., 'Seismicity around Sri Lanka from Historical Records and its Engineering Implications,' *Engineer*, 2020, vol. 53, no. 2, pp. 47-52. Jorge Rodrigues, *Relacion Verdadore del Esantoso Terremoto* (*True Description of the Terrible Earthquake*). This is a four-page pamphlet (Lisboa, 1616).
6. Robert Percival, *An Account of the The Island of Ceylon* (London: C. & R. Baldwin, 1803), p. 114. Zoltan Biedermann, 'Colombo versus Cannanore: Contrasting Structure of Two Colonial Port Cities (1500-1700)', *Journal of the Economic and Social History of the Orient*, 2009, vol. 52, no. 3, p. 435. Sophia Pieters, trans., *Hendrick Zwaardecroon, Memoir for the Council of Jaffnapatam, 1697* (Colombo: Government Printer, 1911), p. 116. Sophia Anthonisz, *Memoir of Hendrick Becker, 1716* (Colombo: H.C. Cottle, Government Printer, 1714), 49. P.E. Pieris, 'Inscriptions at St. Thomas' Church, Colombo', *Journal of the Ceylon Branch of the Royal Asiatic Society*, 1912, vol. 22, no. 65, pp. 385-389
7. James Cordiner, *A Description of Ceylon* (Colombo: K.V.G. de Silva, 1983), vol. 1, pp. 23,51. Kitsiri Malalgoda, *Buddhism in Sinhalese Society 1750-1900* (Berkeley: University of California Press, 1976), p. 191. Anne M. Blackburn, *Locations of Buddhism: Colonialism & Modernity in Sri Lanka* (Chicago: University of Chicago Press, 2010), p. 46.
8. *Saturday Magazine*, 14 March 1835. R.L. Brohier, *Changing Face of Colombo* (*1505-1972*) (Colombo: Visidunu Publication, 1984), p. 29. Cordiner, *Description*, p. 20. J. Penry Lewis, *List of Inscriptions on Tombstones and Monuments in Ceylon, of Historical or Local Interest* (Colombo: H.C. Cottle, Government Printer, 1913), p.1. For the depiction of the banquet in 1772, see Lodewijk Wagenaar, *Cinnamon & Elephant: Sri Lanka and the Netherlands from 1600* (Amsterdam: Rijksmuseum, 2016), p. 73.
9. Lewis, *List*, p. 4. For Tolfrey, see Sujit Sivasundaram, *Islanded: Britiain, Sri Lanka and the Bounds of an Indian Ocean Colony* (New Delhi: Oxford University Press, 2013), p. 105.
10. *Sessional Papers*, 1801-1833, p. 41. *Asiatic Journal*, 1832, p. 50.
11. Stanley J. Tambiah, *Levelling Crowds: Ethnonationalist Conflicts and Collective Violence in South Asia* (Berkeley: University of California Press, 1996), p. 36. Yashodhara Dalmia, *Buddha to Krishna: the Life and Times of George Keyt* (Delhi: Routledge, 2016), p. 59.

12. Jamsheed K. Choksy, 'Iranians and Indians on the Shores of Serendib (Sri Lanka)' in *Parsis in India and the Diaspora*, John R. Hinnells and Alan Williams, ed. (New York, Routledge, 2018), pp. 181-210.
13. Donald M. Stadtner, *Sacred Sites of Burma: Myth & Folklore in an Evolving Spiritual Realm* (Bangkok: River Books, 2015), p. 309.
14. Sagara Jayasinghe, 'An account of the Devotion to St. Anthony during the Portuguese and Dutch occupation in Sri Lanka', *Oriente, (*Fundacao Oriente, Lisbon*), 2015,* vol. 24, p. 86. V. Perniola, *The Catholic Church in Sri Lanka, the Dutch Period, 1712-1746* (Dehiwala: Tisara Prakasakayo Ltd., 1983), vol. 2, pp. 310, 307.
15. Personal communication, Sagara Jayasinghe.
16. V. Perniola, 1985, vol. 3. 1747-1795, p. 496.

Wolvendaal Church

1. Christopher Schweitzer & Christopher Fryke, *Voyages to the East Indies* (London: Cassell & Company, 1929), p. 261. *Grote Atlas van de Verenigde Oost-Indische Compgnie (Comprehensive Atlas of the Dutch United East India Company)* (Atlas Maior, Koninklijk, Voorburg, 2011), vol. 4 (Ceylon), p. 106.
2. Sophia Pieters, trans., *Memoir of Jacob Christian Pielat, 1734* (Colombo: G. J. A. Skeen, Government Printer, 1905), p. 13.
3. Lodewijk Wagenaar, *Cinnamon & Elephant: Sri Lanka and the Netherlands from 1600* (Amsterdam: Rijksmuseum Museum, 2016), 89. Max de Bruijn & Remco Raben, ed., *The World of Jan Brandes, 1743-1808* (Amsterdam: Rijksmuseum, 2004), p. 233.
4. *Grote Atlas*, p. 115.
5. James Cordiner, *A Description of Ceylon,* (Colombo: K.V.G. de Silva, 1983), vol. 1., p. 21. Martin Krieger, *European Cemeteries in South India: Seventeenth to Nineteenth Centuries* (New Delhi: Manohar Publishers, 2013), p. 52.
6. Sophia Anthonisz, trans., *Joan Cornelis Simons, Memoir for his Successor, 1707* (Colombo: Government Printer, 1914), p. 12. J. Penry Lewis, *List of Inscriptions on Tombstones and Monuments in Ceylon, of Historical or Local Interest* (Colombo: H.C. Cottle, Government Printer, 1913), p. 101. Philippus Baldaeus, *A Description of the East India Coasts of Malabar and Coromandel with their Adjacent Kingdoms and Provinces & of the Empire of Ceylon*, Anonymous translation into English, 1671 (New Delhi Educational Services, 2000), p. 153.
7. Hugh Dunthome, *Britain and the Dutch Revolt* (Cambridge: Cambridge University Press, 2013), p. 156. Sophia Pieters, trans., *Hendrick Zwaardecroon, Memoir for the Council of Jaffnapatam, 1697* (Colombo: Government Printer, 1911), p. 77.
8. Cordiner, *Description*, vol. 1, p. 8. R. Raven-Hart, trans., *Heydt's Ceylon* (Colombo: Government Press, 1952), K.D. Paranavitana, trans., *Daniel Overbeek, Memoir for his Successor, 1743* (Colombo: National Archives, 2009), p. 57. Sinnappah Arasaratnam, trans., Julius Stein Gollenesse, *Memoir for his Successor, 1759* (Colombo: National Archives, 1974). p. 86. Henry Yule and A.C. Burwell, *Hobson-Jobson, The Anglo-Indian Dictionary* (London: Wordsworth Editions, Ltd., 1996), p. 138.
9. Pieters, *Zwaardecroon*, pp. 70, 76. Cordiner, *Description*, p. 30. R. Raven-Hart, trans., *Travels in Ceylon, 1700-1800* (Colombo: Lake House, 1963), p. 32. Arasaratnam, *Gollenesse*, p. 86.
10. Pieters, *Zwaardecroon*, p. 76. Raven-Hart, *Heydt's Ceylon*, p. 87.
11. George J. A. Skeen, *Guide to Colombo* (A.M. & J. Ferguson, 1906), p. 81.
12. Pieters, *Joan Cornelis Simons,* p. 21. J. D. Palm, 'An Account of the Dutch Church in Ceylon.', *Journal of the Ceylon Branch of the Roayal Asiatic Society*, 1847-48, vol. 1. no. 3, p. 59.
13. Klaus Koschorke, ed., *The Dutch Reformed Church in Colonial Ceylon (18th century: minutes of the Consistory of the Dutch Reformed church in Colomb held at the Wolvendaal Church Colombo (1735-97).* (Wiesbaden: Harrassowitz Verlag, 2011).
14. S.D. Franciscus*, Faith of Our Fathers: history of the Dutch Reformed Church in Sri Lanka* (Colombo: Pragna Publishers, 1983), p. 23. F. H. de Vos,'Three funerals of Ceylon Dutch Officials in the Eighteenth Century', *Journal of the Ceylon Branch of the Royal Asiatic Society*, 1903, vol. 18 no. 54, p. 123. Susan E. Schopp, 'Up from the Watery Deep: the Discovery of an Armenian Gravestone in the South Sea' in *Les Armeniens dans le commerce asiatiques au debut de l'ere moderne*, Sushil Chaudhury & Keram Kevonian, ed. (Paris: Open Editions Books, 2007), pp. 259-274.
15. Personal communication, Martin Krieger. Krieger, *European Cemeteries*, p. 90. A. Rea, *Monumental Remains of the Dutch East India Company in the Presidency of Madras* (Calcutta: Government Press, 1897), p. 60. Lewis, *List*, p. 113.
16. F.H. de Vos 'Mr Isaac Augustin Rumpf', *Journal of the Ceylon Branch of the Royal Asiatic Society*, 1905, vol. 18, no. 56, pp. 325-333. De Vos, *Three Funerals*, p. 119. Lewis, *List*, p. 108.
17. F.H. de Vos, 'Monumental Remains of the Dutch East India Company in Ceylon', *Journal of the Ceylon Branch of the Royal Asiatic Society*, 1898, vol 15, no. 49, pp. 213 – 287.
18. A.E. Buultjens, 'Governor Van Eck's Expedition Against the King of Kandy, 1765', *Journal of the Ceylon Branch of the Royal Asiatic Society*, 1899, vol. 16, no. 50, p. 53. Fryke & Schweitzer, *Voyages*, p. 246. Baldaeus, *Description*, p. 148. Lewis, *List*, p. 105. Krieger, *European Cemeteries*, p. 31.

19. Lewis, *List*, pp. 106, 142.
20. R. L. Brohier, *De Wolvendaalsche Kerk* (Colombo: Neptune Publications, 2010).
21. J.R. Toussant, 'Dutch Ladies who Lived in Ceylon', *Journal of the Dutch Burgher Union*, 1939, vol. 29, no. 2, p. 36

Ponnambaleshvara Temple

1. David D. Schulman, *Tamil Temple Myths: Sacrifice and Divine Marriage in the South Indian Saiva Tradition* (Princeton: Princeton University Press, 1980), p. 41
2. Personal communication, Crispin Branfoot.
3. George Keyt, 'Music in the Hindu Temple', *Journal of the Dutch Burger Union*, 1983, vol. 61, nos. 1-4, p. 126.
4. For an overview of the temple's history and functioning today, see S. Pathmanathan, *Hindu Temples of Sri Lanka* (Colombo & Chennai: Kumaran Book House, 2006).
5. Stanley J. Tambiah, *Levelling Crowds: Ethnonationalist Conflicts and Collective Violence in South Asia* (Berkeley: University of California Press, 1996), p. 45. M. Vythilingam, *The Life of Sir Ponnambalam Ramanathan*. (Colombo: Ramanathan Commemoration Society, 1971), p. 534. Crispin Branfoot, 'Temple renovation and Chettiar patronage in colonial Madras Presidencey' in *The Contempoary Hindu Temple: Fragments for a History,* Annapurna Garimellla et al. (Mumbai: Marg Publication, 2019), vol. 70, no. 4, pp. 22-35.
6. Kumari Jayawardena, *The White Woman's Other Burden: Western Women and South Asia During British Rule* (New York: Routledge, 1995), p. 137. Elizabeth J. Harris, *Theravada Buddhism and the British Encounter* (London: Routledge, 2006), p. 150. Personal communication, Antonia Behan.
7. For the remarkable discovery of this memoir, see Davish Soneji, 'Siva's Courtesans: Religion, Rhetoric, and Self-Representation in Early Twentieth-century Writing by *devadasis*', *International Journal of Hindu Studies,* 2010, vol. 14, no. 1, pp. 31-70.
8. Soneji, *Siva's Courtesans*, pp. 36, 57, 59. Saskia C. Kersenboom, *Nityasumangali: Devadasi Tradition in South India*, (New Delhi: Motilal Banarsidass Publisher, 2002). p 28. See also Leslie Orr *Donors, Devotees, and Daughters of God: Temple Women in Medieval Tamilnadu* (New York: Oxford, 2000).
9. Marco Polo's description of *devadasis* appears in chapter 174. See Sharon Kinoshita, *Marco Polo, The Description of the World* (Indianpolis: Hackett Publishing Company) p. 161.
10. K. D. Paranavitana, *Journal of Spilbergen: The First Dutch Envoy to Ceylon, 1602* (Dehiwala: Sridevi Publishing, 1997), p. 36.
11. Edmund Jayasuriya, trans., *Hamsa Sandesa* (Colombo: Central Cultural Fund, 2005), p. 49.

Dipaduttamarama Monastery

1. F. F. Martinus, *A Guide to Buddhist Temples, Colombo* (Educational Services, New Delhi, 1990), p. 7. This is a reprint of the 1907 edition.
2. Martinus, *Guide*, p. 10. R.J. Farrer, *In Old Ceylon* (London: Edward Arnold, 1908), p. 38. George J.A. Skeen, *Guide to Colombo* (Colombo: A.M. and J. Ferguson, 1898), p. 90.
3. Kitsiri Malalgoda, *Buddhism in Sinhalese Society 1750-1900* (Berkeley: University of California Press, 1976), p. 220. Stanley J. Tambiah, *Levelling Crowds: Ethnonationalist Conflicts and Collective Violence in South Asia* (Berkeley: University of California Press, 1996), p. 49.
4. Anne M. Blackburn, *Locations of Buddhism: Colonialism & Modernity in Sri Lanka* (Chicago: University of Chicago Press, 2010), p. 34. K. D. Paranavitana, 'Scholar Monks of the Nineteenth Century and the Tragic Transformation of the High Priest Ven. Kapugama Thammakhanda Thero', *Journal of the Royal Asiatic Society of Sri Lanka*, n.s., 1983, vol. 28, pp. 123-164.
5. P. C. Mozoomdar, *Sketches of a Tour Round the World* (Calcutta: S.K. Lahiri & Co., 1884), p. 9. Tambiah, *Levelling*, p. 53. R.F. Young & G.P.V. Somaratna, *Vain Debates: The Buddhist-Christian Controversies of Nineeteenth-century Ceylon* (Vienna: De Nobili Research Library, 1996).
6. Tamara Loos, *Bones Around My Neck: the Life and Exile of a Prince Provocateur* (Cornell: Cornell University Press, 2016). This outstanding study places this Thai prince in the broader regional context.
7. Blackburn, *Locations*, p. 178.
8. Charles Allen, *The Buddha and Dr. Fuhrer: An Archaeological Scandal* (London: Haus Publishing, 2008). Loos, *Bones*, p. 119.
9. Nyanatusita & Hellmuth Hecker, *The Life of Nyanatiloka Thera* (Kandy: Buddhist Publication Society, 2008), p. 27.
10. Personal communication Laura Weinstein and Robert L. Brown.
11. Farrer, *Old Ceylon*, p. 34. Martinus, *Guide*, p. 20.
12. Farrer, *Old Ceylon*, p. 34. Sumet Jumsai, 'Ratna Chetiya Dipaduttamarama, Colombo', *Journal of the Royal Asiatic Society of Sri Lanka*, 2003, n.s. vol. 48. 213-236.
13. *The Buddhast Annual of Ceylon*, 1925, p. 57.

Subodharama Viharaya

1. P.D. Ouspensky, *A New Model of the Universe* (New York: Routledge, Kegan & Paul, 1914), p. 367. *Epigraphia Zeylanica*, vol. 1, p. 227 and vol. 2, p. 68.
2. Carol S. Anderson " 'For Those Who are Ignorant' ": A Study of the Bauddha Adahilla' in *Constituting Communities: Theravada Buddhism and the Religious Cultures of South and Southeast Asia*, John Holt et al. (Albany: State University of New York Press, 2003), pp. 171-88. Senake Bandaranayake, *The Rock and Wall Paintings of Sri Lanka* (Colombo: Lake House, 1986), p. 215. Pers. comm., Kevin Trainor and Vijitha Kumar.
3. For an important source for the 'retreats', see the commentary on the *Majjhima Nikaya*, the *Papancasudani*.
4. Ranjani Obeyesekere, *Yasodhara, The Wife of the Bodhisattva: The Sinhala Yasodharavata (The Story of Yasodhara) and the Sinhala Yasodharapadanaya (The Sacred Biography of Yasodhara* (Albany: State University of New York Press, 2009). John S. Strong, " 'A Family Quest': The Buddha, Yashodhara, and Rahula in the *Mulasarvastivada Vinaya*' in *Sacred Biography in the Buddhist Traditions of South and Southeast Asia*, Juliane Schober, ed. (Honolulu: University of Hawai'i Press,1997), pp. 113-128.
5. For Kandyan era poems on Alavaka, see C.E. Godakumbura, *Sinhalese Literature* (Colombo: The Colombo Apothecaries Co., 1955), pp. 175, 280. David Scott, *Formation of Ritual: Colonial and Anthropological Discourses on Sinhala Yaktovil* (Minneapolis: University of Minnesota Press, 1994), pp. 6ff.
6. Oskar von Hinuber, *A Handbook of Pali Literature* (New Delhi: Munshiram Manoharlal Publishers, 1996), p. 146. N.A. Jayawickrama, *The Sheaf of Garlands of the Epochs of the Conqueror, being a translation of Jinkalamalipakaranam* (London: Luzac,1968), pp. 42-49.
7. Pers. comm., Alexandra Green and Cristophe Munier. Patricia M. Herbert, *The Life of the Buddha* (London: The British Library, 1992).
8. Bandaranayake, *Rock and Wall Painting*, p. 215.
9. James Cordiner, *A Description of Ceylon* (Colombo: K.V.G. de Silva, 1983), vol. 1, p. 67.
10. Bandaranayake, *Rock and Wall Painting*, p. 202.
11. Ibid., p. 284.
12. For this unique mode of depiction in Burma, see Donald M. Stadtner, " '.... if you spill a single drop': Innovation in the *Jataka* Traditions of Pagan', *Orientations*, 2015, vol. 46, no. 1, pp. 2-11.
13. Ranjini Obeyesekere, trans., *Portraits of Buddhist Women: Stories from the Saddharmaratnavaliya* (Albany: State University of New York Press, 2001), p. 17.
14. Marie Gatellier, *'Les Destins de Revati et de Patacara illustres par la peinture Singhalaise', Indologica Taurinesia,* 1999, vol. 25, p. 123-178.
15. Godakumbura, *Sinhalese Literature*, p. 103. For Pagan, see G.H. Luce & Ba Shin, 'Pagan Myinkaba Kubyauk Gyi Temple of Rajakumar (1113 A.D.)', *Bulletin of the Burma Historical Commision*, 1961, pp. 400ff.
16. Bandaranayake, *Rock and Wall Painting*, pp. 214-15. For the Pali sources, see Hinuber, *Handbook*, p. 183, and Frank E. Reynolds & Mani B. Reynolds, *Three Worlds According to King Ruang: A Thai Buddhist Cosmology* (Berkeley: Asian Humanities Press, 1982).

Further Reading

Introduction: The Life of Sacred Sites

Richard Gombrich & Gananath Obeysekere, *Buddhism Transformed: Religious Change in Sri Lanka.* Princeton: Princeton University Press, 1988.

Chandra Richard de Silva, *Sri Lanka, a History.* New Delhi: Sangam Books, 1987.

Stephen C. Berkwitz, 'Buddhism in Sri Lanka: practice, protest and preservation' in *Buddhism in World Cultures: Comparative Perspectives*, Stephen C. Berkwitz, ed. Santa Barbara: Abc-clio Press, 2006.

John Clifford Holt, ed. *The Sri Lanka Reader: History, Culture, Politics.* Durham & London, Duke University Press, 2011.

Anuradhapura: 'A Divine City'

Senake Bandaranayake, *Sinhalese Monastic Architecture: The Viharas of Anuradhapura.* Hyderabad: Orient Blackswan Private, 2009.

Osmund Bopearachchi, *Roots of Sri Lankan Art.* Colombo: Department of Archaeology, 2020.

R.A.L.H. Gunawardana, *The Robe and the Plough.* Phoenix: The University of Arizona Press, 1979).

J.G. Smither, *Archaeological Remains, Anuradhapura, Ceylon: comprising the Dagabas and certain other ancient ruined structures.* London: Cooper and Budd, 1894.

Sigiriya: 'Heaven has Lost its Appeal'

Senake Bandaranayake, *Sigiriya.* Colombo: Central Cultural Fund, 2005.

Nilan Cooray, *The Sigiriya Royal Gardens.* Delft: Delft University of Technology, 2012.

Nandana Chutiwongs et al., ed., *Paintings of Sri Lanka: Sigiriya.* Colombo: Central Cultural Fund, 1990.

Jagath Weerasinghe, *Sigiriya: Managing Heritage with Community.* Colombo: Neptune Press, 2025.

Kelaniya: The Buddha counsels a Snake-King

Jonathan S. Walters, *The History of the Kelaniya.* Colombo: Social Scientists' Association, 1996.

H.C.P. Bell & M. A. Gunasekara, 'Kelani Vihara and Its Inscriptions'. *Ceylon Antiquary and Literary Register*, 1916, vol. 1, no. 3.

Vajira Nalinda Jayathilaka, 'Kalaniya Rajamaha Viharaya Reconstructed in the mid-20th Century: Inspirations and Politics' in *Evolving Traditions of Buddhist Image Houses*, Asoka de Zoysa et al., ed. Colombo: Samkathana Research Centre, University of Kelaniya, 2018.

Kitsiri Malalgoda, *Buddhism in Sinhalese Society.* Berkeley: University of California Press, 1976.

Sri Pada: Adam's Peak

Anne E. Hazlewood, trans., *In Praise of Mount Samanta (Samantakutavannana) by Vedeha Thera.* London: Pali Text Society, 1986.

Alexander McKinley, *Mountain at a Center of the World: Pilgrimage and Pluralism in Sri Lanka.* Chicago: University of Chicago Press, 2024.

Senerat Paranavitana, *The God of Adam's Peak.* Ascona: Artibus Asiae Publishers, 1958.

William Skeen, *Adam's Peak: Legendary, Traditional and Historic Notices of the Samanala and Sri-Pada.* Colombo: W.L.H. Skeen & Co., 1870.

Ratnapura: Saman's Temple

John D'Oyle, *The Diary of Mr. John D'Oyle.* Colombo: Lake House, 1995.

H.C.P. Bell, 'Maha Saman Devale and its Sannasa'. *Journal of the Ceylon Branch of the Royal Asiatic Society*, 1916-1917, vol. 2, no. 1.

P.E.P. Deraniyagal. 'The Saman Sirita, A Hymn to the Presiding Deity of Mount Saman'. *Spoila Zeylanica,* 1961, vol. 29, no. 2.

D.W. Ferguson, 'The Inscribed Mural Stone at Saman Devale, Ratnapura'. *Journal of the Ceylon Branch of the Royal Asiatic Society*, 1899, vol. 16, no. 50.

Attanagalla: A King With Neither a Head Nor a Kingdom

Anne M. Blackburn, *Buddhist-inflected Sovereignties Across the Indian Ocean: The Pali Arena, 1200-1550.* Honolulu: University of Hawai'i Press, 2024.

C.E. Godakumbura, *Hatthavanagallaviharavamsa.* London: The Pali Text Society, 1956.

James D'Alwis, *The Attanagalu-vansa or the history of the Temple of Attanagalla, translated from the Pali.* Colombo: Williams and Mrg., 1866.

Devinuruva: 'in the guise of a wandering ascetic'

John Clifford Holt, *The Buddhist Vishnu: Religious Transformation, Politics and Culture.* New York: Columbia University Press, 2004.

Senerat Paranavitana, *The Shrine of Upulvan at Devundara.* Oxford: Oxford University Press, 1953.

Jorge Manuel Flores, *Os Olhos do Rei: Desenhos e Desclricoes Portuguesas de Ilha de Ceilao (1624, 1638).* Lisbon: Comissao National para as Comemoracoes Dos Descobrument Portugueses, 2001.

Kataragama: 'The grievous disease of love'

Kamil V. Zwelebil, The Tamil Skandapuranam. The Oriental Institute, Prague, 1992.

David D. Schulman, *Tamil Temple Myths: Sacrifice and Divine Marriage in the South Indian Saiva Tradition.* Princeton: Princeton University Press, 1980.

Paul Wirz, *Kataragama: the holiest place in Ceylon.* Colombo: Lake House, 1966.

Gananath Obeyesekere, 'Social Change and the Deities: Rise of the Kataragama Cult in Modern Sri Lanka'. *Man*, 1977, n.s., vol. 12, nos. 3-4.

Trincomalee: 'The Rome of the Orient'

S. Pathmanathan, *Hindu Temples of Sri Lanka.* Colombo: Kumaran Book House, 2006.

Alexander McKinley, *Mountain at a Center of the World: Pilgrimage and Plurarlism in Sri Lanka.* Chicago: University of Chicago Press, 2024.

Alicia Schrikker, *Dutch and British Colonial Intervention in Sri Lanka: 1780-1815*: *Expansion and Reform.* Leiden: E.J. Brill, 2007.

Islam: Mosques and Hermitages

Dennis B. McGilvray, 'Jailani: A Sufi Shrine in Sri Lanka' in *Lived Islam in South Asia: Adaptation, Accommodation and Conflict*, Imtiaz Ahmad & Helmut Reifeld. ed. Delhi: Social Science Press, 2004.

Dennis B. McGilvray, *Crucible of Conflict: Tamil and Muslim Society on the East Coast of Sri Lanka.* Durham: Duke University Press, 2008.

Kalinga Tudor Silva et al., ed. *Religious Interface and Contestations between Buddhists and Muslims in Sri Lanka.* Colombo: International Centre for Ethnic Studies, 2016.

Kandy: The Sacred Tooth Relic

Anne M. Blackburn, *Locations of Buddhism: Colonialism & Modernity in Sri Lanka.* Chicago: University of Chicago Press, 2010.

Dharmaratna Herath, *The Tooth Relic and the Crown.* Colombo: unidentified publisher, 1994.

Anuradha Seneviratna, *The Temple of the Sacred Tooth: History and Architecture of the Temples.* Colombo: Vijitha Yapa Publications, 2010.

B.C. Law, trans.,*The Dathavamsa, A History of the Tooth-relic of the Buddha.* Lahore: Motilal Banarsidas, 1925.

Dambulla: A Vow Fulfilled

Senake Bandaranayake, *The Rock and Wall Paintings of Sri Lanka.* Colombo: Lake House, 1986.

Nandana Chutiwongs et. al., ed. *Paintings of Sri Lanka: Dambulla.* Colombo: Archaeological Survey of Sri Lanka & Central Cultural Fund, 1990.

Ulrich von Schroeder, *Buddhist Sculptures of Sri Lank*a. Hong Kong: Visual Dharma Publications, 1990.

Galle: A Rooster on a Rock

C.R de Silva, 'Galle Four Hundred Years ago'. *The Ceylon Journal*, 2024, vol. 1, no. 1.

K.D. Paranavitana, *Galle Fort: The Heritage City.* Moratuwa: United Printers, 2005.

J. Penry Lewis, *List of Inscriptions on Tombstones and Monuments in Ceylon, of Historical and Local Interest.* Colombo: H.C. Cottle, Government Printer, 1913.

Colombo: 'Such a mixture of nations, manners and religions'

R.L. Brohier, *Changing Face of Colombo (1505-1972).* Colombo: Visidunu Publication, 1984.

Lodewijk Wagenaar, *Cinnamon & Elephant: Sri Lanka and the Netherlands from 1600.* Amsterdam: Rijksmuseum, 2016.

Sujit Sivasundaram, *Islanded: Britain, Sri Lanka and the Bounds of an Indian Ocean Colony.* New Delhi: Oxford University Press, 2013.

Zoltan Biedermann, 'Colombo versus Cannanore: Contrasting Structure of Two Colonial Port Cities (1500-1700)'. *Journal of the Economic and Social History of the Orient*, 2009.

Wolvendaal Church: 'Carnal indulgence their happiness'

Max de Bruijn & Remco Raben, ed., *The World of Jan Brandes, 1743-1808.* Amsterdam: Rijksmuseum, 2004.

S.D. Franciscus, *Faith of Our Fathers: history of the Dutch Reformed Church in Sri Lanka.* Colombo: Pragna Publishers, 1983.

R. L. Brohier, *De Wolvendaalsche Kerk.* Colombo: Neptune Publications, 2010.

Ponnambaleshvara Temple: A Hindu Revival and Shiva's Courtesans

Davish Soneji, 'Siva's Courtesans: Religion, Rhetoric, and Self-Representation in Early Twentieth-century Writing by *devadasi*s'. *International Journal of Hindu Studies,* 2010, vol. 14, no. 1.

Crispin Branfoot, 'Temple renovation and Chettiar patronage in colonial Madras Presidency' in *The Contemporary Hindu Temple: Fragments for a History,* Annapurna Garimellla et al., ed. Mumbai: Marg Publication, 2019.

Saskia C. Kersenboom, *Nityasumangali: Devadasi Tradition in South India.* New Delhi: Motilal Banarsidass Publisher, 2002.

Dipaduttamarama Monastery: The Thai Priest-Prince

Tamara Loos, *Bones Around My Neck: the Life and Exile of a Prince Provocateur.* Cornell: Cornell University Press, 2016

F. F. Martinus, *A Guide to Buddhist Temples, Colombo.* Educational Services, New Delhi, 1990.

Stanley J. Tambiah, *Levelling Crowds: Ethnonationalist Conflicts and Collective Violence in South Asia.* Berkeley: University of California Press, 1996.

Subodharama Viharaya: 'The Buddha saw me'

Carol S. Anderson " 'For Those Who are Ignorant' ": A Study of the Bauddha Adahilla' in *Constituting Communities: Theravada Buddhism and the Religious Cultures of South and Southeast Asia,* John Holt et al., ed. Albany: State University of New York Press, 2003.

Senake Bandaranayake, *The Rock and Wall Paintings of Sri Lanka.* Colombo: Lake House, 1986.

Ranjani Obeyesekere, *Yasodhara, The Wife of the Bodhisattva: The Sinhala Yasodharavata (The Story of Yasodhara) and the Sinhala Yasodharapadanaya.* Albany: State University of New York Press, 2009.

INDEX